W9-CNN-816

FRANZ KAFKA

There is meaning beyond absurdity.
—Abraham Joshua Heschel

Franz Kafka

The Untold Story

George Fabian

Copyright © 2019 by George Fabian.

Library of Congress Control Number:		2019902855
ISBN:	Hardcover	978-1-7960-2056-4
	Softcover	978-1-7960-2055-7

All rights reserved. No part of this book may be reproduced or transmitted
in any form or by any means, electronic or mechanical, including photocopying,
recording, or by any information storage and retrieval system,
without permission in writing from the copyright owner.

Print information available on the last page.

This book is not for sale in the United Kingdom.

Rev. date: 05/06/2019

To order additional copies of this book, contact:
Xlibris
1-888-795-4274
www.Xlibris.com
Orders@Xlibris.com
760122

CONTENTS

ACKNOWLEDGMENTS

The following individuals and teams deserve recognition for helping in one way or another nurture this tome to the press:

Jim Reed, St. John's College, Oxford; Margarete Czepiel, Bodleian Library, Oxford; Reiner Stach, Berlin; Atar Funda, Standesamt Mitte, Berlin; Franziska Bogdanov, Berlin; Alena Wágnerová, Aachen; the team at the Monument of National Literature, Prague; Josef Žabka, Jan Kahuda and the team at National Archives, Prague; Jan Kolář and Hana Mášová, Charles University, Prague; Josef Třeštík, Prague; Marie Poláková; Irena Michalová, Prague; the town of Planá nad Lužnicí; Miroslava Rokosová and Eva Žaludová, Planá nad Lužnicí; Frances Blevis and Jana Riesenfeld-Fabian, Toronto; as well as Judy Walker, who diligently proofread the entire manuscript.

Thanks must also go to Aileen D. Guinto and the team of the publisher, Xlibris. However, none from the above is in any way responsible for the content of this book.

Image credit is due to the following:

-Monument of National Literature, Prague
1, 2, 3, 4, 5, 8, 12, 13, 14, 16, 18, 19, 25, 26

-National Archives, Prague
6, 7, 10, 17, 20, 21, 27a, 27b, 28

-Stiftung Jüddisches Museum, Berlin
9 (courtesy of Eva Bloch)

-Miroslav Šimák
22

-Vladimir Horpeniak
29

-the author's images
15, 23, 24, and 30.

Some photos and images are shown in their raw authenticity.

Copyright permit has been secured from Penguin Random House, New York, to quote from the following English editions of Franz Kafka's texts:
-Franz Kafka, *Diaries 1910–1913;*
-Franz Kafka, *Diaries 1914–1924;*
-Franz Kafka, *Letters to Friends, Family, and Editors;*
-Franz Kafka, *Letters to Felice.*

PREFACE

Few men of letters project as Kafkaesque an image and attract as much creative attention as Kafka himself. In the first seven decades since his death in 1924 alone, an estimated fifteen thousand titles on Kafka were published in major languages.[1] In recent times, his life and works have also inspired numerous soul-searching film, drama, and music productions worldwide and have served as course reading at various academic programs. Kafka comics, operas, and music festivals are supplementing the choices of his fans. A Franz Kafka Way highlights a small seaside resort in the Baltic that hosted him in 1923, and the Franz Kafka Express connects his hometown, Prague, with Munich by rail. In the weightiest display of inspired commercialism, a robotic forty-ton head of Kafka has been erected in Prague. Assembled from several thousands of stainless parts on forty-two levels and propelled by forty-two Siemens motors, this massive structure periodically reconfigures into an array of his similes.

The enduring interest in Kafka confirms him as one of the most enigmatic stars of the literary Pantheon.

Clearly, the body of Kafka's novels, dwelling on trials and tribulations of individuals challenged by inscrutable forces, resonates with cultured readers. His posthumous appeal is also enhanced by the tragic brevity of his life—he died in 1924, just before turning forty-one—and his obsessive concern for secrecy. He destroyed numerous sections of his diaries and, in January 1922, burned much of the received mail (which we may assume was less guarded than his missives). His preserved letters and diaries are likewise notable for metaphorical opacity that leaves a lot to the imagination.

Kafka's penchant for secrecy extended to his oeuvres. Overall, they are quasi-autobiographical. As he put it to his early fan Gustav Janouch, "One tries to imprison life in a book."[2] But they are also both deceptively simple and transparently muddled. He weaves into them personal issues the reader is not supposed to grasp fully. The distinguished crowd of Kafka aficionados (which includes a Nobel Prize winner) accepts that his texts exude a purposeful, 'controlled' intelligence, but the message remains a mystery.[3] In a complementary view, 'Kafka can communicate only with Kafka—and he can't always do that.'[4] Similarly, the author of the most extensive biography of Kafka observes that there must be a master key to comprehending his novels but doubts it will ever be uncovered.[5]

Since Kafka gives up so few secrets, his biographers scramble for any tidbit of relevant evidence or insight. In a British author's hyperbole, 'The scholar who can decipher one erased line of Kafka's diary or prove that his rivals have all gotten wrong the hotel he went to on such and such day in 1913, will be quoted in theses forever.'[6] The Kafka studies have reached a plateau.

As in similar circumstances, further advance in this matter calls for a systematic search both in and outside the box of conventions. Specifically, it must start with reconsidering the assumption so stubbornly held by so many that this shy genius was also a saint.

Kafka himself would undoubtedly be amused by his current pristine image. In his own words, "I write differently from what I speak. I speak differently from what I think; I think differently from the way I ought to think."[7] He also confessed to falsifying or withholding and found "living permanently without lies is as impossible as it is without truth."[8] Several months before his death, he summed up his conduct: "Concealment has been my life's vocation."[9] Beyond doubt, he felt a strong need to obscure the understanding of his life and creations.[10] As has been noticed elsewhere, Franz Kafka qualifies for the moniker of a "talking sphinx."[11]

Venturing into his private closets in some respect involved a revisit of this author's own past. Kafka, for a start, was such a highly idiosyncratic writer in no small part because of his nurture and milieu. Decades later, I frequented his turf centered on Prague's Old Town, attended language seminars on the second floor of the Kinský Palace that housed his high school, took the same courses including his nemesis, Roman law, and, apparently just as him, absorbed the city's unique genius loci that had formed throughout centuries of interaction between Gentiles and non-Gentiles.

Similar to Kafka, my generation learned to accept the notion of life as the aggregate of one's aspirational but paradoxical, even injurious experiences. Does not every good deed eventually get the punishment it deserves? The Hegelian dictum that what is real is also rational made little sense to us (in the quip attributed to Kafka, "Nothing really exists except miracles"). The medieval tale of Golem, the "Jewish robot" as one of his friends put it, resonated with us as well.[12] Could a reader of *The Trial* avoid shiver in the spine on evening walks by the abandoned quarry on Moldau's west bank, the site where the hapless Josef K. might have been executed in cold blood? More than elsewhere, there may indeed exist a realm outside reality in Prague.

Just as Kafka, we also adjusted to a capricious system of values that blurred the truth and fantasy, held public institutions omnipotent, and strapped the individual with an array of bizarre interdictions. Just like him, we approached reading between the lines as a young man's guide to the galaxy. Blanks can be more revealing than words. We also found appealing a one-liner applicable to him—"It is wise to be foolish when circumstances make the effort worthwhile."[13] No wonder that Václav Havel, the grandmaster of absurd theater and onetime Czechoslovak president, also called Prague his home.

The above factors help explain this author's experience as Kafka's interpreter. Exploratory probes suggested there is more to Kafka than a multitude of biographers acknowledge. Complemented by Czech sources, the evidence started conforming with his compatriot Rainer Maria Rilke's gloss, "What we call Fame is nothing but the sum of all misconceptions circulating about an individual."[14] The ensuing research campaign pointed to so far unknown or overlooked sources of Kafka's proverbial feeling of fear, guilt, and shame. Dutifully called into service, they helped clarify other mysteries he confounded the interpreters with.

The resulting narrative may rankle Kafka mavens keen on safeguarding his image of purity and martyrdom. It is backed primarily by Kafka's own words and deals realistically with the subject. Still, in the field straddling fiction and non-fiction, it links some dots by context only and leaves some unconnected. It should be noted that, as other authors concede, similar uncertainties apply to Kafka studies in general. Researching Kafka compares to wading in quicksand. In its core, this book endeavors to explain why and how this gentle public servant grappled with explosive impulses—"demons" in his parlance—and how they impacted his literary production. The reader can expect to gain a better understanding of issues behind such puzzling gems of modern literature as *The Metamorphosis*, *The Trial*, and *The Castle*. More distinctly than elsewhere, Kafka will also come across here as a meticulously programmed wordsmith, so remarkably adept in fictionalizing his personal circumstances and draping them with dry humor.

Introduced is also Kafka's secret love affair that spiced his major texts and may not have played itself out yet: the direct descendants of this alleged sex-abstainer may be living among us.

Whether intrigued or miffed by Kafka's mystique, may you find this biography insightful and stimulating enough to reach for his writings again.

Kafka's 'Tuberculosis'

This inquiry into Franz Kafka's secrets may start with addressing the pivotal issue of his life, his supposed suffering and demise from tuberculosis. The disease allegedly announced itself in his thirty-fourth year. In the popular version relayed by Kafka himself, he awoke in his Prague flat in the predawn of mid-August 1917 with blood in his mouth. He returned to bed, but another hemorrhage and visit to his physician confirmed the diagnosis of pulmonary tuberculosis. This story, as seen below, was eventually discredited by Kafka himself, but let us first put the issue in context.

Tuberculosis was the curse of humankind before the age of antibiotics, affecting mainly the poor. Those affluent or attentive to personal hygiene, including Kafka's class, the urbanized Jewish population, succumbed to it disproportionally less. Moreover, after Robert Koch discovered *bacillus tuberculi* in 1882, civilized countries started developing comprehensive systems of containment and prevention of the disease. The government in the Kingdom of Bohemia, the western part of the Austro-Hungarian Empire, enacted a series of laws between 1902 and 1913, setting specific measures to prevent and fight infectious ailments including tuberculosis. These were followed by executive orders issued by regional authorities and other regulatory bodies.[1]

It is a serious matter to be tubercular today when a refusal to undergo treatment may still warrant arrest and was even more inhibiting in 1917. Physicians, teachers, coroners, and other persons of authority were obliged to report all new cases of the disease or a mere suspicion thereof. A failure to do so or negligence in initiating countermeasures could earn the offending doctor penalty ranging from reprimand or fine to jail time and cancellation of medical license. Concerted efforts under the supervision by state-appointed public health commissioners were to assist the diseased and protect their families, coworkers, and society.

Compulsory measures were comprehensive, starting with a thorough disinfection of the diseased, his personal belongings and residence. For illustration, the Prague magistrate demanded a systematic sterilization by steam and chemical means of the tubercular's body discharges, clothing, bed and bed linens, dishes, furniture, bathroom, toilet facility, and clothing of all caregivers. The walls had to be scrubbed up to two meters' height with disinfectants of varying kind and strength, all according to a meticulous protocol. Soft items were supposed to be carted off in bags for steam disinfection in special sanitation stations.[2]

The tubercular persons were expected to live as much as possible in isolation, avoid all contacts with children, use separate dishes, and carry spitting cups to contain tubercular sputum—a repulsive, highly infectious mix of decaying lung matter, blood, and body fluid. There was no escape from this regime: the patient's change of address had to be reported to authorities, and his freedom to move around let alone travel abroad was severely restricted.

Similar stringent rules existed in other parts of Central Europe, Kafka's roaming grounds.[3]

Were Kafka and his family ever subjected to any of these restrictive measures? Not at all. Was he ever denied entry into a country he wished to visit, be it Germany, Austria, Italy, France, or Denmark? No, he was not. These facts alone put in serious doubt his status as a sufferer from pulmonary tuberculosis—and far more of the same is still coming.

Blood discharge can have numerous causes, but more often than in lungs, it originates in the upper respiratory system. On his first visit after hemorrhage to the family doctor Mühlstein in August 1917, Kafka was indeed diagnosed with bronchial catarrh, an inflammation of the upper tips of the lungs and breathing tube that carries air to them. It can be a marker of tuberculosis, but that was not Kafka's case. Mühlstein, an internist, took the patient lightly, merely prescribing three bottles of further unspecified drink and advising him to return in a month or right away if blood reappeared. Kafka's condition was not infectious.

According to his account, Kafka coughed blood again but less. Back at Mühlstein's office, he was found somewhat emaciated but not at acute risk.

City dwellers, in particular, can be asymptomatic carriers of the tubercular bacillus, he was told, but even that apparently was not his case. Mühlstein assured the patient he posed no threat of infecting others, thus effectively ruling out tuberculosis.

At this point, as we will see, Kafka's mind was set on getting time off work, a next-to-impossible goal for a civil servant exempted from fighting in the Great War 1914–1818. This could change instantly if diagnosed tubercular, but when Kafka visited again Dr. Mühlstein two weeks later, on or about August 29, the latter confirmed the patient was free of the disease. The diagnosis had not changed—bronchial catarrh.

Kafka visited Dr. Mühlstein for the fourth time on September 3. With results of the X-ray exam and sputum test in, Mühlstein confirmed even more resolutely the catarrh. The lungs proper were untouched. Kafka's case was not even suspicious and thus reportable. Considering the patient's age, there was little danger that tuberculosis could eventually develop, Kafka reported, alluding to the fact that tuberculosis attacks primarily children and juveniles. Mühlstein advised ample food and fresh air but prescribed no medicine. Above all, he denied the patient's request for a pass from work. If tubercular, Kafka would have been furloughed indefinitely.

Without delay, Kafka underwent another examination in the morning of September 4 (1917), this time by Prof. Gottfried Pick, an internist and director of the Laryngological Institute at the Prague University. This crème de la crème expert was also unperturbed. He confirmed Mühlstein's diagnosis. The patient was not tubercular. In a critical shift, however, Pick recommended three months' leave for recovery.[4] This set the precedent: Based on his bronchial catarrh and assorted health issues, Kafka managed to extricate himself from work for several months in 1917 and repeated similar feats on other occasions thereafter.

It needs to be pointed out that bronchial catarrh was the only lung condition Kafka was ever positively diagnosed with. Fixated on his tuberculosis but lacking any convincing proof thereof, his biographers either ignore this or at best struggle to square the circle. Thus, the prominent Kafka specialist has suggested in the first-published volume of his biography that pulmonary catarrh was a 'standard diagnosis' for tuberculosis in Kafka's days.[5] It was not. The authoritative *Pathology and Therapy of Internal Diseases* by Josef Thomayer, the fifth edition of which appeared in Kafka's time, clearly differentiated between *catarrhus pulmonum*, pulmonary catarrh, and pulmonary tuberculosis.[6]

While tuberculosis may manifest itself in inflamed lung apexes, it is much more than that. The equivocation of lung inflammation with tuberculosis is untenable. Not accidentally, then, the same author, in the second-published volume of his biography, rewrote the argument to give the impression the good-humored Dr. Mühlstein failed to diagnose Kafka's tuberculosis competently.[7]

The accusation of negligence or incompetence likewise lacks credibility. The detection of tuberculosis was an elementary subject in all medical schools and reached a sophisticated level in Kafka's time. X-ray technology (for which Wilhelm Röntgen received the Nobel Prize in 1901) was widely available and, along with other diagnostic tools such as tuberculin test and sputum analysis, allowed a firm diagnosis. Even if we assume for a second that both Mühlstein and Pick erred, Kafka was subsequently examined by at least a dozen qualified doctors in Prague and elsewhere before his pensioning in 1922 alone. Yet, though even a mere suspicion of tuberculosis was reportable, none of his examiners raised a warning flag. It is unlikely in the extreme that they all concealed or failed to detect the disease, the conduct that would endanger their careers and the lives of both the patient and his family.

Moreover, Kafka's authentic diagnosis of 1917, inflammation of lung apexes, was no surprise to him. He was tagged with this condition as early as 1907 and diagnosed with the same again and again until his last year. It would be rather odd to assume that a succession of doctors, supported by laboratory personnel, for seventeen years misdiagnosed tuberculosis for the same chronic ailment. Does not the reverse thought make far more sense—namely, that a bronchial catarrh was Kafka's real respiratory problem? The text below supports this contention, addressing also the issue whether Kafka in the last weeks of his life struggled with the rare tuberculosis of larynx.[8]

Kafka's personal conduct befits a nontubercular status. Employed at an institution committed to health preservation, he regularly dealt with tuberculosis. In fact, he was a member of a team exploring current approaches to coping with the disease. Its symptoms, prevention, and good hygiene were the topics familiar to him. Personally, he washed his hands several times a day and considered tuberculosis "very upsetting, not only because of the constant danger of infection but above all because this continual illness is filthy . . . I can only watch with disgust when the others [infected] bring up sputum."[9] We may safely assume he found his health problems consistent with the doctors' diagnosis.

Being free of tuberculosis would explain why such a conscientious, fastidious person showed absolutely no interest in subjecting to the treatment thereof. In truth, Kafka cared little for his doctors' advice in general, visiting them primarily to extract time off. His preference was natural healing methods, he claimed, but followed them sloppily and eventually denounced naturopathy as quackery.

Equally striking was his unconcern about infecting others, his family, lovers, coworkers, and children in particular. It was common knowledge in his days that tuberculosis is deadly to kids. Boarding them with an untreated tubercular amounts to criminal negligence. It must have been with the firm understanding of his noninfectious status that nobody minded his sharing the family apartment at Oldtown Square with his sister Ottla and her infant daughter Věra, or his vacationing with both of them in close quarters in 1922, or taking vacations with little Věra and her two-month-old sister Helena in 1923, or spending time with his other sister Elli's young children in the Baltic the same year.

In sum, there is no firm evidence of Kafka's lung tuberculosis, just a nebulous, evasive flutter.[10] The entries in his diaries for the critical period in 1917 and subsequent segments that could shed light on his supposed appointment with tuberculosis have been expunged forever. The absence of a direct proof is not the proof of absence, of course. But a wide spectrum of facts still to be presented below further contradicts the image of a tubercular Kafka.

The key to untangling this conundrum suggests that his health issues were a far better match with the wasting-away disorder, *Schwindsucht* in bygone German. It denoted a serious weight loss that typically occurred at the time of famine. In sharp contrast to tuberculosis, it was a noninfectious condition reversible with better nutrition, but it could lead to death if untreated. Kafka referred to *Schwindsucht* with regard to his situation. It is food and drink denial leading to ever worsening emaciation that will indeed be identified here as a major factor in his demise.

For now, then, the informed reader is asked to ponder the imponderable—namely, that Franz Kafka's tuberculosis may be a tall tale.[11]

This complementary question is due now: Why did the affluent Kafka deprive himself so drastically of the necessities of life? Addressing his health handicaps in late August 1917, he contended having been shackled by them for the past five years. Lungs, he rephrased it to Felice Bauer, were not responsible for his problems: "I don't believe this illness to be tuberculosis, at least not primarily tuberculosis, but rather a sign of my general bankruptcy."[12] A major personal failure the onset of which, without medical attestation, he pegged to a specific year, 1912? To solve this puzzle, we need to untangle other secrets of Kafka's life and writings first.

BACKGROUND

Located at the crossroads of Europe, Franz Kafka's hometown of Prague was a unique place notable for the intermingling of peoples and cross-fertilization of ideas. The East met the West there. The predominantly Czech population had, for centuries, been challenged by German settlers in conflict and cooperation. Politically, Prague had been the capital of the Czech kingdom consisting of two core lands, Bohemia in the west and Moravia in the east. In 1526, however, the Czech lands became part of the Habsburg Empire centered in Vienna, and Prague gradually regressed into a provincial capital.

Both sides of Franz Kafka's family tree belonged to the Jewish Diaspora that had been present in the Czech lands as far back as written history goes. The rationalizing reforms of Kaiser Joseph II in the 1780s expected Jews to Germanize their names, but Kafka's ancestors opted for the Czech word meaning "jackdaw." Franz Kafka's paternal grandfather Jakob was a robust person who earned his living as a kosher butcher in a small Jewish community centered on Osek, a village in Southwestern Bohemia. His grave can be seen to this day at an abandoned Jewish cemetery at the nearby village of Radomyšl. There were perhaps twenty to thirty Jewish families in the region, not enough to run a full Yeshiva school.

Since the Diaspora shied away from education in Czech, Franz Kafka's father Hermann (1852–1931) apparently received only rudimentary tutoring focused on Judaism. As the fifth child in the family, he started eking out a living as a delivery boy for his father and embraced Czech as his first language in constant interaction with Czech populace. His Czech was fluent but untutored and strictly phonetic in written form. Three years in compulsory military service also helped his German, which, however, retained a Czech accent and was likewise less than correct grammatically.

Short of formal education, Hermann Kafka excelled in business because of his vitality and acumen supplemented with an unusual knack for math. His granddaughter Věra recalled in 2014 that even as an old man, he managed with ease to solve in his head complex mathematical calculations his family tested him with. This faculty of abstract thinking was probably inherited by his son Franz and gave him a critical edge—the ability to conceptualize with astonishing effectiveness his stories.

While the Kafkas overall were notable for their drive, the maternal side of Franz's family tree, the Lövy clan, belonged to the better established and more affluent middle class. Rooted in the town of Poděbrady in East Central Bohemia, they prospered after the Habsburg Empire dismantled anti-Jewish regulations in the 1860s. Among Kafka's maternal uncles, Alfred and Joseph Lövy were adventurers trotting the globe, while the youngest, Siegfried, also a bachelor, was a country doctor in the Moravian town of Třešť (Triesch). Another uncle, Rudolf, likewise a bachelor, was a low-key individual who also irked the family by converting to Catholicism.

Their elder sister and Franz's mother, Julie (1856–1934), was, in Max Brod's words, "a quiet, pleasant, extremely clever, not to say a wise woman."[1] Her dowry helped Hermann Kafka set a firm footing in Prague as a merchant in millineries in the 1880s. Though the marriage was apparently arranged, Hermann and Julie were compatible and became loving parents. Living and running their shop in the hub of Prague's Jewish community centered on Oldtown Square, they worked long hours catering both to Jewish and Gentile customers.

Franz was the eldest of Kafkas' three boys but, since his two younger brothers died as infants, also the only one. Born on July 3, 1883, he grew up in well-defined circumstances marked by attendance at the elementary German Boys' School on the Fish Market, bar mitzvah at 1896, and the Oldtown German gymnasium, a demanding high school attended mainly by Jewish students. Meanwhile, in 1889 and 1890, his sisters, nicknamed Elli and Valli, were born, followed in October 1892 by the third sister, Ottilie, nicknamed Ottla.

The 1890s saw major shifts in Kafka's country. For the start, the Czech nation, so far dominated by the German-speaking, Vienna-based Habsburgs, was on the upswing again. Inspired by the past glories of the Czech kingdom, this renaissance found a solid complement in the advancing industrialization of the Czech lands. By the turn of the century, the spirit of confidence was also expressed in a large sanitation project in Prague that reshaped much of the ancient Jewish quarter Josefov between the Oldtown Square and Vltava (the Moldau). The Old-New Synagogue was left standing under the street level to remain the focus of Jewish life in the city.

The Czech resurgence also manifested itself in rising assertiveness against all things German, in particular the German minority in Bohemia. Jewish citizens had become more than innocent bystanders. Apart from traditional Gentile prejudice, they now coped with a double jeopardy because of their preference for German language and education. Anti-Semitism manifested by the Dreyfus case in France also infected Bohemia in 1898, in the form of the Hilsner affair, supposedly involving a ritual murder. Although the future president of Czechoslovakia T. G. Masaryk courageously resisted the hysteria, the prospect for Jews seemed just as uncertain in Czech lands as elsewhere in Europe.

By 1900, Jews constituted 60 percent of German-speaking inhabitants of Prague, but their numbers hovered around 25,000 out of the total population of 450,000. Further, they started conceding grounds to the Czech element. While in the 1895 census 75 percent of Prague Jews declared themselves linguistically German, in the 1910 census 55 percent of them considered themselves linguistically Czech. No less than 90 percent of their children, however, attended German schools.

Hermann Kafka's interests suffered little by this Czech upsurge. He was a lukewarm religionist, eschewing yarmulke and kosher food and attending a synagogue at Jindřišská Street on special occasions only. The service at the synagogue was in Czech. His shop sign was also in Czech, and at home, he communicated primarily in Czech peppered with German and Yiddish words. His affinity with Czechs served him well in business. When anti-Jewish riots broke out in Prague in 1898, his shop was left undisturbed. A closet socialist who dreamed of a just social system, in everyday life, Kafka senior was steadily climbing the ladder to an upper-middle-class status.

His son Franz, however, grappled with difficult life choices. He may have been impacted by childhood memories, claiming in 1921 that as a little boy, he had been crushed by his father.[2] This could have referred to his father's occasional assertion of paternal authority such as his banishment to the balcony for whining or merely a justification of his real and perceived failures in adult life. However, he was far more burdened by the unending search for identity.

Perhaps more than his father and other family members, Kafka felt spiritually rooted in Jewishness, and his closest companions were all Jewish. But his commitment to the Jewish cause was tempered by reluctance to display it in conditions of anti-Semitism. Eventually, as he admitted in *Letter to His Father* (1921), he also failed to find in Judaism a counterbalance to his father's pragmatism. Tepid if not opportunistic was also his interest in Czech affairs, even though he had learned passable Czech from parents and maids and casually followed Czech culture. His formal education was German and so was his outlook and ambitions. True, he would not stand up when *Wacht am Rhein*, the hymn of German nationalists, was sung in a pub. But he also never accepted that the Prague streets were signposted in Czech, referring to them and other localities in their German equivalent even after the establishment of Czechoslovakia in 1918.

The eclipse of German interest in his hometown and the threat of anti-Semitism impacted Franz Kafka's already sensitive psyche and left him questioning himself and the security of his existence. "Fear . . . is part of me and perhaps the best part," he quipped in 1920, expressing the attitude that was far from unique among Prague Jewry.[3] The word "fear" reappears in his diaries and letters like a refrain in Greek drama.

On graduating from high school in 1901 with 'very good' in geography, history, Greek, and philosophy,- and satisfactory in German, math, natural sciences, and French,- he matriculated in the German section of the Prague University. First, he enrolled in chemistry but soon switched to law. In spring 1902, however, he failed the freshman course in Roman law. This blow prompted him to explore the alternatives. He took summer courses in art history and, in October, traveled to Munich, pondering enrollment there in German studies.

However, the grass was not greener in the Bavarian metropolis, and Franz eventually resumed the study of jurisprudence in Prague. An indifferent student, he passed (but barely) his state exams and received a doctor of law degree in late spring 1906. After articling in a private law office, he began a one-year legal practice at the state court in Prague in October of that year.

By all accounts, Kafka made the impression of a quiet, composed young adult with natural predisposition for goodness. In his self-assessment of 1920, "My misfortune is that with my brain and heart I regard all people as good."[4] In his close friend Oskar Baum's recollections, he indeed acted in an unfailingly gentle way. On the visit to a Berlin aquarium, he was caught speaking to a fish. Max Brod too found him gentle and kind, commanding an unusual degree of respect, the essence of which was hard to fathom. Brod traced it to his way of communication—compact, always meaningful, and "full of sad humor."[5]

Kafka's traits contrasted with those of the Kafka clan, defined by him as strength, health, appetite, and self-confidence. But he also ascribed weaknesses and failings to these qualities and expressed affinity with the Löwys. In another self-assessment of 1922, he drew comparison with his uncle Rudolf Löwy, a modest, shy bachelor. As he saw it, however, the uncle was not pulled apart by the same ambition. Franz Kafka set for himself exceptionally high criteria for self-esteem and gratification, but these did not include a career in jurisprudence, and his personal traits were not supportive of it.

For illustration, after this trained lawyer signed a lease for an apartment in 1914, he could not recall the terms when confronted by his landlord: Embarrassed by his helplessness, he hired another lawyer to draft a new lease. Years later, Milena Jesenská bluntly observed, "He does not understand the simplest things in the world . . . this whole world is and shall remain mystery for him. A mystical enigma."[6] Lost for everyday life, Kafka felt comfortable in his well-defined precincts.

Pondering his career, he opted for the predictability of employment. In October 1907, thanks to Uncle Alfred Löwy's intervention, he was hired as a clerk at the Prague branch of the large insurance company Assicurazioni Generali. But he worked long hours, from 8:00 a.m. to 6:00 p.m., and soon started looking for another work.

On completing a course on workers' insurance at Prague Academy of Commerce, in July 1908, he began his second, and as it turned out the last, job in the legal department of the Institute of Workers' Accident Insurance, a semi governmental body of approximately 250 employees that set safety standards and recompense for injured workers in Bohemia. The position was well suited to his character. In private life, he showed compassion with underdogs, weeping over the case of a young mother who, out of poverty and desperation, strangled her infant girl. As a manager of the family asbestos business, he was clearly distressed by the workers' conditions. Leaning as a youngster to anarchist socialism and its protagonists, Peter

Kropotkin and Gustav Landauer, he put together a draft of a workers' collective in his later years.

Kafka traveled extensively throughout Central Europe, but none of the visited places appealed to him enough to leave his hometown permanently. Even Munich, arguably as close in spirit to Prague as any German city, did not have enough allure. As his friend Johannes Urzidil put in perspective, Prague was a unique, lively body of Czechs, Germans, and Jews; a wellspring of aspirations, talents, and accomplishments.

Within this miniscule universe, it was the Jewish enclave in the Old Town that supplied Kafka with much of his inspiration, challenge, and support. Along with his friends, mainly sons of well-to-do Jewish parents, Franz frequented cafes in downtown Prague, primarily Café Louvre and later Café Arco. Sensitive and private for the most part, he observed the scenery from "somewhere in the corner."[7] Of limited social drive, he found himself comfortable in a small circle of friends. Max Brod would recall that in those situations, "his tongue sometimes ran away with itself in the most astounding manner." A large crowd, on the other hand, intimidated and suffocated him.[8]

Max Brod (1884–1968) was not Kafka's first friend but certainly figured as the most influential. The eldest child of a cultured well-situated family—his father, Adolf, was a deputy director of the Union Bank in Prague and his mother a pretty socialite—Brod was diagnosed with a spinal curvature at the age of four. Forced to wear braces in gym classes, he grew up slightly deformed. However, he was also an extrovert who dressed elegantly and possessed restless intellect, trying his mettle as a novelist, poet, dramatist, critic, composer, and musician. Along the way, he also established a reputation as a womanizer.

Unlike his Jewish friends who almost uniformly saw the future bleak, Brod attended a Catholic high school with extra sessions given by a rabbi and formed an optimistic outlook on life. Committed to reason, decency, and racial tolerance, he would build bridges to the Czech culture, introducing his Jewish community to Czech writers such as Jaroslav Hašek and Petr Bezruč, as well as composer Leoš Janáček.

Imbued with optimism, in the fall of 1902, the precocious Brod gave a lecture at the Jewish students' club on Arthur Schopenhauer and Friedrich Nietzsche, two stalwarts of German philosophy. As could be expected, he found the skeptical rationalist Schopenhauer more congenial than Nietzsche, a provocative nihilist who turned the values of society upside down. Kafka attended the lecture, a tall, dark, handsome teenager with so much going for him—yet brooding and pessimistic. After the lecture, he confronted Brod over his critique of Nietzsche, the first of numerous occasions that revealed a gulf of separation between them. And yet this was one of the defining moments of Kafka's life for he would strike a lifelong friendship with Brod primarily beneficial to him. Just like there would not have been Karl Marx as we know him without Friedrich Engels, Kafka would probably have remained a struggling regional author without Max Brod's unfailing support and encouragement.

In 1904, already at ease with his new friend, Kafka addressed him with existential musings and a sense of togetherness: "We burrow through ourselves like a mole and emerge blackened and velvet-haired from our sandy underground vaults."[9] The following year, he and Brod allied with two similar-minded individuals, Felix Weltsch, the future librarian, and Oskar Baum, another gentle character who had lost his sight in a brawl between the German and Czech students and earned a living as a music teacher. Though their friendship was repeatedly tested, they would remain exceptionally loyal to each other throughout the years.

Kafka's parents Hermann and Julie

HERRMANN KAFKA, PRAG I.
Zeltnergasse 3.
Galanteriewaren en gros Geschäft.

Logo of the family business

Kinský Palace: the family business was on the ground floor
to the right, Kafka's gymnasium on the floor above

Preschooler Kafka

Teenage Kafka

Max Brod

Felix Weltsch

1902: RESORTING TO "SAW DUST"

A revolt against the established norms gripped the transatlantic world in the first decade of the last century, manifested across the board in new advances in science, arts, and cultural sensitivity. Albert Einstein saw his theory of special relativity published in 1905, Pablo Picasso and his confreres broke the tradition of figurative painting with cubism, and the musical avant-garde Alban Berg, Arnold Schönberg, Claude Debussy, and Igor Stravinsky, most prominently, found new modes of expression that defied nearly all Western music of the past 350 years.

The *le fin de siècle* in Vienna and by extension Central Europe was seemingly more frivolous, associated with three *w*'s, waltzes, women, and wine. The reality, however, was likewise cross-textured with convention-defying trends that, among other effects, attacked the taboos of lifestyle and sexuality. Richard Strauss's opera *Salome* (1905) perhaps best exemplified the new wave. Following Oscar Wilde's drama, Strauss composed arguably the most shocking opera ever: the teenage Syrian princess. Salome, in unrequited love for John the Baptist and herself the object of incestuous lust by her stepfather, King Herod, in revenge, asks for John the Baptist's head, and when she receives it, severed, declares love for it, caresses, and kisses it passionately on the lips before she herself is killed. *Salome* ran into censorship problems or was banned in major operatic houses of the day.

Among the factors that accompanied if not underpinned this flowering of creativity and decadence was a rampant drug abuse. The drug of choice from time immemorial until the nineteenth century was opium, complemented after the 1850s by its derivate, morphine. In consequence of the standoffish attitude of governments and authorities throughout much of the century, armies of addicts had formed in the industrialized and developing regions of the world alike.

The young Viennese physician Sigmund Freud (1856–1939), not averse to experimenting with drugs himself, joined the bandwagon of detoxification. By all signs, his first patient, the twenty-five-year-old Bertha Pappenheim, known in history as Anna O., coped with a debilitating dependence on morphine. Freud tried to straighten her out with hypnosis, the method propagated in France, but the experiment did not work.

Meanwhile, a new, supposedly miraculous substance was gaining acceptance on both sides of the Atlantic—cocaine. The extract from coca leaves harvested in South America, it was legal and seemingly harmless. Coca-Cola was the best known cola-based product that came on the market in the 1880s; others included mates of coca, coca wine, and coca lozenges. Cocaine use skyrocketed when the pharmaceutical company Merck started mass-producing it for the Bavarian army in 1883.

Making it the subject of his scientific curiosity and paid by manufacturers of the drug, Freud wrote enthusiastic articles on cocaine, the best-known being "On Coca" (1885). He touted the drug as an anesthetic, aphrodisiac, mind booster, appetite stimulant in case of wasting diseases, and treatment of morphine addiction. However, when he administered cocaine to his friend and morphine addict Ernst von Fleischl-Marxow, his assumptions proved tragically wrong. The latter quickly developed a double addiction to both drugs and died of emaciation in 1891.

The tragic story of Fleischl-Marxow could by no means halt cocaine from gaining popularity. In the late nineteenth century, a variety of cocaine concoctions had become fashionable across the national and social divides, primarily not only in the artistic community but also among the royalty—Queen Victoria of England and Tsar Nicholas II of Russia—the popes, and politicians including Winston Churchill. Cocaine became an enticing addition to the drug subculture that flourished by 1900 in various parts of the globe. The drug abuse was by and large legal but regarded as improper, even more so in Central Europe where appearances really mattered.

Yet, the Viennese society—literati, artists, doctors, soldiers, and politicians—experimented with every possible substance, from narcotics such as opium and opiates to cocaine and the freshly discovered barbiturates. The lure of drugs entrapped even the Imperial family. The pharmacy prescriptions discovered after the fall of the Habsburg dynasty in 1918 revealed that the Grand Dukes Otto and Franz Ferdinand, as well as the Crown Prince Rudolf, had been taking opium, morphine, cocaine, heroin, and codeine. The Kaiser Franz Joseph, who ruled the empire since 1848 and had the reputation of a stodgy disciplinarian, was consuming morphine, cocaine, codeine, as well as arsenic and caffeine. His wife, the empress Elisabeth, developed a taste for opium, morphine, cocaine, cannabis, and codeine.[1]

Like the Imperial family, most drug users managed to keep their enthusiasm for narcotics private. Only those who blatantly overstepped the social norm became newsworthy, among them Kafka's acquaintance Otto Gross. Son of Kafka's professor at the Prague University, Gross was a member of Freud's circle who started carving his own niche in psychiatry. Under the influence of cocaine and opiates, however, he veered into the whimsical. One of his pet projects was the camp Askona where nudity and licentiousness were considered the prerequisite of freedom next to drugs. A cult figure increasingly subservient to narcotics, he was falling apart both morally and physically, was repeatedly committed to an asylum, and eventually died as an emaciated junkie in 1920.

Kafka probably first encountered Gross in 1907. As a monographer points out, there was striking affinity between them.[2] Ten years later, meeting accidentally on a train, they plotted a journal devoted to combatting resistance to free will. Almost certainly, this was meant as a spoof on the addicts' lack of resistance to drugs. Kafka showed an interest in the project that, however, did not get off the ground. He still continued to express understanding with the half-deranged eccentric and suspected murderer who also fathered children with four different women. Remarked Kafka retrospectively on Gross, "I felt the warmth of a certain personal connection glowing from it."[3]

After Gross hungered to death, Kafka, facing the same prospect, in 1922, wrote one of his most poignant short proses, "The Hunger Artist." The same year he also objected indignantly to his friend Werfel's lampooning of the deceased.

Did Kafka partake in the drug festival of his contemporaries? In the uncontested view of a German biographer, he 'resolutely' avoided all stimulants, including faddish drugs of the literary bohemia. The age was rife with drugs, only Kafka was clean.[4] How does the author know? His is merely a guess stemming from the widely held conviction that Kafka was a white lily; he could do no harm to or deceive himself and others.

Such platitudes, however, are misleading without qualification. Based on evidence accumulated here, Kafka carried in himself a moral compass but, when forced by circumstances, behaved like a mortal and feared retribution.

This ambivalence applies to drugs as well. Though the heavily sanitized sources offer no direct evidence of his addiction, this cannot be accepted as evidence of his abstention. Once again, the absence of proof is not the proof of absence. Kafka acted like a drug addict, expressed himself like a drug addict, and suffered from health problems that paralleled those of the Imperial family and were symptomatic of substance abuse. Drugs can define one's existence and creative dispositions, and this certainly holds true for him. By failing to explore this potential minefield, Kafka's biographers are nowhere near comprehending numerous aspects of his life and work.

The available evidence points to 1902 as the year when the nineteen-year-old Kafka crossed the bridge to the world of drugs, never to return. Nineteen years later and in a circuitous mode as ever, he implied he had resorted to drugs to prove his worthiness to his father, and his ambition had prevented him to "quit the battlefield" ever since.[5]

This fatuous course of events can be reconstructed from the preserved evidence. Thus, in early April 1902, Kafka still admonished his early friend Oskar Pollak: "You often become quite sick. Then I feel sympathy and cannot do anything and say anything." And again, castigating Pollak with words pointing to the latter's drug dependence: "Only the wicked criticaster . . . inhabits you, and he is a subordinate devil whom, however, you should shake off."[6] The letter was written from the position of an onlooker.

The same spring, however, in his freshman year at the Faculty of Law, Kafka failed the introductory course in Roman law. Come hot summer, two volumes of the textbook still lay at his desk in the family apartment in Celetná Street, and he was at a loss how to dispense with the "disgusting Roman law between my teeth."[7] What a shame if he failed the repeat!

Vacationing with his uncle Siegfried Löwy in Třešť, Franz pondered but felt uneasy about his options. In August 1902, then, another uncle of his, Alfred Löwy, arrived in Prague. He was a highly respected member of the family living in Madrid and active as entrepreneur and business manager in charge of Spanish railways. Kafka considered him the closest relative, in some respect closer than his parents.

Entertaining an eerie notion that the uncle Löwy might help him somehow out of his predicament, Kafka returned from Třešť to meet him in Prague. The uncle indeed made a recommendation that the recipient found straightforward but creepy. On hearing it, Kafka reported on August 24, he dropped into silence and avoided mentioning the subject again in two days that he spent with the uncle in Prague.

What was this unctuous advice? Years later, Kafka would recollect his trouble with exams in 1902 and write apocryphally that for a few months before (re)taking them, and "in a way that spoke severely of my nerves, I was positively living, in an intellectual sense, on sawdust." The phrase has so far defeated his interpreters' imagination: intellectual sawdust? In Kafka's critical qualification, it was the kind of substance that had "already been chewed for me in thousands of other people's mouths." He meant the peasants of South America for whom, since time immemorial, chewing coca leaf had been one of their few pleasures. We can accept that cocaine was the "creepy" substance Kafka that resorted to in August 1902 and found it exactly to his taste.[8]

While recreational users take cocaine for the high, brain characters appreciate its capacity to temporarily sharpen the mind. This evidently was the property that Kafka expected to benefit from, but the choice placed him in an awkward situation. There was no glory in confessing to an artificial boost of brain capacity. Consistent with his penchant for secretiveness, he concealed his new stimulus from Uncle Löwy and merely hinted it to Oskar Pollak, pleading for understanding. "All right, I began cautiously," Kafka summed up his introduction to the world of drugs.[9]

Cocaine can be digested, inhaled, injected, or sniffed. Which form did Kafka find congenial to his lifestyle? Long before the Internet made this search technique standard, the Sherlock Holmeses of the day filtered evidence for key words relevant for the case. Alas, a few months into his cocaine habit, in another story for Pollak of December 1902, Kafka mentioned becoming restive by letting his nose "sniff the air of the room"; how "stuffy, stale and unaired" this air was. Kafka rarely gave his interpreter a second chance. On the balance of probabilities, this was an allusion to cocaine sniffing, the most popular form of the drug's intake.

Soon, the super-sensitive Kafka started expressing values consistent with drug use. Low self-esteem was one of them. He characterized himself as "Shamefaced Lanky" with gray eyes, skinny fingers, pitiful legs, woolen socks, and appalling way of handshaking. Reflective of the oppressive nature of drugs, he also felt responsive to both "my god and my devil" and began invoking hell and "the death of us."[10]

The metaphor of one's entrapment in a cave, symptomatic for drug addiction, also showed up in Kafka's writings early, complemented with a nightmare of gasping for air. He compared himself to a "caveman who rolls a block in front of the entrance to his cave . . . but then, when the block makes the cave dark and shuts off the air, feels duly alarmed and with remarkable energy tries to push the rock away."[11]

The use of cocaine in moderate quantity may produce little physical impairment. As a teenager, Kafka played soccer and tennis, rode bike, swam, rowed a boat, and dated attractive girls. Yet, in retrospect, he perceived his initiation to cocaine as a setback. As he would claim in 1913, he had felt unfit for ten years. Indeed, while completely healthy in 1902, already the following year, he became concerned about his well-being. Thus, not yet twenty years old and amid his second-year university courses, he took a two-week nature cure in a sanatorium near Dresden.

This was the first of his numerous stays in various curative or recreational institutions—seemingly an absurd habit given his age. Visiting Leipzig and already worried about weight loss—one of the side effects of drug use—he consulted a local doctor who recommended a cake consisting of eggs, flour, butter, and a lot of sugar. This calorie-rich creation flavored with orange and lemon helped stabilize his weight.

Clearly, Kafka was striving to smooth the path to his major goals, the university degree and a career as a writer. According to his friend Hugo Bergman, he expressed the desire to write as early as 1894, at the age of eleven. As the twenty-year-old, a live-in maid would recall, he composed and engaged his sisters to perform theater sketches, among them a piece on George of Poděbrady, the Czech king of the fifteenth century.

However, cocaine may have helped Kafka pass law exams but little else. The substance stimulates the cognitive function rather than imagination, and its effect wanes fast as the drug metabolizes in blood and liver. It was not suitable for the storyteller he aspired to become. The texts that Kafka penned before and during his cocaine period (prior to 1907) have survived only in fragments; they are lively but evidently not good enough to meet his own expectations.

Where would Kafka go as a writer if he continued on the same path? In September 1903, he sent Pollak a bundle of his writings, so close to his heart. Would the recipient comment on it? Probably encouraged by the response, Kafka soon announced that fragments of a novel would follow for a review. So far, he appreciated Pollak as a window to the world. The recipient, however, was probably reserved about Kafka's texts and eventually left Prague for Vienna to mature into a respected art historian. The two drifted apart. If Kafka continued writing, it was for his drawer only.

By 1906, the extended Kafka family was doing quite well. Herr Kafka's business prospered in 12 Celetná Street; Bruno Kafka, a son of his cousin, received a doctorate in law in 1904 and embarked on a distinguished academic career to eventually become president of the university and a liberal politician. There were lawyers, doctors, and entrepreneurs among Franz's relatives. His friend Max Brod, one year younger, was preparing his first novel for publication. Franz also tested his luck by sending one of his stories to a Vienna competition in 1906. However, it failed to generate interest and has never resurfaced.

From his mathematically gifted father, Kafka probably inherited the capacity for framing complex thoughts in his head. At the university, he also took courses conceivably meant to enhance his writing talent. Thus, he became familiar with the writer's craft, showing awareness of composition and cadence of sentence. So many powers seemed to be tied to his stake; he wrote in self-assessment, wondering whether they could become useful to him personally and the country. Cocaine, however, was not the medium to activate them. Since passing his university exams in the spring of 1906, Kafka had little use for this drug except for recreational purposes. In early 1907, possibly in consequence of his New Year's resolutions, he embraced a new stimulant in his quest to become a respected writer.

1907: THE FAUSTIAN COMPACT

Out of other substances Kafka could conceivably enhance his talents with, the most alluring was opium and its natural derivatives or opiates. Opium, in particular, apart from its appeal as a recreational drug, became the favorite medium in the early nineteenth century for boosting one's creative juices, primarily by purveying rich, semirealistic dreams. As the self-styled 'pope of opium' Thomas de Quincey famously put it, if an opium user deals with ox, he dreams of ox. However, the opiatic dreams distort reality, space, and time. The drug thus mediates an alternate universe, the *paysage opiacé* or opiatic landscape as the poet Charles Baudelaire observed. Research suggests the unprecedented agglomeration of talent in the nineteenth century, the age of romanticism, can be plausibly linked with the widespread, unfettered indulgence in this narcotic. Opium was the quintessential *drogue romantique*.[1]

Both the creative and political elites of the nineteenth century had for decades ignored or belittled the adverse impact of opium. As the tide at last turned against this drug in the 1880s, one of its numerous alkaloids came in the vogue—morphine. Named after the mythical Morpheus, the god of dreams, it was both cleaner and more powerful. Few creative minds conceded the role of morphine in their work. Perhaps the most accomplished was Jules Verne (1828–1905), the pioneer of science fiction fathoming space travel, undersea exploration, and the modern urban landscape. He paid his dues with an "Ode to Morphine," the closing sentence of which reads, "Ah, pierce me 100 times with your needles fine and I will thank you 100 times, Saint Morphine."[2]

A strange never-told-before case of Sigmund Freud and his stumble into psychoanalysis also fits the story here. As already mentioned, early in his medical practice in Vienna of the 1880s, Freud experimented with methods of beating addiction to opium and morphine. Neither hypnosis nor cocaine proved to be effective, but he must have realized that the addicts' dreams— no matter how phantasmagorical—were rooted in reality. With some justification, he came to assume that dreams convey a rational kernel or confession, which people are either unaware of—or too shamed to reveal—in regular intercourse. After mining testimonies of his patients and possibly his own experience for fifteen years, Freud attempted to 'untwist' them—that is, to give them a realistic explanation—in *On Interpretation of Dreams* (1899).

This groundbreaking compilation assigned sexual connotation to a vast array of dreams—the attribution that few have ever since confirmed. It would appear that Freud, a child of the licentious age, imprinted *On Interpretation of Dreams* with his idiosyncrasies. Still, his generalizations laid the foundation to psychoanalysis, the discipline that considers the brain to be a depository of suppressed memories or impulses, subconscious or unconscious, that need to be addressed for the benefit of the patient. Freud's concept of the subconsciousness mirrors the phenomenon of opiatic dreams.

In his long but troubled life, Freud probably understated his personal involvement with opium and opiates. So did countless others, either unwilling to share their fame with a narcotic or be stigmatized for drug abuse. In consequence, though the rolls of those who died primarily of addiction would be long, their death was ascribed to one or more side effects, in particular respiratory failure and wasting away. Both the addicts and their care providers effectively participated in denial, deception, and self-deception.

Kafka, in Max Brod's testimony, was keenly interested in Freud and his theories highlighting the role of dreams (he denied, though, the efficacy of psychotherapy). It was a natural progression when, in his quest to become a respected writer, he revisited his Faustian bargain in early 1907. Two years later, he would imply he expected the change to be propitious to his writing but detrimental to his health. On balance of probabilities, he opted for the dream-sponsoring morphine. The shift was simple: though recognized as addictive, morphine was easily available on prescription as a pain reliever and relatively cheap. In Kafka's days, it was delivered primarily with hypodermic needles.

Did Kafka give up cocaine? Since both narcotics share some side effects, the answer is inconclusive. On one subsequent occasion, he hinted serving two devils. However, addiction to cocaine develops more slowly, especially if the drug is taken for a purpose (as Kafka did in 1902) rather than for pleasure. That said, the cocaine-related terms such as 'sniffing' no longer showed in Kafka's texts from 1907 on, while the characterizations germane to opiates began multiplying. We can assume that this medium in 1907 imparted Kafka with what he called a "special nature of my inspiration,"[3] or as he would put it repeatedly to Brod, "false hands that reach out to one while one is writing."[4]

Physical discomfort attributable to opiates impacted Kafka's life already in the spring of that year. At best recorded by biographers but never placed in a context, his mysterious ailments included nervousness, depression, hallucinations, alternate spells of chills and hot flushes, fever, and obstructed swallowing. Severe headaches also started visiting him, prompting him to compare them to the feeling a pane of glass must have at the moment of cracking. Constipation became so serious that a refusal to take a laxative ruined his trip to Lugano and Milan in 1911. His sleep patterns also changed: whereas in the past he had a "prodigious addiction to sleep,"[5] he began complaining about insomnia, the typical side effect of opiates (and counteracted by more of the same).

A culturist with a figure that attracted covetous glances from the opposite gender, Kafka also started to comment disparagingly on his physique. Observing his extremities in December 1908, he realized how much they had deteriorated in the past two years. Now and later, he would despair when undressed over his body and over a "future with this body."[6]

In contrast to frequenting swimming spas in the past, he also became reluctant to show in a bathing suit. In this, he paralleled Otto Gross, who, though possessing the lithe body and mind of Casanova, also felt ashamed showing disrobed or only partially robed. Why so? Intravenous drug users inject through their extremities, the practice that leaves needle traces and scars. In a more advanced stage, blood vessels collapse and the extremities become covered with sickly, bluish spots.

"My afflictions . . . are now appropriately walking on their hands," quipped Kafka in 1907 on what almost certainly was the habit of shooting morphine into his forearms.[7]

Soon, he noticed another effect of opiatic addiction so distinct from the impact of cocaine. It was a pronounced difficulty to rationalize turmoil brought about by the drug, "a war or something of the sort." The factors that inspired him were "so unusual" and their tempo "so jangled" that he failed to keep the pace with them. At times, the effect was outright frightening: "Like rifle bullets I fly from one [subject] to another, and the accumulated excitement . . . is quite enough to make me tremble."[8] The attendant irresolution, the typical plague of opium slaves, added to Kafka's inborn tentativeness.

Long term, his character and lifestyle were also undergoing symptomatic changes. For example, in his past, Kafka had been keenly interested in public affairs and politics, flirting with anarchism and socialism. Much of that evaporated in his twenties when he started living as if behind a glass wall. Positive attitudes and activism typically get suppressed in an addict. As Kafka's contemporary and another addict Jean Cocteau noted, "Opium desocializes us and removes us from the community . . . Opium is anti-social."[9] Kafka was turning indifferent to public life and declared the idea of helpfulness at odds with his nature.

Consistent with his new drug, his diet was also changing. Opium and opiates often produce aversion to alcohol and meat products. As Cocteau put it, "Opium and alcohol are mortal enemies."[10] Accordingly, the same Kafka who had been "overfed by meat and all good things" and enjoyed beer in the past now embraced vegetarianism and shunned alcohol. For the rest of his life, he tried to escape the "ordeal of eating meat."[11]

Equally striking was his incipient intolerance of sound. This too is the typical side effect of opium and opiates; often it is aggravated by another symptom Kafka also complained about—ringing inside the ears. Thus, any background noise drove him to despair. As he described the situation at home, "When the breakfast clatter ceases on the left, the lunch clatter begins on the right. Doors are now being opened everywhere as if walls were being smashed." Even a broom sweeping the rug in the adjoining room sounded "like the train of a dress moving in jerks."[12] He bought special earplugs to isolate himself from noise, but the result was disappointing. Irked by the household rattle, he dubbed the family apartment the "headquarters of the uproar" and morphed his discomfort into a short story, "The Great Noise."

Most telling of Kafka's taste for drugs was his face. The skin of opium and opiates users often darkens with unnatural hues. Karl Marx's face was so dark that he earned the lifelong nickname Moor. In more recent times, Elvis Presley, addicted to powerful opiates and opioids, was almost black from shoulders up when he died in 1977. Kafka was no exception. Already in 1910, Max Brod described him in his novel *Stefan Rott* as having "great grey gleaming eyes, which stood out in strange contrast to his brown face under his thick coal-black hair" (*rot* means "red" in German).[13] Kafka's face darkened still more in the following years to the point that his last companion, Dora Diamant, considered him a North American Indian when they met in 1923.

Within several weeks on morphine, Kafka found himself addicted. As he coped with the unforgiving narcotic, his perception of the world also grew dim. When Brod mentioned Gnosticism, the doctrine contending the world was created by Demiurge, the evil God, he answered God did not have such a radical relapse, just a bad day. His self-esteem was as low as before, as expected from someone who loses self-control (in a quip credited to Abraham Joshua Heschel, "The sense of dignity grows with the ability to say No to oneself").

Little wonder that Kafka struck a tone of resignation and nihilism as early as May 1907: "I really am hopeless, but nothing is going to change me . . . My future is not rosy and I will surely . . . die like a dog."[14] Thus spoke a freshly minted lawyer with so much going for him careerwise. Turning also paranoid like other drug users do, he came to suspect the whole world conspiring against him and his best friend Brod evolving into a future enemy.

The conscientious Kafka clearly anticipated some of these handicaps but hoped his new regime would benefit him as a writer. Did it? Shortly into his opiatic days, in February 1907, he destroyed most of his old writings, depriving us of a chance to chart safely his evolution as a novelist. Still, more than a dozen short stories or fragments of this period have been preserved, and they show two different writing styles. About half of them are conventional realistic texts that, we may assume, predate 1907.[15] The rest are short stories that reflect his new mode and/or anticipate other texts.[16]

Kafka's change of direction in 1907 shows in the "Description of a Struggle," the oldest preserved longer text of his. He seems to have been working on it intermittently between 1904 and 1908.[17] Divided into three sections, it is rather disconnected and stylistically incongruous. Section 1 presents a square narrative, relating walk and talk of the storyteller and his "acquaintance" through familiar quarters of old Prague.

After this unadventurous opening comes section 2, titled "Diversions or Proof That It's Impossible to Live." Penned in 1907–1908, it alludes to Kafka's switchover from cocaine sniffing to morphine in 1907. After experiencing "so many pleasant diversions," the narrator realized that his life was monotonous and his lungs were suffocating from "unbreathable air, from outraged things." So "it really was necessary for you to be taken somewhere else," he assured himself. In his new setup, there is "good air" and "it's gay here," but, he questions, "Isn't it also perilous?"

Section 2 also reflects the impact of his new medium. First, Kafka here draws on dreams occurring in half-sleep and hence receptive to impulses from outside. They straddle fantasy and reality. The narrator's sleep seems deep and dreamless, yet, in fact, all night long, he is interrupted by someone's talk from which he, the narrator, can distinguish only isolated words. The outcome is Kafka's new, shall we call it supernatural, representation of the world tainted with violence.

This too is consistent with the impact of opiates that, modern research shows, can result in expressions of brutality, self-mutilation, suicide, and murder. Kafka's literary predecessors betrothed to the drug, from Edgar Allan Poe to Robert Louis Stevenson, built violence into their texts. Our kind, quiet, unassuming Franz Kafka also becomes a purveyor of gratuitous sadomasochism in section 2. Transposed into a somnambular landscape, the narrator rides his acquaintance like a horse, kicking him in the belly to make him more lively. He also presses his hands around his neck, giving him a choke. When the latter injures his knee, collapses, and is no longer of any use, the narrator tells us that he leaves him there on the stones and whistles down a few vultures.

On abandoning the maimed acquaintance so mercilessly, the narrator floats late at night over the moonlit landscape toward the "terrifying moon." Eventually overcome by experience to which he is unaccustomed and succumbing to stupor, he settles down in half-sleep.

The link to reality? It comes by weaving into the text persons close to Kafka, the habit that would show in all his major works. The lame acquaintance and victim of the narrator's sadism is apparently mimicry for Max Brod (with whom Kafka had a dispute in 1907). The rich, effeminate "fat man" in subsequent segments of the "Description," whom the narrator truly loved, may have been a cover for the precocious Franz Werfel, an inspiring *auteur* who had shown little appreciation for Kafka's texts. Both characters' life ends violently; the "acquaintance" commits suicide, bleeding to death from a self-inflicted stab wound, and the fat man drowns.

The elementary sense of loneliness, common to addicts, also shows in this section: "I have done nobody any harm, nobody has done me any harm, but nobody will help me." It is complemented by the feeling of resignation in the fat man episode. Thus, the narrator observes the latter's struggle for life in the stream of a river, hoping to "learn something about this apparently safe country." However, the fat man dissuades him from rescue attempts, claiming that his plight is nature's revenge. The narrator watches impassively as his beloved friend is swept over the waterfall.

The reader discerns the pattern that would resurface most prominently in *The Trial* but not as drastic yet: toward the end of "The Description of a Struggle," the narrator effectively refutes his own postulate that "it's impossible to live," assuring himself, "No one loves you . . . But you go on living. You don't kill yourself."[18]

Kafka apparently restarted "The Description of a Struggle" as an ambitious project, a showcase of his enhanced skills. However, his choice of subject was uninspiring, and he lacked both the prerequisite personal experience to feed his dreams and the skill to convert them seamlessly into prose. In the comment of his biographer, Kafka here shows 'utter incapacity' to match words with the objects they are supposed to designate.[19]

Two other pieces of Kafka's prose testify to his progress as the morphine-sponsored writer in 1907. "The Vulture" is a short story of a scavenger hacking at the feet of the helpless narrator. Too weak to defend himself, the narrator lets the vulture eat him away. It is a variant of the Greek myth of Prometheus in which eagle or vulture nibbles every day on the liver of this demigod chained to the rock. This ancient parable may have fictionalized the trauma of addicts whose liver is slowly but surely degraded by opium consumption, and hence, little wonder that it resonated with the nineteenth-century addicts such as Mary Shelley and Karl Marx.[20] Before long, Kafka too was to cope with liver problems inflicted by opiates.

Another fragment of interest is "Wedding Preparations in the Country." Kafka worked on it during the first half of 1907, apparently banking on his new power of imagination. Opiates, it must be noted here, produce the sense of two parallel brains, often in competition with each other. Robert Louis Stevenson, himself a morphine user, exploited this in *Strange Case of Dr. Jekyll and Mr. Hyde* (1886). Kafka gave this experience a new twist.

His "Wedding Preparations in the Country" revolves around a diffident bridegroom who imagines deputizing his dressed body to the wedding while staying in bed. With an enhanced eye for detail—another effect of opiates—the writer furnished the text with rich minutiae, but his intent to expand it into a novel again came to nothing.[21]

Kafka's struggles were observed by his friends and classmates. The quiet, introspective son of a medical doctor Camille Gibian stood closest to him but shot himself to death in 1905 (another schoolmate committed suicide already in 1902). That left Max Brod as his most trusted comrade. Having a deformed spine must have given Brod some discomfort and pain for which opiates were the only reliable remedy (until aspirin was introduced in 1898). Yet almost certainly, he had not developed an addiction or condoned the use of drugs for creative purposes.

Not accidentally, therefore, Brod was disturbed by his friend's new lifestyle. From 1907 on, he clearly made an effort to divert him from drugs and the mode of writing they sponsor. Thus, already in February of that year, using a drama review he penned as a message board, he identified Kafka as a representative of the "high culture of German penmanship," next to Heinrich Mann, Kurt Wedekind, and Gustav Meyerink.[22] Kafka had not yet published anything, but Brod was undoubtedly privy to some of his texts and made this unprecedented gesture to assure his doubting friend of his natural talent. There was no need for stimulants.

Kafka, however, was an obstinate listener. Signs of estrangement appeared already in the spring of 1907 as he suspected Brod of shunning him. In mid-June, he tried to comfort Brod with the first chapter of "Wedding Preparations in the Country," approximately fourteen pages of text. The latter would claim he liked the story, but whatever his real response was, Kafka abandoned this project too.

Brod again attempted to boost Kafka's self-worth. In the summer of 1907, he convinced his publisher, Axel Junker in Stuttgart, to use Kafka's drawing for his first book of verse, *The Path of the Lover*. The debut as an illustrator did please Kafka, who, in mid-August, expressed to Brod his bittersweet gratitude. However, his nagging self-doubts persisted.

Just like Don Quixote, motivated dreamers need a Dulcinea—and Kafka was no exception. He was constantly on the lookout for females charmed by his ambition. On vacations with his uncle in Třešť in mid-August 1907, he met a girl that seemed to fit the bill. Hedwig Weiler, hailing from Northern Bohemia, had taken respite in the town from her studies in Vienna. Behind her back, she earned his gentle ridicule as someone who, because of her protruding teeth, could not close her mouth. Yet she also captivated him instantly with her strikingly red cheeks as well as interest in languages and philosophy. Before long, she was asked to transfer to the Prague University and give lessons to children so they could start living together. This prospect made Kafka tremble with excitement and gave him hope for a contended life. He also opened a secret bank account.

In a rehearsal of his future dating conduct, he also turned Hedwig into a witness to his innermost feelings, a sense of isolation and unworthiness: "I have no social life . . . I am a ridiculous person." With his mind darkened by addiction, nothing seemed to be working to his expectations, and the outlook was just as dim. He was unhappy to the point of confusion and felt incapacitated but not by real sickness: "A few minor ailments, a little fever, a little frustrated expectation put me to bed for two days." He and Weiler soon parted but kept trading letters, still tinted with his torments.[23]

Unsure about his career as a writer, in the second half of 1907, Kafka contemplated less illustrious alternatives. With well-paying salaried positions hard to find, in mid-August, he told Brod he might take courses in commerce and Spanish and, with his uncle's help, find work in the Spanish world. Would Brod join him? Kafka, of course, was an antithesis to his enterprising father or uncle Löwy. With the latter's help, however, he eventually landed his first salaried job with the local branch of the Italian insurance company Assicurazioni Generali. But from the onset, Kafka found his job too long and dreary and a salary of eighty crowns inadequate. What a terrible week, he summed up his early work experience on October 9. Later in the month, he was ready to concede the employment would change little in his unhappy state.

After five years on drugs, the twenty-four-year-old Kafka was, as a detailed medical exam for his employer found, healthy but fragile. Diagnosed with light inflammation of the tips of lungs—probably the side effect of both cocaine sniffing and shooting morphine—he was underweight at sixty-one kilograms for his height of 1.82 meters. He also felt frustrated both at work and with his writings and, feeling rotten, preferred not to talk to anyone. His mind had darkened so much that he dubbed Pařížská Street (Nicklasstrasse) the family lived on a "Suicide Lane" and summed up his life by a quip, "One must earn one's grave."

The following year, Kafka's fortunes improved somewhat. For one, Brod's close friend Max Bäumle died, and from then on, so Brod in retrospect, his relations with Franz grew deeper. Thanks to Brod again, in March 1908, eight of Kafka's short stories appeared in the first issue of *Hyperion*, a trendy periodical published by the Viennese literate Franz Blei. Still, it was an inconspicuous assortment. When Brod read these pieces to Franz Werfel and Willy Haas, both future men of letters, their reaction suggested Kafka's name would not cross the borders of Bohemia. Was this the ticket to fame?

Kafka was appreciative of Brod's support, claiming he not only loved him more than himself but also doubted his insecure nature could benefit. Again, while he produced little of significance in 1908, his personal and health woes widened to include occasional fainting spells and hand tremor that prevented him from writing. He handled it with humor, informing, in one instance, Brod that the initial letter of his name was too inconvenient to be put it down on the paper decently. Though living at his family expense, he also lacked money but on occasion still found his new lifestyle enjoyable. "All one needs for this is empty wallet, and I can lend you that if you like," he cheekily observed.[24]

While Brod on his graduation accepted employment in the post office, in July 1908, Kafka landed a plum job at the Institute of Workers' Accident Insurance in Prague. However, better pay, shorter hours, and a more congenial atmosphere did little to suspend his sense of isolation. He wrote less than three months later, "Nobody can stand me and I can stand no one." In inexplicable unhappiness and desperate to find someone who would merely touch him in a friendly manner, he went to a hotel with a prostitute.[25]

Inspecting his bare arms by the yearend of 1908, he effectively conceded that syringes ruled his life: "As I realized before washing up this morning I have been in despair for two years."[26] Not yet twenty-six years old, he had lost his stamina and felt so tired and dull owing to the lack of sleep. Worse yet, as drugs were losing their effect, Kafka's writing almost came to a standstill in 1909. That year, he wrote on Brod's instigation and published only one original text, "The Aeroplanes at Brescia." It is a travelogue about their joint trip to Riva and Brescia in Italy, recounting the observed flight of airplanes, the most recent wonder of technology.

In March 1909, two sections from "Description of a Struggle" were also published in *Hyperion*, and Kafka tried to revive "Wedding Preparations in the Country." He penned two more chapters, more realistic probably to please Brod to whom he again submitted samples with a self-deprecating comment. Brod was impressed. As he would recall, "I was overpowered and delighted. I got the impression immediately that here was no ordinary talent speaking, but a genius. My efforts to bring Kafka's work before the public began from that moment . . . Franz resisted."[27]

By the yearend of 1909, Kafka felt depleted; "On the last rung of my ladder . . . resting quietly on the ground and against the wall."[28] He toured Western Bohemia, hoping it would help somehow, but it did not. The way back to drug-free days seemed foreclosed, but a change of direction was desirable.

1910: "THE GENERAL UPROAR WITHIN ME . . . WHICH I HAVE NO TIME TO COMMAND"

As on the similar occasion in the past, the advent of 1910 prompted Kafka to revise his drug regime. Looking back in mid-December 1910 at "my present condition which has already lasted almost a year," he noted, "I do not even know whether I can say this condition is new . . . I have had similar ones, but never one like this."[1] Apparently, he continued with an intravenous delivery of a substance that gripped him just as morphine: "I am nothing but a mass of spikes going through me; if I try to defend myself . . . the spikes only press in deeper." He still experienced pain but effectively stopped perceiving it in "sheer urgency" to inflict it upon himself.[2] He was still trapped in a vicious circle.

The invasive nature of his new experience suggests that, rather than dropping opiates totally (which could have been excruciatingly hard), he opted for another opiatic alkaloid but of higher potency than morphine. On the scale of probabilities again, it was heroin. Feeling cranky but determined to start afresh, he complemented it with having his stomach pumped.

Based on real-time information, heroin was a preferred choice for those tempted by opiates in 1907. This derivate of opium was discovered in 1895 by a German scientist Heinrich Dresser working for a German pharmaceutical eventually known as Bayer. The company staged a trial with thirty-five morphine addicts, administering them heroin. Two patients committed suicide from withdrawal symptoms, but twenty-seven were 'cured' inasmuch as they lost craving morphine. Without much delay, in 1898, Bayer started marketing heroin with fanfare as a safe substitute for morphine. What a relief! Philanthropists began offering free samples of heroin to morphine addicts.

From Kafka's perspective in 1907, however, this anti-morphine also touted as a remedy for insomnia seemed to be lacking the property attributed to morphine, the capacity to induce a dreamy otherworld. We can assume that, unsure whether heroin would help his creativity, Kafka stayed clear of it in 1907.

Marketing heroin eventually became a monumental flop. It would turn out that this drug rapidly metabolizes into morphine and is twice as potent. By 1910, evidence was mounting of the compound's affinity to morphine and its wicked addictiveness, but this may have not donned fully on Kafka yet. He switched to the drug that carried a great risk—and yet was easily available. Heroin and opiates in general had become prescription drugs, but their use was unregulated in the Habsburg Empire.

As we know, Kafka already found it difficult to handle the transition from cocaine to morphine in 1907. The impact of heroin, then, was overwhelming. As he observed in May 1910, there was "always something in me to catch fire, in this heap of straw that I have been for five months." This fire had been "consumed more swiftly than the onlooker can blink his eyes" (and yet he did not regret this "unhappy time").[3] Physical discomfort and health concerns also started asserting themselves when Kafka, exploring his "abilities" in evenings, experienced a tight chest and blood pounding in his head.

It would have been more tolerable if heroin significantly enhanced his writing, but that was not the case. True, in March 1910, five of Kafka's short stories were published in *Bohemia*—a slim picking from his pre-heroin phase. However, his expectation to grow tall with the "might of weeds"—a customary barb at the opiates derived from the gel of poppy cones—had not materialized. Instead, he found himself unable to write anything satisfactory in the first five months of 1910 and began assuming the "weeds" would not compensate him even though they "all were under obligation to do so."[4]

There was a good reason for it. In general, Kafka tried to write between 8:00 p.m. and 11:00 p.m. and go to bed then. However, similar as morphine, heroin did not conform to his needs. The drug delivered bursts of uncontrolled creativity, followed by dulling the central nervous system that made him drowsy for hours. Thus, Kafka spent much of the night semiconscious, dreaming vividly but unable to record anything. "My whole body warns me against every word . . . before it lets me write it down . . . The sentences literally crumble before me."[5] Sleeping "alongside" himself, Kafka awoke at around 5:00 a.m. full of dreams but dazed and without time to work them over.

Due in the institute by 8:00 a.m., he was forced to delay creative refashioning of his dreams and associations until next evening or later. By that time, these usually receded in his short-term memory. Thus, he had no chance to command what he called "the general uproar within me." The spells of conscious and subconscious also lost distinction in Kafka's life. He began assuming he was awake for no more than five minutes at a time. His sense of time blurred accordingly: everything looked to him like one day without any mornings, afternoons, and evenings.[6]

Kafka's diaries reveal frustration over his inability to exploit high-potency substances. At one point, he observed that others, like the Japanese jugglers, can "scramble up a ladder" that "just goes up in the air," resting on the raised soles of someone lying on the ground. "I cannot do this." How precarious this calibration of talent and drugs can be![7]

What a wretched life, Kafka again pitted himself already in July 1910. While conceding his woes were self-inflicted, he turned the arrow against society: his parents and relatives harmed him "out of love," and this made them even more culpable. In fact, Kafka tried to convince himself that a "multitude of people . . . my parents, several relatives, individual visitors to our house, various writers" were all responsible for his distress because of their expectations and complacency.[8] Even his education worked against him in some respects. In a mental process typical for addicts, this supposedly mild-mannered young man raised the specter of murder: his misery was "like a dagger . . . and no one . . . can be sure as to whether the point of the dagger won't suddenly appear sometimes in front, at the back, or from the side."[9]

Meanwhile, physical handicaps kept testing his body. He tried to keep his exercise regime but gave it up already in March 1910. Muscle pain—the addicts called it rheumatic pain—attacked his shoulders, back, legs, and arms. Failure to replenish the opiate or attempts at withdrawal also generated pain, Kafka realized again. Hence, resistance to the drug or "courage," as he put it, "leads only to cramps . . . and we will stay with our cramps, don't be worried," he humored himself.[10]

The cramping feeding tube or esophagus—and the resulting pain on swallowing—also began to plague him seriously. Days multiplied when he involuntarily fasted on tea. To alleviate his craving for food, he adopted the seemingly odd practice of "fletcherizing," or chewing each bite of a meal for several minutes. It helped gulping food and drink down in moments of lessened pain. Later, he would also claim to deliberately cultivate a facial tick. It was deliberate inasmuch facial contortions are yet another side effect of opiate use.

The peculiar form of opiatic half-sleep interspersed with dreams again robbed him of a meaningful respite. In fact, it was the power of his dreams, Kafka claimed, that prevented him from sleeping. Probably because of sleep deprivation, Kafka was also losing coherence, repeating a specific claim in his diaries three times with minor variations.

More physical distress was in store for him. Heroin could be delivered by injection, orally, or by snorting. Kafka apparently continued injecting as in his morphine days. Thus, though girls still found his body "kissable," blemishes inflicted by needles made him uncomfortable. There was no escape: When he resisted the temptation of the drug, the craving returned in force. The agony of withdrawal overwhelmed the pain of injection and led to relapse. Kafka tried to convince himself he suffered no pain, but it did not bring a lasting relief. "A bullet would be best. I shall simply shoot myself away," he summed up his desperation in late spring of 1910.[11]

Like other opiates and drugs in general, heroin is metabolized in the liver. By the fall of 1910, Kafka's liver had obviously been overtaxed, punishing him with gout, a grossly swollen foot because of the accumulation of liquids. It caused no pain but put in doubt his forthcoming trip to Paris with Felix Weltsch, Max Brod, and his younger brother Otto. Eventually, Kafka did travel to the French capital, but the opiates exacted another more serious toll. While in Paris, he was nearly incapacitated by a sudden outbreak of boils. This painful bacterial disease produces abscesses as big as fists that eventually burst with pus, soiling garments and fouling the air with stench. Rare in the general populace, boils apparently served as yet another safety valve of the overworked hepatic system, disproportionally afflicting opium abusers from Coleridge, Heine, Marx, and Engels to Richard Wagner.[12]

Kafka promptly returned to Prague, in poor shape, feeling like in a grave, unable to walk or sit because of the pain: "Everybody regards me as an improbable apparition. . . the doctor declared himself horrified by the appearance of my backside." Kafka's back was dotted with five painful boils, but even more painful was attendant skin rash, another typical plague of addicts to opium.[13] During the examination, he also had a brief fainting spell but covered up all this for the sake of his employment.

This was not the last time Kafka suffered from such an ignominy: there are more references to boils in his life, some direct, some implied. Just as in cases of other addicts such as Bismarck, the eruptions forced Kafka to avoid both work and friends. At times, he tried to refrain from social contact for days, recusing himself from meeting even his trusted friend Max Brod.

All this notwithstanding, Kafka had apparently done a lot of writing in 1910 but again destroyed most of it. Inability to produce anything up to his standard further extended his insecurity and gloom: "My doubts stand in a circle around every word, I see them before I see the world."[14] This and the sum of imagined or actual sufferings made him feel living a dog's life with no help or escape. Expressing the sense of futility common to drug addicts, this comfortably encamped scion of an upper-middle-class family felt suicidal in the world that was collapsing on him.

Kafka's nihilism was confirmed by a disheartening slight. As he recorded it in January 1911, his chatty uncle glanced through a page of his writing and handed it back, saying to the onlookers, "The usual stuff." He said nothing to Kafka. Commented the offended, "With one thrust I had in fact been banished from society."

In the wake of this humiliation, Kafka felt completely deflated, in need to start afresh like a baby. In response, he revised his daily regime to accommodate better what he called the "special nature of my inspiration." While so far he had been striving to write between eight and eleven in the evening, now he extended his active hours until 2:00 a.m. and compensated with afternoon naps. The adjustment, he hoped, would give him a chance to record his richly textured dreams afresh. Almost instantly then, new somnambular stories appeared in his diaries, and just as instantly, Kafka brimmed with confidence. "I can do everything . . . When I arbitrarily write a single sentence . . . it already has perfection."[15] Did he learn to "juggle the ladder" after all?

His euphoria was quashed by the reality. Above all, Kafka was a civil servant expected to account for his comfortable salary. He specialized in accident prevention with focus on two accident-prone categories, the woodworking industry and quarries in Northern Bohemia. Thanks to his lawyerly background and by nature a conscientious person, on the whole, he was undoubtedly performing well, visiting numerous businesses, writing well-reasoned papers for his superiors, and upgrading his expertise through courses and conferences. As early as 1909, he was commended as an "eminently diligent worker of exceptional talent and exceptional sense of duty."[16] In addition, his aspirations as a writer were also well known and respected by his superiors, his immediate boss, Chief Inspector Eugen Pfohl, and managing director Dr. Robert Marschner. The latter was a cultivated intellectual who eventually made his name as a Goethe scholar.

There is also little doubt, however, that drugs exacted their toll—late arrivals, headaches, sleepiness, fatigue, muscle pain, cramps, and absences intermittently marred Kafka's work performance. Already in 1909, only twenty-six and less than two years at work, he was granted his first three weeks of medical leave.

The extension of active life until 2:00 a.m., then, added to Kafka's woes, in particular by depriving him still more of precious sleep. Thus, in February 1911, he sent Pfohl a morning message that, trying to get out of bed, he "simply folded up" and would not show up at work. He added that he might be turfed out of Pfohl's department on coming to the office the next day but hastened to assure his superior he loved him like a son. In truth, as seen below, Kafka's relationship with Pfohl was more complex and his opinion of him less charitable.

Mixing the career of a devoted public servant with drug dependency began to burden Kafka's conscience and sense of job security. He alluded to this on numerous occasions. Already in December 1910, he expressed the dread of his precarious office standing. In one of his frequent moments of candor, he mentioned a "horrible double life from which there is probably no escape but insanity."[17] In another cathartic revelation, he confessed to being ready to give notice several times because of this "dreadful impediment in my life."[18] Alternatively, he deemed himself deserving termination because of his recurrent incapacity to execute his office duties adequately. Kafka was in fact promoted to deputy department head in 1911.

Concerned about Franz's mounting troubles, his mother, Julie Kafka, approached Oskar Baum in early March 1911, asking him to set his head straight. According to Brod, hers was a moving letter, but motherly love could not move the mountain. True, the ensuing trips that Kafka took with Brod to Italy and Paris gave him anything but a license to drug fest. But then, Kafka went alone to a sanatorium in Erlenbach, Switzerland, in September 1911, with a predictable outcome. Just as after his other solo vacations he had taken since 1905 in various locales of the Czech lands—Liboch, Třešť, and Zlaté Hory (Zuckmantel)—he returned with little appreciable improvement of his health.

His craving for intravenous opiates also remained as strong as before. In September 1911, he spent an entire evening discussing with another aspiring writer and visual artist Alfred Kubin their common problem of flatulence (which alternates with diarrhea in addicts). When, toward midnight, Kafka accidentally exposed part of his arm, the sight prompted Kubin to cry out, "You are really sick!" The forearm must have been discolored because of repeat syringe injections.[19]

With boils fresh in his memory, Kafka was exposed in 1911 to other health issues consistent with the abuse of opiates. His joints were aching and skin itching all over, his face showed red blotches, and headache bordering on agony made itself at home on the left side of his skull. Turmoil and perplexing convulsions left him agitated and confused. Paralysis temporarily disabled his arm, and tremor caused his left hand to repeatedly clasp his right hand by the fingers. A weak heart troubled him at times. His attempt to facilitate swallowing by an intensive chewing of food was ineffective, obstructing, as he phrased it, the linkage between stomach and mouth. Most damage was inflicted by his insomnia as even on closing his notepad at night, vivid dreams continued to deprive him of a genuine sleep.

Unable also to write consistently, in early October 1911, Kafka subjected to one of his recurrent spells of self-reflection. As before, he was fully confident of his creative abilities. Obliquely, he also expressed his belief that to make them flourish, they needed to be nurtured externally: "It is a matter of more covert powers which are of an ultimate significance to me."[20] It was his sleep-deprived nights that facilitated mining his rich opiatic dreams (conversely, when Kafka slept relatively well, he was unable to write). Still, the problems with opiates persisted, mainly because of their arbitrary surges. Kafka had "no time to command . . . the general uproar" within him and no willpower to restrict it.[21] Thus, many amazing nocturnal images in his head dissipated before he could record them next day.

A solution seemed near at hand: if he could control his nightly séances and remain reasonably conscious, could he also write throughout the night? His intent proved unworkable. Even if he somehow managed to stay awake until early morning, the resulting sleep deprivation wreaked havoc on his life.

Thus, though Kafka was promoted at work in 1911, his new sleep regime left him still more exhausted if not incoherent and impaired his office performance. On October 24, counsellor Lederer summoned him to discuss his health issues and delved into Kafka's life in such a detail that the latter lost his calm. It was so unnatural for him, he commented. There undoubtedly followed similar conflicts that Kafka managed to defuse and retain the goodwill of his superiors. Their benevolence, however, failed to attach him to his work. Kafka now believed, not without justification, that the office robbed him of a chance to be creative at night. Before long, the twenty-eight-year-old started imagining the moment he would be free. He needed time for snoozing to compensate for his nightly exploits.

His quest for expendable time, however, crossed his family's concerns. In December 1910, he was still able to claim he had almost never quarreled with his parents: the mood at home was exceptionally peaceful. The same month, however, Kafka's eldest sister, Elli, married Karl Hermann. Six years her senior, he was one of eight siblings of a family rooted in a village in Midwestern Bohemia. In consequence of this arranged marriage and possibly on Franz's suggestion, the Kafka family opened in 1911 a factory in Prague specializing in heat-resisting asbestos products. Kafka senior provided seed money, and Franz promised his time for what essentially was meant to be a meal ticket to the newlyweds.

Alas, the start-up did poorly, and Kafka was expected to honor his word. Since his office hours ended at 2:00 p.m., he had time to spare before dinner. His impracticality and lack of business acumen were no secret; the family probably also hoped the extra assignment would help straighten his lifestyle. From Kafka's standpoint, on the other hand, tending to the factory robbed him of precious afternoon naps and the opportunity to extend his writing time at night.

Reluctant to yield, Kafka earned the displeasure of his father. Herr Kafka mentioned again and again how good life the young generation had and, even worse, voiced suspicion his son lacked the drive. Was he following the path of his uncle Rudolf Löwy, who lived contently as a convert and bookkeeper? Frictions began spoiling family life. For illustration, Herr Kafka, annoyed by an unwelcome visitor, minced no words dismissing his son as a bad person in the presence of relatives. "I have written myself almost into a hatred of my father," commented the dejected

Kafka junior. In afterthought, he jotted down in his diary on November 2, "This morning, for the first time in a long time, the joy again of imagining a knife twisted in my heart."[22]

A few days later, Kafka also wrote the first draft of "In Headquarters of Noise," one of his memorable short texts. A mild censure of his family, the article accused his closest relatives of addiction to clatter and was eventually published in a Prague paper. Irritated by his family, Kafka was too unfocused to write anything consequential, and when he applied his pen to another short story, a sort of self-portrait, the title was self-explanatory, "Bachelor's Unhappiness."

Max Brod, as usual, followed closely his best friend's struggles and resolved to intervene again. In November 1911, he proposed to Kafka penning jointly a novel to be titled *Richard and Samuel*. The prospect of cooperation with the so far much more successful author flattered Kafka and made him instantly enthusiastic. The collaboration, he assumed, would release the best in him, and great moments would follow. Without delay, Kafka began working on the novel to the exclusion of other texts.

As he toiled with abandon, by mid-November, Kafka once again began expressing the frustration with his inability to master the swells of unnatural inspiration. He conceived something good "only in a time of exaltation, a time more feared than longed for."[23] However, these spells of creativity—Kafka also called them "astonishing convulsions"—were accompanied by chest tightness and blood pounding his brain. With his head on fire, Kafka struggled to snatch dreams and ideas for belaboring next day, and even when he managed to put them on paper eventually, the result seemed inadequate, timid, and, above all, incomplete in comparison with the fullness of his somnambular experience. In addition, after a night of bewildering frenzies, he struggled to keep himself awake and coherent at work. "I yawn at the directors, at my chief, the clients, in short at everyone who happens to get in my way," he observed in embarrassment.[24]

Constantly challenged by his afflictions, the twenty-eight-year-old exclaimed, "Nothing can be accomplished with such a body," and expressed premonition of dying before the age of forty.[25]

Still worse, after a few weeks of working on *Richard and Samuel*, it became obvious how far apart Kafka and Brod stood as writers. The latter's earnest, moralizing prose clashed with Kafka's idiosyncratic storytelling. "I and Max must really be different to the very core," Kafka noted in his diary after recording a semifictional dream that Brod would not care for.[26]

By December 8, Kafka finished the first chapter of the joint novel, feeling he had given it everything and left little else to sacrifice. Content with the result, he barely concealed aching to write all his angst out of him into the "depth of the paper."[27]

Yet Brod was not pleased, despite his meddling in Kafka's text. It made the latter apprehensive about his style, so foreign both to Brod and family. While he had anticipated the new regime to make him a better writer, now he regretted carrying "weights I cannot get rid of."[28] As Christmas of 1911 was nearing, Kafka hoped to find more time for writing but instead spent holidays inactive. The project of *Richard and Samuel* was abandoned. Meanwhile, Kafka began investigating another source of inspiration.

1912: 'CIVILIZING THE APE'

Kafka himself regarded the year of 1912 as the turning point in his writing. It indeed marked his conversion into a penman of distinction. In addition, he also singled out that year as the end of his "innocent innocence" and the onset of serious health problems with no point of return. Were his health and creative watersheds related? The text below presents them as a binary consequence to his prolonged search for writerly prowess.

That search included other authors. An exceptionally omnivorous reader, Kafka was paying special attention to predecessors showing affinity in lifestyle and production. How were they able to deliver such masterpieces as *Faust*, *Madame Bovary* or poetry of Heine's caliber? By 1911, he also started delving in personal lives and creations of Goethe, the German man of letters Heinrich von Kleist, Gustav Flaubert, Charles Dickens . . . They were—no surprise for the nineteenth-century writers— either opium smokers or consumers of the drug in the form of laudanum, opium diluted in alcohol. In the case of von Kleist, his addiction can only be surmised on the basis of his health problems that closely paralleled those of opium takers. The enigmatic Kleist, who committed suicide at the age of forty-one, also left behind a body of work that was dreamlike, ironic, and grotesque. This was the direction Kafka seems to have already been trending to but so far without much success.

Another inspiration in his search for new direction appears to have come from an unexpected source. For much of his life, Kafka was ambivalent about Zionism striving to establish a Jewish homeland in Palestine. "I admire Zionism and am nauseated by it," he would claim.[1] But there also was Hasidism, the movement laying emphasis on Jewish tradition and mystic aspects of life here and now. It emanated from Eastern Europe and

Russia but began attracting the attention of Western Jewry by the turn of the century. Martin Buber, Kafka's acquaintance and unconventional exponent of inclusive Judaism, published a selection from Hasidic stories in German. Reflective of the collective experience of the tribe, the Hasidic mind had developed the habit of communicating through fables and parables rich in paradox and absurdities. In the defining wisecrack of Hassidic sage Abraham Joshua Heschel, "There is a meaning beyond absurdity."

Kafka read Buber's anthology and was further exposed to the Hasidic perspective with the visit to Prague in 1911–1912 by a Yiddish theater troupe from Lemberg (today Lviv in Western Ukraine). Neither Yiddish nor Hasidism had many devotees among Prague Jewry, but Kafka was captivated by these visitors trying in primitive conditions to portray the absurd frailty of life. He struck a friendship with the leading actor Isaak Lövy and developed an odd infatuation for his female counterpart Madame Tschissik, who was married and a mother of two. In response to a lukewarm reception of the group, in February 1912, Kafka organized its recital and delivered opening remarks in Yiddish—the only public lecture ever of this very private person. He was disappointed that his parents did not attend.

There is little doubt that the Lemberg troupe and the Hasidic spirit in general reinforced Kafka's propensity for dark humor, irony, and irreverence. Five years later, he would still intone that Hasidic stories were the only Jewish literature in which he "immediately and always feel at home."[2]

By 1912, Kafka also discovered and started paying serious attention to Fedor Dostoevsky (1821–1881). Another night owl who died of degradation of the lungs, Dostoevsky was carted to the grave followed by students carrying shackles—a gesture symbolizing the writer's living in a prison inside of himself. Kafka, who on numerous occasions expressed a similar despondency, found in Dostoevsky psychological and health problems he was familiar with. He purchased the diary of this great storyteller and, reading through, could hardly hide his excitement: what a rapture.[3]

There also was, of course, much to learn from Dostoevsky's craft, the blending of tragedy with the comic and grotesque, of personal angst with social critique, and buildup of the story with telling phrases and judiciously orchestrated scenes. Dostoevsky seems to have also impacted Kafka with the pivotal notions of unknown guilt, 'crime and punishment,' and suffering as liberation. Who else but this remarkable wordsmith would preach the counterintuitive, Enjoy the toothache!

Kafka's horizon was expanding by 1912. While the prevailing tone of his texts so far had been earnest and bitter, he now aspired to complex stories incorporating the above-mentioned elements. With this retooling in process, he took another exploratory step. A few days after sparring with Brod over *Richard and Samuel*, he visited another friend Felix Weltsch.

One year his junior, Weltsch also graduated from the Law Faculty and added to his qualifications a doctorate in philosophy. In 1909, he began working at the National and University Library in Prague but devoted his discretionary time to philosophy and journalism. Along with Brod and Kafka, he also paid Friday visits to the 'saloon' of Berta Fanta, wife of a pharmacist on Oldtown Square. Her house, *Zum Einhorn*, was frequented both by the local avant-garde as well as by Jewish notables visiting Prague. As a repeat visitor, almost certainly he was exposed to more than stimulating ideas.[4]

In the evening of December 22, 1911, then, Kafka visited Weltsch and witnessed a startling situation. His host's attic flat was overheated and filled with nauseating smoke, but Weltsch himself enjoyed that, his face distorted with excitement, perplexity, and stupor. Unable to coax him into allowing fresh air in let alone into going for a walk, the amazed Kafka watched for an hour his friend's shenanigans. What a revolting experience! Kafka doubted whether he would leave the room as a friend.

At noon on the very next day, December 23, however, he revisited Weltsch and then both went to see another friend, Oskar Baum. Subsequently, Kafka walked to Weltsch's home, and both were sorry to part. On following visits to Weltsch, Kafka usually again found his room overheated and full of foul air and blamed it for Weltsch's health problems.

Weltsch's favorite pastime that Franz Kafka experienced—the reader is asked to accept as a working hypothesis—was opium smoking.

Only few secrets had not been shared by such close friends as Kafka and Brod. We may assume that the visit to Weltsch challenged again Kafka's bond with Brod, already tested by discord over *Richard and Samuel*. Amid reciprocal unease, Kafka started questioning their friendship, and the planned reading from his diaries on New Year's Eve that he looked so much forward to did not take place. "We were not in tune," he commented thereafter, blaming Brod for the estrangement.[5] He also experienced problems at work, but these were settled with yet another letter to his boss.

Kafka wished to concentrate all his forces on writing, to the neglect of everything else, private life, joy of sex, eating, and drinking. But smoking was not to his taste, and he also realized that opium would make his isolation even worse. On the last day of January 1912, Weltsch brought him books about Goethe—the same Goethe who, in *Maxims and Reflections*, invoked opium as his favorite narcotic and struggled with drug degradation in his last years. Kafka read them with zeal but summed up his impression as "Goethe's revolting nature." This notwithstanding, Kafka recorded that Goethe also found infinite delight in creating. Living as a writer with opium was not such a burden?[6]

This so far had not been Kafka's experience with opiates. Again and again, in the early months of 1912, he despaired his writing skill, and rereading his old notebooks meant re-experiencing misery in a more compact form. A glance at his pre-1912 texts that have survived in his diaries indeed shows little intricacy. Recorded Kafka in October 1911: a dream about a donkey that looked like a greyhound and walked erect on human feet. His fantasy also involved such subjects as a vivid play of colors in his room or a vision of Napoleon who stepped out of the wood. On the whole, he wrote down series of individual images that were bizarre rather than sophisticated, not the stuff that would set him apart from his predecessors.

Another conflict at home over the asbestos factory in early March 1912 drove Kafka again into suicide mood, followed by his burning of several old papers. Among the destroyed texts apparently was the first version of "The Man Who Disappeared," intended as a chapter of a longer epic about a young man's misfortunes in the USA. A few days later, he returned to this project, this time collecting pertinent information from a variety of sources. Still, he did not progress far, blaming his office and factory work for slackness.

Social pressure on Kafka was relentless. His father, Hermann, fared exceptionally well, preparing to relocate his business from Celetná Street to larger premises at Kinský Palace in Oldtown Square. Since 1906, he was no longer selling to retail customers. Both the Czech and Jewish communities were bursting with life. Albert Einstein, already famous for his theory of special relativity, spent a very productive academic year 1911–1912 at Prague University. In 1912, he began referring to time as the fourth dimension. Frequenting the musical and literary circles of the Jewish community centered on Oldtown Square, he almost certainly played his violin at Fanta's and met both Kafka and Max Brod. The young conductor of great promise Otto von Klemperer also visited in the spring of 1912. In March of the same year, another prominent Ashkenazi born in Moravia, Gustav Mahler, had his Symphony No. 8 premiered in Prague.

Among Franz's friends, the seven years younger Franz Werfel just published in Germany a collection of poems *Der Weltfreund*, which became an instant success. Even the blind Oskar Baum had already issued his second book describing his solitude, *Das Leben in Dunckeln* (*Life in the Dark*). His dearest friend Max Brod was on a tear, crisscrossing Central Europe on lectures and live presentations. On March 17, he performed his musical compositions at a club of German women artists in Prague. Next day, Kafka, himself short of musical talent, wrote down in an apparent fit of jealousy, "I was prepared for death at any moment."[7]

How could Franz prove his worth? On reflection of his dry spell in writing, on April 1, he examined various options but found it outright scary to comment on them in his diary. "I am afraid to write about it." Did he resolve on another "unctuous" way out of his feeling of inadequacy? Apparently, he did but waited for the opportune time impatiently: "I haven't been able to make use of a single moment."[8] The opportunity came a few days later, during the long Easter weekend.

On Good Friday, April 5, the world's biggest ship, the *Titanic*, arrived in Southampton, England, dressed in flags to drum up publicity for its maiden transatlantic voyage that would end ten days later in a tragedy, killing 1,503 of its passengers off the coast of Newfoundland. The very same day, Franz Kafka, in search of excellence, also embarked on what turned out to be his Titanic.

He described this fatuous turn of events almost five years later in the "Report to an Academy."[9] Ostensibly, this is a satire about a chimpanzee captured in Africa and civilized in Europe. "With an effort which till now has never been repeated I managed to reach the cultural level of an average European," the ape boasts. This may have been Kafka's sarcastic comment on 'civilized' countries tearing themselves apart in World War I. But primarily, this puzzling story describes in delicious humor how Kafka became a captive to opium smoking.

At the onset, Kafka writes in the first person, admitting that although he had "excellent mentors, good advice, applause, and orchestral music," he took the path to his present "yoke" freely and essentially alone. All his escorts shied away to preserve their status. Still, seen from a five-year perspective, he had no regrets: "I could never have achieved what I have done had I stubbornly set on clinging to my origins, to the remembrances of my youth." Opium was a rewarding path for this aspiring writer.

Then Kafka retells his falling into this gratifying but inglorious trap through an ape named Red Peter—probably a pun on his own reddening complexion. Shot at and injured during a hunting expedition, he was left with a scar that he covered with pants (Kafka's needle scars were hidden under his sleeves). Once captured, he was confined to a small cage from which there was no escape. "I was pinned down," Kafka alludes to his morphine/heroin stage. Any attempt to get out of his cage, right or left, or any direction, was fruitless. But his captivity offered an intriguing option. Through the bars, he observed the crew sitting in semicircle around him, drinking or only grunting to each other while smoking their pipes. Smoking! "It was so easy to imitate these people . . . I could soon smoke a pipe like an old hand." He also learned to spit in the very first days. Bottles of schnapps, however, did not agree with him: the smell of it nauseated him.

On reaching Europe, this ape that found taste for pipe smoking opted for performing on the variety stage and managed to gain some respect among humans. Freedom, however, was not to be his choice. He merely cast off apehood to join the race track of humans. Then a visitor came and asked, "How long have you actually been living among us?" Answered the Red Peter, "Five years. On the fifth of April it will be five years."[10]

That takes us back to Good Friday, April 5, 1912. With the time off his work, Kafka obviously ventured in opium smoking that evening—to record it next day as an event both triumphant and regrettable. He wrote cryptically on Easter Saturday, "Complete knowledge of oneself. To be able to seize one's abilities like a little ball. To accept the greatest decline as something familiar."[11]

In expectation of a "sudden walk," he imagined how, as a result of this "decisive action" in late evening hours, one becomes energized by a sudden fit of restlessness and feeling of relief and freedom. "With limbs swinging extra freely in answer to unexpected liberty you have procured for them, . . . you recognize with more than usual significance that your strength is greater than your need to accomplish effortlessly the swiftest changes." This also was the time, Kafka noted, when family faded away and one's ego grew in stature.[12]

Did Kafka extend his opium-smoking days in April 1912? Probably not. His diary might tell more—if there was not a monthlong gap in starting April 7. Circumspection was warranted. In the first decade of the century, the world had been gripped by a major epidemic of narcotics. The heavy health toll eventually mobilized the international community. In January 1912, nearly all transatlantic countries signed the International Opium Convention in The Hague. It declared opium, morphine, and cocaine harmful substances, restricted their use to medical purposes, and subjected to controls both their production and distribution. Though specific legislation was not yet coming to Kafka's hometown, our lawyerly writer knew well the vice was both injurious and illicit.

In addition, Max Brod tried to counter Kafka's doubts again, this time with a charm offensive. In May, he and Kafka published a joint travelogue, "The First Long Train Journey," and the same month, they attended together a cabaret in Lucerna on Wenceslaus Square. Kafka gushed how wonderfully beautiful evening it was, claiming he loved Brod more than himself. Yet he also castigated himself for deception and wrote a letter to his opium tutor, Weltsch, the very next day, proposing that they address each other with the familiar *Du* instead of the formal *Sie*. From this point on, as Kafka put it, Weltsch had become his good friend, not just an acquaintance.

We may assume that a subtle tug developed between Brod, who tried to restrict Kafka's drug intake, and Weltsch, who probably hawked the opium's stimulative property. Late in May, on White Sunday, May 27, the trio went for a joint excursion that, in Kafka's assessment, did not go well. But Brod held a trump in his sleeve. On the subsequent trip to Germany, he and Kafka visited Goethe's place in Weimar and on a return trip stopped at Rowohlt publishing in Leipzig. The publisher Kurt Wolff, a young upstart with a bias for young authors, already knew and respected Brod, but Kafka was a dark horse. In Kafka's observation, Wolff was a "beautiful man of about 25, to whom God has given a beautiful wife, several million marks, and the inclination to be a publisher."[13]

In Wolff's recollections, Kafka had the "most beautiful eyes" but otherwise gave the impression of a sick man. A decade of drug abuse had already shown in the appearance of this twenty-eight-year-old son of a prosperous Prague family.[14]

What mattered, however, was that—undoubtedly on Brod's appeal—Wolff invited Kafka to submit for publication a new, original work. For

Kafka, it was just as much burden as honor. In preceding months, he could not compel himself to any systematic writing. His heroin/morphine regime no longer provided the necessary boost.

Yet opium entailed risks. True, it could be consumed mixed with alcohol, in the brew known as laudanum or theriak. This is the least injurious form, but, just as other morphinists, Kafka had developed an aversion to alcohol. The other choice was smoking opium, but he was not keen on smoking and no doubt educated himself on the dangers of inhaling. Compared with 'clean' laboratory morphine or heroin, opium smoke is a composite of over fifty alkaloids that flood the respiratory and endocrinal systems with irritants and toxins. Kafka's tutor, the twenty-eight-year-old Weltsch, spent extensive time bedridden already in the summer of 1912 and, in Kafka's words, developed a "secret partiality for boils exceeded only by . . . fondness for iodine," the disinfectant used to combat them. Just as Kafka, Weltsch also struggled with weight and hearing loss. "How **that** has knocked him down," Kafka marveled, avoiding the identification of the root cause.[15] Presaging his own health problems, Kafka also observed Weltsch's "hypochondria" lodged in his lungs and larynx.[16]

So far, he had accepted a Faustian deal, risking health degradation by opiates for excellence in writing, but a switch to opium called for caution. In the hope of clearing his mind, our aspiring writer approached the general practitioner Dr. Kohn, who attested to his "digestive disorders, low body weight, and a series of nervous problems" and recommended at least a four-week cure in a reputable institution.[17] Kafka instead encamped for much of July 1912 at a sanatorium in Harz Mountains in Central Germany, hoping to start a project for Kurt Wolff. However, he spent time there reading the Bible, and when he sat down in the writing room, he used up an hour and a half there usually alone and without writing. As days passed by, he registered his inability to write or, more properly, a profound displeasure with his current production.

Accordingly, his resistance to a new external stimulus was weakening. In his diary, he broiled against the voices counselling against mixing drugs. He would prefer to be possessed by only one devil, but that was not his case. His devils should either battle it out until only one is left or defer to one great devil. This can be read as justification for replacing the opiates by opium.

Torn apart by conflicting impulses, on return from Harz Mountains, Kafka regretfully informed Brod he could not complete the collection of stories for Kurt Wolff, and therefore, the book project was off. In fact, his stories were complete but on rereading seemed inadequate. He felt better texts were within his reach and this should dictate his next steps, he informed Brod on August 6. But he lacked the courage to take the plunge.

Then, on August 13, Kafka had a chance meeting at the Brod's with a businesswoman from Berlin. Four years his junior, Felice Bauer was intelligent, reasonably attractive, interested in Jewish affairs, and knowledgeable about literature. Her distant kinship with Brod also spoke in her favor. With no convincing proof, the biographers tend to credit her with inspiring Kafka to a sudden surge of literary deftness that followed. Their meeting of August 13, 1912, therefore, is deemed to have been a moment that 'changed the face of German literature, of world literature.'[18]

Far from denying the so-called weaker gender's role in the enrichment of humankind, the Felice Bauer case is far more complex. For sure, she did inspire Kafka. In aftermath to their encounter, he resolved to submit the assortment of stories to Kurt Wolff for publication after all. In a draft letter to the publisher, he suggested that even with the greatest skill and the greatest understanding, the bad in them was not easily discernible. The collection eventually appeared as a thin book titled *Meditation*.

Rather than being instantly transformed into a confident author, however, Kafka spent the next month in the same mental limbo as before. Remorseful for wasting his days, he psyched himself up to better days with the new medium: "My horrible calm interferes with my inventiveness." Impatiently, he was shoring up courage to make the decisive step.[19]

In afterthought, was Felice Bauer the desirable prize? Their parting on August 13 was less than auspicious. Kafka's first impression of her, recorded weeks later, was unfavorable: "Bone, empty face that wore its emptiness openly. Bare throat. A blouse thrown on. Looked like a servant in her dress . . . Blond, somewhat straight, unattractive hair, strong chin." This became his "final verdict" about Felice Bauer the moment they had been seated at Brod's.[20]

However, other positive developments in the following weeks encouraged him to take the critical step. In early September, his uncle Alfred Löwy arrived in Prague, the same uncle who had been present during his past drug milestones in 1902 and 1907. This forceful go-getter may have, directly or indirectly, expressed understanding for Franz's another bold act. In addition, publisher Wolff subsequently confirmed that *Meditation*, a collection of stories Kafka had submitted, would indeed be published. Kafka was to become a bona fide author. In this situation, on Sunday night of September 15, he at last tossed away his qualms about the new medium. How do we know?

As he would put it six weeks later, his weekdays had been a "merciless mechanical grind," but for the last six weeks, "Sunday for me has been a miracle, the glow of which I begin to see on waking Monday morning." Sundays, the only days off work then, had become his "springboard for pleasure."[21] If 'sniffing' and 'spikes' pointed to his prior use of cocaine and intravenous opiates, respectively, the key word Kafka used to describe his new Sunday pleasure was "glow," the term associated with the slow-burning morsel of opium jelly in the pipe. The glowing "miracle" that he began experiencing in earnest on September 15, 1912, can plausibly be ascribed to opium smoking.

Kafka joined the rarified caste that, in the words of another accomplished opium smoker Jean Cocteau, found a taste for "the age-old perfection of this exquisite poisoning."[22]

Feeling confident now, Kafka also dared to approach Felice Bauer. In the first letter to her of September 20, he wrote, "My life is determined by ups and downs of writing, and certainly during a barren period I should have never had the courage to turn to you."[23] Two days later, on another Sunday night, September 22, he was at it again. Thanks to his newly discovered prowess, he recorded in his diary, "The Judgment," the story heralding a writer of promise.

"THE JUDGMENT"; *THE METAMORPHOSIS; AMERIKA*

There is a great deal of hypocrisy regarding the use of drugs as performance enhancers. On one hand, society bans them in sports and vilify the athletes caught doping. The classical case is that of the Canadian Jamaican sprinter Ben Johnson who won a magnificent one-hundred-meter dash at the 1988 Olympics in Seoul, only to be stripped of his gold medal and all records for using anabolic steroids. In the attendant quip, he went from hero to zero in 9.87 seconds. The more recent affair involved the American cyclist Lance Armstrong. Having beaten a cancer associated with an elevated intake of growth hormone, Armstrong won seven times the Tour de France, arguably this planet's most grueling sport event. Extensively tested but never caught during his racing career, in early 2013, he confessed to having benefitted from illicit drugs and blood doping. Other cyclists have no doubt resorted to the same but lacked the prerequisite talent and grit to own the podium. Lance Armstrong certainly ranks as one of the greatest sports figures and symbols of human perseverance, but the asterisk of a cheater sticks to him.

Performance-enhancing drugs are banned in sports on account of both fair play and health concerns. Yet, throughout the last two centuries at least, cultural and political elites have routinely used and abused them—and countless have had their health impaired or died of overdose—in an effort to augment their success. In this context, drugging oneself to the grave adds rather than detracts from one's allure. An assortment of pop culture stars, writers, poets, painters, and musicians have benefitted from this double standard. William Burroughs, the intriguing beatnik author and self-confessed "junkie," was one of those who profited from his indulgence in opiates such as heroin. A cheater perhaps but still claiming a place in the limelight, with Norman Mailer calling him the only American writer conceivably possessed by genius.

Considering things more equitable, is not the public at least entitled to know that the cultural icons' wings may have benefitted from external drafts?

The substance Franz Kafka resorted to in mid-September 1912, opium, has a long history. Homer in *Iliad* described the effect of Helen's of Troy cup, including 'forgetfulness of pain and the sense of evil.'[1] Apart from being a recreational drug, opium has always been appreciated as a performance booster. On his attempt to subdue India in the year 326 BCE, Alexander the Great distributed it to his soldiers to augment their stamina and dare. On the destructive side of the ledger, the Roman emperor Nero was apparently driven to cruelty with an opium concoction invented by his physician.

As opium became more affordable by 1800, its use started climbing steadily both for recreational purposes and as the holy grail of creativity. Numerous Romantic figures of prominence, writers, poets, composers, painters, and politicians—including Lord Byron, Edgar Allan Poe, the stars of French Romanticism, Goethe, Richard Wagner, Bismarck, and Karl Marx—indulged in this mesmeric substance. In addition to endowing the Romantics with an intriguing mix of sensory pleasures and sense of self-empowerment, opium enhanced the characteristics that co-defined the age—inventiveness, imagination, and moodiness, both mellow and harsh to the extreme. Opium does not create talent; it may allow it to shine brighter. It is hard to disconnect this *drogue romantique* from the unprecedented agglomeration of talent and creativity in the nineteenth century.[2]

As the Romantic generation died out by 1900 and governments started curtailing access to opium, cocaine became the drug of choice. Opium, opium smoking in particular, had been driven underground but still flourished in Paris and in Central Europe as a refined expression of counterculture. In Paris, as late as 1916, there still were some 1,200 opium-smoking parlors in existence frequented by devoted "opiofiles."[3] In Vienna, Freud and his circle of passionate "smokers" looked contemptuously on ordinary tobacco puffers. Among Kafka's friends and compatriots aspiring to literary fame too, some exhibited habits, visions, literary styles, and health problems consistent with the use of opium or opiates.[4]

Does Kafka's "The Judgment" bear any association with the drug? Ostensibly, it narrates the tragic fate of an alienated young man Georg Bendeman who tries but fails to reconnect with his father. Sentenced by him to die, he rushes across the street to the bridge, swings himself over the railings, utters, "Dear parents, I have always loved you," and jumps to his death. His fall is unnoticed by the traffic crossing the bridge. Life goes on uninterrupted.[5]

"The Judgment" is clearly reflective of Kafka's circumstances. The protagonist's fiancée, Frieda Brandenfeld, is a cover for Felice Bauer to whom (or rather, to "FB") Kafka dedicated the story. The phrase "a giant of a man" is consistent with Kafka's perception of his father, Hermann. The friend with a discolored skin is, according to Kafka, modeled on his uncle, but as Brod pointed out, this figure also bears traces of the Hasidic actor Isaak Löwy.[6] Georg also sends this friend not one but three letters about "the engagement of an unimportant man to an equally unimportant girl." Kafka's sarcasm suggests that this unimportant man was Max Brod, who, in 1912, became engaged to marry Elsa Taussig—and had earned Kafka's displeasure by attempts to dissuade him from drugs. Shortly before writing "The Judgment," Kafka parted tensely with Brod, who, along with Weltsch, left for a trip to Italy.

By general consensus, this slim story marks a 'literary breakthrough' in his writing career.[7] Kafka here set a new standard in richness and consistency of presentation, reversing along the way the narrator's role from that of an occasional dispenser of violence to its victim. As his biographer marvels, 'Suddenly, without guide or precedent,' Kafka reached another level of writing skill, 'fully equipped with the "Kafkaesque" inventory' that marked his mature style.[8] Remarkably, Kafka accomplished that in one night, after chasing the elusive excellence for more than a decade. By any measure, this was a feat defying a natural process. Kafka himself declared in this context that the "demon" was behind his writing drive; alternatively, he called "the ecstasy" a precondition of literature.[9]

Sensitive biographers surmise Kafka's rearming was the fruit of his new lifestyle but are unable to elaborate. All things considered, until a more plausible explanation is offered, Kafka's new 'hallucinatory yet focused state of mind'[10] that so suddenly enhanced his talent in September 1912 can be ascribed to opium.

The impact of the drug is discernible in circumstances and contents of "The Judgment." Notably, Kafka penned the story in one sitting, during the night of September 22 to 23, with finishing touches done at around 6:00 a.m.—in itself an unusual exploit. Opium smokers are, in general, night owls, and the drug is known to temporarily boost concentration and perseverance. That night, indeed, Kafka ignored fatigue as he began experiencing "strangest fancies" that perished and rose again in a "great fire." Barely finished and his bed still untouched, he walked into his sisters' room and read them the story. More than a year and a half later, he would still recall the ecstasy of how the story burst forth with exceptional ease. But it remained embedded in his mind merely as a "specter of the night," the meaning let alone the details of which he would have hard time recalling.

Not accidentally, in a sort of self-confession, Kafka admitted his new mettle was both exciting and reprehensible. In the context of "The Judgment," he jotted in his diary, "Conviction verified that with my novel-writing I am in the shameful lowlands of writings." But he instantly posited, "Only *in this way* can writing be done, only with such coherence." Only in this way reminiscent of Freud, he believed, he could find the joy of writing something exquisite.[11]

Equally important for his life and work, this retooling would also remain firmly fixed in Kafka's mind as injurious to his health: he would pin again and again the beginning of his morbidity to the year 1912. Still more explicit, he would claim that his "wound" opened for the first time in one long night in 1912.[12] As his health woes multiplied, he would be viewing that year as the beginning of his slide to death.

On completing "The Judgment" in the early Monday morning of September 23, then, Kafka excused himself from work, advising his superior Pfohl he had been struck by dizziness and slight fever. Still pulsating with excitement, he arranged the reading of "The Judgment" to his friends at Oskar Baum's apartment. The event took place on September 24 and overwhelmed him. Toward the end, his hand was shaking and he had tears in his eyes, he would recall. His best hopes had been confirmed.

He could also hardly wait for Brod and Weltsch to return from Italy. Right at Prague's central railway station on Sunday, September 29, he proudly relayed his nocturnal effort that resulted in "The Judgment." Quite uncharacteristically, he also dared to outline his next project, a surrealistic novel on America. Presented with a fait accompli, Brod dryly noted in his diary, "Kafka, in ecstasy, is writing through the nights," and two days later, "Kafka in incredible ecstasy."[13]

What specifically in opium was of benefit to Kafka? Most consequential, it is a less powerful narcotic than morphine and heroin, the derivatives that had been preventing him from instantly recording his dreamy associations. At 1/50 of morphine's strength, it does not knock out the user completely. It may dull one's cognitive capacity, but it keeps him in a state of near consciousness. In the testimony of Jean Cocteau, "Opium nourishes a state of half-dream."[14] Smoking opium, then, allowed Kafka to write down his somnambular fancies at once, or to put it in his terms, the "miraculous glow" enabled him to "juggle the ladder" for much of the night.

The new reality called for adjustments in Kafka's daily regime. Afternoon sleep, a failure in 1911, now provided a meaningful respite for his night adventures. As the night set in and, we interpolate, he lit up the opium pipe that befogged his brain, he felt a "tremendous desire to write; the demon inhabiting the writing urge" took over.[15] Semiconscious, he started plying his pen at ten thirty to eleven thirty and would go at it on occasion until early morning. He would still find it difficult to sleep soundly, but it suited him well for the time being. "My mode of life is devised solely for writing," he summed up the new arrangement.[16]

Apart from "The Judgment," Kafka penned two other texts of distinction in the fall of 1912, *The Metamorphosis* and the initial chapters of *Amerika*. All three are vaguely autobiographical, dealing with a subject that never goes out of fashion, the father-son relationship. In Kafka's texts, the father is excessively harsh and unfair, indifferent to or a source of his son's struggles and ultimate demise. Also, while in "Description of a Struggle" the protagonist was witness to or inflicted harm on others, here he assumes the quintessential Kafkaesque role, a victim of adverse circumstances. What motivated Kafka to reverse himself in these three stories? As the above paragraphs imply, it was his perception of his new drug regime as lethal and premonition of a premature death that began tainting his writings.

On completion of "The Judgment," Kafka started a short story titled "The Stoker," intended as an introduction to a novel. However, a new crisis at home collided with his work. One source of discord was the asbestos business run by his brother-in-law. It needed another infusion of capital, but Herr Kafka was unwilling to commit more money. Alfred Löwy was approached for a loan—an embarrassment for the whole family. Kafka junior shared the blame for the initiative in setting up the business and for reluctance to lend a hand in running it.

There was more to his woes, however. Between 1907 and 1913, the Kafkas lived on the upper floor at 36 Pařížská Street (formerly Nicklasstrasse), a no longer existing building on the bank of the River Moldau. After the eldest daughter married in 1910, the family of five, noisy canaries and maid, shared a medium-size apartment with little to hide. Franz himself occupied a small unheated room between his parents' bedroom and the living room. Thus, when he began smoking opium in September 1912, even with his windows always open, the place filled with obnoxious fumes.

There was uproar on the domestic front, Kafka junior reported to Brod on Monday, October 7. His mother had not even come home for dinner, blaming him for neglect of the factory and for something else he would not specify. Even his youngest sister, Ottla, ordinarily on his side, deserted him now. The family had good reason to be concerned about him, Kafka admitted. The revulsion against his new lifestyle made him think of jumping out of the window.

The concerned Brod instantly wrote to Frau Kafka, warning her among other things that her son was at risk of suicide. There was a history of suicide in the family. In 1901, Kafka's cousin Oskar Kafka, one year younger and extrovert always full of jokes, shocked the entire clan by taking his life. Without delay, Frau Kafka responded to Brod, confessing to being very upset but helpless. The only remedy she envisioned was to relieve Franz of his work at the asbestos factory behind her husband's back. The intervention frustrated Kafka. Rather than giving up on opium, however, he decided to mine the furor around it artistically.

On Sunday, November 17, Kafka started a new story, *The Metamorphosis*. The following Sunday, even with windows open and his room as cold as a grave, the whole family except the maid left the apartment—to avoid foul smoke, we can assume. Reliance on the new medium would explain why Kafka, as many addicts do, exhibited a confused mind when writing *The Metamorphosis*. He mixed up the names of persons in the story and no fewer than six times named the main protagonist "Karl" instead of "Gregor." Feeling isolated and suicidal—and believing he and his father now hated each other amicably—Franz completed this sixty-page brainteaser within a few weeks.[17]

Ostensibly, *The Metamorphosis* is about a young commercial traveler Gregor Samsa who, living with his parents and sister, wakes up from uneasy dreams to find himself transformed into a gigantic insect with numerous thin legs, hardened back, and brown belly. Barely able to move, embarrassed, and dejected, he tries to conceal his hideous transformation from his family by keeping his door locked but not for long. Through a series of minor confrontations, his pitiful conditions become known to others, and even his mother and sister treat him more with disdain than sorrow. Cut off from interaction with the outside world and maltreated by his father, he eventually dies just before dawn, all along thinking of his family with tenderness and love.

Quantities of guesswork have been published on this taxing story of fifty pages, including an exhaustive volume ten times that long. There is little doubt that Gregor Samsa's tale elaborates some aspects of Kafka's family life—to such a detail that Samsa's home has the layout of Kafkas' apartment (only the occupancy of Kafka's and his parents' rooms is reversed). Yet despite the intense scrutiny, *The Metamorphosis* contains 'many more secrets' that—in view of a foremost biographer— may never be clarified without a detailed knowledge of Kafka's life.[18] Conversely, Gregor Samsa's misadventures may shed light on the writer himself. In response to his youthful follower, Kafka himself declared *The Metamorphosis* to be "not a confession . . . [but] in a certain sense—an indiscretion" and took an abrupt farewell without elaborating.[19]

Alas, it hardly comes as a surprise that central to *The Metamorphosis* is Kafka's—partly inborn—low self-esteem, now made still worse by injurious lifestyle. Elsewhere, in his correspondence, he now imagined living and writing in conditions similar to Gregor's, in a spacious cellar, with food being brought in and always left outside the cellar's entry. In *The Metamorphosis*, the onset of Gregor's troubles is effectively dated to 1907, the year Kafka ventured into opiates. For reasons we do not learn in the novel, Gregor is guilt-ridden for having put his family in ill repute and isolation—just as the real Kafka expressed elsewhere the growing feel of shame, despondency, and loneliness.[20]

Kafka's lack of self-respect, so typical for addicts, also helps explain his selection of insect imagery. His was not a unique choice. The images of insects were employed by—or lived in the dreams of—numerous luminaries of the nineteenth century, among them Goethe (bugs), Richard Wagner (giant grasshoppers), Bismarck (ants), and Dostoevsky (a variety of insects). The above-mentioned were reputed users of opium or opiates except for Dostoevsky, whose personal trials and health problems leading to his death in 1881, however, were likewise consistent with the after-effects of these drugs.

These creepy-crawly associations stem from the sense of self-hate, debasement, and repulsiveness generated by drug abuse, the research suggests. The addicts' fantasies could be far more revolting, of course: a century earlier, de Quincey famously recorded the nightly scare of encountering monstrous crocodiles underground, and Freud's friend Fleischl-Marxow, who eventually died from addiction-related hunger, in his dreams fought snakes crawling under his skin.

Kafka resorted to insect metaphor on other occasions—in his older text "Wedding Preparations in the Country" and in his correspondence, when he imagined crawling like a vermin or being a flabby worm of the earth. Like in other addicts, this fixation was obviously the effect of his muscle cramping that made him immobile from time to time. He had to "work hard just to crouch, pressed to the ground" on his belly, confessed the thirty-year-old to Felice Bauer.[21] In another self-confession, he was barely able "just to crouch and lift the corpse a little bit above" him.[22]

The same misfortune befell him on November 17 (1912) as, unable to stand up on his limbs, he failed to join the family for Sunday breakfast. The very same day, he renounced contacts with Felice Bauer for the first time and started the story of Gregor Samsa, who is so cramped that he can hardly breathe let alone lift his head or turn around.

There are other striking parallels between Kafka, the addicted writer, and his antihero in *The Metamorphosis*. Just like Kafka in his semi-dreams, Gregor Samsa crawls over everything, walls, furniture, and ceiling—all the while the whole room is "reeling around him." Just like Kafka, Gregor also accepts the lack of sleep for reason, spending long sleepless nights, "scrambling for hours on the ladder." Scrambling on the ladder? The reader recalls Kafka regretted his inability to do this—meaning, to write consistently—when on high-potency opiates. With opium he, alias Gregor Samsa, could 'scramble on the ladder' for hours indeed. Just like Gregor is concerned when the boss shows up to investigate his truancy from work, so Kafka feared his disconsolate lifestyle might cost him his job. He was ready to throw himself at his boss's feet to keep his job, he confessed to Brod.

One of the most puzzling aspects of *The Metamorphosis* involves "apples." They are weapons in the hands of the sadistic father who tosses them at his son-insect. One lands on his back and causes inflammation. It gives Gregor an incredible pain culminating in a "total derangement of his senses." As nobody ventures to remove this rotten something, the wound disables Gregor for more than a month. Biographers gasp for interpretation, which is near at hand: the apple episode is a metaphorical rendering of Kafka's struggle with boils, the revenge of the opiates that so inconvenienced him and other addicts. Often the size of a fist or apple, these putrid growths indeed inflict severe pain, numbing one's senses, and take a month or more to heal.

Segments of *The Metamorphosis* refer specifically to opium smoking. Those beholden to the habit, for example, excrete darkish sweat during their hot spells that discolors sleepwear and bedding. The real Kafka was embarrassed to admit to Felice Bauer the "indescribable peculiarity" of his linen.[23] Gregor too leaves behind a brownish, stinky liquid, upsetting both his sister and his mother. In Kafka's hilarious sideline, the former runs into the next room for an aromatic essence to help her mother recover from a fainting fit.

Far more invasive, of course, was opium smoke. In real life, Kafka mentioned with irony "the dreadful things happening in our house" to his acquaintances.[24] In *The Metamorphosis*, then, he describes in a riotous overstatement his family's consternation over foul air in their apartment and, specifically, in his stinking "dungeon." Thus, on entering Gregor's room, the mother tears open the window despite cold weather and leans out as far as she can, gasping for air. His sister acts in the same embarrassing way. In these moments, we learn, Gregor is ready to crouch, trembling under the couch.

The sister grows accustomed to consider herself an expert in Gregor's affairs in defiance of her parents, but eventually, she too stops pleasing him. Others in the household are less accommodating. The servant girl is disgusted and begs for permission to leave. Her wish is granted on condition of confidentiality. As Gregor resumes his air-fouling activity, his sister Grete observes, "He is starting all over again . . . the thing has to go."[25] She neglects bringing him food or hurriedly pushes any food that is available into his room with her foot. She also cleans his room as hastily as possible with one sweep of the broom, and the family starts arguing as to who should do the cleanup.

Then comes Gregor's sad finale so uncanny in foreshadowing Kafka's own fate. His universe is now confined to a bed and sofa, and in his lethargy, he accepts living in a dusty room. Ultimately, only his sister gives him a degree of comfort and compassion. Even this must end as starvation and illness take their toll. Just like Kafka, Gregor cannot eat properly. There is plenty of food in his family, of course, and the lodgers are stuffing themselves, but food has no charm for him. When he puts something in his mouth, it is as a pastime; he chews on it for an hour or so and usually spits it out again (Kafka here describes the habit of excessive prechewing of food he adopted a few years earlier). In Gregor's imagination, a standard fare turns into spoiled cheese, old breadcrumbs, and chewed-on bones. No longer able to swallow without discomfort, he rejects almost with revulsion even his favorite drink, milk.

His inability to take food cannot be alleviated easily: his family knows only from hearsay how to feed him properly. As a result, he suffers from extreme hunger and expects to die of starvation. As he indeed succumbs to hunger overnight, his emaciated body is handled by a domestic with a broom. Seeing his corpse, she calls out, "Come and see, the thing has croaked." The summoned family observes the dried-up cadaver with a mixture of amazement, piety, and relief, "Thanks be to God."[26]

The Metamorphosis is an evocative story that bears the stamp of Kafka's ripening flair for metaphor. In a friendly view, it is 'one of the few great and perfect works of poetic imagination.'[27] Kafka himself was far more critical. Subsequently, he would confess to "great antipathy" to *The Metamorphosis*: "Unreadable ending. Imperfect almost to its marrow."[28] Written in the spur of a moment, the story indeed is short on sophistication and closes with clutter. One of few major works of his published in his lifetime (in the fall of 1915), it nevertheless put him on the literary map as a writer of promise.

On completing *The Metamorphosis,* Kafka turned his attention to a novel that Brod would eventually publish as *Amerika* (the alternate title is *The Man Who Disappeared*).[29] It is ostensibly the story of a young man's transatlantic voyage to and adventures in the United States. Kafka never ventured across the Atlantic, but members of the Kafka clan did starting in 1904 (and their descendants still live in North America). He worked on the novel earlier but abandoned it only to see his interest piqued again in 1912. His immediate inspiration was a series of lectures and a book by the Czech MP Dr. Soukup, a socialist detailing his experience overseas.

No doubt Kafka returned to the project confident of new powers of imagination that opium mediated. In the expert testimony of Jean Cocteau, "One of the wonders of opium is to transform instantaneously an unknown room into a room so familiar, so full of memories that one thinks one has always occupied it."[30] This enhanced capacity to evoke the unfamiliar in absorbing detail allowed Kafka, in Prague, to project "himself alone" in New York or "go to Frankfurt for the second time" in one day. *Amerika* was, in his words, a "remembrance of a dream."[31]

Not accidentally, of Kafka's three major works, *Amerika* has the most references to the words "smoke," "smoking," "pipe," and derivatives—altogether twenty-two. It also has far more references to "the High" than *The Trial* of 1914 (there is none in *The Castle* of 1922).[32] As Kafka put it in the novel, almost everyone owned a pipe, and smoking imparted the feeling of luxury. The main character, Karl, also acquired a pipe for himself "and soon got the taste for it"—and just like Kafka was incapacitated on occasion.[33]

Kafka, who expressed the fondness for pipe smoking also as Red Peter in "A Report to an Academy," hoped to produce in *Amerika* a narrative on par with Charles Dickens, another opium user.

The novel is about Karl Rossman, a stand-in for Kafka, who is unjustly accused by his father of impregnating a maid at the age of sixteen and banished overseas. Further in the text, Kafka explains the real seducer was the maid, about thirty-five, who often prayed to a wooden crucifix in her small room next to the kitchen—and occasionally made passes on the pubertal youngster. She eventually gave birth to a healthy boy, who was baptized and given the first name of Karl's uncle. However, Karl's parents, anxious to avoid scandal and payment of alimonies, unceremoniously packed him off to America.

According to Brod, the plot reflects an affair that young Kafka had with a French maid. The Kafkas indeed engaged a French-speaking governess in 1899, Celine Bailly, a Belgian. Kafka himself would later confess that as a "precocious city boy" at age sixteen, he indeed had a risky sexual affair exposing him to "great dangers" that he had been blissfully unaware of. He managed to extricate himself with the assistance of his father, who, however, minced no words advising him to seek prostitutes instead.[34] This counsel probably damaged Kafka's psyche and turned him against his father—the sentiment expressed in the novel.

Miss Baily is apparently personified in *Amerika* as the vulgar Brunelda, the fat praying mantis by someone's characterization who indeed makes passes on Karl. Apart from that, the novel conveys Kafka's world of 1912. The teenage Karl exhibits similar health, mental, and existential grievances as the adult author, including an extraordinary lack of appetite, cough, and spasmodic muscles that force him to stumble "on all fours."[35] He also wears cotton in his ears as Kafka did to insulate him from noise. Karl's maternal uncle, an American senator, who first accommodates and then abandons him, has "Jacob for a Christian name"—a playful reference to Alfred Lövy, a convert to Christianity. One of the female figures, the piano-playing Clara with whom Karl quarrels, seems to be modeled on Felice Bauer with some features of Ottla.

Supposedly roaming America, Karl also revisits his hometown in the dreamy chapters 5 and 6. The occasion is his arrival in search of work to Rameses, a fictional "big town." In the "Hotel Occidental," he encounters a German-speaking head cook who used to work for Prague's "Golden Goose" (a five-star hotel on Wenceslaus Square still in existence today). She quickly develops a liking for him, hires him as a liftboy, and offers him accommodation in her living quarters that bear resemblance to Kafka's apartment. She is a good-hearted woman, kind to him as if he was her son, Karl observes. One of three females in Kafka's major works who provide accommodation to the chief protagonist, she approximates Kafka's mother, Julie.[36]

The head cook is assisted by Therese, a young typist/secretary or simply "the girl." Much of this chapter is devoted to the interaction between her and Karl. Working long hours, she feels lonely and attaches to him instantly, paying late evening visits to his room and welcoming him to her place. Soon, they start taking walks and doing errands in the city together; they also argue and reconcile with the head cook's intervention (who usually takes Therese's side). Therese has no secrets from Karl, stands behind him right or wrong, and weeps profusely when he runs into existential problems. She is set in circumstances and exhibits characteristics akin to those of Kafka's sister Ottla. Lurking from behind the stage is the headwaiter, a person of some authority in this context resembling Kafka's father, Hermann.

As in his other texts, Kafka narrates in chapter 5 and 6 issues that seem rooted in his real-life experience. They revolve around a street man, Robinson by name, whom Karl invited to his residence. The two have the history of some physical tenderness—Karl attempts winning Robinson over by stroking his hand, and the latter leans on him when riding in a car. This time, Robinson is found in Karl's bed after an overnight stay, incapacitated by a sudden spasm and demanding money before leaving.

It is an embarrassing moment possibly implicating Karl in homosexuality and abuse of intoxicants.

While the latter mulls his response, the headwaiter wastes no time to apprise the head cook about her "angel boy" and his escapade. Both the head cook and Therese are spellbound and upset when Karl is quizzed and admits the validity of the charge. Interested in Therese's response, he takes note of her sobbing. The affair spills over into the chapter 6 with a widening narrative.

Ultimately, it's not Karl's indiscretion in the residence but his unapproved absence from work that matters (in real life, Kafka missed work on completion of "The Judgment" a few weeks earlier). Karl is dismissed for dereliction of duty, allowing Kafka to resume roving through the imaginary American landscape.

Dependent on Soukup and contemporary Americana, Kafka committed some factual errors in *Amerika*, most notably claiming the Statue of Liberty has a sword in her raised arm. In general, his narrative followed other European observers mixing praise and criticism of American society. Himself a vague egalitarian and suspicious of modernity, he disapproved of American industrialism, conspicuous consumption, wealth disparities, and lack of compassion. "In this country sympathy was something you could not hope for." His uncle has ten different offices in one building; houses for the rich are larger and taller than need to be and are surrounded by high walls and guarded by watchdogs. Welcome to gated communities!

Yet despite this "extraordinary waste of space," "several families live in one little room" in New York, Kafka also observes.

Kafka's attempt to produce a disciplined novel did not meet his expectations. In the second half of January 1913, he abruptly ended work on *Amerika* and eventually dismissed it as a complete failure. The novel lacks a focus. Kafka still hoped to mine the surreal world spanning dreams and reality, but this fusion was difficult to sustain.

FELICE BAUER: "THERE ARE STILL SOME HORRIBLE CORNERS IN ME THAT YOU DON'T KNOW"

Felice Bauer (1887–1960) was a dedicated and levelheaded Berliner, modishly attractive, and successful at work. When Kafka met her in Prague in August 1912, she was the executive secretary at Lindström, a company selling office gadgets, most notably parlograph, a recording device predating dictaphone. In today's world, she would probably climb high on the executive ladder. Apart from gender discrimination, she was hampered by disconsolate affairs at home that forced her to support her four siblings.

Kafka's first impression of her physique was unfavorable, and the passage of time changed that little. The biggest drawback was her teeth, especially a golden one. In Kafka's eyes, she had no sex appeal, yet she was obliging, extremely patient, and conscientious. She also shared his interest in literature, Zionism, and vegetarian diet, and suffered from similar neurotic indispositions, nagging self-doubt, sleeplessness, and nightmares.

In five years of their epistolary contact, Franz and Felice exchanged approximately one thousand letters and postcards. Whereas he destroyed all her mail, Felice eventually sold all but the most sensitive missives in her possession to the New York publisher Schocken. Those never made public, we may assume, consisting of what Kafka himself called "inaccurate . . . imprudent, dangerous letters." Clearly, the reconstruction of what transpired between him and Felice Bauer can never fully reveal their secrets.

In direct contact, Kafka praised his Berlin acquaintance lavishly. The pleasure of writing to her instilled him with a sense of infinity, he intoned with Old World charm. He also displayed a sharp memory in recalling the circumstances and minute details of their first meeting. Soon, however, he began a campaign of discounting himself as a prospective groom: his energies were pathetically fragile, he was the thinnest person, and his life was determined by quirks of his writing. Felice should know he worked well into night, went to bed usually with slight chest pain and upset stomach, and hardly slept. In consequence, he arrived in his office in the morning barely able to perform his duties adequately.

Kafka held a choice job, working six hours a day to earn a very comfortable income. An average industrial worker in Bohemia toiled eight to nine hours, six days a week, for one-sixth of his salary. He enjoyed the benevolence of his office superiors and free upscale accommodation with his parents. The root of his discomfort was not material.

Before long in his letter exchange with Felice, he indeed hinted at not being the master of himself: "If there is a higher power that wishes to use me, or does use me, then I am at its mercy."[1] His mother was justifiably concerned about him, he added, giving no details. Soon, he also ruled out another meeting with Felice. In his justification, even though he looked anything between eighteen and twenty-five years, she would find him unbearable because of his personal impediments. Apart from staining his linen, they handicapped him with "catarrh-infected throat."[2] Opium smoking, as we know, produces both bronchitis and darkish sweat stains on bedding.

The recurring self-doubt continued to impact his interaction with Felice. Weeks into their mail exchange, he suggested that their contact be reduced to one letter a week—and reversed himself a few days later. Bewildered, Felice secretly approached Max Brod for advice. He replied that Kafka was an uncompromising artist who deserved to be tolerated for moodiness and eccentrics. "In the afternoon he is exhausted, so all that is left for the 'profusion of his vision' is the night. This is tragic."[3]

Calling Kafka's nightly bursts of creativity tragic? In the follow-up exchange between Felice and Brod, the latter tiptoed around his friend's nocturnal exploits that he found so objectionable. Greatly worried, behind Kafka's back, he also sent an eight-page letter to Frau Kafka, imploring her to pay attention to her son's problems. In retrospect, he would describe his step as an extremely brutal intervention. In mid-November (1912), Kafka's mother also received a concerned message from Felice. In response, she asked for her help in changing Franz's eating and sleeping habits and his daily routine in general.

Kafka became privy to this correspondence and responded with contrite tenderness: he loved Felice so much and placed so much hope in their friendship. But he also confessed to having "this one hopelessly black spot" that his doctors could not cure.[4] In search of explanation, numerous authors assume it was impotence or fear thereof—or fear of a venereal disease—that held him back.

This surmise is definitely invalid. Kafka called his handicap a "minor, fleeting illness" that, at the same time, was also his "much coveted . . . pleasure."[5] He would restate this in different permutations in letters to Felice and would refuse to reform when asked to do so. Besides, this handicap also gave him troubles at work. A "dreadful impediment" or "weights" started obstructing his work performance as early as in 1908. In addition, he felt a similar impairment when on vacations. Wrote he to Brod from a sanatorium in Riva, "If only that *one* thing would loosen its hold over me, if only I did not have to think of it constantly . . . By comparison with this, nothing has any meaning and I merely keep travelling around inside these caverns."[6]

We may safely assume that the "black spot" he coveted was not some sort of sexual inhibition or deviancy but his insatiable taste for drugs and its consequences—a powerful deterrent to social life let alone intimacy.

For illustration, Kafka saw nothing but horror when a full plate was placed in front of him.[7] He tried to mask his opium-induced difficulty to swallow with *fletcherizing*, endless chewing on each morsel of food. To his embarrassment, his father covered his face with a newspaper at suppertime rather than watch this silly habit. Projecting this situation into *Amerika*, Kafka described how the main protagonist Karl offends Miss Clara by not eating his meal because of the "constraint under which he had suffered during the whole dinner" and the resulting lack of appetite.[8] Kafka could expect to raise the eyebrows of Felice Bauer's family by repeating his routine in Berlin.

The separation between him and Felice suited him well, he knew. He appreciated her being a distant security and source of strength unperturbed by personal contact. As a biographer notes, 'The important thing about her was that she did exist.' To her chagrin, Kafka ruled out resolutely visiting Berlin over Christmas 1912. Haunted by her tears, he compensated by a contrived chat about family, friends and his health conditions. Thus he implored her in December 1912, "Never fail to tell me, dearest, where you are, what you are wearing, what is it like around you."[9] Come New Year's Eve, the drugged Kafka, age thirty, was once again tied to his bed, confessing how glad he actually was being unable to be with her.

We can assume that as Felice Bauer entered his life, opium smoking became Kafka's favorite form of drug intake primarily responsible of his health problems. In coming years, his writings would incorporate references to a "long thin pipe," "triumphant pipes," pipes that hang in the stand; "our day-to-day smoking," smoking as "our unthinking habit," smoking "timidly in spite of all routine," smoking the pipe in "half-sleep"; smoking as an act of liberation from "fetters of everyday life"; and "the pleasure of smoking" unknown to so many. He would also muse about the singularity of smoking and a link between smoking and art.[10]

By the yearend of 1912, however, Kafka's initial fascination with opium was on the wane. The resistance of his family and Max Brod to his new stinky routine undoubtedly accelerated this process. Perhaps critical was his failure to manage his time effectively: he was constantly craving for sleep. Once Brod again proved aloof to his new style of writing, Kafka's motivation to grab the pencil declined as well. Consequently, he stopped working on *Amerika* in January 1913, never to complete the novel, and observed himself sinking into a hole as a writer.

In early February (1913), Kafka visited the same Weltsch who had introduced him to opium smoking. This time, he perceived the host quite critically, "as usual in an overheated room full of foul air . . . almost unbreathable air." To make him stay, Weltsch opened the door to the adjacent cold room, obliging Kafka to listen and converse in his overcoat. It was an unpleasant experience but not unknown to the guest. Weltsch was coping with "hypochondria" that, Kafka observed, is lodged in his lungs and larynx.[11] Kafka himself would eventually identify the same organs as the focal point of his own health problems.

Uncertain about his new lifestyle, in late February 1913, Kafka joined Weltsch for a stroll and reluctantly listened to his pep talk. Weltsch's words seemed extremely sensible, but Kafka reserved a decision. As he mulled his options, on March 1, he still reported spending time on lonely evening walks. At home, he barely spoke to anyone safe perhaps Ottla, and her goodwill was also wearing thin.

The next day, March 2, Kafka apparently curtailed the smoking routine that had set him so sharply apart from the family. Keeping company to his mother and father, he stayed in the living room that evening and tried to write to the sounds of their card game. He also advised Felice Bauer that his production would be impacted from now on. While his recent writing had given him courage to approach her, he now realized this creative phase was disappointingly short-lived.

In the follow-up letter of March 3–4, Kafka advised Felice he was a different person from the one she had so far corresponded with. The change was not a "transformation into a new state [but] . . . rather a relapse into an old and no doubt lasting one." Three days later, he again disassociated himself from the writer of his first letter to her: he had been "completely thrown back" onto his old tracks.[12] As part of his retrenchment and probably also to please Max Brod, Kafka now discarded 550 "worthless" pages out of about 600 pages of a further unidentified text.

We may assume that Kafka returned to intravenous opiates in March 1913. This was possible because of cross-tolerance among the different forms of opium, permitting a substitution of one by another. The inflow of obnoxious fumes into his body subsided, certainly to the relief of his family and Max Brod. Reconsidering his treatment of Brod, Kafka now regretted he had never been completely candid with him, neither in minor nor in important matters. With both sides anxious to reconcile, Kafka was now able to report a pleasant evening at Max's. In another joyful moment, his mother ventured into his room again and kissed him good night—something that had not happened for years.

Even the father, Hermann, now earned his admiration for being able to put up with the extended family relying on his largesse. Though the father was a cautious type foreseeing hazard everywhere, he also possessed a strong character devoid of proclivity to lie, his son observed.

For a few years, there would be no major conflict between Kafka and his closest relatives.

However, the string of his handicaps attributable to opium and opiates was uninterrupted. Obstruction in swallowing still topped Kafka's concerns, and he reported it with sad humor: "This morning I had to regret that my principles would not allow me to eat anything."[13] On occasion, he justified his starving as an attempt at cleansing his system. Other features of his health woes included headaches, insomnia, constipation, 'neurasthenia,' the addicts' favorite term for mental anguish, as well as watery eyes and running nose, a sort of virtual cold that affects the addicts year-round. In Kafka's apt observation, this problem was largely hypochondriacal; he suffered from a cold that actually was not a cold (in Cocteau's testimony, opium indeed has its own cold, shivers, and fevers that do not coincide with cold and heat). Increasingly, Kafka expressed the feeling of a healthy unfit: he walked home like a sick man, weary of the distance still to be covered, but not ill. Not thirty yet and his hair was graying. As needle marks reappeared on his arms, we may assume, he again preferred small, less frequented bathing establishments and usually toward evening.

With the abrupt stop to his writing, Kafka shifted his attention to Felice. But she was far from enamored by *Meditation*, his first—and slim—book. Her favorite was August Strindberg, whose twenty-seven volumes of collected works she possessed. She appreciated other writers as well, but a mere mentioning of them made Kafka jealous. Gripped by anxiety, sometimes he could not even write to her, let alone enthusiastically entertain a trip to Berlin. He felt so uncomfortable on expectation his lifestyle would turn off both Felice and her family. Eventually, he resolved on visiting Berlin over the Easter holidays (1913) and meeting with Felice alone, principally to tell her that "you have been misled by my letters" and show her "who I really am."[14] Was he really prepared to reveal his "hopelessly black spot"?

On Saturday, March 22, he sent Felice a telegram "still undecided" and then boarded the train and arrived unannounced in Berlin late in the evening. Next morning, he desperately tried to alert her of his presence. But she had already made other plans, and the couple spent merely a few hours together walking around Grunewald Park. In their second meeting in eight months, there was little opportunity for Kafka to spill his personal secrets. On the return leg, he stopped in Leipzig on March 25 to meet his publisher Kurt Wolff and his compatriot, now editor, Franz Werfel.

Back in Prague, Kafka struggled with lack of sleep, exhaustion, and angst but promised Felice to divulge his secret in a day or two. But then, he had a suicidal dream—and waffled again. On March 28, he pleaded for patience: she deserved to be told everything quite brutally, but he was not in a position to do that. Several days later, he sent a soulful letter to Brod, tinged with self-contempt. Describing one of his recurrent nightmares, he was stretched out on the ground and "sliced up like a roast," and with his hand "slowly pushing a piece of this meat toward a dog in the corner." At the same time, he showed heartfelt sympathy for Felice, calling her truly a martyr. He felt responsible for upsetting the entire ground "on which she used to live happily and in harmony with the world." All this served as a backdrop to his dramatic claim: "Yesterday I sent my great confession to Berlin."[15]

However, no letter of this nature exists, and if he really sent one, his confession was not clear enough. A few weeks later—in a letter to Brod—Felice summed up her experience: "I don't know why it is, he [Kafka] writes to me fairly often but his letters never come to the point, I don't know what it's all about, we have not come any closer to each other and for the moment there is no hope."[16] It may also be that she preferred not to comprehend his opacities.

A plain disclosure of his "black spot" could damage his standing with her, of course. Getting free of addiction was the preferred route, and Kafka apparently resolved to attempt it, this time with family support. He conferred with his clan to find a way back from his quandary, Felice was told. In early April 1913, he indeed began working with a gardener in the Prague suburb of Nusle, in cold and rain and wearing only shirt and pants. His goal was to "escape self-torture" by doing some strenuous manual work. Pushed aside was his involvement in the family's asbestos factory.[17]

There is little doubt Kafka sought to overcome addiction on previous occasions and failed. Drug abusers in general cope with withdrawal symptoms that inflict extreme mental and physical pain. They return to the drug not to get high but to avoid being sick. Just one puff, one needle or pill may be enough to bring relief—and restart the cycle. One of Kafka's acquaintances, Jan Dvorsky, also tried a self-cure from Kafka's afflictions by outdoor gardening and, failing in that, poisoned himself in February 1913. Others, in the grip of 'neurasthenia,' the favorite runabout for addition, shared his fate. Kafka's attempt in the spring of that year likewise led nowhere. On May 3, he admitted his resistance to ghosts of night had been fading until it became mere sham. Despite having the family on his side, "I did not find the way."[18]

His desperation flared up again: he recorded the image of a "pork butcher's broad knife that quickly and with mechanical regularity chops into me from the side and cuts off very thin slices which fly off almost like shavings because of the speed of the action."[19] He also feared setbacks in the office and suffered from the physical impossibility of handwriting—one of his recurring problems shared with other addicts.

At this point, Felice was challenged by problems in her own family, in particular by the pregnancy of her sister Erna and by her delinquent brother Ferdinand. In consequence, she showed less attention to her troubled suitor in Prague. Kafka wasted no time to complain in writing. Her supposed lack of trust combined with his defects made him feel uncertain and tinged his letters again with artfulness and insincerity: "My love makes the words stick in my throat and floods every syllable I mean to write."[20] With his mind in disarray, he also claimed wishing her to be free of himself—and then resumed complaints about her silence.

Kafka's detoxification attempt was motivated by understanding his visit to Berlin could not be postponed indefinitely. Failure to beat the addiction, therefore again heavily burdened his conscience when, at last, he resolved to make the trip. His two days in the German capital on May 11 and 12 were oddly anticlimactic. Quartered at Hotel Askanischer Hof on Königgratzer Street, he met Felice's family and spent time with her alone on a trip to the popular lake Nikolassee. Intimacy was off again if only because any attempt at disrobing would reveal needle marks on his arms. Aware of his discomfort, she did not ask probing questions.

In retrospect, Kafka would characterize his conduct in Berlin as craziness; in contact with Felice's family, he felt "so small, and everyone stood as huge as giants all around me . . . I must have made a very nasty impression on them." Guilt-stricken and ashamed of his physical condition, once again, he missed courage to disclose his addiction. Thus, in afterthought, he also let Felice know they still had a "number of terrible things to discuss" before getting out of the woods. She did not know what imprisoned him and made him the "unhappiest of men."[21]

Mulling his options, Kafka found nothing more urgent than to mail his disclosure to Felice's father but meekly predicted it would lack clarity. Tormented by uncertainty, he then changed his mind again: the letter would be for Felice's eyes only. He still needed five more days and several drafts before settling on the final text. It amounted to yet another tiptoeing around his drug dependence.

There still existed certain problems that Felice was vaguely aware of but did not take seriously enough, Kafka intoned. She should know that though rarely if ever sick, he had not been in perfect health and missed the sense of well-being for the past ten years. This burden was apparent almost at all times—a reference primarily to his weight loss. It had prevented him from talking, eating, and sleeping naturally, from being natural in any way. However, no one took his problems seriously enough, or they were overlooked for his own sake. In particular, his own family ignored them in a "conspiracy of silence." This, however, would not be possible in an intimate relationship.

Out of the sense of responsibility, Kafka implored Felice to a heart-to-heart talk so he could divulge the nature of his "great plight" that imperiled their cohabitation: "I cannot bear the concern because I regard it as too great." Felice should also convey to her mother that his trip to Berlin had "both meaning and purpose, but lacked the man to accomplish either."[22]

As the anguished Kafka waited impatiently for response from Berlin, besieging Felice with messages of despair, Max Brod came to his rescue again. He sent her another letter, probably repeating the claim of his friend's genius and frailty. But Felice may have not been a stranger to the world of drugs. Time after time, her brother Ferdinand was embezzling money from customers' accounts and sold whatever he could steal at home, possibly to feed his drug or gambling addiction. On Brod's prompting, then, she sent Kafka a telegram that probably was mildly reassuring. It was followed by her promise to write every day again. His secret liability, Kafka could assume, had been accepted as a fact of life.

To understand Kafka's follow-up conduct, his ambivalent attitude toward women must be noted. Similar as his favorite writer Kierkegaard, who admitted to immoral credo of losing interest in women he had conquered, Kafka likewise treated them as a scalp collector; they lost appeal once under his spell. For this reason, also, Felice Bauer started fading as the object of his fantasies in the spring of 1913—while Kafka began scoring as a writer. In May, "The Stoker," the first chapter of *Amerika*, was published by Kurt Wolff. This event that left him in high spirits because he considered the story really good, a rare praise of his own text. Even his father was apparently interested.

The following June, "The Judgment" appeared in *Arcadia*, followed by *The Metamorphosis*. The response was lukewarm, but it gave a boost to Kafka's burdened psyche. More than ever before, he felt confident of having a "tremendous world" in his head but needed seclusion for writing, and neither the office nor Felice allowed for such luxury.[23]

Conflicting impulses again impacted his conduct. In mid-June 1913, he drafted a marriage proposal—and at once began raising trifling, repetitious arguments against. The word itself, marriage, made his knees shake, even when merely writing it on a postcard. Could Felice be happy with someone like him, such a sick and miserable man who could hardly walk and was incapable of coherent reasoning or even telling a story properly? As for family life, he found it distasteful and nauseating to watch his father and family make a fuss about cute children. Felice also needed to know his position at work was unstable; there were squabbles in the office, all his fault, and they were bound to recur. If all this was not a potent deterrent, was she aware she would have to move to Prague and settle in a small house on the outskirts just like her sister in Budapest for whom she felt so sorry? Would she not be embarrassed? Marrying such a loser with an odd lifestyle would force her to live far more modestly than she could imagine—she, in his mind, a big spender unwilling to travel third class.

Scrupulous to a fault or buying time, he even suggested that a doctor be asked to rule on his suitability for matrimony, stipulating it should not be his family physician to ensure impartiality. Even then, Felice was admonished she could not trust even a doctor of her choice. As a monographer puts it, Kafka 'pleaded the case against himself like an advocate using all available means.'[24]

Meanwhile, Frau Kafka contracted an agency to investigate Felice and her family. The report arrived from Berlin on July 1, in her son's opinion both shocking and intensely funny. Kafka hastened to assure Felice these routine reports could not be fully trusted; certainly no information agency would be capable of telling the truth about him (addiction was not considered a disease but an alternate lifestyle). But she discounted his laments, and in early July, Kafka told his mother they were engaged.

Directly or by implicit, however, he kept the self-demotion campaign on. He was unable to talk with anyone including his parents, hated all his relatives, and was capable of tormenting even Felice hardheartedly. Above all, he continued to be absurdly terrified of their common future mainly on account of his weakness, which was both self-inflicted and unmanageable. It turned him into a "man without self-control […] When dealing with myself I am powerless."[25]

The lack of genuine interest in matrimony was affecting his conduct steadily. In July 1913, he disingenuously informed Felice that the apartment he had chosen for them would be available only in ten months. Worse yet, rather than joining her for summer holidays, he vacationed with his parents in Radešovice, just outside Prague. Plainly hurt, she curtailed letter writing and took her vacations on the Isle of Sylt in the Baltic. It prompted him to more self-flagellation and spells of silliness. When she suggested Herr

Kafka could clarify the situation with the Bauers in Berlin, he responded by inviting her for a few hours to Prague on her return from the Baltic, a detour of over six hundred kilometers for her. As for his travel plans, he claimed to have dreams about Felice almost every night but for a multitude of reasons preferred to eschew a trip to Berlin despite their engagement.

Unbeknown to Felice, on July 21, he jotted down in his diary a page-long "Summary of all the arguments for and against my marriage." It shows a dramatically split personality. On the one hand, Kafka reasserted his incapacity for living as a single; he could not bear his current personal trials let alone the challenges of old age. On the other hand, he believed he needed solitude to retain his dedication for writing. Marriage would never allow him to be alone, he feared, and would never offer him the luxury of early retirement. If alone he might quit his job one day, he assumed, but not if married.[26]

Unbeknown to Kafka, the perplexed Felice, meanwhile, asked a graphologist to look at his handwriting. On learning the results, the irritated Kafka disputed most of them. He was neither very determined nor extremely sensual or good-natured. On the other hand, he considered himself thrifty, both from necessity and thanks to inborn sense for austerity, he claimed on August 14.[27] Deep down, he realized that his "black spot" would continue draining his resources, health, and mental capacity.

With this overarching handicap, Kafka also continued to shape the arguments against a marriage accordingly. Though his encounters with Felice were so rare, he felt they have been marred by the countless moments of total estrangement. With her in mind, he envisioned monasticism as an ideal, enduring form of marriage: "Coitus as punishment for the happiness of being together. Live as ascetically as possible."[28]

Accordingly, more self-denigrating letters followed. Could Felice imagine austere life with the man who was "peevish, miserable, silent, discontented and sickly"? Apart from not being a good marriage prospect and having no capacity for family life, he also found office work unbearable: it conflicted with his "only desire and only calling, which is literature." At the same time, Kafka conceded having neither money to live independently nor strength to earn living as a writer.[29] Has a prospective groom ever disqualified himself so mercilessly?

The stressful situation took a toll on Felice Bauer as well. She broke down with headaches and heart palpitations. "Your dear, suicidal letter received today," responded Kafka.[30] He not only reproached himself for tormenting her but also asserted his own woes were far greater than those he inflicted. One night, he even experienced a frightful "attack of madness, the images became uncontrollable, everything flew apart until . . . a Napoleonic field marshal's black hat came to my rescue."[31] On more than one occasion, he wished, as other addicts do, to be lying several stories underground.

There also was some resistance to Felice at home, or as Kafka willingly amplified it, audible warnings. Apparently, his father wanted assurance she would not need his money if married. An awkward condition this was, of course, predicated on doubts whether his addicted son with a fabulous income could support the family. Herr Kafka was, therefore, ready to visit the Bauers in Berlin, discuss legitimate worries about the marriage, and condone it if they still welcomed his son into the family. The junior Kafka was agreeable with the idea that would relieve him from the burden of confession. Thus, suddenly, he also found words of appreciation of his father's "strong character." In contrast to him, he had "no proper appreciation for money (I may have inherited from my father avarice in little things, but not, alas, his acquisitiveness)."[32]

About the same time, the end of August 1913, a letter arrived from Felice's father. As Kafka read it, she had failed to divulge to him the aspect of marriage that might imperil it. Since Herr Kafka's trip to Berlin did not materialize, Franz responded to Herr Bauer with a letter of clarification. In it, once again, he denigrated himself as cunning, aloof, unsociable, glum, and selfish, and a hypochondriac who hardly talks even with his closest relatives. But he still shied away from even alluding to the nature of his dreadful secret.

Somehow wishfully, in one of the follow-up missives, he claimed Felice already was familiar with his inner inhibitions that he tried to suppress so resolutely. Since no answer came in time or was depressing, once again, he felt the need to say farewell to her, and she once again turned for advice to Brod.

In early September, Kafka got a chance for a relief from his neurotic quandary. An international congress for first aid and hygiene was held in Vienna, and he took part along with his bosses Pfohl and Marschner, both slated to deliver reports. Overstaying for several days in the Austrian capital, he also attended a Zionist congress dealing with the issues of peripheral interest to him. The spare time gave him a chance to satisfy his hushed-up cravings. Research into addiction shows that a change of location enhances the doping effect of drugs. Within a few days in Vienna, Kafka indeed developed an alarming insomnia, fever, heart pain, and ravaging headaches. Apparently drugged up, he spent his time in the hotel, oblivious to goings-on let alone to writing.

Still in poor shape, he took advantage of his Vienna presence to travel farther south, visiting Trieste and Venice first. He found Venice captivating but felt "not sufficiently coherent to write anything coherent," he reported to Brod on September 16. In retrospect he wished he could "tear those days in Vienna out of my life."[33] His next destination was Riva, a resort on the picturesque Lago di Garda that hosted him and the Brod brothers already in the summer of 1909.

The sanatorium of Dr. Hartungen on the northern shores of the lake, then still in the Habsburg Empire, catered to the upper class. Its clients included the writers Heinrich and Thomas Mann, as well as Sigmund Freud. All submitted to a medical examination to ferret out those with contagious diseases including tuberculosis. Kafka passed the exam. Like similar establishments, the sanatorium frowned on conventional medicine, placing emphasis on the fashionable natural healing. The calorie-rich diet and communal dining supported those like Kafka who suffered from undernourishment. Feeling distaste for meat, Kafka could nevertheless opt for a vegetarian meal. During his stay at the sanatorium one client, a jovial Austrian general shot himself dead.

Kafka's regime at the sanatorium was not drug-proof. After five days, he wrote to Brod that his health would be better if only he could shake off "one thing" that held him inside underground caverns. Trapped there by drugs, he also saw no escape from the lethargy and despair. He could neither talk nor write, he confided to Brod midway through his stay in the sanatorium.

Kafka's afflictions and laments did not prevent him from functioning normally throughout the years. While in Riva, he dated a German miss from Lübeck, Gerti Wasner. Despite her immaturity and illness, Kafka reported, she was a real well-adjusted person who also happened to be a Christian. He fell for her fast, but the romance ended with her tearful departure after ten days. She meant so much to him, he recalled in retrospect.

It appears that this fling in Riva motivated Kafka to further loosen the bond with Felice Bauer. The idea of spending time with her on a honeymoon filled him with revulsion, he confided to Brod. Somehow incongruously, he felt unable to live both with her and without her. Under these circumstances, was his relationship with Felice sustainable? Back in Prague on October 13 and finding it hard to readjust, he suffered from more terrible headaches and struggled as ever to get a few hours of restless sleep. At this point, another siren appeared on his horizon, dispatched by none other than Felice Bauer.

Kafka and Felice Bauer in 1917

Grete Bloch in the 1930s

Karel Šviha whose affair inspired Kafka to *The Trial*

Adult Franz Kafka

Kafka's doodles

Golden Lane, a romantic cubicle for two

GRETE BLOCH

In late October 1913, Kafka received a letter from Fräulein Bloch suggesting a meeting on her forthcoming stopover in Prague. In a matter-of-fact response, he thanked for the invite and promised to comply: "Of course I shall come."[1] She arrived in a fur coat that turned him off, but his reserve vanished fast. Margarete (Grete) Bloch (1892–1944) was a delicately built Berliner, far more agile and animated than Felice Bauer. A graduate of a commerce academy, she too was successful in the men's world and similarly supported her family in Berlin. Prague was on her way to Vienna where she was about to start working for a local distributor of office gadgets Lopresti.

Though she apparently arrived to plead Felice's case, a mutual attraction quickly developed between the thirty-year-old Kafka and this twenty-one-year-old messenger whom he described as a rather unusual girl of immense vivacity. They met two days in a row, and Kafka accompanied her to the railway station. Biographers, however, hold an unfavorable view of Bloch as a spoiler of Kafka's romance with Felice, a pretender set on engraving herself in his life. It is true that, compared with Kafka's voluminous correspondence with Felice, his letters to Bloch are available only for the period October 1913 to October 1914. Kafka's publisher Schocken at first showed no interest in them, and those eventually published have been heavily sanitized. Obviously, there was a lot of the controversial to tell—and to conceal.

Undoubtedly, the most tantalizing question mark concerning Grete Bloch is whether she bore Franz Kafka a child. Twenty-four years later and hiding from Hitler in Italy, she approached Max Brod to correct an unfavorable comment on her in his biography of Kafka. Brod should know she had been close to Kafka and had been forced to carry alone the "misfortune" that concerned Franz as well. Almost certainly, Brod already was aware of or sensed the nature of that "misfortune" and the subsequent correspondence with her confirmed his hunch.[2]

Far from piggybacking on Kafka afterlife, Bloch revealed her secret in more detail in a private letter of April 1940. Reminiscing on that "magical city" of Prague she visited five years earlier, she mentioned stopping at the grave of a man who, notable for his mastery, "meant so much" to her. This man, deceased in 1924, "was the father of my boy, who died in Munich in 1921 just before he reached the age of seven . . . far away from me and from him." In her words, she and the child's father parted during World War I and met only once before their boy succumbed to fatal illness.[3]

Kafka biographers have for decades dismissed Bloch's claim as unfounded and improbable. Yet far from being a publicity seeker, she held on to the secret until long after Kafka's death and divulged it to her confidant only when the Nazi onslaught on Jews—of which she would also become a victim—was already under way. She wrote the 1940 letter feeling her life was coming to an end. Her claim of Kafka's paternity was accepted by Brod—a rare step by someone otherwise bent on covering up for his friend. Just as she, he was motivated by historical accuracy.

At least one other friend of Kafka, Dr. Ernst Weiss, was also aware of Bloch's pregnancy and tried to mediate a resolution in 1914. Eventually, a photo of Bloch and her son was uncovered, confounding the naysayers. But they still argue, on the flimsiest evidence, that Kafka needed not be the father: Grete Bloch allegedly could not figure out whom she bedded at the time of conception. Kafka's sensuous correspondence with Bloch, another of his recent embellishers claims, "did not lead anywhere."[4]

This and following chapters effectively confirm Bloch's claim—and unveil another major yet unknown aspect of Kafka the man and novelist.

It all started in the first week of November 1913. Apprised by Grete of troubles in the Bauer family and feeling good about her attention, Kafka suddenly brimmed with confidence: "If it would only remain! If I could go in and out of every door in this way, a passably erect person." Without mentioning Grete's visit, he promptly advised Felice Bauer that, owing to "discoveries" he had made about himself recently, he would travel to Berlin for the weekend after all.[5]

Uninvited, he arrived in the German capital late in the evening on Saturday, November 8, to find out next morning that Felice could spare one hour only. They spent it strolling in the popular park Tiergarten. She promised to return later the same afternoon and accompany him to the train station but failed to show. They would not communicate for weeks. His masculinity hurt and feeling unwanted and unappreciated, he dropped the reservations about Grete. Toward midnight of his first day back in Prague, November 10, he wrote her a long letter disclosing how pleasantly surprised he had been with her appearance and how much Felice had disappointed him.

As the days without Felice's letters were adding up, his self-esteem evaporated again. Short on confidence, he confessed in late November: "I am an incapable, ignorant person who . . . would be fit only to crouch in a kennel." Intentionally he walked through the streets frequented by prostitutes, flirting with the "exciting" prospect going with one of them.[6]

Also in November 1913, the Kafka family—now consisting of the parents, Franz, Ottla, and a maid—moved to the Oppelt House at the corner of the Oldtown Square and Pařížská Street (Nicklasstrasse), one of the choicest locales in Prague. The entrance to the premises at 6 Oldtown Square was protected by an ornamental wrought-iron gate and wide dark oak panels. Their sunny six-room rental on the top floor with bay windows offered precious views of the Old Town and a glimpse of Petřín Hill (the building, short of the top floor inhabited by the Kafkas, is marked today as Staroměstské náměstí 5).

A bigger living space and two entrances offered more privacy and better conditions for writing. Kafka had not produced anything worthwhile in several prior months, and the lull added to his malaise. We can assume he returned to opium on landing at Oldtown Square, and this brought about renewed frictions at home. How furious he was with his mother: just talking to her irritated him to the point of screaming. A Saturday evening at the Brods made him likewise realize their friendship was again challenged. On the other hand, a visit to Felix Weltsch brought some relief. Seated in the rocking chair, he engaged the host in banter about the "disorder of our lives."[7] The shared "disorder" they commiserated about, the reader recalls, was the taste for opium.

Kafka nevertheless failed to restore his self-confidence and motivation for writing in the closing weeks of 1913. The unresolved private affairs contributed to his lethargy. Could Grete Bloch substitute for Felice Bauer as his good luck charm? It did not take him long to realize that, compared with the young and rather unsophisticated Grete, Felice was more a woman of substance and independent mind, a better fit for someone with literary ambition.

By late November 1913, he once again idolized Felice as "clear, pure, original, distinct, and lofty, all at once."[8] He also restarted sending her letters, but they went unanswered. Distraught, he asked his friend in Berlin, Ernst Weiss, to intercede on his behalf, in vain. In another missive, he disclosed his affair in the Riva sanatorium—apparently to make Felice jealous—but still received no response. Impulsive and contradictory, he bade her farewell only to change his mind and suggest matrimony. Almost instantly, however, he began backpedaling again: she had to understand marriage would not change him, and that would impact her as his spouse terribly. Felice underlined this sentence and sent a postcard promising a reply.

It prompted Kafka to more backtracking: does Felice realize she would lose her independence and worry-free life in Berlin by moving to the provincial Prague, unfamiliar with the language and living with a morose husband? By this, he messaged that he would not be moving to Berlin. And was not it her suggestion after all to drop the idea of marriage and just go on with letter exchange? As before, it suited Kafka best if Felice lived far away. No wonder she was in no haste to answer.

At this point, Kafka cared little for Grete Bloch. In December, he drafted a warm letter to her but apparently failed to mail it and then neglected to answer her two missives. When she arrived in Prague and called his office in January 1914, he was not available. In the meantime, however, Felice had been ignoring his entreaties for two months and failed to answer a letter from Frau Kafka as well.

In this situation, Kafka came to appreciate Grete Bloch's persistence. In late January, he apologized for having treated her so lightly, blaming it on his mind so blindly fixated on Felice. The piano-playing Grete, that "lively, cheerful . . . perfectly normal and healthy child," caught his attention at last. Encouraged by her responsiveness, he quickly became personal, inquiring about the man in Munich she had mentioned. He also expressed delight realizing she wished to have something to do with him. Then he popped up the question: "By the way, how do you spend your Sundays?" Could she make a "mad dash" to Prague?[9]

By February 11 (1914), however, a postcard from Felice arrived at last—this thanks to Grete's intervention, Kafka assumed—and he restored his preferences fast. On the eve of Weltsch's marriage, also, he realized that Felice remained in centerfold of his dating interest. He confirmed this to himself with a melodramatic entry into his diary on February 14: "There will certainly be no one to blame if I should kill myself, even if the immediate cause . . . appears to be Felice's behavior."[10] Four days later, he obliged Grete to write him regularly—and behind her back started plotting another get-together with Felice in Berlin.

On Friday evening, February 28, then, Kafka arrived in Berlin and next morning made an unannounced appearance at Felice's office. She had plenty of family problems, and the two spent only a few hours together on Saturday and Sunday. During another walk in Tiergarten, his once athletic body ravaged by drugs could not keep up with her pace; this thirty-one-year-old lagged behind to the point of prostrating himself, "humiliated more deeply than any dog." Understandably, when he begged her to say yes to marriage even if she did not love him enough, she did not answer. On his part, he would observe that Felice hardly ever finished the sentence in seventeen hours combined they had spent together. He also sensed her fears about a joint future and doubted her willingness to put up with his idiosyncrasies and leave Berlin.[11]

Sunday afternoon was the time for intimacy, and Felice firmly promised to come to his hotel. She failed to show up. He used the idle moments in Berlin to visit his acquaintance Martin Buber, a proponent of humanistic Judaism. On his return trip, he stopped in Dresden for a chat with Robert Musil, his Prague friend working as an editor of the prestigious periodical *Neue Rundschau*.

Already from Dresden, he sent a postcard to Grete on March 1: "Have been to Berlin. It couldn't have been worse. Next thing will be impalement." A day later, he added a harsh recount of his Berlin misadventure, claiming Felice had left it to his discretion whether they break up. Hence he passed on to Grete as the main purpose of his life, "a sound and firm resolution enabling me to go on living alone, without Felice." Alone, not with Grete.[12]

Grete was depressed in her Vienna perch, suffering from headaches and feeling abandoned by her family. Kafka suggested exercises, vegetarian diet, more thrift—and started wooing her again. Apologetic it took him so long to appreciate her, he proposed another meeting and, when she proved agreeable, hammered the point. "Do come, do come if it is at all possible," even if for one afternoon, he implored her on Friday, March 6. "I shall be quite bearable; I shall be unbearable only if you don't come."[13]

There followed a sequence of fast-paced steps that can be reconstructed in the rough from fragmentary evidence. Kafka and Grete also used undocumented means of communication, telegrams, and telephone, available to them at their workplaces.

First, Grete promptly agreed to come to Prague on Sunday, March 8. However, Kafka changed his mind fast. Rather than meeting in Prague on Sunday, he suggested a date at a venue somewhere halfway between Prague and Vienna on Saturday evening. That would allow them spending the night and much of Sunday together. "Do write and tell me. Then we can study the timetables and find a nice place."[14]

Grete resisted out of respect for Felice, but Kafka responded the latter was aware of his fondness for her. He and Grete Bloch indeed met in hastily arranged circumstances that weekend of March 7–8. That place probably was Gmünd, a border town between Austria and Bohemia, the Bohemian part of which is known as České Velenice. Located midway on the railway line between Prague and Vienna, the town would be associated in Kafka's mind with Grete Bloch until his rendezvous there with Milena Jesenská in 1920. On that occasion, he would confess, "I am helpless confronted by 'Grete' . . . I like looking into your [Milena's] eyes. That's about it, exit Grete!"[15]

It must have been a hot tryst, judging by a few details that Kafka would record with lawyerly circumspection. Thus, the first day back in Prague, on Monday, March 9, he penned a four-and-a-half-page-long entry into his diary. The revolving point came at the last, seemingly unconnected sentence: "It was Sunday afternoon, they lay in bed in one another's arms. It was winter, the room was unheated, they lay beneath a heavy feather quilt."[16]

The previous segments of that entry, however, concerned Felice Bauer. They were introduced by Kafka's confession of love for her and consisted of musing on his "dependency" and inability to get rid of issues that troubled her. He also wrote down worriedly that Felice was essential for nurturing his writing career. In addition, he realized that, if asked to choose his next domicile, he would prefer Berlin over Vienna. The Austrian capital was associated with Grete but unpopular with him and his Prague confreres as a center of reaction and clericalism.

The same Monday, March 9, Kafka also directed a long letter to Grete. It is available only in a censored form, omitting his instant reaction to the weekend events. In the preserved rump, there understandably is no complaint about having missed her over the weekend. Instead, Grete was assured of his discretion: "No, dear Fräulein Grete, we won't mention **this** again." He also pleaded with her to leave Vienna, suggesting Prague or Frankfurt as alternatives.

But Kafka apparently returned from Gmünd with something bothersome. "Had I had the opportunity on Sunday, I would gladly have told you all about it in person," he also wrote to Grete on the ninth. It appears that during the weekend date, he discovered or found a confirmation of something that made her still less desirable as a mate. It could have been her lack of enthusiasm for his stories, in particular "The Stoker," or her health. As shown below, she was compromised by the same afflictions as Kafka. Far from identifying the source of his discomfort, however, in the same letter of March 9, Kafka merely admitted a new contact with Felice and ruled out meeting Grete again at Easter.

Obviously, in the wake of his fling with Grete Bloch, Kafka resolved to rekindle his writing career in cohabitation with Felice. Yet he feared she was slipping from his grasp and even felt certain antipathy for him because of the "overpowering evil forces" that ruled his life. This obstruction, he wished to believe now, could be overcome with her help. Stretching it still further, he foresaw hard luck for himself unless he married Felice. To that goal, Kafka was now willing to leave his work in Prague and transfer to Berlin, the city he considered impersonal and intimidating.

For obvious reasons, Grete was not fully informed about his meandering thought. Kafka merely assured her he would not pass over the "affair" with her in silence, but exactly this he tried. As he parsed it, his relationship with Felice was "too strong, perhaps indissoluble"—and independent from his relationship with Grete. Effectively, he relegated his bond with Grete to second tier. And, by the way, Grete should know that he invited Felice to a meeting in Dresden instead of Berlin.[17]

Once Felice ruled out coming to Dresden, however, Kafka was back to courting Grete. On Friday, March 13, he suggested another date. He would be "delighted to sit opposite you, to talk to you . . . go for a walk with you." As enticement, he added the above-mentioned image of her "lying out of breath on the checked featherbed" and continued in the past tense: "In those days Frl. Grete was little perplexed but recovered and has improved steadily, though she refuses to believe it." Grete was reminded she had enjoyed the intimate moments with him despite the primitive setting.[18]

Kafka proposed a meeting in Gmünd, probably the place of their date the past weekend. Grete was dejected and struggled with incessant headaches but submitted to his wishes. So surefooted now, he warned her the date would be off should he arrange a weekend rendezvous with Felice instead. He probably arrived in Gmünd by an express train at 7:00 p.m. on Saturday, March 14, half an hour earlier than Grete. This time, she did not wear a fur coat as on previous occasions. Kafka would remember his sigh of relief on seeing her in a "nice traveling coat, at last without furs, and you actually looked freer, cleaner, brighter."[19] They stayed in one of the two hotels near the railway station and returned to their respective domiciles on Sunday evening. No other documentary evidence of this tryst is available, but the lack thereof is also supportive: Kafka left for posterity no letter or diary entry from the weekend of March 14–15. Six years later and only then, he would recall the Gmünd setup to his another romantic interest, Milena Jesenská.

Gmünd became to Kafka the symbol of an erotic feast he would keep returning to. If things did not work out with Felice, he approached Grete again on Wednesday, March 18, they should reunite at Gmünd the following Sunday: "I definitely deserve that Sunday . . . surely as viewed from on High." Apparently, more than sex was on his agenda. A few days later, he assured Grete lustily that the "mere anticipation" of [another] meeting at Gmünd had given him "more pleasure than anything else for some time." With no hesitation, he called her "the best, kindest, and sweetest creature . . . a Child of Spring."[20] Yet the same day, he also wrote a letter to Felice's parents, asking them for information regarding her infuriating silence.

Come the weekend of March 21–22, Kafka apparently stayed in Prague. In a lengthy letter, he assured Felice of his love and blamed his silliness for an endless chain of surprises and disappointments. He hoped to start a new life either by marrying her or by giving notice and leaving Prague. Felice should also know he already started looking for a job in Berlin. This time, Felice rewarded his perseverance by suggesting another meeting in Berlin for Easter, but nothing came of it. With Grete on a visit in Budapest, Kafka probably spent the nearest weekend of March 28–29 in Prague again.

Meanwhile, he and Grete still tested each other for willingness to another fling. Giving her a glimmer of hope, he claimed if things did not work out satisfactorily with Felice, then she would be free and he too but for one day only. In that case, he would come for Easter to Vienna. He also no longer wanted Grete as his go-between to Felice, arguing she was unaware of details and what she knew could be untrue. "I also falsify and withhold," he explained. Behind her back, he in fact pondered an engagement to Felice.

As Grete again responded in a welcoming manner, he also started plotting a program for his visit to Vienna. There was a small window of opportunity to meet there, but it closed fast. On April 5, Kafka assured Grete in a letter that has been heavily censored that he "wasn't about to forget about Gmünd, nor about Vienna."[21] Intent on keeping his choices open, he also tried to recruit her for joint travel to Berlin for Easter, but Grete recused herself. In this situation, he at least relieved his conscience by giving Felice a notice that he liked Grete very much.

Over the Easter weekend of April 11–12, 1914, then, Kafka visited the Bauer family in Berlin once again. He was apprehensive as, in particular, his inability to swallow needed to be covered up. In retrospect, he assessed the image he projected in Berlin as someone "ill, sometimes absurd, usually silly and occasionally too sly by half."[22] But considering his background and aspirations, he was a catch. Felice agreed to an engagement to be followed by a marriage in September; she also expected to terminate her promising career with Lindström and move to Prague. Ten days later, the engagement of Fräulein Bauer and Dr. Kafka was announced in *Berliner Tagblatt*.

THE 'TRIBUNAL IN BERLIN,' JULY 1914

On return from Berlin, Kafka reflected on the odd nuptial courtship there. In a letter to Felice Bauer's mother, he described himself as loving Felice no less than she did. But apparently, while in Berlin, he and Felice spent merely fleeting moments alone and even did not exchange a kiss. It was not his fault, he responded now. True, he was so distracted and inattentive during those two days, but she did not give him the chance, and he was too indifferent to ask for it, Kafka shifted the blame. "There are times when I want to thank God that we are not living in the same town just now." In truth, he found himself and Felice to be complete opposites—not a reassuring prospect for marriage.[1]

Caught in a quandary, Kafka obviously found consolation in more drugs. Being "overstimulated" was one of the "ugliest and most frequent states" of his life, he observed.[2] His hand was heavy, he confided to Felice, and when there was no news from her, then it became completely paralyzed and made him incapable of doing anything, not even putting the engagement announcement in a Prague paper or packing up the book for her father. By the same token, he claimed artfully Felice's virtual kiss evoked in him the feeling of darkness and frenzy and pleaded with her for patience. "Everything will become clear and we shall be the most united of couples."[3]

In truth, Grete Bloch still cast a heavy spell over him. When she wrote she could not understand his engagement, he retorted he felt a true longing for her and would love to hold her hand. In his obsession, he even asked Grete to invite Felice for a joint trip of all three to . . . of all places, Gmünd!

Grete wanted to end the affair and asked for her letters back, but Kafka balked. He was aware of her loyalty and had no intent to drop her: "I shall be delighted with every moment you spend with us." She could also be sure he would not mishandle her patentable innovation they discussed "that day in the hotel room"—probably a reference to their second rendezvous in Gmünd. And how "lovely and free" he would feel again in Gmünd . . .[4]

As Grete hesitated, Kafka approached Felice: it would be great if she joined him in Gmünd for a day. Effectively, Felice was asked to travel three extra hours south of Prague to the place that witnessed his tryst with Grete. And since Gmünd did not appeal to Felice either, he went back to Grete. He imagined going to Berlin with her by train, "squeezing your hand . . . lovely journey!" And if this prospect failed to enthuse her, he still wanted her to witness Felice's anticipated arrival in Prague.[5] Keeping the flame alive, Grete sent him photos of herself instead.

Felice indeed visited Prague between May 1 and 5 (1914), principally in search of an apartment. It was Kafka's parents who found and rented a pleasant dwelling for the couple on Dlouhá Street, in a walking distance from Oldtown Square. But Felice already sensed her fiancé's detachment and treated him with mistrust. On the other hand, he felt again distracted by her golden tooth. They also quarreled over the apartment. Felice barely left Prague that he resumed wooing Grete.

In a letter that might have eventually landed in Felice's hand, he implored his part-time lover to accept a ménage à trois. Once he would be married, Grete should come and live with him and Felice for some time. They would have a pleasant life, holding each other's hand. In contrast to Felice, he also opened up to her more about his drug dependency, calling it an "enormous hypochondria, which . . . has struck so many and [has] so deep roots within me that I stand or fall with it." Since Grete also suffered from insomnia, Kafka suggested valerian tea, but he himself frowned on such a natural therapy, knowing the root cause of his sleeplessness was his "pretty unhealthy way of life."[6]

Toward the end of May 1914, preparations were nevertheless finalized for the formal engagement of Kafka and Felice. In spite of insomnia, headaches, and bouts of coughing so bad he feared being torn apart, he still tried to convince himself the marriage would bolster his ability to write. With his family in attendance, the two became engaged in Berlin over the weekend of May 30–31. After mulling this moment for so long, however, Kafka was spectacularly unmoved. The engagement ceremony made him feel like a criminal bound in a corner and watched by policemen, but, he also observed, Felice suffered the most.[7]

In truth, he could no longer bear the prospect of marrying her. Thus, while she resigned from her Berlin company in anticipation of moving to Prague, behind her back, Kafka effectively ruled out a joint Prague existence. Getting out of the city now figured as his prime goal, and with this in mind, he approached an acquaintance with whom he had not communicated for ten years. His engagement to Felice was effectively stillborn.

Why this change of mind? Apparently, it was connected with his lover again. Grete Bloch was pregnant, the fruition of their secret encounters in March 1914. Abruptly returning to Berlin by the end of May, she was only in her third month but already attracted the suspicious eye of her mother and felt uneasy about her dress. Kafka was probably aware of or guessed her pregnancy. He invited Grete to the engagement ceremony with assurance that no matter what, her unaltered dress "will be viewed with . . . the most affectionate eyes." She could also rest assured that he had not divulged anything to Felice Bauer.[8]

During the stay in Berlin, May 30–31, then, Kafka took stock of Grete. What he saw made him remorseful. In a follow-up letter, he blamed himself for writing only about himself and "at first even deceitfully"; how much she must have suffered because of his shenanigans. And in contrast to past lustiness, he began treating her with tenderness and concern. He pleaded with her to avoid exerting herself by writing to him and to leave her office earlier.[9]

Conscience was pricking him, but he was not ready to renounce his engagement to Felice. His noncommittal attitude drew a sarcastic reaction from Grete: surely his predicament was not unavoidable. Kafka replied with his staple argument, reminding her that his questionable health offset his good features. Apart from morbid irritability, he singled out insomnia, claiming sleep deprivation for four consecutive nights left him on the verge of passing out. The unconcerned Grete dismissed his complaints as "nothing." Still reluctant to break with Felice, he at least assured Grete that her letters were and would remain confidential.[10]

A verbal intercession was preferable. Kafka's friend Ernst Weiss, a medical doctor and writer, was to travel from Berlin to Prague in late June. However, he had been introduced to the pregnant Grete in May, possibly at the engagement ceremony, and clearly wished to foil the impending marriage. In Kafka's words, he became an enemy of Felice Bauer. Thus, acting from Kafka's viewpoint "on account of my news," Weiss arrived in

Prague already on the sixteenth for a two-day visit in an apparent effort to mediate. Kafka considered the situation horrid, but to his relief, Grete obviously raised no demands. He still offered helping her get a job with a large underwear manufacturer in Prague. "Do you want to? Would it be possible? I should be pleased."[11]

Grete, who probably expected him at least to cancel the engagement with Felice, did not respond. It raised fears in him of the "real misfortune, of which I know nothing directly, only by intolerable threats. How about the main reasons for your silence?" he alluded to her pregnancy, adding a verse from the Bible.[12]

In retort, Grete suggested a telephone conversation in the hope of getting some sense of his intentions. Kafka instead insisted on a face-to-face, assuring her nothing had changed. He was "merely being tossed to and fro . . . be patient with me."[13] But then, on June 30, he disclosed he would meet Felice either in Dresden or in Berlin and wanted her to be present.

Grete sensed the worst. In a letter, the copy of which ended up in the hands of Max Brod, she reproached Kafka bitterly. "Could anything appall me more than your letter of yesterday . . . I suddenly see the situation so clearly, and am in despair." While she had been ready to accept his engagement with Felice as a stroke of good fortune for both of them, she was no longer inclined to condone it. In truth, if Kafka honored the engagement, she would face "an infinite responsibility to which I no longer feel equal."[14] She realized she may have to become an unwed mother.

In her follow-up letter, Kafka was told bluntly that Felice should find a man her equal, "cheerful, high-spirited, intelligent, and thoroughly good"—not exactly him. Kafka replied defiantly that Felice was, after all, his fiancé, adding that his "friendship" with Grete could not be shaken by any possible disclosure. This again signaled her pregnancy would not prompt him to abandon Felice.[15]

On Friday, July 10, Kafka arrived in Berlin, ostensibly on his way to vacation in the Baltic. There is no indication Felice was supposed to join him. Judging by the absence of his letters to her following their Berlin engagement, relations between them was already tense. Reporting to his sister Ottla from Berlin on the tenth, Kafka was prepared to be at his obfuscating best: "I write differently from what I speak, I speak differently from what I think, I think differently from the way I ought to think." Since this too was revealing, he ended with this postscript: "You mustn't show my letter or let it lie around. You had best tear it up."[16]

Next day, July 11, 1914, Kafka took a taxi to face what he would call a "tribunal in the hotel." Somewhere in Berlin, he met with three young women, all potentially enamored by him—Felice Bauer, her sister Erna, and Grete Bloch. Others, Ernst Weiss in particular, may also have been present. Grete Bloch just topped the fourth month of pregnancy, and it undoubtedly showed on her slim figure. Since Kafka resisted a renunciation of his engagement, she felt justified to seek redemption or take revenge. She provided Felice with one or more letters from him. In retrospect, he would comment to Felice, the letter(s) had almost disgraced her.[17] Confronted with his duplicity, Kafka would recall, Felice stroked her hair, wiped her nose, and then unloaded on him "much studied, hostile things she had long been saving up." Having little to say in defense, he assumed the mask of indifference. Emotions depleted, the meeting closed with a tacit understanding the engagement was over.

Kafka enjoyed the freedom. He left the hotel together with Fräulein Bloch. In Askanischer Hof, they were served by a spirited waiter, but a disappointment awaited them in the hotel room. It was a hot Saturday afternoon, and heat was also reflected from the wall across the street. A noisy courtyard and bad smells added to the feeling of a "boiler factory." Bed was their next destination. Beneath the bedcover, however, they surprised a bedbug. "Crushing it is a difficult decision," Kafka would recall ambivalently. The chambermaid was summoned and pretended astonishment: "There are no bedbugs anywhere; only once did a guest find one in corridor." This foreclosed Kafka's another amorous festival. Little do the biographers care about the lowly bedbug's role in the history of world literature: Kafka's life might have taken a different path had he reconnected with Grete Bloch that Saturday afternoon in Berlin.

On second thought, Felice showed up in the hotel, "in spite of the fact that everything was already settled." Kafka accepted an invitation to her parents' home in Charlottenburg. He would recall this visit as follows: "Her mother's occasional tears. I recited my lesson. Her father understood the thing from every side . . . They agreed that I was right, there was nothing, or not much, that could be said against me. Devilish in my innocence. Fräulein Bloch's apparent guilt." When Felice's parents and aunt waved after him on leaving, he realized he would still be a welcome addition to the family.[17]

The same evening, Kafka sat on a bench on Unten der Linden, troubled by stomachaches and a painful liver but pensive. He decided to forgo the Sunday revisit of the Bauers, despite Felice's telegram exhorting him to come. Instead, he sent a letter to her parents by courier, blaming her for ruining the prospect of marriage. In truth, it was Kafka who had readily backed out of the engagement. In afterthought, he would deem the letter both dishonest and coquettish.

In a gesture defiant of both Felice and Grete, he spent Sunday afternoon with Erna Bauer, Felice's elder sister. They chatted, sipped wine, and flirted at a fashionable restaurant on the River Spree in Stralau, watching cruising ships depart up and down the river. Next morning, July 13, Kafka left for Northern Germany and eventually joined Weiss and his girlfriend for a two-week vacation in the seaside Danish resort Marienlyst. On the return leg to Prague, he stopped in Berlin on July 26 but met Erna again rather than Felice or Grete. For several months, Kafka and Erna Bauer would engage in an epistolary flirt to the point of contemplating joint Christmas holidays.

From Marienlyst, Kafka informed his parents of the events in Berlin. Only a fragment of his letter is preserved, and it shows him both in an accusatory and defensive mood. As he put it, the Berlin adventure was not a disaster considering the circumstances. Rather than holding a job with no worthwhile prospect, he claimed, it would be better to quit and leave Prague because his life there was leading nowhere. He should attempt living as a freelance for two years in Germany, perhaps in Berlin or in Munich, and devote time to literary work. Overall, he wanted his parents to believe his duplicity had a silver lining: the breakup with Felice restored his freedom of action and thus contributed to his and his parents' welfare.

The trainload of disgust and self-hate at last caught up with Kafka on his return to Prague. His diary for August 6 reads, "Full of lies . . . incompetence, stupidity . . . I discover in myself nothing but pettiness, indecision, envy, and hatred against those who are fighting and whom I passionately wish everything evil."[18] He was also aware of his growing attachment to another woman: there was certain relationship, he observed, that he felt distinctly but was unwilling to entrust to the paper.

OTTLA KAFKA

In the conventional perception, Kafka was an ascetic whose propensity for self-denial extended to sex. For various reasons, be it impotence or fear of contracting a venereal disease, he is believed to have had 'fear of sex . . . a haunting fear of sex,'[1] This view is massively contradicted by reality. There is little doubt that, no matter how gentle and considerate, Kafka was an individual of strong and diverse sexual drives. Even in his last year, when he could hardly walk or talk, his last companion still found him unusually sensuous. He became sexually active at the age of sixteen and grew up aggressively heterosexual, a skirt chaser cavorting with prostitutes on occasion. Not yet thirty, he also described in his diary a "seduction" of a girl in Jizerské (Iger) Mountains in Northeastern Bohemia, the region he indeed made visits to. By today's standard, it was a brutal rape.

Told at first in third person, the perpetrator makes a brief attempt to "persuade" a girl on a joint stroll along the riverbank. Failing in that, he throws her on the grass and assaults her as she lies there "unconscious with fright." His lust quenched, he carries water from the river in his cupped hands in a frantic revival effort. To his relief, she regains consciousness even though her eyes are still closed because of fear and humiliation. Legal repercussions cross his mind but not for long: she is just a plain girl, the daughter of a landlord where he spends a summer vacation to restore his "delicate lungs."

Circumstances suggest this was not merely the record of a dream. Kafka had developed the habit of writing down potentially embarrassing aspects of his life in a third person. He likewise starts in the third person here, but then confirms he was the one who poured water on the luckless girl.[2]

Several years later, when his sister Ottla attended a school in Jizerské Mountains, Kafka initiated what can be regarded as an attempt to close the above affair. Referring to himself as "Herr K.," he directed Ottla to deliver his letter to "Fräulein K.," who, in his characterization, was afraid of any form of coercion and herself fought against it with tenacity to forestall it. Possibly alluding to the raped girl's ongoing trauma and blackmail, he claimed there already had been "a good many scenes." Still, Kafka felt blameless as the—further unspecified—"case" had occurred between "agitated people."[3]

Parallel with his initiation to heterosexual life, Kafka also exhibited strong homoerotic tendencies. As an adolescent, he showed deep attraction for Oskar Pollak, his cultivated schoolmate at the gymnasium and early university years. In his letters, mixing infatuation with shame and fear, he wanted to kiss Pollak's hands out of gratitude for walking with him. He also registered shudders when being touched stark naked by another obviously male person. This homoerotic bent, not unusual in the teens, lingered in Kafka into adulthood. As has already been noticed elsewhere, homosexual impulses on occasion cropped up in his texts, and he never showed disgust with them. In 1917, Max Brod mailed him remarks about Hans Blüher's book on eroticism in history, calling it "a hymn on pederasty." The recipient instantly asked for details about this volume that put on a pedestal male homosexuality in contrast to the "lower" heterosexual love and family.[4]

Apart from Pollak, in real life, Kafka recorded suggestive entries regarding other male friends and acquaintances—Franz Werfel, Isaak Löwy, Felix Weltsch, and Robert Klopstock. In a fragment of *The Trial*, Kafka also rendered a homophile passage about the painter Titorelli (as suggested below, the cover for Weltsch). During a visit, Josef K. strikes the painter's cheeks, who pretends not to notice it. Tormented by this inertness, K. nevertheless derives great pleasure from the situation, knowing well that Titorelli is a frivolous person who will eventually grant his "desire."[5] Similarly, the protagonist of *Amerika* has an erotic encounter with another male in his room.

Kafka's sexual lust was quite indiscriminate. Thus, in 1912, he described sensual pleasure watching two prepubertal Swedish boys with blond hair and long legs so shaped that the best way to get at them would be with the tongue. Among the few periodicals he subscribed to as a young adult was *Ametyst*, a glossy publication published by Franz Blei in Vienna. Mirroring the attendant sexual revolution, it did not shy away from such issues as pornography and bestiality. It helped Kafka to build in secret his own pornographic collection. Along the way, Kafka had numerous trysts with prostitutes and eroticism tinged his major works from *Amerika* to *The Castle*.

Habitually ignored by biographers is a high level of intimacy between Kafka and his sisters. It started early and extended well into their adulthood, underpinned by his treatment of them as a tyrant enforcing total obedience. They "loved him and worshipped him as kind of a higher being," observed Gerti Kaufmann, the daughter of Elli.[6] Their compliance went well beyond the ordinary. In recollections of Anna Pouzarová, employed by the family as a governess in 1902–1903, when it was not too cold the three sisters, on his orders, exercised naked on the carpet in the big room. Elli was fourteen or fifteen; Valli, twelve; Ottla, eleven; and Franz nineteen.[7] Though nudity engrossed Kafka's generation, and nudist camps had mushroomed everywhere. Kafka himself spent time in at least one of them, a sanatorium at Jungborn. However, the sexes were usually separated when bathing. Kafka's conduct was highly improper among adult relatives, certainly in his milieu. As Pouzarová implied, he got away with it because the Kafka children usually spent the day at home alone while their parents tended the store.

How far did this intimacy go? His eldest sister, Elli, had been at first unattractive in his eyes but eventually earned his accolades as "cheerful, carefree, brave, generous, unselfish and hopeful."[8] Married in December 1910 to a handsome clerk, Karl Hermann, she remained, in her younger daughter's testimony, more devoted to her brother than to her husband and children. She already was a mother of two in June 1914, when Franz recorded in his diary: "Elli says: 'The most beloved darling, I am longing for your elastic body.'"[9]

His middle sister, Valli, turned out less susceptible to his influence and more observant of her parents' wishes. Yet, reflecting on her engagement, Kafka jotted down in his diary in September 1912: "Love between brother and sister—the repeating of the love between mother and father."[10]

It is a fair assumption that an intimate relationship with his sisters did not register with Franz Kafka as an absolute taboo.

Felice Bauer got a glimpse of his wacky standard a few months into their mail exchange. In January 1913, Kafka sent her a photo of his sisters Valli, age twenty-two and freshly married, and Ottla, age twenty-one, naked: "I am glad you found Ottla attractive . . . The other naked one is Valli, whom I don't expect you recognized."[11] Felice had already been warned of his unconventional manners by Brod. Still, she responded with a distressed letter that in turn prompted Kafka to show concern about her health: "Dearest; are you afraid? . . . Do we have a total collapse? . . . Are you crying? . . . It means you despair of me."[12] Kafka's follow-up letters allow for observation that Felice started treating him with more reserve.

With two elder sisters sidelined by their marriage, the youngest, Otilie, moved to a privileged position in Kafka's life. Born in 1892 and nicknamed Ottla, she was cheeky, stubborn, hot-tempered, and—as quite common for youngest child in the family—rebellious. At least since her teenage years, she had also been keenly observant of her brother Franz, his private life, and—according to the governess Pouzarová—expressed misgivings with his dating habits. On leaving a junior college for girls, no later than age seventeen, she started helping out in her father's shop and eventually worked long hours from 7:45 a.m. to 4:00–5:00 p.m., sometimes until closing time. Her daily routine offered few opportunities for socializing, and her interest in men was discouraged. When she advised her vacationing parents of a possible romance in 1910, her mother, Julie, interceded, "You are still a child. Your two sisters are first in line. You still have a long time ahead of you."[13] As Ottla's chances for a private life outside the family were limited, she and Franz were growing closer to each other.

A pattern developed: like a child, Ottla demanded Franz's special attention, and he complied warmly. Thus, already in his first known letter to her of December 1909, he wrote from Plzeň (Pilsen) that memories of those delightful hours passed with her at their club remained his only pleasure. In another letter from Varnsdorf of May 1911, he promised to bring her something back if only because she cried before his departure. Even in conflicts, tenderness prevailed with Kafka readily assuming the blame. When in June 1912 he improvidently addressed a letter to the family from Weimar, he corrected fast: he would gladly write to her only as well.

Along with her sisters, Ottla also performed a useful role in Kafka's aspirations as a writer. He liked reading new texts to close friends to gauge their response. Compared with Max Brod or Oskar Baum, who tended to be critical, his sisters were more patient and supportive. "I have reconciled myself to reading badly to everyone except my sisters," Kafka jotted down with his understatement in January 1912.[14]

Like her sisters, Ottla had a superficial education and little interest in books but showed reverence for his creations. For this reason, also, he considered reading to her particularly satisfying. In turn, he cultivated her artistic sense and was so pleased hearing her recite Goethe's poems with the "right feeling." Thus, while Ottla did everything to demonstrate her devotion, Kafka reciprocated with warm, appreciative words: "She loves me very much, blindly she considers everything I say, do, or think, to be good, but at the same time has much sense of humor of her own."[15]

Kafka's venture into opium smoking in mid-September 1912, we can assume from *The Metamorphosis*, caught his youngest sister off guard. In the ensuing uproar, she at first sided with the family but soon changed her mind. In late November, Kafka reported humorously that Ottla kept him company, cracking nuts, eating more of them than she gave to him, and usually making their lives enjoyable. With Felice Bauer on the doorsteps, Ottla made sure she stayed on his mind—and Kafka willingly accepted. His affection was evolving into a fixation devoid of reality: at one point, he described Ottla as extremely tall like other members of their father's family. She was not.

While he gathered no vibes for Felice, speaking as a man-beetle in *The Metamorphosis*, he described touchingly his sister Grete Samsa (who displayed the characteristics of Ottla). Moved by her playing violin so beautifully, he could not resist not making eye contact with her. It was obvious she would "stay with him on her free will . . . bend down her ear to him" no matter what. And if she burst into tears, he would "kiss her on the neck, which, now that she went to [her parents'] business, she kept free of any ribbon or collar."

So engrossed Kafka was with his youngest sister that in closing *The Metamorphosis*, he broke the rules of composition and made Grete the center of the narrative. In his description, Grete blossomed into an "increasingly lively and vivacious daughter," a "beautiful and well-proportioned young woman." No wonder he eventually dismissed *The Metamorphosis* as indiscretion, "imperfect almost to its marrow" and specifically singled out the ending as unreadable.[16]

The entrance of Felice Bauer also made Ottla still more persistent in seeking Franz's attention. In February 1913, he planned a business trip to Litoměřice (Leitmeritz), the town about fifty kilometers north of Prague, at first as a day trip. With Ottla insisting on coming along, however, he consented to travel a day earlier, on Sunday evening, and spend the night with her in a hotel. Their father, Hermann, already wary of his children's growing fondness for each other, surprised Franz by raising no objections, probably because he had relatives in Litoměřice and Ottla was a better family ambassador.

The joint trip pleased Kafka enormously. In a letter to Felice, he admitted devotion to his sister and pleasure of having her in Litoměřice: "The same thing will be repeated."[17] He left little doubt that Ottla was central in his life now but still resisted her attempts to invade his space. When, for example, she and the governess pressed him for details of his private life, he responded with extreme annoyance.

Physical appearance mattered to Kafka. Compared with her elder sisters, Ottla stood out also in this respect because of her youthfulness. In 1913, he started to have private moments with her in his bathroom. In one of those situations, pleasurable and not quite innocent, Kafka recalled in his diary being "on fire" when describing to her a funny film. "Why can I never do that in the presence of strangers?" he wondered. It is not clear whether the encounter was also in the nude, but it certainly aroused in him conjugal flashes. "The broadening and heightening of existence through marriage," he followed up. On second thought, however, he effectively ruled out Ottla as a mate: "I would never have married a girl with whom I had lived in the same city for a year." But then, the stigma of incest was countervailed by a sensuous observation, "A band of little golden beads around a tanned throat."[18]

Gregor Samsa, the reader recalls, experienced a similar arousal when observing his sister Grete in *The Metamorphosis*.

A few days after this bathroom intimacy, he revised his opinion again in "Summary of all the arguments for and against my marriage." Torn between the inability to withstand life alone and compelling reasons to stay unmarried, the best solution was cultivating the bond with his sisters. In their presence, he was "entirely different . . . fearless, powerful, surprising," in a similar disposition as when writing. Kafka referred to "sisters," but the elder ones had already married and moved out. Certainly, they and their husbands also cared little for his existential texts let alone drugs. He rarely spoke to them, he observed elsewhere.[19] It was Ottla, so highly esteemed by him as a human being, in whom he also found the most appealing soul mate.

This further contributed to his vacillations regarding Felice Bauer. Both the Berliner and Ottla appear to have read him this way and acted accordingly, the former with melancholy and restraint, Ottla with tempestuous possessiveness that on occasion turned annoying. After his affair in Riva in the fall of 1913, the regretful Kafka promised her another bathroom intimacy, but she apparently started jealous tantrums. This time, he dismissed her outburst as completely unfounded. It was advisable to draw the line because of her habit of repeatedly testing his patience.

A good-hearted female in search of an idol she could care for, Ottla found her brother. She began emulating him and proved extremely adaptable in this, showing interest in literature, taking up exercise, and embracing vegetarianism (in which she persisted through much of her life). Kafka offered support and tutoring, for example, by reading aloud to her from other masters. Though lukewarm religiously, she also discovered Zionism, in her mind more an escapism than a commitment to the cause. The idea of emigrating together to faraway Palestine also gave Franz some hope he would leave his devils behind one day. Meanwhile, she spent her free Sundays volunteering in an institute for the blind.

As he had been drawn deeper into her life, Kafka also showed a proprietary instinct. In January 1914, he jotted down "Ottilie's love affairs" in his diary and then, as a third person, a story that occurred in Šluknov (Schluckenau), another town in Northern Bohemia that Kafka visited on work assignments: A "sister" told her elder brother that, according to a card reader, his fiancée was deceiving him; he had good reason to be jealous. If this was not upsetting enough, the sister also confessed to an erotic encounter with her teacher. On hearing it, the brother became ferociously inquisitive about the details. The sister allayed him, claiming it did not go beyond kisses: "What are you thinking of? I am a virgin" (Ottla was twenty-two). Besides, she assured her brother, she felt as if lying in his arms.[20]

Kafka's fling with Grete Bloch in the spring of 1914 apparently did not register with Ottla as a threat. Calling her childish, he described humorously her insistence on writing the address on his parcel to Grete, despite being berated for her small and almost illegible handwriting.

His renewed courtship of Felice Bauer in the spring of 1914 followed by the engagement, however, was a blow to her. Kafka assumed sending her to the Bauers ahead of the family would break the ice. Frau Bauer indeed issued a warm invite, but neither Felice nor Ottla was thrilled. There clearly was no love lost between them. Voicing the sense of rivalry, Felice responded in the manner that led Kafka to take Ottla's side. He would not have sent his sister to Berlin on the strength of her last letter, he answered

Felice: "Not entirely without my approval Ottla is defiant now and does not want to go at all. I don't think that's a bad thing."[21]

Though Ottla eventually traveled with her mother to Berlin on May 27, her truculence added to the tense tone of the engagement ceremony. Assessing in retrospect its impact on Felice, he noted, "What was merely a passing occurrence to the others, to her was a threat."[22]

On return to Prague, both the freshly engaged Franz and Ottla plunged into despair. They felt as if their cocoon had been shattered mercilessly. Dejected and unable to bear it at home after the business close, they ran away into the hills encircling Prague and, acting like teenagers, clambered on trees and shook them while swinging down the slope. Ottla neglected to send the courtesy 'thank you' letter to the Bauers and intended to skip the wedding. Torn apart by conflicting allegiances, Kafka asked for advice from an acquaintance, who, in view of the circumstances, counseled leaving the country.

It was in no small measure his attachment to Ottla that negated Kafka's engagement to Felice Bauer. On reaching Berlin again on July 10, he effectively assured his sister that cultivating the bond with Felice was not on his mind. The "tribunal in the hotel" next day worked further in Ottla's favor. While Kafka lost much of his interest in the Berlin sirens Felice Bauer and Grete Bloch, she was morphing into an invisible black star that kept him from straying afar. With no inspiration whatsoever by Felice Bauer, he was also kissed by the muse again in the second half of 1914.

1914: The Second Burst
of Creativity

Disaster descended on Kafka's world in the summer of 1914. Since the end of the Napoleonic wars a century earlier, the Old Continent had enjoyed relative peace, punctuated merely by regional conflicts. In the hot summer weeks of 1914, however, a conflagration of unimaginable proportions erupted—World War I, also known as the Great War. Two military blocks intertwined by dynastic ties, one consisting principally of Germany and Austria-Hungary, the second of France, England, and Russia, started tearing each other apart, each anticipating a short road to a glorious victory. Pride mixed with prejudice infected the warring countries as both the draftees and volunteers were leaving for the frontline amid cheers of bystanders. Few dared to resist the nearly universal war hysteria, perhaps most notably Lord Bertrand Russell. From Kafka's friends, it was Max Brod, an indomitable humanist, who voiced an antiwar sentiment.

Mildly favoring Austria-Hungary but sedated by his lifestyle, Kafka recorded in his diary the earthshaking events and attendant chauvinism with ostentatious indifference. Indirectly, however, he stood to benefit greatly from this man-made cataclysm as a writer. How so?

As we know, Kafka lost his writing capacity in the front months of 1913. By June of that year, he still referred confidently to the "tremendous world I have in my head" but was at a loss "how [to] free myself and free it without being torn to pieces." Itching for new exploits as a writer, he would a "thousand times rather be torn to pieces," but the proper stimulus was missing.[1] He wrote nothing of significance since early 1913, even failing to deliver a book manuscript to the publisher Wolff. In justification of his lethargy, he admitted to Grete Bloch his inspiration had to come from outside: "I have no control over my capacity for writing. It comes and goes like a phantom."[2] This "phantom" deserted him in the early months of 1913 when, in consideration of his parents, he abandoned opium intake. Almost certainly, his abstention persisted after the Kafkas moved to the top floor of 6 Oldtown Square.

The outbreak of the Great War changed Kafka's situation meaningfully. First, the risk of him being drafted in the Austro-Hungarian army was averted when, on the intervention of his bosses, he was declared indispensable with no time limit at the Institute of Workers' Accident Insurance. It amounted to an act of favoritism. His brothers-in-law were less fortunate. By the end of July, Karl Hermann, the husband of Elli, and Josef Pollak, the husband of Valli, were both called to the army. For Franz, this was a God-sent opportunity to gain privacy. He vacated his room at Oldtown Square in favor of Elli and her two children, to start living alone, first, at Pollak's place at Bílkova Street, then at Hermann's flat at Nerudova Street uptown.

Solitude, the cherished solitude! Already on August 6, 1914, Kafka was exhorting himself: "My talent for portraying my dreamlike inner life has thrust all other matters into the background; my life has dwindled dreadfully." To restore his writing potential, he needed a stimulus again. While others performed "in lower regions with greater strength," he required to "waver on the heights."[3]

Two days later, again "in the grip of inspiration" on Saturday evening, he indeed resumed writing intensively. His inspiration was not Felice Bauer. He had not been communicating with her for two months; in fact, he had come to regard her as inconsequential for his life and possibly interfering with his work. His restored creativity again rested on his somnambular experience and his lifestyle of 1912–1913, when he took naps in the afternoons and plied his pencil at nights. This is what Kafka did in August 1914. As before, he was productive not when sleeping soundly but in half-sleep, and, as before, his effort was neither kosher nor permanent. He anticipated exploiting his reacquired creativeness to a "despicable degree."[4]

We can assume that Kafka again fortified his writing skills with opium in August 1914. The result was a sudden, almost miraculous revival of his writerly prowess. In contrast to 1912, however, he did not feel as raptured and controlled better the challenge of the drug. Pleased overall with his effort, in October, he managed to get two weeks' vacation and devote still more time to writing, staying at his desk until five in the morning and on one occasion until seven thirty.

In the upsurge that would last about five months, he worked on such memorable pieces as *The Trial*, "The Penal Colony," "Memories of the Kalda Railroad," "The Village Schoolmaster," a chapter of *Amerika* ("The Man Who Disappeared"), and various minor prose. Once again, as another biographer observes, these works were replete with 'characters, scenes, and landscapes . . . vivid, as though he were hallucinating.'[5] Kafka himself called them "personal proofs of my human weakness"—an apparent allusion to his drug stimulus.[5] Traces of it can be detected in most of the above-mentioned works, in particular in his ambivalent handling of violence.

As we know, violent associations occupied Kafka's mind since 1907, parallel with his foray into intravenous opiates. After his return to syringes and opiates in March 1913, he started conjuring up masochistic images of self-mutilation. A "daily prey to fantasies," he imagined pushing slices of his body to a dog in the corner.[6]

In April 1913, he also jotted down a dream of a "mass of teeth fitted together, exactly as in children's jigsaw puzzles," uniformly guided by his jaw in a sliding motion.[7] Stored along with other similes in his mind, this image became socially relevant with the ongoing slaughter of the Great War. In the autumn of 1914, then, Kafka used it as a muster for the torture machine in "The Penal Colony." This is Kafka's darkest text graphically depicting gruesome torture as a welcome event. As he subsequently wrote to the publisher Wolff, the story was reflective of the agony of "our times in general" and even more of his personal life: his own times had been distressing "for an even longer period than the times in general."[8] Lament of a seasoned drug abuser.

In the story itself, a European visitor of a remote island, the "researcher," witnesses the sadistic torture of a luckless man, as a punishment for sleeping while on duty (the insomniac Kafka also dozed off at work regularly). The torture device consists of two adjustable panes of needles each etching the sentence into the victim's back in blood. The shorter needle both pierces the body and sprays a jet of water—an allusion to the dual function of a syringe. In the old days, we learn that the writing needles let drop an acid, but the practice is no longer permitted—possibly a reference to the 1912 international ban on narcotics.[9]

The condemned man behaves in ways attributable to a syringe drug addict. Indifference to own fate is particularly striking. He does not know his sentence, and there is no point telling him for he will learn it on his body (needle marks will tell). He also puts up no resistance, of course. Showing no fear of the needle contraption, he calmly examines it at close quarters before being strapped to the bottom section of it facedown, naked, gagged, and drowsy. Once in a while, the machine needs fresh space for writing—just as an addict needs healed skin for new needles. The tortured does not have the strength to scream and eventually loses all desire to eat. Similar as Kafka practiced it, the man rarely swallows food outright; he only rolls it around his mouth and spits it out into the pit. On occasion, he even vomits. Just as Kafka, he is a thin man.

Once in a while, the condemned man also seems to have recovered entirely, and the supervising officer declares him free, but then the nightmare returns until the victim accepts his guilt and becomes submissive "like a dog." Kafka here morphed his real-life experience: the never-ending string of attempts to beat the addiction and relapses indeed brings about resignation to a life of agony. Just as drug addicts in general earn little understanding, the visitor too shows no empathy for the victim.

In another symptomatic turn of events, the supervising officer himself cannot resist the lure of needles and their discharge. He disrobes and willingly submits to the same silent, revolting piercing—in expectation of pleasure. However, the machine does not deliver the anticipated masochistic gratification. Instead of "writing" and delivering the exquisite torture, it jabs the officer until a great iron spike goes through his forehead.

Watching this lethal effect of needles does not deter the original condemned man at all. When the attending soldier commands him to go home, he takes the order as a punishment (it is so hard to give up opiates amid excruciating withdrawal pain!). So hooked on his torturous regime, he drops down on his knees, imploring the soldier to let him stay. Similar as Kafka, the condemned man eventually relinquishes the torture by needles for . . . smoking! In the company of a soldier and the visitor, he goes to a dilapidated teahouse, "a long, low, cavernous room, its walls and ceiling stained by smoke" that makes the impression of a certain historic tradition. The description fits the traditional opium smoking den.[10]

In "The Penal Colony," Kafka presented a complex, imaginative story too gruesome to elicit much appreciation at a time dominated by reports of millions maimed and slaughtered in the war.

Similarly revealing is "Memoirs of the Kalda Railway."[9] While "The Penal Colony" primarily reflected Kafka's past with intravenous opiates, the "Memoirs" drew on his fresh memory. Written in "I" form between August 15 and 21 (1914), it is ostensibly about a loner who participated in railway construction in distant Russia—struggling with symptoms Kafka struggled with in Prague.

The most burdensome was a heavy cough: "The fits of coughing were so severe that I had to double up when I coughed . . . I thought my coughing would terrify the train crew, but they knew all about it." This "wolf's cough" attacked him at night and was so oppressive that the storyteller was forced to kneel on the bunk and press his face into his skin to silence his howls. He waited tensely in expectation some vital blood vessel would burst and "put an end to everything," but nothing of that nature happened. The loner was then advised the common remedy of opium smokers—tea. On taking it, he felt immediately a relief as the cough had somewhat subsided.

Like the authentic Kafka, the loner also coped with other symptoms consistent with addiction. Fever tired him a great deal, he lost resilience; sometimes his whole body trembled, forcing him to lie down and wait until he came to senses again. The reprieve involved going to "Kalda"—probably meaning a health resort—and staying there until his conditions improved.[11]

Kafka's new bout of creativity in the second half of 1914 was again sabotaged by his mental and physical quandaries, sleeplessness, headaches, and falling motivation. In search of approbation, on November 20, he read "The Penal Colony" to Max Brod, who, as we know, disapproved of Kafka's forays into the world of drugs. The metaphor on tribulations of a syringe user left Brod unenthusiastic, to chagrin of the author. Kafka read "The Penal Colony" once more at Werfel's with Brod and Pick present on December 2. He had nervous twinges prior to the readi ng, suggesting a high level of anxiety, and the feedback from his close friends was again far from encouraging. "Go on working regardless of everything," Kafka urged himself in the aftermath, confident of the quality of his recent writings. In astute though dark self-appraisal, he expressed belief that his best works stemmed from his capacity to "meet death with contentment." Death, of course, was already perched in his mind as the possible outcome of his drug-inspired writing career. This thirty-one-year-old now resigned to dying provided the pain was not too great.[12]

At the same time, his relations with Brod were challenged again. At an afternoon visit to "B." on December 15, the unusually irritated host scolded him for "debility, blankness and stupidity almost." Kafka's reaction: "It's a long time since I have had a purely private conversation with him, was happy to be alone again."[13] The strife with Brod focused on Dostoevsky, Kafka's forerunner both in artistic direction and health degradation. In Brod's conformist opinion, Dostoevsky was wrong profiling too many mentally ill persons. Kafka retorted they were not exceptional specimen of humankind.

In a defiant mood, Kafka instantly penned another shorter story (on December 18), "The Village Schoolmaster," also known as "The Giant Mole." Ostensibly, he was poking fun here at the *sancta ignorantia* of the educated. The central figure is a schoolmaster who smokes a pipe, and his place stinks of tobacco. He has also written a pamphlet about the giant mole seen in the countryside, hoping this would help him to fame. But his discovery is disputed by a prejudiced savant who dismisses it as a great joke. Thus, the pamphlet is ignored by readers, and the schoolmaster earns bad reputation rather than recognition. Seen in the context, this tale about the pitfalls of challenging the established norms reflects Kafka's friction with Brod over his resolve to make a dent as an unconventional writer. There may be a legitimate world beyond what is perceived as reality and normalcy.

By the yearend of 1914, Kafka traveled with Brod and his wife, Elsa, to Kutná Hora (Kuttenberg) in East Central Bohemia in what appears to have been an attempt at reconciliation, but his trip had only a limited impact. Probably in early February 1915, and on a verge of resignation, Kafka started another short piece, "Blumfeld, the Elderly Bachelor."[14] It offers the most explicit rendering of his experience as an opium smoker. This bachelor is fond of long water pipes with the bowl that he stores in a rack—the typical paraphernalia of opium smoking. In the evening and semidarkness, he chooses one, fills it with particular care, lights it up . . . and spends hours watching a "magic," two small white balls that keep jumping around him, occasionally bouncing off the floor, producing rattle.

Blumfeld tries to corner them but struggles with numbness, dizziness, and gloom. Overcome with adversities, he almost collapses, stops smoking, and falls into a dreamless sleep. In the morning, awakened by the landlady as usual, he takes breakfast and washes in "cold, exceedingly refreshing water"—the traditional step to recovery by addicts. He also realizes the two magic globules that so fascinated him at night are, in truth, two ordinary children's balls.

In the second part of "Blumfeld," Kafka apparently addressed the flip side of his nightly adventures—his neglect of the asbestos factory. The storyteller is the manager of a linen plant owned by Herr Ottomar who rarely shows up and is ignorant of new methods of management and unappreciative of Blumfeld's work. He also undermines Blumfeld's authority by dealing with his underlings and saddles him with incompetent, troublemaking assistants. Herr Ottomar can be considered a stand-in for Herr Kafka, who raised concern about his son's absences from the factory in late 1914. In a display of narcissism that would repeat itself, Kafka started offloading his bad conscience on his father.

THE TRIAL

The most distinguished work Kafka produced in his second outburst of creativity in 1914 was *The Trial*. This baffling novel's challenges start with the form. In contrast to Kafka's previous—mainly linear—texts, the manuscript of *The Trial* consists of not necessarily sequential segments with text added in free space, indicative of the author's haste to record his ephemeral inspiration. Max Brod, to whom Kafka entrusted the file in 1920, arranged these loose bundles for publication in 1925. The less-than-perfect consistency of the text conjures up still more lose associations, further enhancing the novel's inscrutability. Speculations abound as to what inspired Kafka to this haunting narrative, in particular, because, unlike his other stories, the novel has little prehistory in his texts, and many pages of his diary that could elucidate its genesis have been destroyed.

In view of the previous chapters, it does not come as a surprise that the title and the lead story line are again reflective of Kafka's dependency by drugs—the association already noticeable in the stories of Georg Bendeman and Gregor Samsa. Carved to his image, the novel's protagonist Josef K. struggles with the same health problems— spasms of coughing, sudden weakness, nausea, lack of appetite, deafened ears, further unspecified "attacks," immobility—as well as the feeling of isolation, despondency, the "bars inside," and futility of resistance. The torture inflicted on Josef K. occurs in his rooms; both the torturer and the tortured have a tanned skin and are subject to the same pain and humiliation; they seem to be identical. The notion of self-inflicted agony and demise, not unusual in addicts, permeates the novel. Similar as his imaginary predecessors Bendeman and Samsa, K. is also shamed by his pitiful conditions and, just as the author himself, regards death as an atonement for and liberation from his trials.

In an insightful quip, K. goes placidly to death for self-regard and the 'survival of his image.'[1]

The Trial, however, was penned in response to unique circumstances. As we know, the global convention signed in The Hague in January 1912 proscribed the recreational use of cocaine, opium, and opiates, restricting them to medical purposes only. However, Austria-Hungary was not a party to the convention. Because in part of a powerful narcotic lobby, Vienna abstained from signing, the only 'civilized' country to do so, and failed again to sign when asked retroactively.

The limbo evidently mattered to the conscientious civil servant keen on holding to his cushy job. Indirectly but forcefully, in *The Trial* and elsewhere, Kafka would express the sense of straddling the borderline between innocence and culpability. In his nimble lawyerly frame of mind, he was both guilt-free and guilty as a recreational drug user.

In the novel, then, Josef K. is one day "captured" or "arrested"—just as Kafka fell for drugs—without warrant and restrictions on his personal freedom. A trial expects him, not a conventional one, but a trial "by word of mouth." It primarily concerns his reputation, but Kafka adds other meanings to the text.

Josef K. knows the charge against him, and so do his potential backers. All sense that his "acquittal"—read: recovery from addiction—is unlikely. Should he resist at all? In chapter 8, Kafka lets Josef K. admit—one might say rightly so considering the agony associated with detoxification—that "it is often safer to be in chains than to be free." In the 'escape from freedom' warp, Josef K. wishes to believe his arrest is meant to protect his own interests. Ambivalent about his guilt, he eventually accepts the surreal case against him in spite of residing in a "country with legal constitution . . . universal peace, all the laws . . . in force."[2]

The "false hands" that, in Kafka's words, guided his pen when working on *The Trial* also come through in images associated specifically with opium. A young man in the doorway smokes the pipe, Josef K. smokes a "cigar" resting on a sofa at night—the typical posture of opium smokers—and just as in Kafka's earlier works such as *Amerika,* the air is depleted and spoiled, fouling the premises of the court and atelier of the painter Titorelli. Josef K. grasps for air that, however, is "too thick for him." He perspires, suffocates, and, in general, feels unwell because of the stifling conditions in the room. The terms "smoking," "smoke," and "pipe" show repeatedly in this slim volume.[3]

Some telling events must seem absolutely incomprehensible to the uninitiated reader. For example, on examining Josef K's nightshirt, the warders take it away as evidence of his guilt. Why? As we already know, users of opium and opiates stain brownish their wardrobe and bed linen, and Kafka obviously was no exception. The tarnished nightshirt is proof of K's "crime" and ground for punishment.

Similar to Gregor Samsa in *Metamorphosis*, Josef K. is also concerned about the impact of his bad health on his work; though coming to office early, he is already exhausted and issues instruction to admit no one. His workday is filled with petty assignments and casual interaction with the deputy manager and the office staff in anticipation of a more rewarding life after work.

If dependence on drugs supplied the guiding motives for *The Trial*, Kafka still needed populated stage. He chose the trial format. Why? Biographers surmise it was the confrontation with Felice Bauer in Berlin, in July 1914, that 'spawned the key images and scenes' of *The Trial*. But not accidentally, they offer no supporting evidence.[4] In truth, Kafka remained in full control of the events in Berlin, and the outcome was liberating rather than enslaving, antithetical to the novel's gist.

Beyond the biographers' vistas is the affair that shook Prague society in the first half of 1914 and impacted *The Trial* in a major way. Almost completely overlooked, here is the real-life story behind this jewel of world literature.

The central figure was Dr. Karel Šviha, a lawyer and in quick succession a judge, mayor of a regional town, and a politician. Elected at the age of thirty-two to Parliament in Vienna for the reformist People's Socialist Party, he became the caucus whip two years later. An upstart in the camp of Czech progressives mildly opposed to the Habsburg monarchy, he had bright prospects until, to use the opening phrase of *The Trial*, somebody slandered him: in early March 1914, the central organ of Czech conservatives, *Národní listy*, published an anonymous report alleging he was a paid police agent.[5]

The ensuing uproar, closely followed by both the Czech and German press, brought to the fore the key elements found in *The Trial*, starting with the puzzling conduct of the accused. As it would turn out later, Šviha had met with the police president Klíma at Prague headquarters on Bartolomějská Street on several occasions. These meetings were of a political nature, intended to keep open a channel of communication with

Archduke Ferdinand d'Este, the heir to the throne (whose subsequent assassination in Sarajevo triggered the Great War). Šviha's colleagues in the party were aware of these goings-on and participated in preparing background briefings and memos for the archduke.

However, Šviha was also coping with assorted personal issues—bronchitis, neuralgia, physical weakness, passivity if not lethargy, a nervous tick in the face, and constant lack of money. Despite his wife's significant dowry and his comfortable income as a judge and MP, he lived in severe financial straits. After his rich cousin and supporter died, Šviha, as it would show later, indeed accepted payments for his reports to the police president. Also for this reason, his response to the accusation was far from vigorous. Expected to make a statement in Parliament, he excused himself on the grounds of illness, instantly raising more doubts. A "tribunal" of six respected members of the Czech establishment was hastily convened by the leading right-wing politician Karel Kramář and found Šviha guilty. Almost instantly, also, the public tarred him as a traitor, his party threw him overboard, he was forced to give up his parliamentary seat and membership in the party, and the parliamentary club of Czech political parties excluded him from its ranks. In one week, Šviha was politically assassinated based on spurious evidence.

The police could have exonerated Šviha. However, he failed to ask for a police statement, and when the boss of his party demanded it, the Prague police chief's response was 'No comment.' There remained no option but to sue the editor of *Národní listy* Heller for defamation. The trial, which took place amid mass hysteria in mid-May 1914, was heavily stacked against Šviha. While the right wing of Czech politics hoped to score political gains by his denunciation, the left lacked the conviction to lend him support. The main witness for the defendant, a secretary in the police president's office, was not properly sworn in and merely testified she had seen Šviha coming for a meeting with her boss.

Šviha took the stand but further damaged his cause with palpable lack of vigor and nervous demeanor. The only notable witness for the plaintiff was Thomas Masaryk, the future president of Czechoslovakia. True to his reputation as a myth debunker, he argued the allegation of Šviha's spying was unproven and absurd. The slanted court proceedings violated established legal norms. On May 15, 1914, the jury had its say. As the excitement was mounting across the city, a crowd of ten thousand gathered in front of the court building on Charles Square, cordoned off by the police. At 10.15 p.m., the verdict came: by unanimous vote, the twelve jurors found the defendant had grossly defamed Šviha— and equally unanimously labeled Šviha a police confident. Paradoxically, the plaintiff was both wronged and guilty. Amid shouts of "Shame to Šviha" and "Shame to Masaryk," he left the building by a back exit, a 'dead' man never to step into the limelight again.

The *Prager Tagblatt*, the liberal German daily in Prague that Kafka read, followed the trial closely and devoted an entire page to the judgment. He and Šviha shared a background in jurisprudence, mild socialist tendencies, and tarnished personal lives that defied black-and-white categorization. The trial blurred the distinction between innocence and guilt, reality and innuendo, and rational and absurd. Arguably more than any other singular event, the Šviha affair impacted *The Trial* and Kafka's work in general with a . . . Kafkaesque tinge.

The preserved tidbits of evidence suggest Kafka started mulling a story along the lines of *The Trial* in the aftermath of the Šviha case, but it was not until living on his own that he applied his pen to it in August 1914.

The first two chapters of *The Trial* plainly echo the Šviha case. Similarities abound, starting with a morning 'arrest' and the follow-up disregard for judicial protocol. Just like Šviha, Josef K.'s has two handlers who take care of his case, indifferent executors of history in the making. The public opinion in *The Trial* also splits into two "parties," the left and right, and even though Josef K. feels affinity with the left, he too gets no support from that camp. Similar as in the Šviha trial, Josef K.'s proceedings are dominated by the more powerful right wing that has a field day exploiting its political opponents' embarrassment. If Šviha was God-sent to the right, Josef K. paradoxically also earns the right wing's burst of applause and shouts of "bravo." Just as in the Šviha trial, a crowd of spectators outside awaits the outcome of K.'s case.

Eventually, Kafka widens focus in *The Trial* to provide a biting comment on the deplorable political and legal culture exposed by the Šviha trial. Already during the first interrogation, Josef K. finds the two factions that previously seemed so irreconcilable drifting together, pointing fingers alternatively at him and the examining magistrate. The audience, inclined to accept K.'s guilt, becomes subdued and indifferent. As he resorts to attack, K. observes both the left and right wear "the same badges . . . making pretense of party divisions." In truth, they belong to one old boys' club, keeping their interests uppermost in their mind.

Toward the end of chapter 2, Kafka leaves the Šviha story to weave into the narrative his personal circumstances. The most pressing issue that confronted him in the fall of 1914 was the pregnancy of Grete Bloch. We know that, carrying his child, Grete returned to Berlin from Vienna by June 1. He offered to find her a job in Prague, but nothing came of it. According to Grete's friend, she was a proud person. In mid-October 1914, then, Kafka received her letter and found it bewildering. It mentioned Felice Bauer's undying interest in him, but Grete's prime goal undoubtedly was to nudge him toward cohabitation or marriage. His mind was split. On one hand, he felt certain he wished to live alone, meaning without Grete. Yet, though he worked on *The Trial* until 3:00 a.m., he played with the letter all through the evening and felt again enormous temptation in spite of everything.

In a duplicitous response, Kafka, on one hand, wrote Felice that his fling with Grete had been the outcome of her [Felice's] disinterest in him and his "odious . . . peculiarities." At the same time, he also assured Grete that his reconciliation with Felice was out of question; it made him "miserable to think that for some incomprehensible reason Felice may be deceiving herself." But after the "tribunal" in the Berlin hotel, he was in no hurry to accommodate Grete either. He merely thanked her for the letter, adding inconclusively, "I have always considered your interest to be genuine and unsparing of yourself."[6] He also recorded but eventually destroyed what undoubtedly were delicate entries in his diary.

Kafka, nevertheless, kept Grete Bloch in mind while working on *The Trial.* Introduced awkwardly and out of context in chapter 3 is an imaginary novel, *How Grete was Plagued by her Husband Hans.* Hans was the name of Bloch's brother, a boisterous medical student whom she supported. Chapter 4, then, fictionalizes an unsettling event that involved Bloch. The chapter has been deleted from the authoritative German edition of the novel as an irrelevant fragment, even though Kafka adjusted the ending of chapter 3 and start of chapter 5 to fit it in.[7] Evidently, he found the issue dealt with in chapter 4 pressing enough to address it in the novel.

The chapter ostensibly depicts an episode in a "boardinghouse" that, apart from Josef K., is the home to three other people, most prominently Frau Grubach. She is one of several matronly figures in Kafka's texts (the others are featured notably in *The Metamorphosis*, in *Amerika*, and in *The Castle)* who control the real estate Kafka's alter egos covet. Living in a space filled with furniture, rugs, china, and photographs, and employing a maid, she is described as affable, always eager to have a talk with K., her boarder; indeed, she venerates him and "absolutely believes" whatever he says. The thought that he might move out brings her to tears. This figure approximates Kafka's mother Julie and the "boardinghouse" the family apartment at 6 Oldtown Square in Prague.

The living quarters are shared by Fräulein Bürstner, a "typist" who works long hours and comes home late. In Frau Grubach's words, she is a good girl, kind, decent, punctual, and industrious. K. believes she is smitten with him, "an ordinary little typist who could not resist him for long." The initials FB suggest she represents Kafka's would-be bride Felice Bauer, but this impression wanes in the long closing segments of the first chapter. Rather than a distant pen friend, Fräulein Bürstner becomes K.'s banter partner and wiling recipient of his kisses, first on the lips and face, and then on the neck and throat (he keeps his lips there for a long time). Neck and throat, the reader recalls, were parts of his sister Ottla's body Kafka coveted to kiss.

The necking of K. and Fräulein Bürstner is not quite proper, prompting them to conceal it from the cohabitant Captain Lanz, described in the novel as "a tall man . . . with a tanned, fleshy face" and a nephew of Frau Grubach. In fact, Fräulein Bürstner is terrified that Lanz might get a whiff of what is going on. The circumstances suggest that while Lanz is an alter ego of Hermann Kafka, Fräulein Bürstner is a stand-in for Ottla Kafka rather than Felice Bauer.

The "boardinghouse" is then visited by "FB's friend," in this context, Felice Bauer's confidant Grete Bloch. Whether invited or on her own initiative, Bloch obviously embarked on another trip to Prague one autumn Sunday in 1914 to gauge the Kafka's response to her pregnancy. The visit can be plausibly dated to Sunday, November 22, 1914, when Bloch was in her eighth month.[8]

Accordingly, chapter 4 introduces the visitor as a German girl called Montag, the German word for "Monday" (Bloch's birthday was Monday, March 21, 1892). She is "a sickly, pale girl with a slight limp"—that is, slightly handicapped just as the pregnant Grete was. Fräulein Montag is supposedly expected to be vetted as another resident of the boardinghouse, but her case is far more contentious and incriminates Josef K. in some way. In anticipation of her arrival, Frau Grubach already suffered greatly, and Fräulein Bürstner was so upset she stopped communicating with K. It drove him to insanity, prompting Frau Grubach to ask, "Why is Herr K. taking such an interest in Fräulein Bürstner?"

Fräulein Montag's visit then further stirs emotions. As both she and Frau Grubach are moved to tears, K. tries to calm them down but feels coresponsible for the mayhem and offers to move out. When the Fräulein starts pacing the hall, Frau Grubach tells K. that she offered help but the visitor is self-willed. The landlady maintains Montag should not become a boarder anytime soon but might move in later. However, as K. sees it now, she should be allowed to move in outright. For the time being, she could be accommodated in Fräulein Bürstner's room.

Frau Grubach's vacillation and tears leave K. exasperated. But his attitude hardens when the Fräulein Montag summons him to the dining room. Described as pacing again (Grete was apparently displaying her rounded figure), she delivers a grim message that he has "long foreseen." No detail is given of the problem except that it accords "very well with all the persecution" K. endured that Sunday morning from other boarders. He cannot resist taking an almost sarcastic look at the perturbed Frau Grubach. The case is so touchy that he too starts sobbing.

An intervener appears on the scene, Captain Lanz. We know that Herr Kafka was not fond of Felice Bauer, and, accordingly, Lanz takes Fräulein Montag's side. This instantly arouses ill feelings in K. He seeks solace in the room of Fräulein Bürstner, only to realize that she has packed her belongings and left the boardinghouse. This Fräulein Bürstner is not a friend of the visitor after all. While Lanz and Fräulein Montag converse in low voices at the door of the dining room, glancing heavily at Josef K., he retires to his quarters, sheepishly "keeping close against the wall."

As Grete Bloch returned to Berlin reconciled to giving birth to her child out of wedlock, Fräulein Montag does not make any appearance in *The Trial* beyond chapter 4.

The credibility of this reconstruction is augmented by the evidence of a concurrent crisis in Franz Kafka's life. It should be recalled that he inherited oversensitivity from his maternal side including the record of suicide. Thus, just as Josef K. cries, Kafka was so upset on receiving Grete Bloch's letter of October 25 that he could not write. He even refrained from tending to his diary between November 13 and 23. After Bloch's Prague visit that month, then, he plunged into an "utter despair," finding it impossible to regain his balance. Living on the borderline of insanity, he strained mightily to recover.[9] Nothing extraordinary occurred in the fall of 1914 to explain his sudden desperation other than Grete's pregnancy and the prospect of having an out-of-wedlock lovechild. "It is certain that I shall live on alone (if I live at all—which is *not* certain)," he eventually recorded his mood.[10]

He also composed a sort of last will and addressed it to Max Brod: "Dearest Max, my last request. Everything I leave behind me . . . both at home and in the office, or whenever anything may have got to . . . is to be burned unread the last page."[11] Kafka did not take his life, but there is little doubt that the Grete Bloch affair was another factor responsible for the title *The Trial*.

On returning to the main track of the novel, Kafka stealthily introduced another relative, Uncle Karl or Albert K. Described in chapter 6 as a "petty squire from the country," he is apparently a stand-in for his uncle Siegfried Löwy, the country doctor from Třešť in Moravia. Always in a hurry on visits to the city, the uncle calls on Josef K. in the office and inquires about his "trial." Since Josef K. is reluctant to divulge the details in presence of his colleagues, the two discuss his case walking on the street. The uncle, noticing his nephew has become visibly thinner, grasps the situation fast.

After a period of silence, the uncle asks, "But how did this happen? . . . Things like this don't come down on one suddenly, they roll up for a long time." To relieve his nephew from severe pressure, he invites him for a holiday in the countryside: this, in a sense, would enable K. to get away from the charges. K. frowns on his uncle's growing interest in his cause, claiming he can manage his case more effectively. His recalcitrance upsets the uncle, who now fears that K. could become a disgrace to both himself and the family. A consultation with the uncle's friend is desirable.

At this point, Kafka, in a clever twist, sends K. and his uncle for a talk with Dr. Huld, the advocate. The face of this "ordinary" lawyer has a "long beard attached"—a phrase suggesting he is a secular Jew. Similar as Josef K. and, for that matter, Kafka, he also resides at the top floor and copes with numerous health issues including bad heart, insomnia, short breath, hearing problems, and difficulty of speaking. Despite his ill health, Joseph K. gets an interview with him at any hour he chooses. Dr. Huld, the advocate, unmistakably bears the features of the advocate Dr. Franz Kafka. Thus, in the segment of *The Trial* that relates Joseph K.'s arrival along with his uncle to the advocate Huld, Kafka effectively meets Kafka.[12]

The advocate's character helps the writer to introduce other guises starting with Leni. Described as a young girl with dark eyes and pale cheeks, she is an office worker just as Fräulein Bürstner earlier in the novel or Therese in *Amerika*. Actually, she is a morphed Fräulein Bürstner who declares already in chapter 1 her intention to start working in a lawyer's office in one month. Accordingly, Fräulein Bürstner does not show in the novel past chapter 4 or, for that matter, alongside Leni—and the latter is "new" in Huld's office.

Just as Therese and Fräulein Bürstner have emotional ties with the principal male, so Leni is Huld's conscientious *Pflegerin,* or caregiver, interacting with him intensively, fixing his bed and food. But she also intermingles with Captain Lenz and instantly bonds with Josef K., addressing him in familiar German *Du* (Thou)—the habit not customary for casual acquaintances in Kafka's day. Leni's physical appearance and her contentious character and conduct—and the novel's context—lend credence to her being another stand-in for Ottla Kafka.

There may be a reason why Kafka's biographers shy away from this association: Leni, apart from being the suspected lover of the advocate, has no qualms soliciting intimate moments also from Josef K.

We know that already in *The Trial's* segment on Fräulein Bürstner, Josef K. gets erotically entangled in his living quarters with someone who can be more comfortably identified as Ottla Kafka than Felice Bauer. The first explicit intimacy between K. and Leni also takes place at night in the advocate's top-floor office. It occurs on her initiative, but huddling on the bench, they admit their attraction to each other is abnormal. "A queer way to behave," Leni remarks to his assent. Amid her attempts to elicit tenderness—"You don't like me in the least"—he thinks of "this cherishing little creature that appears to have some incomprehensible passion for me." "Do you have a sweetheart?" Leni asks K., knowing he does. He promptly produces a snapshot of his girlfriend, the description of whom resembles Felice Bauer. As we know, however, Kafka did not trade letters with Felice in the fall of 1914, and Leni accordingly dismisses Josef K.'s assertion. She still accuses him of having abandoned her for his incommunicative girlfriend. Clearly, Josef K. and Leni have a lengthy history.

At this point, Leni also proudly mentions her precious asset coded by Kafka as a web of skin between her two fingers. Josef K. is pleased with this finding. It is probably an allusion to Ottla's virginity of which she assured her brother several months earlier. When K. kisses her at last, she becomes ecstatic and bends over him, biting and kissing him on the neck. "You belong to me now," she wishes to believe. K. is not entirely thrilled by the attention of this "little girl." The wording in the novel gels with Kafka's somewhat condescending characterization of Ottla elsewhere as "small" and submissive to him.

Leni's infatuation with K. does not go unnoticed. The uncle holds a disparaging view of her and treats her rudely. Frustrated, he bangs K. against the house door for cavorting with this "little trollop, who is obviously the Advocate's mistress." Her conduct not only hinders a satisfactory resolution of K.'s case but also brings the sick advocate to the verge of collapse and death.

Leni's tender care contributing to Huld's demise? This oxymoron probably reflects Kafka's hunch, expressed both by himself and by Brod, that Ottla's tolerance of his drug abuse was deleterious to his health.

Just as Kafka felt in 1914 unease about Ottla's persistence, Josef K. eventually also becomes uncomfortable with Leni's attention. When she reappears in a large and well-furnished kitchen that, one can assume, stands for the Kafkas' place and tries again to make a physical contact, he rebuffs her: "I don't want you to kiss me now." He also finds outright repulsive her suggestion to spend the night together and scorns her another pass on him.

Leni targets with similar meddlesome coquetry also the Advocate Huld. She knows exactly how to coax him, points her lips in his direction as if giving a kiss, and flaunts her taunt figure. Just as K., however, the advocate remains stubbornly unresponsive despite his reputation as her lover.

Alongside with weaving personal circumstances into the narrative, Kafka adds more text echoing the Šviha trial and his own experience as an articling court lawyer and litigator for his employer. Thus, he claims, through Josef K. in chapter 7, that behind the case, there is a vast organization at work—meaning, the court system. It is corrupt and incompetent from the highest rank down to "retinues of servants, clerks, police and other assistants, perhaps even hangmen." Opportunistic to a high degree; they all justify their existence by persecuting "innocent persons" like him.

True to his libertarian leanings, Kafka makes more scathing observations about the court system in connection with K.'s appearance at the court: it is rigid, out of touch, capricious, rife with favoritism, rigged against the accused, and guided by political expediency rather than facts. Inequality in capacity and rank mars judges' performance and adds uncertainty and the scent of ridiculousness to court proceedings. As many others, Kafka concurs with his favorite penman Charles Dickens that the law can be "a ass—a idiot." No wonder that, with the Šviha affair in fresh memory, Kafka's friends were amused when listening to the introductory parts of the novel.

Highlighting the judicial system's absurdities allows Kafka to restate that K.'s case cannot be handled through conventional legal channels. Thus, K. sidesteps the advocate and seeks the counsel of Titorelli, the court painter living in the attic, which also serves as court premises. The name is pseudonym, we learn, and K. is familiar with the real person. Based on leads Kafka provides, the "painter" is a mimicry for his close friend Felix Weltsch with whom he shared "disorder of our lives" in the form of opium smoking. Just like Weltsch's room, Titorelli's space is filled with stifling air that leaves the visitor gasping and his head swimming. "That's both uncomfortable and unhealthy," objects K., echoing Kafka's reaction to a visit at Weltsch's. Like Weltsch, Titorelli does not mind: there is no point airing the place.

Titorelli is just as knowledgeable as the advocate about the torture and, for that matter, about charges that K. has drawn upon himself. During a lengthy conversation with the visitors, he makes points that can be best interpreted as an outline of the addict's options. Thus, he asserts he has never encountered a single case of final acquittal—that is, beating the addiction—and K. should not expect that either. There may have been acquittals in the past, but this is the stuff of legends. K. has two choices—a postponement of the case, implying a containment of the drug, or an "ostensible acquittal," a temporary solution since the acquitted man is rearrested soon. In plain words, withdrawal pains force the addict to resume doping.[13]

Kafka found both personally unpalatable, and he did not ordain them to K. either. Since a permanent "acquittal" was not a realistic way out, ending one's life remained the option. As the story nears its tragic closure, K. loses his supporting cast. There is no longer Frau Grubach, Fräulein Bürstner, and Fräulein Montag. Leni, the caregiver, still shows. In her last appearance, she uses fists to clear her way to him. But far from enamored by her pestering, he tries to get away to another room. When he attempts to close the door and she blocks it with her foot while trying to reach for him, he grabs her hand and squeezes it so hard that she lets go with a whimper. K. then locks the door, thus stressing the separation. The painter Titorelli is written off by the unhappy parting scene: K. leaves his host's place tottering with handkerchief pressed to his mouth to avoid the intoxicating air.

Walking away from Titorelli, K. is also determined to dismiss his shadow, the advocate Huld. He does it in chapter 8 amid another harangue against the lawyers. That leaves K. isolated. In the final scene as a free man, apparently taking place in Prague's premier church, St. Vitus Cathedral, K. encounters a prison chaplain who informs him from the pulpit that the case is going badly, "you are held to be guilty." There comes an instant retort from K. "But I am not guilty, it is misunderstanding . . . We are simply men here, one as many as the other." His case is not that exceptional in the less-than-perfect society. "That is true, but it does not make you less guilty," answers the priest.

As the story transcends into the philosophical, Kafka delivers through the priest one of the most poignant passages in world literature, the story of a country man who comes to the "court" seeking *Recht*, the German word meaning in this context most appropriately "justice." A doorkeeper stops him, the first of many guards controlling passages from hall to hall. He cannot get admittance now, he learns, but may gain entry later. Settling on a stool next to the door, he engages the doorman in small talk and showers him with gifts. As days and years go by, he also makes many futile attempts to get in. Growing old and frail, in expectation of death, he asks in a whispering voice why in all those years, nobody has come seeking admittance than him. The doorman replies, leaning to him, "No one but you could gain admittance through this door, since this door was intended only for you. I am now going to shut it."

Is admittance to one's destiny or justice really attainable? In the prison chaplain's words, "The Court makes no claims upon you. It receives you when you come and relinquishes you when you go." The court or fate is indifferent to the individual; it does not determine one's life. The individual alone does.

On the eve of his thirty-first birthday (Kafka turned thirty-one on July 3, 1914), K. is visited by two taciturn men. He guesses their intent and accepts the futility of resistance. The trio, walking through the moonlit city, ascends several steeply rising streets to reach a small stone quarry on the edge of an urban settlement. K. is stripped to the waist and, shivering in the night cold, waits until a suitable spot is found, at a loose boulder near the cliff. A butcher's knife is demonstratively passed from one man to another, giving K. a chance to grab it and drive it into his own chest. However, he lacks the courage to become his own executioner. It is his "last failure." One of the men does it for him. Dying "like a dog" is a shameful but appropriate end for an addict who cannot control his destiny, Kafka implies in the last sentence of *The Trial*.

WARTIME:
"WHAT A MUDDLE . . . WITH GIRLS"

As Kafka feared, his second explosion of creativity was also of limited duration. We may assume that after returning to opium in August 1914, the stimulus again began waning, and his daily regime turned out to be unsustainable. He hoped to compensate for his nocturnal exploits with afternoon naps but usually managed to get to writing not earlier than 11:00 p.m. and lost much of sleep if he worked past 1:00 a.m. The schedule took a heavy toll, mainly in sleeplessness. Thus, he was facing the same old quandary: if, for one or other reason, he could not belabor his dreams through the night, they faded away. From the end of January 1915 on, Kafka, the writer, described his situation as the "complete incapacity," "complete standstill," and "unending torments." Soon, he felt "incapable in every respect," "finished," or at best unsure how to proceed.[1]

In this situation, the attendant symptoms of ill health had become harder to cope with. By January 1915, Kafka again recorded horrible afternoons, incessant headaches, and heart pains, and wrote in self-assessment, "I destroy myself."[2]

It would appear that, in response to new reality, Kafka reduced smoking opium as too taxing to his health. Reduced but not suspended. In one of his quips incomprehensible to biographers, he asked, "Could I endure any other air than prison air?" and answered, "That is a great question or rather it would be if I still had any prospect of release."[3] There still is a plethora of references to his deleterious habit after February 1915. Thus, during his checkup in 1916, he was advised, "Not too much smoking, not too much to drink, more vegetable meals," and lie down quietly at night and sleep.[4]

At times, Kafka referred to smoking a pipe in half dreams or invoked a scene of reading a newspaper and "puffing away mightily at my pipe." There are also other telling allusions in his writings—to "a long quite thin pipe"; pipes that hang in the stand; "pleasure of the pipe"; pipe smoking as a discreet, special habit in spite of all routine; a day-to-day pipe smoking; "triumphal" pipe smoking; and pipe smoking that removes "fetters of everyday life." Rolling out his last piece of prose, Kafka also raised the question of "relationship between art and pipe smoking," admitting the issue is controversial.[5] Based also on additional evidence below, opium remained Kafka's favorite recreational drug even after its effect as a creative stimulant ebbed.

It does not necessarily mean Kafka in 1915 suspended the intake of other narcotics. A gruesome dream he recorded in late January 1915 probably marked the return to his old routine. It was about a blade "driven with such incredible precision between my skin and flesh that it caused no injury. Nor was there any wound . . . I did not bleed." Evocative of "The Penal Colony," this imagery suggests Kafka resumed shooting opiates intravenously, no matter how contemptuous he considered it now.[6]

Morphine and heroin, of course, were too violent and their effect too short-lived to give him a significant boost. As before, he resumed lamenting that he could not track the stories through the night; they fell apart and disappeared. Dreams were "exploding" in his frazzled sleep.[7] Accordingly, another phase of low productivity in his writing started in early 1915. He blamed the family asbestos factory for the lull, claiming he could not resume writing so long as he was expected to tend to the business. In truth, he failed to show up there for over a month at a time. During the remaining war years, Kafka penned merely shorter stories, most of them for the drawer.

Symptomatic of his syringe regime, and also in response to war carnage, his production again revolved around a physical violation of the body. This man who did not seem capable of swatting a fly, invoked homicide in his writing, imagining "with your own hand to throttle down whatever ghostly life remains in you . . . with the eyes of an animal, . . . [with] no compunction," in the name of the "final peace of the graveyard." In a somber, violent piece "Fratricide," Kafka extolled the "bliss of murder," exclaiming "the relief, the soaring ecstasy from the shedding of another's blood!" There were "plenty of men who know how to murder people," reads another line of his. Even a seemingly cute animal, half kitten, half lamb, "can lie for hours in ambush, but it has never yet seized an opportunity for murder." In another short piece, the nomads were "tearing morsels" with their teeth out of the flesh of a living ox.[8]

In the same time, Kafka continued to explore for inspiration other kindred spirits and sources. As we know, he already showed a keen interest in Dostoevsky; now he added to his reading list other Russians—Herzen, Belinsky, Bakunin, and Gogol—and summed up his impression as the "infinite attraction of Russia."[9] He also took notice of his older contemporary August Strindberg, the Swedish writer exploring the trendy subject of the subconsciousness. Personally, Strindberg had similar spells of despair as Kafka, and the hero of his novel *By the Open Sea* copes with similar afflictions like sensitivity to noise.

A side effect of Kafka's reluctance to tie the knot with Felice was his discovery of Søren Kierkegaard (1811–1855). This brooding Danish philosopher and writer articulated existentialist anguish that contributed to his breaking off an engagement, supposedly to assert priority of his writing over married life. Kafka observed Kierkegaard's case was very similar to his: "He bears me out like a friend." But he was also appreciative of Kierkegaard's idiosyncratic concepts such as 'guilty-non-guilty' and propensity for saying the opposite of what one thinks, either by stating seriously what one does not mean or putting as a joke something he means seriously. The reader is left to sort it out. "Kierkegaard pilots the undirigible blimp so superbly," Kafka quipped as he himself leaned toward the same mode of expression.[10]

Still closer on Kafka's horizon were Jewish affairs and Judaism, but not the ceremonial routine of them. As an adult, he compared boredom he felt as a boy in the synagogue to monotony of his office life. His interest in Hasidism, so strong in 1911–1912, was also receding in war years, all the while the Jewish refugees from war zones in the east were flooding Prague. Reluctant to ally himself with the cause, he also declined an invitation of his acquaintance Martin Buber to contribute to his periodical *Der Jude*. Kafka likewise turned deaf when his accomplished friend Robert Musil visited Prague in military uniform in April 1916 and asked Kafka for contributions to *Die Neue Rundschau*, the prestigious magazine he edited.

Meanwhile, no longer able to sustain his writing regime, he continued cultivating his private interests. Grete Bloch should still have ranked high in his considerations. Precisely in due time after bedding him in March 1914, she gave birth on December 21 to his son Alexander Ludwig

Hans-Werner Bloch. In a truly Kafkaesque twist, the father was listed as Hans Werner Bloch, the name of both Grete's father and brother.[11] Kafka, however, had apparently turned indifferent to the mother's plight and his own progeny, refocusing instead on Felice Bauer. It did not go well with his friend Ernst Weiss, another Bohemian Jew and a surgeon increasingly moonlighting as a writer.

Writing in German, Weiss belabored rough subjects of contemporary society, including rape, incest, and drug addiction. In many respects, he mirrored Kafka's opinion, for example, in registering the corruptive effect of drugs (which he also indulged in but judiciously). In personal contact, Weiss also tried but failed in the summer of 1914 to convince Kafka into abandoning of Felice Bauer in favor of the pregnant Grete Bloch. Already on the joint vacation in Marienlyst that summer, he gave Kafka to read the manuscript of *Franziska*, a novel describing a passive man's botched relationship with two women. Kafka was anything but charmed. Aware of Grete Bloch's predicament but unable to change Kafka's mind, Weiss eventually broke off the friendship and charged his erstwhile friend with "creeping malice."[12]

In Kafka's new reasoning, however, reconciliation with Felice could help him as a writer. He would not be able to write any more, he observed on November 30 (1914), unless he managed to have her back. Accordingly, he restarted a letter exchange with her, placing hopes on their next date in Podmokly (Bodenbach), a small town in Northern Bohemia straddling the border with Germany. The arrangement forced Felice to apply for a visa because of wartime requirement. "I shall see Felice. If she loves me, I do not deserve it," he commented on.[13]

The get-together on January 23–24 (1915) was their first without bystanders. Kafka expected a "new" Felice, but the two days they spent together proved him wrong. They had no open quarrel; civility ruled as they walked peacefully side by side. But the air was full of negative vibes. She did not hesitate to correct his Prague German and voice criticism of his two elder sisters, calling them shallow. Even worse in Kafka's eyes, she neglected to ask any question about Ottla. Finding her behavior irritating, Kafka was in no mood to foster tenderness. In retrospect, he commented that he never experienced with her that "sweetness one experiences with a woman one loves."[14] With Grete Bloch and Ottla casting long shadows, Kafka and Felice Bauer were not much interested in each other.

Three months later, Kafka made a timid attempt to restore contact with Felice, suggesting they spend together Whitsun in Bohemian Switzerland. As he put it, coming alone would be best, but she could bring anyone she liked. That apparently was a green light for taking along Grete Bloch, now the mother of his boy.

Over the weekend of May 23–24, Kafka, together with Felice Bauer and Grete Bloch, indeed visited a resort near Dresden. The only evidence is a postcard they jointly dispatched to Ottla. There followed another tête-à-tête with Felice in the West Bohemian spa Karlsbad in June 1915 that obviously led nowhere and a "truly horrible journey" to Ústí nad Labem [Aussig], another town in Northern Bohemia.[15] Kafka's relationship with Felice cooled off again; their communication became sporadic, and postcards replaced long letters and focused on trivia. Kafka complained that silence would be more desirable. His offer in December 1915 to visit Berlin remained unanswered.

Meanwhile, the Great War was giving Kafka more opportunities for womanizing. After the initial illusions about a short and glorious victory evaporated in both warring camps, the generals who dictated war policies since late 1914 resolved to bleed the enemy to surrender. In the monstrous war of attrition that followed, losses of human life were accumulating rapidly, reaching millions before long. In 1916, even Britain was forced to institute a draft. By the war end in 1918, the senseless carnage would have annihilated an entire generation of the innocent. As recruits headed to the front, a shortage of young males developed at home.

Kafka, who, in Max Brod's testimony, attracted women at all phases of his life, did not resist the temptation. Despite his worsening shape, in June 1916, he looked back at his record: "What a muddle I've been in with girls, in spite of all my headaches, insomnia, grey hair, despair . . . there have been at least six since the summer. I can't resist . . . [to] admire anyone who is admirable and love her until admiration is exhausted."[16] In Marthe Robert's quip, Kafka became a collector of women's favors.

War also impacted his work at the Institute of Workers' Accident Prevention. His mandate there, to prevent and compensate workplace injuries, had become so absurdly meaningless, compared to the waste of life in the war. Social norms were also obliterated by the influx of war refugees, injured soldiers, need for amputations, and care for the amputees, and widespread deprivations in civilian life. As vice secretary, one of Chief Inspector Pfohl's three deputies, Kafka had a supervisory authority over thirty employees, and he took part in the drive to help injured soldiers. But he was bored and frustrated in his Spartan office furnished with a desk, cash box, conference table, cloth chair, and telephone; surely, he also resented the restrictions on his writing regime and use of drugs. A ban on vacations for war exempt in force since 1915 further narrowed his options.

Thankfully, his standing in the office remained solid, and he continued to successfully approach his superiors for favors. It was not merely his demeanor and proficiency that allowed him this. The institute's director Marschner, a cultivated lawyer who treated Kafka like his son, was a portly, fragile man who shared his most obvious liability—heavy cough. So did his immediate boss, Chief Inspector Eugen Pfohl (1867–1921). According to a contemporary report accusing the institute of mismanagement, Pfohl was in the center of it, a mercurial ruffian and Marschner's wicked spirit. Kafka himself characterized him at one point as "raging."[17] True to his habit, he portrayed his superiors accordingly in his texts, starting with *Amerika* (1912).

Chapter 6 of *Amerika* introduces circumstances that approximate the institute. In this setting, the "hotel" that Karl works in is effectively controlled by two individuals, the headwaiter and the head porter. While the former is a person of some authority, bearing resemblance to Marschner, the head porter, or Feodor, is modeled on Pfohl. Portrayed in absorbing detail as a tall, bulky, irritable man with whiskers and glasses to whom the headwaiter defers, he is also a pugnacious bully who lets it be known that "naturally, all the service staff who come in contact with me have to obey me absolutely."

Initially, Feodor shows hostility to Kafka's alter ego Karl. On hearing that Karl had actually spent a doping night with Robinson and promised him money, however, he vows, "As long as I keep hold of you, you are not thrown out"—and starts abusing him physically. Karl, on his part, realizes it is a good idea to stick with his "mortal enemy" who now dares to clutch him "in a sort of hug." In his view, the head porter's overtures need to be accommodated despite pain they inflict.[18]

Several months after abandoning *Amerika*, in September 1913, Kafka and Pfohl lodged for a few nights in a Vienna hotel, and the former recorded in a bittersweet tone, "Antipathy towards P.[fohl]. On the whole a very decent man. Has always had an unpleasant little gap in his character, and out of this very gap—now that one is constantly on hand to see—he creeps out in his entirety."[19] Shortly thereafter, Kafka also noted a new "laughing, boyish, sly, revealing" Pfohl who stuck his right hand in his pants as though to show another side of his.[20] Married in 1890, Pfohl was the father of two children.

Kafka returned to his employment status in *The Trial*, portraying similar characters in similar circumstances— except that this time, the bank assessor Josef K. handles the office intrigues more confidently. The chapter "Advocate-Manufacturer-Painter" introduces the director/manager who is well disposed to K. but unhealthy, suffering from chronic cough. The deputy manager is again a "dangerous" man whose deep facial lines speak more of his ambition than age (Pfohl was forty-seven in 1914). He takes advantage of the director's unsound condition to shore up his own influence. K. feels he could challenge the deputy but refrains from resisting this shift of power, in part because he senses his "case" is not quite unknown and his own reputation is waning.

In the fragment "Public Prosecutor," earmarked for *The Trial*, the otherwise struggling Josef K. again becomes proxy to describe Kafka's good standing at work. It partly stems from K.'s legal savvy that is sought by his colleagues, "all scholarly, respectable and relatively powerful gentlemen." His competence is also appreciated by the director, a weak, ill, coughing man weighed down by his responsibility. He has a weak spot for K. and treats him as a son. This director/manager, just like the ailing headwaiter in *Amerika*, can be identified with the institute's aging Dr. Marschner (who had a weak spot for Kafka).

Josef K., however, enjoys a far more personal rapport with his junior boss Hesterer, another mimicry for Pfohl. An "invalid with a chronic cough," Hesterer also is, similar to Feodor, the head porter in *Amerika*, or the deputy manager in the main text, a loud, assertive individual "as respected as . . . feared." If he cannot convince his opponents, he at least frightens them. We learn that K. is superior to Hesterer because of his better legal judgment (in contrast to Kafka, Pfohl was not a lawyer), but the two share the same pains and engage in a "soundless dialogue." Breaking the office barrier, they become so close that "all distinctions of education, profession and age" are obscured. Hesterer entertains K. in his apartment as both indulge in drinking alcohol and smoking in defiance of the former's casual girlfriend. Hesterer also does not shy from physical contact. However, if the head porter in *Amerika* crushes Karl's limb, Hesterer and Josef K. are seen one evening walking together intimately with locked arms. Since K.'s privileged position is well-known, the proud writer reveals, other colleagues come to him to intercede on their behalf. "In general quite polite and modest toward everyone," K. complies gladly within the limits of rank and table.[21]

In another fragment, "Struggle with the Deputy Manager," Kafka then describes how Josef K., by an astute use of psychology and nurturing the feel of intimacy, keeps his superior engaged despite his own "state of weakness."[22]

After denigrating himself so often in his writings, in these two fragments, Kafka raised to a subtle defense of his professional status. But they defied the *Trial*'s thrust, and he never completed them at any length deserving inclusion in the main text.

We can assume Kafka judiciously exerted his charisma to gain influence with Pfohl, possibly a fellow addict and bisexual bully. This hypothesis is the most plausible explanation of Kafka's dare and mind-boggling perks he was receiving during the war, all attributable primarily to Pfohl's intervention. Thus, already in December 1915, after a spell of torturing headache and insomnia, he approached Pfohl requesting a release from work. His three options were a termination of employment, volunteering for the military, and a long leave of absence. Termination was a nonstarter, and Pfohl rejected it outright.

Volunteering belonged to the same category of fantasies. For one, though in general supportive of Austria's war effort, Kafka was absolutely unfit for the living hell of the front line, both on account of his character and lifestyle. In the yearend balancing in December 1915, he regretted he had not gone away in 1912 (the year he started with opium) and thus remained "in full possession of my forces, with a clear head."[23] In contrast to his muscular frame in the past, he already looked undernourished in war years and described himself as emaciated. At times, according to reminiscences of his acquaintance Nelly Engel, he was so incapacitated he could not leave his room at Dlouhá Street. He also spent weeks struggling with a sort of imbecility, almost certainly induced by drugs. As he summed it up, there were certain decisive issues that ruled out his volunteering.[24]

Pfohl was well aware of this too. He proved willing to give Kafka one week's holiday provided he would spend it . . . sucking candy bars full of iron. This mineral is known to boost red blood cells, but there is no indication that Kafka ever suffered from anemia. Iron supplements, however, had been a traditional home remedy against the aftereffects of opium indulgence. In discussion with Kafka, Pfohl also mentioned that, himself being very sick (he had less than six years to live), Russian candy bars would benefit him as well. In fact, he suggested taking the iron treatment jointly.

Pfohl's proposition obviously fortified Kafka's self-confidence. He became still more assertive in pressing for extra benefits and found his superiors unusually accommodative. "The things they are prepared to put up with from me at the office surpass all office traditions."[25]

An oversupply of iron causes, among other problems, heart palpitation. This afflicted Kafka more than once and again in the spring of 1916. Visiting a specialist in April, he was diagnosed with cardiac neurosis. The suggested therapy was electrical shock treatment, but he promptly canceled the next appointment. What benefit would it have treating the consequences of a condition? Knowledgeable about health issues, he obviously connected his cardiac neurosis with iron and his taste for drugs.

The April visit to the specialist failed to advance Kafka's "prime desire" and "only possible salvation," which he now identified as to be free from his job. Plotting his next move, in early May 1916, he petitioned the director again, either for a long leave of absence without pay—by which he meant a half or entire year—or for cancellation of his exemption from military service.

Apart from his salary, Kafka had no means to live on, and his petition was, as he put it, a "complete lie." The director likewise took it as a bluff. The applicant was offered instead a generous three weeks' vacation, which, as a war exempt, he was not entitled to.[26] He resolved to spend it in the West Bohemian spa Marienbad, an incredibly beautiful place in his mind, and talked Felice Bauer into joining him.

Marienbad is known for carbon dioxide and iron-rich springs that could alleviate Kafka's health problems. Located amid lush hills and meadows, it also was suitable for romantic encounters. Felice greeted him warmly at the town's railway station on July 3 and, throughout her stay, proved constantly accommodative. However, they lodged in adjacent rooms, door to door, with keys on either side, and Kafka apparently spent the first night alone and woke up, in his hyperbole, "imprisoned in a fenced enclosure which allowed no room for more than a step in either direction."[27] The following Monday, he moved to a more attractive room but still felt miserable and suffered from excruciating headaches. A "series of frightful days spawned in still more frightful nights." He spent time reading the Bible.[28]

What was going on? For one, he just happened to suffer again from boils, those revolting, painful eruptions that surely deflated his amorousness. But boils were the side effects of his indulgence in narcotics, and Kafka needed both the space and time to replenish them. Lodging side by side with Felice restricted his opportunity for a fix. The more attentive she was, the more irritating to him. While feeling pity for her, he also recorded in his diary, the "hardship of living together . . . Impossible to live with F. Intolerable living with anyone."[29]

At this point, Kafka was also discouraged knowing that Felix Weltsch struggled in his fresh marriage not the least because of his "disorder." Weltsch's wife, Julie, a pianist, cordially resented Kafka's visits, no doubt occasions filling the apartment with nauseating fumes. At times, she even sought overnight refuge with Weltsch's parents.

After nearly a week of this misery in Marienbad, things abruptly improved for Franz and Felice. In what sense? We may assume that until now, Kafka avoided an explicit disclosure of his taste for drugs or, as he put, his "odious peculiarities."[30] In Marienbad on July 10, however, he must have confessed to his addiction in full. "Much has been torn open that I wanted to shield forever," he would put it to Brod a few days later. And Felice, almost certainly not surprised, turned out accommodating again. Franz gushed, "When she came toward me in the big room to receive the engagement kiss, a shudder ran through me . . . I have never had that kind of intimacy, except for two cases."[31] What a relief!

In a joint letter to Felice's mother of July 10, the couple claimed that so far they "tackled things in the wrong way."[32] They decided to get married after the war and live in Berlin. In view of Kafka's expensive drug habit, they also agreed to keep their money separate. On the day of Felice's departure, July 13, they confirmed the accord by visiting Kafka's mother, Julie, who vacationed with her daughter Valli in Františkovy Lázně (Franzesbad), another West Bohemian spa.

Next day, Kafka informed Felice that not one but two communications had arrived from Grete Bloch, a postcard and a telegram, but there supposedly was nothing in them that warranted Felice's instant attention. It would appear that Grete, the mother of Kafka's son, had been waiting for a favorable turn of affairs. The Marienbad tryst was, therefore, a cruel blow to her. The postcard and telegram almost certainly announced her decision to give up the one-and-a-half-year-old boy for adoption.

The first literary hint of possible adoption comes in a fragment Kafka penned in late spring of 1916—a dream about Hans and Amalia, two children invited by a "stranger" to visit a "magazine"—meaning, a warehouse. While Amalia is pushing Hans indoor, the weary boy resists, deterred by the chill air inside and distrust of the stranger who, like Kafka, has difficulty breathing. Eventually, the stranger drags the struggling and screaming Hans in through a "hole" with Amalia holding on to her brother's feet. The story can be interpreted as a metaphor of Kafka son's resisting separation from his mother.[33]

It was apparently after Kafka's rendezvous with Felice Bauer in Marienbad in June 1916 that Grete took that heartbreaking step. On August 9, then, Kafka asked Felice to pass on "kindest regards to Frl. Grete. What does she think of the home?" By the "home," he probably meant the family in Munich that had adopted his son. Kafka was also anxious to learn how Grete coped with "it" and what it meant to her.[34] The feedback distressed him again. He wrote to Felice on September 1, "I am deeply disturbed by Fräulein Grete's suffering; I am sure you won't desert her now . . . By being kind to her, you are acting on my behalf as well." He also asked Felice twice to keep Grete on her bandwagon. Conscience was catching up with him again.[35]

Grete Bloch would later claim she visited her son in Munich only once and only for a few hours. Kafka may have been present: in the fall of 1916, he penned another text suggesting he had also met his son— still a toddler—at the home of his adoptive parents. Hans, "the lawyer's son . . . sitting on a crate leaning upright against the wall," is visited by a "stranger." He is shy at first and resists the stranger's attempt to reach for him. However, the stranger does not budge, and Hans eventually gathers the courage to move closer and finally even touch him. The stranger utters some words, but his unusual pronunciation hampers communication with the boy (Kafka's German had a Prague inflection).[36] Grete Bloch stayed on Kafka's horizon, but the direct communication between them apparently ceased.

Felice Bauer, however, was not the beneficiary of Kafka's detachment from Grete. In August 1916, reading "Essays against Monogamy," he excerpted a sentence almost meaningless on the surface: "All the beautiful phrases about transcending nature [of monogamy] prove ineffectual in face of the primordial forces of life."[37] Strictly speaking, Kafka was right: for much of its existence, humankind had been living in much looser forms of cohabitation than monogamy. Cognizant of that, the modern anarchists, Kafka's confreres, elevated free love to one of their defining postulates. After a long soul-searching then, in late August 1916, Kafka found himself unable to act decisively regarding Felice. More than ever before, he was torn apart by conflicting emotions that, however, were turning in her disfavor.

THE GOLDEN LANE

We have last come across Kafka's youngest sister, Ottla, as the truculent Fräulein Bürstner and flamboyant Leni in *The Trial* (1914), the temptress to two of Kafka's alter egos in the novel, Josef K. and her lawyerly boss Huld. In real life, her infatuation with her brother continued to be a problem for the twenty-five-year-old. Separation could release her from the unnatural bond, Kafka realized. As he blamed himself gallantly in January 1915, "I have really kept her down, and indeed ruthlessly . . . she is strong enough, once she is alone in a strange city, to recover from my influence." A plan was hatched that month to send her away to Berlin in the hope of speeding up her emancipation and acceptance of Felice Bauer. But nothing came of it if only because of the mutual dislike and rivalry between the two young ladies.[1]

That meant Kafka regularly felt the need to rebuff Ottla's advances. On a trip to Budapest with his eldest sister, Elli, he chastised her for persistent invitations to visit her room, while she had not frequented his. He admitted having paid little attention to her affairs but claimed there was a "special reason" for that.[2]

Two months after Ottla nixed her relocation to Berlin, in March 1915, she introduced Franz to her potential suitor, a Czech clerk Josef David. Kafka was welcoming. When David was shortly drafted in the army, he sent him a postcard with a whimsical drawing and inscription of cordial greetings. With David away, however, Ottla was step by step relegating Felice Bauer to the background. In April 1916, she joined Franz on a two-day business trip to Karlsbad and made sure it was noted: she added kind regards above her name to Kafka's postcard to Felice. It was a minor coup for her.

At this point, however, Herr Kafka started grumbling, and Kafka junior promptly invited Felice to a date in the Dresden area. Once again, Ottla's possessiveness irritated him greatly. On a business trip to Marienbad in May, noticeably annoyed, he responded to her whining letter that it was fine to have separate lives.

Kafka's joint vacations with Felice in Marienbad was not welcome news to Ottla, especially after she learned that their relationship had improved. Feeling good now, Felice repaid Ottla with an invitation to visit them for a few days: "It is glorious here. You can see how well things are going for us . . . by the fact that tomorrow we are visiting your Mama." It was an exercise in rhetoric for the very next day, Felice returned to Berlin. In the same letter, however, trying to placate Ottla but in a slap to Felice, Kafka also grandly assuaged his sister, "Next we will travel together into . . . I hope, the free world."[3]

Marienbad, notwithstanding Ottla's attempts to ingratiate herself to her brother, started paying off in the second half of 1916. Kafka devoted far more time to her, discussing such intricate authors as Schopenhauer and Dostoevsky and undertaking joint Sunday excursions to Prague's outskirts clad in vibrant autumn colors. Her physical attraction tempted his senses as before. He wrote to Felice in early September 1916, "Ottla is expecting me at the swimming bath; the blood—quite unsolicited—is racing through my head again."[4] At the same time, the growing feeling of intimacy with his sister evoked in Kafka the notion of God's wrath.

"Going off again with Ottla," he wrote to Felice on September 10, adding that recently they visited two beautiful places near Prague, "both as silent as the Garden of Eden after the expulsion of man." To break the silence, he read her from Plato while she taught him to sing.[5] Earlier, after an evening walk home with Ottla from Malá Strana across Charles Bridge, he jotted, "God's rage against the human race . . . the unexplained prohibition, the punishment of all (snake, woman, man)."[6] The reader will run into more of these biblical associations related to Ottla.

In Berlin, Felice Bauer could not but be displeased with this turn of events. In mid-October, she observed bluntly it would not be her greatest pleasure to sit at the table with all members of his family. Kafka responded by claiming hostility to his father and mother but praising Ottla lavishly. In his opinion, she was an ideal mother, a perfect balance of such opposite virtues as humanity and pride, empathy and detachment, and devotion and independence. Confronted by the annoyed Felice, he backtracked, "I merely mentioned her good, partly excellent qualities . . . compared with her mother's. I never meant to conceal that at the same time she may well be rather complacent, intellectually calculating."

At this point, Felice became more assertive. We can assume that she sent Kafka an ultimatum regarding his addiction, mentioning Felix Weltsch. While the latter's wife detested Kafka's visits, Felice, in turn, asked Kafka to terminate his association with him. (Apparently, Ottla expressed a similar wish the following year.) In a retort to Felice of October 23, Kafka confirmed the claim of his "arrangement" with Weltsch was correct but not new. "Your threat, Felice, will be impossible to carry out, except with the help of a straight-jacket." The Berliner had to understand his lifestyle was irreversible and nonnegotiable. And how lovely the countryside was yesterday, he turned the page![7]

As Kafka's relationship with Felice was souring again, he arranged a public reading of "The Penal Colony" in the Gallery Goltz in Munich. With no need for a visa, Felice also attended. The event that took place on November 10–12 fell far short of expectations. For one, Kafka could not handle public reading well. Chronic bronchitis stripped his voice of resonance, and his delivery was interrupted by spells of heavy coughing. In addition, the stomach-churning story found little enthusiasm at a time saturated with news of real carnage at war. One listener fainted during his presentation; others left before it ended. In retrospect, Kafka would admit the "grandiose failure" of the evening: "I have abused my writing as a means of getting to Munich, where otherwise I have no intellectual ties."[8]

This could not positively impact his already strained relationship with Felice. The only Munich moment he would recall was their quarrel in the pastry shop. They apparently parted without much regret and without a follow-up chitchat, prompting him to complain again about her silence.

At this point, the restless Ottla seized the initiative. She had already reserved and, in late November 1916, took the possession of a small dwelling at the Prague Castle complex, some twenty minutes' walk uphill from the Kafkas' home and business at the Oldtown Square. It was situated in a tiny alley called Alchimistengasse (today Zlatá ulička, the Golden Lane) that used to lodge the guards, servants, and traders since the late Middle Ages. An accommodation just one grade above sleeping in a dumpster, this cubicle of sixteen square meters accessible through a low door was, in Kafka's words, "so small, so dirty, so uninhabitable, with every kind of defect."[9] He advised against renting it, but Ottla went ahead anyway, had it painted, and furnished it with a few pieces of bamboo furniture and a plank bed. Paper-thin walls were no barrier to noise, and the fecal stench fouled the alley along with coal smoke—that is, if coal was available.

In the fragment "The Pail Rider," Kafka described the wartime misery as follows: "All coal spent, the pail empty, the shovel useless, the stove breathing cold, the room blown full of frost . . . I must have coal."[10]

Kafka was renting a freshly built, comfortable place with balcony in 18 (now 16) Dlouhá Street, not far from both his family and work. From any practical standpoint, he needed Ottla's cubicle like a hole in the head. He who hated noise and cherished privacy, upper-middle-class comfort, and clean air! If Ottla were motivated only by helping with his writing, she would have been much more effective in Dlouhá Street. Sharing the place at 22 Golden Lane had no practical justification. It suited the relationship that had progressed beyond the siblings' customary affection. The parents were not welcome here; in fact, Ottla kept them in the dark about the location.

Nor were Felice Bauer nor Josef David truthfully apprised of the circumstances. Ottla wrote to David that her brother wanted to have her little house for a few days only, and she gladly complied because it was otherwise unoccupied. On his part, Kafka explained to Felice that after returning from Munich, he started looking for a flat but eventually accepted Ottla's hospitality.

So Ottla rushed from the Oldtown Square to this romantic hideaway at noon, opened the tiny window to let the foul air out, and restarted the fire for Franz, who came for his afternoon sleep. She returned after work to prepare evening meals and watch her brother's shenanigans. Thrilled by his presence alone, she felt intense joy and was so sorry to see him leaving for his flat, usually around midnight. Franz, on the other hand, came to appreciate his night strolls back to Dlouhá Street. Walking cooled off his overcharged system.

Kafka, or someone else, expunged *en bloc* his diary entries from late October 1916 to early April 1917. This hiatus has foreclosed any chance to be privy to his impulses and experience during his first cohabitation with Ottla. It appears, however, that his appreciation of her started waning by the end of 1916. He told her the cubicle deprived each of them of independence. Furthermore, he confided to Felice Bauer that not everything was perfect with Ottla: "However sweet and self-sacrificing she may be, when she is in a bad temper she cannot help letting me feel it once in a while."[11] He kept coming aware his absence would make his sister unhappy. Ottla too was losing interest in Golden Lane and eventually deputized the family's Czech maid to care for the place.

Kafka spent New Year's Eve alone, and when the opportunity came, he relinquished his flat in Dlouhá Street in early March 1917 and rented a two-room flat on the second floor of Schönborn (Colorado) Palace. Situated on the slopes of Petřín Hill and today the site of the U.S. Embassy at Tržiště 15, this was an upscale accommodation, and Kafka seems to have moved in for real.

It needs to be pointed out, however, that his talent was not wasted. Thus, when back in July 1916, his Leipzig publisher Kurt Wolff inquired about his new texts, Kafka replied he had nothing at hand, calling it a penalty for having wasted his energies in recent times. Starting the fall of 1916, however, Kafka harvested a modest crop for his past effort. In October, "The Judgment" was published as a book, and *The Metamorphosis* appeared in *Die weissen Blätter*; a month later, it also came out as a book. Thanks to Wolff's initiative, he also received money attached to the Fontana Prize. This award went to Carl Sternheim, who, independently wealthy, could afford the gesture. Kafka was cited for "The Stoker," *The Metamorphosis*, and *Meditations*.

Motivated again, Kafka was quite productive between the fall of 1916 and spring of 1917, penning several small jewels. In July 1917, then, Kafka sent a collection of thirteen stories to the publisher Wolff in Leipzig. Both sides were pleased. Compared with his past production, his new prose was less violent and more sophisticated and introspective. In the controversial piece "Jackals and Arabs," which has earned him unfair accusations of anti-Semitism, Kafka took a critical look at the conflict between Jews and Arabs in Palestine, "a very old dispute, so it might be in the blood." A visitor from the north asks, "What is it that you jackals want?" to receive this answer, "We have nothing but our teeth for everything we want to do, good and bad . . . We must have peace from Arabs, air to breathe." Writing this on the eve of the Balfour declaration that would lay ground to the Jewish homeland, Kafka wondered, in 1917, how to put an end to this "strife dividing the world."[12]

About the same time, he rendered with humor his entrapment by opium in the "Report to an Academy" and wrote other tales on the same topic. In "Prometheus," he returned to the topic that intrigued him, this time reviewing four legends concerning the Greek demigod who, chained to a rock, sees his liver continuously nibbled on by a vulture or eagle. Since liver is an organ typically degraded by drugs (but can grow back), the myth of Prometheus can be considered an allegory to the addicts' tribulations—and as such attracted creative interest of Kafka's nineteenth-century predecessors, opium users such as Mary Shelley, Goethe, and Marx.[13]

An addict's helplessness is also conveyed in "The Hunter Gracchus": "Nobody will read what I say here, no one will come to help me," and even if they came, "every door and window would remain shut . . . the thought of helping me is an illness that has to be cured."[14] The reflection on opiatic boils once again shows in "A Country Doctor," completed in 1917. Reminiscent of Kafka's treatment of boils in *The Metamorphosis*, it is a hallucinatory story of a boy both healthy and ill. Near the hip in his right side is an open wound as big as the palm of adult hand. On a closer inspection, it is filled with thick worms "with small white heads and many little legs."[15] In a gesture bordering on tasteless, Kafka dedicated this revolting story to his father, who, without saying anything else, asked him to put in on his night table.

In the meantime, the Great War was taking a heavy toll both in trenches and at heartlands. Following the dictate of attrition, both warring camps mobilized all their resources, which, however, proved inadequate. Food rationing, rising prices, and hunger became commonplace, feeding the spirit of despondence and revolt. Drastic reprisals including executions had so far stifled dissent but not for long. In March 1917, a revolution broke out in Imperial Russia, followed in November by another revolution, of exhaustion, which brought to power a new political breed, Lenin and the communists. In Bohemia, the general war malaise exacerbated the tension between Czechs and Germans with Jews caught in between. The strife also impacted Kafka's workplace as his colleagues divided into a Czech and German camp in the fall of 1917. With disruption of families, public life, and economy, society seemed to be splitting at the seams.

Mindful of his status as a public servant, Kafka refrained from commenting meaningfully on events. In a few texts, he merely voiced a mild concern about the Habsburg Empire's waning fortunes, most notably in "The Great Wall of China." Ostensibly about the strength and failings of Chinese emperors, the allegory effectively blamed the Viennese court for failure to rally the empire's nationalities for the war. Despite all adversities, the "salvation of our fatherland" was in the mind of many, but without an effective leadership, "this burden and suffering . . . will be our demise."[16]

At the same time, neither Kafka personally nor the family and their business on Oldtown Square experienced any serious hardship let alone hunger during the war. It was his ever-restless sister Ottla who, in the wake of the failed cohabitation at Golden Lane, conceived another action in line with the angst of the day. Leaving her father's business, in mid-April 1917, she moved to and started to manage a farm owned by the family of her brother-in-law Karl Hermann in the West Bohemian village Siřem (Zürau).

She already had prior discussion with her father about studying agriculture. It would give her a chance to escape parental control and start afresh elsewhere, possibly in Palestine. The Siřem option was more realistic, but still, Ottla was a city girl with no knowledge whatsoever of farming. Her decision irked the family, in particular the father. Besides losing a conscientious sales help, he doubted her staying power and ulterior motivation. Ottla's sharing with her brother a place the address of which she kept secret (22 Golden Lane) and her overall conduct already grieved him. Was her choice of the remote locale such as Siřem another trap for Franz? Herr Kafka tried to accept her move in resignation, but when she visited Prague in early August, he poured it on her. As she reported to Josef David, he started berating her for leaving the shop as soon as she walked in and, in the evening, talked about her and Franz with great displeasure.

Ottla probably also felt slighted by Franz's reservations to their shared life at Golden Lane. But after a month in Siřem, she wrote him a letter that called for an immediate response. Kafka replied he had already felt abandoned, but her letter was a harbinger of a better time. In early June, he finally visited Siřem, and the bond was renewed. Later the same month, he assured Ottla he would come back but not before September. That summer of 1917, he also started learning Hebrew, the sign of giving some consideration to Ottla's dream of their joint existence in Palestine.

With an unerring sixth sense or forewarned, Felice Bauer made an appearance in Prague in early July. On the way to her sister in Arad in Hungary, she used the stopover as a bid to reclaim Kafka. They may have resolved to renew their engagement, and Kafka accompanied her on the trip to Hungary, but his mind and heart stayed in Bohemia. There is no mention of the engagement in his diaries or letters. He returned from Budapest, leaving Felice to complete the journey to Arad alone. On the way home, he told an acquaintance, the Prague poet Rudolf Fuchs, that he considered parting with her. According to Brod, he indeed declared with a surprising calm back in Prague that the romance was over. "He even seemed to feel well."[17] The battle he had been fighting inside himself for five years was resolved in Felice's disfavor.

Later in July, Kafka mailed his sister by a sheepish, meandering letter, clearly a solicitation of her goodwill. Ottla promptly visited Prague and got an earful from her father but also reconnected with her brother. The latter subsequently told Frau Kafka of his intent to secure a longer vacation for a stay in Siřem. Toward mid-August, so he would claim, he experienced a sudden bout of bad health that indeed cleared him for joining Ottla in the Bohemian countryside.

1917: A "Mental Tuberculosis"

In March 1912, recalling his experience as a girl conqueror, Kafka also mentioned his effort to restore his "delicate lungs."[1] They were indeed delicate years before he made an issue of it. He suffered from pulmonary catarrh or bronchitis as early as 1907 and was rediagnosed with this condition again in 1917. Exactly how his mind meandered in the summer of 1917 toward aligning his lung problems with tuberculosis will never be known. Kafka eventually tore out the entries in his diary from August 11 to September 14, the critical period between his hemorrhage and his first days in care of his sister Ottla in Siřem.

It is not even certain whether and in what form his—supposedly tuberculosis-heralding—blood discharge in mid-August occurred. Did it happen predawn in bed, as he reported to Ottla in late August 1917, or did he just spit "something red" in the swimming pool on a hot August day, as he relayed it to Milena Jesenská three years later?[2] We know for sure that, irrespective of hemorrhage, the doctors did not diagnose him tubercular; in fact, Kafka was not even a passive carrier of the TB bacillus (someone asymptomatic who can still transmit the disease). Hence, his doctor Gustav Mühlstein also felt certain that he was no risk to infect others.

It should be noted that blood discharge more likely originates in the upper respiratory tract than in lungs anyway. For someone diagnosed with bronchitis like Kafka, the likeliest culprit was opium smoke that floods the entire respiratory system with irritants and toxins. Opium smokers learned to cope with blood coughing just as with the reoccurrence of boils and weight loss. Kafka himself, as we know, accepted this nexus, dating the onset of his serious health problems to his initiation to opium in 1912. There is no record of him discharging blood again after 1917, but his health was steadily deteriorating—the consequence of what he phrased as "giving the devil his due."[3]

On one hand, the absence of tuberculosis was good news to him. Incorrigibly fastidious, Kafka considered this disease obnoxious. This was in line with the general perception of the tubercular who were shunned, if not ostracized, by society. But the attitudes were changing. Ever since Puccini's *La bohème* premiered under Arturo Toscanini's baton in 1896, the operagoers from New York to Australia could not keep their eyes dry over the tragic fate of the lead character Mimi. She dies, feverish, coughing violently, and presumably tubercular but never identified as such in the opera. Somewhat perversely, the disease began garnering empathy in addition to horror.

Kafka, apart from being a keen observer of social standards, was serving on his institute's committee examining new trends in avoiding and treating tuberculosis. He was well aware of the subject's specifics. Could symptoms similar to that of tuberculosis earn him time off?

Whatever the form and extent of Kafka's blood discharge in mid-August 1917, he failed to extract any concession from Dr. Mühlstein on the first visit. About two weeks later, August 29, he visited Mühlstein again. We know about the outcome from his letter to Ottla postmarked the same day. Kafka at last mentioned here his blood episode and the doctor's diagnosis, bronchial catarrh. Claiming to feel much better now, he reported on the twenty-ninth that the doctor did not change his mind. He was free of tuberculosis. Mühlstein still ordered an X-ray and a sputum test to confirm his noninfectious status. In Frau Kafka's opinion, Mühlstein was a knowledgeable doctor well respected for reducing her husband's heavy night cough.

Kafka, however, did not wait for results. In the same rambling letter of August 29, he showed resolve to capitalize creatively on his health liabilities. In his new, contrived reasoning, they were quite compatible with tuberculosis, and hence, he could pass as tubercular. To consider him as such, therefore, was "the only right" approach. Accordingly, he now declared himself, timidly, a sufferer from "this mental disease, tuberculosis." In another version of his self-diagnosis, the "head in the time of need has spawned the lung disease."[4] The whiff of tuberculosis, he hoped, would give him a strong ground for eight to ten days' leave (he would be out indefinitely if truly tubercular).

This has been sufficient for generations of biographers to assert, employing various spins, that Kafka 'was convinced, rightly, that he had tuberculosis.'[5] Kafka and tuberculosis have become binary terms, never questioned even if the evidence points elsewhere. Closer to the truth, Kafka was well aware that the adverse effects of narcotics—mainly the compromised respiratory system, cough, and weight loss—paralleled those of pulmonary tuberculosis and resolved to use them as such in late August 1917. The reader is asked for understanding if, to counteract the biographers' routine fixation on Kafka's tuberculosis, this tome rarely misses the opportunity to correct the myth.

In late August 1917, then, Ottla was assured that Kafka's condition was not contagious and issued him an invitation to Siřem. Energized, he promptly relinquished the apartment in Schönborn to return to the family quarters at Oldtown Square and occupy her room temporarily. Reporting this to Siřem, he slipped into erotic ambiguity: he had filled Ottla's room completely, not with furniture but with himself.

His doctor, Mühlstein, however, was a stumbling block. Visiting him for the fourth time in three weeks on September 3, Kafka left disappointed again. Backed by test results now, the doctor resolutely denied him time off work. Should his troubles persist for a few months, Mühlstein suggested, he might be injected with tuberculin for peace of mind. Invented by Koch supposedly as a cure of tuberculosis, tuberculin was increasingly accepted in Kafka's age merely as a diagnostic tool of the disease. Its unpleasant side effects, however, deterred the would-be recipients, and Kafka ruled out Mühlstein's suggestion outright. Why such an aggravation if the test would likely be negative? Clearly annoyed by the uncooperative doctor, Kafka denounced him for ignorance, of contradicting himself, and of wanting to know everything.

On short notice, Kafka visited Prof. Gottfried Pick from the Prague University in the morning of September 4. This crème-de-la-crème expert confirmed Mühlstein's diagnosis, bronchial catarrh. Just like Mühlstein, Pick failed to detect even a suspicion of tuberculosis that would make the patient's case reportable. But Pick proved more accommodative than Mühlstein, recommending a three-month stay in the countryside. Kafka called it a "passport to eternity."

While at the end of August he hoped that, with protection of his boss Pfohl, he would be able to wring eight to ten days free, Pick's memorandum whetted his appetite still more. On September 6, Kafka asked the institute for either an early retirement or a three-month leave of absence. He realized an early retirement was out of question for a thirty-four-year-old nontubercular, but requesting it buttressed his chance of getting a more substantial time off. In self-assessment, he felt "playing out again a sentimental comedy" not without lying on his part.

As expected, his bosses Pfohl and Marschner rejected a retirement outright. However, as compassionate professionals guided by the mantra of health preservation, they harbored tender feelings for their thin, coughing colleague. Without even filing a pertinent petition, Kafka was approved for three months of leave of absence. His case was far too nonstandard for the formal approval process. A short notice in his file dated September 14 merely stated he would be absent from office on account of his bronchial catarrh. Intent on keeping his truancy under the lid, Kafka told his family the break was meant to heal his nervous conditions.

His choice of victimhood was astute, offering both a convenient cover for drug addiction and a respite from the hated work. He wrote to Ottla on September 4, "There is justice in this illness . . . something altogether sweet," compared with the state of his affairs in past years.[6] The same day to his publisher Wolff, "The disease which for years now has been brought on by headaches and sleeplessness has suddenly broken out. It is almost a relief."[7]

A sweet relief? As Kafka's contemporary and specialist in drug addiction observed, "One cannot use morphine long enough without . . . conceptions of truth and falsehood becoming more and more cloudy."[8]

Kafka's fervent desire to encamp with Ottla in Siřem upset Max Brod. It was him who arranged the fast-track examination by Pick. However, he also forewarned the professor about Kafka's "reckless" lifestyle and probably suggested fitting conditions. Pick, then, formulated his memorandum accordingly. The leave of absence he proposed was conditional on Kafka taking an arsenic cure. Kafka, to be sure, was recommended arsenic on other occasions. Why arsenic? Taken in the form of Fowler's solution, it was another traditional antidote to such side effects of opium as boils and weight loss. Among other famous people of the past, Karl Marx was forced to consume it at the behest of his best friend and bread giver Friedrich Engels when completing his masterpiece *Capital*. Marx hated arsenic, and so did Kafka.

The latter would have been well served by following Pick's advice, though. Apart from hemorrhage and insidious weight loss, he was coughing at night and coped with night sweats, shortness of breath, and raised temperature. Thus, readying his luggage for travel to Siřem, he encountered resistance of his well-meaning friend.

Certainly not fooled by Kafka's pretense of tuberculosis, Brod objected to his rejection of arsenic and his choice of Siřem. He wished to see Kafka in a bona fide sanatorium, preferably in Switzerland or Italy, and undergo a serious cure for his afflictions. Kafka, on the other hand, repeatedly claimed vacation, not recuperation, was on his mind when plotting the Siřem escapade. The discord unresolved, Brod obliged Kafka to a joint visit of Professor Pick on Monday, September 10. Brod wanted to present his objections, Kafka reported to Ottla.[9]

Little is known about that Monday meeting. Skimpy evidence suggests Kafka was obliged to stop his weight loss voluntarily and, obliquely, to scale down his drug intake. Wasting no time, he left for Siřem on Wednesday, September 12. In retrospect, he recognized how lucky he was in obtaining a three-month vacation as an "active civil servant" exempt from war duty and how much he owned it to his association with tuberculosis: "The remarkable thing, which I have finally begun to realize, is that everyone is excessively good to me . . . in matters great and small."[10] No wonder he perceived his health issues "more like a guardian angel than a devil" that entered his life at the right point. Free as a bird for now, Kafka hoped Professor Pick's requirements were not going to "profoundly spoil this long free time" ahead of him.[11]

Strikingly thin Kafka

Kafka's signatures

Kafka and Ottla in Siřem, 1917

Siřem: Kafka wished to live here with Ottla forever

Kafka, bottom right, in Matliary

Milena Jesenská

PARADISE IN SIŘEM

Only eighty kilometers west of Prague, Siřem was a world apart from the refined city Kafka called his home. For one, access by public transportation was patchy in the age when car ownership was still rare. The visitors commonly took two trains from Prague to the nearest railway station Měcholupy (Michelob). The rest of the journey, some five kilometers, had to be negotiated by foot or coach. Consequently, the travel time to cover the distance was three and a half hours or more. The nearest post office in Bišany (Flohau) was also five kilometers away but in the opposite direction.

The village itself was a cluster of seventy-four houses straddling the main road with the hint of a center anchored by a water fountain and a Catholic church. There also were three beer pubs and an elementary school, serving 350 inhabitants, all German speaking, but no electricity and no light in the evening. Located in backwoods of economic activity, the village depended on agriculture and particularly hops, the ingredient that for centuries gave Bohemian beer its intriguing taste.

The farmhouse that Ottla had taken possession of was owned but not occupied by the family of her brother-in-law Hermann. There was a small garden adjacent to the house and some hop acreage, but most of the twenty-hectare farmland was uncultivated. Ottla had no farming experience and quickly antagonized the farmhand. With only one horse at her disposal and no farming equipment, she was restricted to tending to a pig, goats, and geese, and to cultivating the weedy garden. This forced her to buy produce such as milk and eggs in the market and made her family wonder why she could not supply even potatoes. In fact, Ottla and Franz were receiving regular parcels including foodstuff from their mother in Prague. The Siřem venture amounted to Ottla's version of Marie

Antoinette's Petit Trianon. No wonder it met with the disapproval of both her family and her friend Josef David, who, in a letter from warzone, called her Siřem enterprise a "funny farming."[1]

Apparently mindful of appearances and tensions that their crammed space at Golden Lane had generated, Ottla and Franz at first settled in separate quarters in Siřem. While she lived in the single-floor house rented from the Hermanns, he moved into a room on the second floor a building nearby. As local sleuths would later determine, the Hermanns sold this house to a local farmer in 1914, and it was unoccupied at Kafka's time. It would be torn down after the Second World War as the village depopulated.

On arrival, Kafka tried to convince himself he never felt better healthwise. The only health issue he would confess to in the village was inner weaknesses. It started asserting itself soon after arrival, he claimed in an obvious allusion to doping. There is an oblique reference in his letters to doing unspecified "business" while in Siřem with Weltsch, and a complaint that all his "Prague connections" left him in the lurch, in particular the main "supplier" who had lowered his profile afraid of denunciation.[2]

That notwithstanding, Kafka was proud of his deftness in securing vacations with the help of tuberculosis. The association gave him "an immense support a child gets from clinging to its mother's skirt."[3] Echoing his opinion and worry-free, Ottla opined that God must have sent him "this disease . . . without which he would not be able to leave Prague."[4] But the semblance of reality needed to be upheld even vis-à-vis his closest friends. Thus, as early as September 5, Kafka discreetly asked Brod and Weltsch to "warn" people of his tuberculosis short of mentioning the matter to his parents (that would not be his option if he were truly tubercular). The same figment was passed to Felix Weltsch a few weeks later. This time, it allegedly was his physician Mühlstein who had taken a second darker view of his health: "There was tuberculosis of both the right and left lungs, which, however, would clear up fairly soon."[5] The word "tuberculosis" also received prominence in Kafka's key letter to Felice Bauer. Resorting to outright prevarication, he wrote her, "Without going into all the medical details, the outcome is that I have tuberculosis in both lungs."[6]

The concerned Felice promptly announced her intent to visit Siřem. In the past, Kafka often pleaded for her presence, but not this time. He tried to dissuade her by a telegram that, however, was not dispatched, nor was a parting letter he had composed. She reached Siřem in the afternoon of September 20, after a long journey, and settled in Franz's room while he obviously lodged with Ottla. There was a palpable tension in the air. Almost certainly, she realized the true change in Kafka's life was not his health. Still, she took a trifle communication between them with quiet demeanor bordering on fatalism.

Prior to her departure next day, Felice stepped out of the house, but Franz did not follow for a long time. Joining her eventually, he claimed to have been looking for her. The unflappable Berliner remarked she heard him talking inside. Standing on the steps and gazing over the village square, they merely engaged in an insignificant chatter. In his recapitulation, she was unhappy about the pointlessness of her trip, his incomprehensible conduct, about everything. He was tormented but not unhappy. His heart was elsewhere. As she was leaving Siřem late in the evening in a carriage driven by Ottla with him staying put, he thought of her as an "innocent person condemned to extreme torture" and of himself as a repulsive torturer. In afterthought, he rebuked himself, "You have destroyed everything without having really possessed it."[7]

Within a week, Kafka received three letters from Felice, once a coveted treasure, now the items of indifference. It took days before he read them, and when he did, the content made him defensive again. He came to appreciate Felice's calm and collected demeanor now. Replying in an exculpatory tone, he pointed out that he had tried to avoid lies in his communications, and she was not unaware of his private war in the past five years and suffered because of it. She needed to be reminded now that his was not a tuberculosis from which he could recover but a condition that could not be reversed: "I will never be well again."[8] Indirectly but firmly, Kafka again intimated that his Faustian involvement in drugs was not negotiable, and this made him unsuitable as a partner for life.

A few days later, Weltsch, who knew about Kafka's afflictions firsthand, also disputed his claim of tuberculosis, calling it a "false theory." This elicited the following obfuscation: "I am not obstinate, . . . I am in possession of the original documents and can hear the lung."[9] But then, Kafka himself began issuing a series of ambivalent statements. He wished Brod to believe that his brain and lungs "came to an agreement without my knowledge" with brain in the lead.[10] His "medically certified illness" was in fact a trap he had fallen into, a "borrowed" or symbolical disease the standard medical treatment of which would be equally symbolical and ineffective.[11]

As he phrased it to Felice Bauer, his body had for years been a battleground between good and evil, meaning abstinence and addiction. In consequence of this war with an ever-changing frontline, he had grown pathetic and shameful. Hence, "I don't believe this illness to be tuberculosis but rather a sign of my general bankruptcy."[12]

Similar to other addicts, Kafka also showed remorse. Calling himself a Tartuffe, he found it so hard to "lie in obtaining the vacation." Now and other times, he also feared divine retribution. "I am too calculating, and the Bible tells us what the fate of reckoners will be," he quipped to his friends.[13] Giving up the ground to Felix Weltsch, Kafka eventually tried to settle the issue with him as well, suggesting that "in spite of all lies," they understood each other.[14]

Ottla seconded him. On a visit of Prague in late November, she told the father there was no need to worry. Obviously, she meant it as reassurance that her brother's health posed no risk to him or anyone else. By the same token, she feared the father, knowing the situation, would be upset at his son's long idling in Siřem. However, she left believing he took it in strides.

Free from the family oversight, Kafka began exhorting himself on arrival to Siřem to make a new beginning as a writer. Part of this rewind was a destruction of his recent texts including, presumably, copies of his "monstrous" letters to Felice Bauer and entries in his diary. Both of them probably threw light on his decision to declare himself mentally tubercular. "Tear everything up," he told himself as he restarted his diary in a new booklet.[15]

In early September, the publisher Wolff suggested to Kafka a new book consisting of his minor prose. It could have included "A Report to an Academy," which earned words of appreciation by his friends. Despite his good intentions, however, Kafka was much too engrossed in private affairs in Siřem to respond to the offer. Even recording his life in Siřem made him uncomfortable soon. Eventually, he would either destroy or care not to make entries in his diary between November 11, 1917, and June 26, 1919. Parallel or in place of a diary, he resumed compiling a sort of extemporaneous commentaries, now reflecting his experience in the village. Max Brod would assemble them into a slim tome and publish as *The Blue Octavo Notebooks*. Included is a collection of aphorisms that Kafka himself numbered and titled "Reflections on Sin, Suffering, Hope and the True Way."

As his other texts, *The Blue Octavo* notes, his aphorisms in particular, correlate well with scraps we know about Kafka's personal life in Siřem. In the apt observation of a biographer, in Kafka's parables, the third person can easily become the first person.[16] One can certainly comprehend a few ghastly entries in the notebooks. For illustration, referring to his old nemesis, boils, Kafka rendered them now as "a smelly bitch that has brought forth plenty of young [clusters], already rotting in places . . . who continue to follow me faithfully everywhere, whom I am quite incapable of disciplining . . . until finally . . . the pus and worm-ravaged flesh of her tongue laps at my hand."[17]

Above all, however, the above texts show that temptation of flesh in Siřem overshadowed Kafka's handicaps. It is notable that, just as K. in *The Trial*, Kafka was the target rather than initiator of carnal advances; this was the case of his "seduction." In his metaphor, "A cage went in search of a bird." In another quip, "He who seeks does not find, but he who does not seek will be found." The attention was far from unwelcome. "Sweet snake, why do you stay so distant, come closer," Kafka jotted down early on.[18] Subsequently, reflecting on his "morning in bed," the writer of *The Blue Octavo* felt "terribly puffed up" by an ever-seductive subject.[19] In mid-October, then, he revealed to Brod that love had become the centerpiece of his life in the village. In his words, "All the previous times were but illusions, only now I truly love." He became a "happy lover" wishing to "live here always."[20]

Who was his entrancing lover in Siřem? One of the two servants that Ottla employed? He found both unapproachable; nay, he felt inhibited in their presence. Does perhaps his neighbor Frau Feigl, a mother of seven little girls fit the profile here? His relationship with the people in the village was so loose, he reported to Prague, that the locals considered him Herr Hermann, the owner of the place.

It was his sister Ottla who pivoted Kafka's life in Siřem. When she left for Prague for a few days, he was so depressed, feeling "low-spirited, lumpish, leaden-stomached" and unable to function.[21] Her presence was the only reason Kafka wished to live in the village forever, deprived of nearly all perks of civilization, oblivious to his health and writing mandate. Difficult to accept as it may be to some, the object of Kafka's fleshly love in Siřem was his youngest sister, the woman he also considered the ideal mate.

We know that he equivocated love between brother and sister with a love between mother and father. His bond specifically with Ottla was abnormally personal already prior to Siřem. A respected biographer has noted that a still more intimate relationship developed between the two siblings in 1917, but neither he nor anyone has proffered an explanation.[22] In truth, as early as September 18, Kafka himself disclosed to his best friend Max Brod: "I live with Ottla in a good minor marriage; marriage based not on the usual intense high currents but . . . on the low voltages."[23] His "minor marriage," Brod would learn subsequently, included breakfasting in bed.

Sex between siblings was socially or legally permissible in numerous societies of the past and still is today, with varying restrictions, in many countries including Brazil, Portugal, Spain, France, Belgium, the Netherlands, Sweden, Russia, India, Japan, and Israel. It was a taboo in the Austro-Hungarian Empire and Germany even though, as somebody quipped, if Freud is to be believed, everyone would be sleeping with their close relatives given half a chance.

Kafka was far from uncomfortable with attachment to a single woman. Always attentive to scriptural authorities, he had excerpted the Talmud to make the point that a man without a woman is no person. Felice Bauer's claim on him, however, had constantly been challenged by his attachment to Ottla. The former's humiliating departure from Siřem, then, brought the two siblings still closer together. "A sunray of bliss," Kafka described the situation in *Blue Octavo*. As his "marriage" to Ottla was coming to bloom, he looked still further, to procreation. It is not entirely a crime for someone health-challenged to have children, he noted, adding that Flaubert's father was tubercular.[24] The notion that even someone burdened with a major debility could give life to a healthy child found domicile in his mind.

Meanwhile, on a stopover in Prague, Felice Bauer apprised Brod of the situation in Siřem. Her account, including an observation about Kafka's indifference to food, left Brod upset. In reaction, he mailed a letter to Siřem on September 24, berating his best friend for treating Felice so shabbily for she meant well. He also reminded Kafka that the health issues he shared with Weltsch—and manifested by bronchial catarrh— were reversible. Their acquaintance the poet Robert Fuchs had certainly managed to recover, and Brod himself would also straighten his life in similar circumstances. Kafka, however, lacked the prerequisite self-control and neglected the therapy. A reduction of drug intake, Brod implied, would alleviate both Kafka's catarrh and eating disorder.

Brod's frustration extended to Ottla, whom he considered too much under her brother's spell, despite all her care and love. "A caregiver must be able to dictate, but she only seems to follow you." In addition, he cared to mention that Kafka was missing the "deeper realm of real sexual life," effectively signaling his disapproval of the siblings' bedroom sharing. Kafka should summon courage and present himself for another checkup to Professor Pick not later than October 10 as he had promised.[25]

By this time, Kafka had given up on the nature-cure theories, dismissing them as wrong as their psychological counterparts (by which he meant primarily Freudian psychotherapy). In response to Brod's harping, he conceded a deeper realm of sexual life was closed to him in Siřem but also ruled out compliance with medical advice (which revolved around detoxification). As before, he preferred independence in handling his afflictions, in practical terms a status quo. Besides, what if Pick took him away from Siřem, "the best place for me"? Brod ought to be reminded again that his lifestyle was not negotiable: "The reasons you give for the need to get well are very fine, but utopian. This assignment you give me might have been carried out by an angel hovering over my parents' marriage bed."[26]

At this point, Brod resolved to come for a visit. However, Kafka fended him off with a letter addressed to both Max and his urban wife, Elsa. While he was "thriving among all the animals," would the Brods appreciate unglamorous life in Siřem, surrounded by pigs and goats? Several days later, he marshaled more arguments against their visit to the household that, the Brods should be warned, a stranger was bound to find "mismanaged, rife with little inconveniences and even unpleasantness." If all this failed to deter them, they should come for a day trip only on Sunday and return to Prague by the evening train. There would be no point staying overnight.[27]

In place of Brod but probably on his instigation, Frau Kafka visited Siřem on September 30. Herr Kafka would not show up, undoubtedly displeased with his children's defiance of social conventions. That suited his son well. As the weeks were piling up for him and Ottla in a nearly complete isolation, however, their cohabitation showed fissures. By late October 1917, they started quarreling about minor things. The temperamental Ottla may have punished him by ceasing communication. Thus, around October 23, Kafka wrote a short prose, "The Silence of Sirens." Prefaced "Early morning in bed," this lighthearted piece tells how sirens, motivated perhaps by the "utter bliss on Odysseus' face," resolve to become silent. Odysseus observes from close the "poise of their necks, their deep breathing, their eyes brimming with tears" but "being a man of so many viles . . . such a cunning fox," ignores their silence. And not surprisingly, the sirens no longer want to lure anyone; all they want is to "catch a glimpse for as long as possible of the reflected glory in the great eyes of Odysseus."[28]

On October 29, Kafka underwent another checkup in Prague by Professor Pick after all. The latter opined that the patient should return to work. His view apparently was not communicated to the institute, but Kafka, feeling sad and restless, and dreading Prague, nevertheless started looking for new accommodation in the city. Yet before long, he entrusted the search to his mother and returned to Siřem on November 2.

His discord with Ottla was still lingering. "When a sword cuts into one's soul," the main thing is to "keep a calm gaze, lose no blood, accept the coldness of the sword with the coldness of a stone," he admonished himself on November 7.[29] He also recorded "sheer impotence" and, as late as November 12, mentioned, "Long time in bed, resistance."[30] The conflict between the siblings was apparently resolved by Kafka taking a conciliatory attitude again. As he put it to Brod, there was "some kind of alien element" in his sister, but he accepted it: "Here I can submit."[31]

The follow-up must be reconstructed without the benefit of his diaries. Presumably reflecting a reality that was uncomfortable, he stopped making entries onward of November 11 or destroyed them later. Thus, his *Blue Octavo*, including "Reflections on Sin," remains the most authentic source on his private life in Siřem and quite an illuminating one.

It should be mentioned here that opium can temporarily act as an aphrodisiac. This may explain why the thirty-four-year-old Kafka, though suffering from shortness of breath and cough that prevented him on occasion from walking and talking, became again possessed with physical sex by mid-November 1917. Here are the terms that he expressed now and never before or after: "the man in ecstasy," "gladiator after the combat," "asphyxiation," "you have girded your loins in a most laughable way for this world," as well as the triumphant "A. is a virtuoso, and Heaven is his witness." To get into this elevated stage of gratification, "it took the intercession of the serpent."[32]

The serpent's intercession also turned Kafka in Siřem associable. Apart from being aloof to the neighbors, he started neglecting communication with the family and resisting visits even of his closest friends. Actually, as he put it to Oskar Baum, he would have welcomed all of them in the first week and perhaps in the second, but things changed since the third week. He lost the rationale for inviting them. Why did Kafka suddenly turn into a recluse? He looked for "complete solitude in order to solidify certain adjustments," he fogged the answer.[33] More than anything else, we may assume, he needed no witness to his blossoming romance with Ottla. To dispel his friend's suspicion, he portrayed her as constantly and heroically at work in the household. In truth, the hop harvest season had ended, and Ottla employed two maids for domestic chores.

Max Brod was unrelenting in the effort to reform his best friend and apportion the blame for his failings. In the aftermath of Kafka's latest checkup by Professor Pick, he reproached Felix Weltsch in whose apartment Kafka had been introduced to opium smoking and probably engaged in it there after his family's resistance forced him to give it up at home. Weltsch now wondered why he, and specifically his living quarters, had become "an innocent target of these controversies."[34] On November 8, Brod also issued a direct challenge to Kafka, vowing to force him in cooperation with his parents to relocate to a sanatorium in the south unless he changed his ways. He also announced firmly his arrival in Siřem for early December 1917.

In this situation, Kafka found a convenient scarecrow, mice. Would not his urbanite friends find the rodent repugnant? Framing it as the incurable failing of Siřem, in mid-November, he reported to Weltsch a dreadful night, when not one but a "whole swarm" of mice leaped down together from somewhere. The critters, he claimed, had left him defenseless and speechless, and eventually spoiled everything. Even the smell and taste of the rustic bread was mousy, he wished Weltsch to believe. Max Brod too learned about the "plague of mice" in Siřem that even a borrowed cat failed to stop. The nocturnal visitors and the weird cat with "pricked ears and glowing eyes" evoked "sheer terror" in Kafka.[35]

Dutifully retold by biographers, these mice stories have amused generations of readers, but neither Weltsch nor Brod. The latter penned a sarcastic retort. "Your mouse letter . . . has almost floored me," he told Kafka, advising him to relocate into a "mouse-free" sanatorium.[36] It prompted the recipient to backpedal in mid-December: "A misunderstanding: the mice caused me no sleepless nights except for the first fantastic one." Similarly, he assured Oskar Baum that his mice alarm was only in fun.[37] Baum and his family could visit as it pleased them now. Weltsch received an open invitation retroactively on December 20: "If only you had come . . .

everything I am and have in Siřem . . . would have been at your disposal."[38] No longer keen on visiting, Brod found various excuses to stay clear of Siřem. So far as we know, during Kafka's nearly eight months' stay in the village, he would meet him only at the railway station in Měcholupy.

Mice also served Kafka to break other awkward news. Reporting on the invasion of the freewheeling critters to Brod, he claimed that to escape them, he moved to his sister's quarters. In consequence, he was nearly incapable of writing in the evening, and mouse caught up with him even there. Furthermore, since he and Ottla were also having "breakfast in the bed" and were getting up late, his day was short and offered little time for writing as well. Still, a relocation to a sanatorium was out of the question, he informed Brod, claiming his health was unfailingly good: "Even Dr. Pick said nothing about the south."[39] How much Kafka enjoyed the "small marriage" with Ottla in the cold Bohemian village!

All this, however, cumulatively impacted his conscience. As he put it defensively during the Siřem escapade, he was not really following the demands of a supreme judgment but rather living up to the standard of humanity. "My sole concern is the human tribunal, which I wish to deceive . . . though without practicing any actual deception."[40] Indeed, he simulated tuberculosis to effect the release from work and his engagement to Felice Bauer; he pretended mental exhaustion to justify both to his parents; he was in an incestuous relationship that needed camouflage; and he resorted to white lies to fend off his friends' poking visits as long as possible.

"There is marked impairment in the ethical feelings of previously honest persons" who succumb to drugs, a contemporary specialist observed.[41]

In an unsparing self-review of mid-November 1917, Kafka blamed himself for failing "as has no one else around me . . . I cannot acquit myself properly here." Perennially invoking suicide, he now accepted the prospect of "a wretched life and a wretched death." Overall, he described his fate by the last sentence of *The Trial*: "It seemed as though the shame was to outlive him."[42]

In spite of his secular exterior, Kafka can be characterized as a religious atheist; his overall sense of morality, sin and evil had a religious connotation. Thus, *The Blue Octavo* notes show him struggling mightily to reconcile with the Bible and Ten Commandments. The biblical "evil" crops up in this text in a variety of permutations. It is everywhere and in everything, part of human frailty: "The ulterior motives with which you absorb and assimilate Evil are not your own but those of Evil." True, "one must not cheat anyone," but that requires self-control. Since self-control was not Kafka's strength considering his lifestyle, he wished to restrict himself to "tell fewest lies" rather than to "give oneself the fewest opportunities of telling lies."[43] (One can detect in this an echo of the Great Inquisitor in *The Brothers Karamazov*.) Lacking self-control, he could not resist the opportunities offered by evil and hence needed deception and lies to cover them up.

One source of Kafka's Evil was obviously drugs. A "horde of devils" drove him "into the Good" by "pin points pricking" him all over, he alluded to the effect of syringes. And once the good clawed him, he sadly fell back into evil.[44] Kafka's life was a series of temporary emancipation from and relapses into narcotics.

Still more burdensome for the writer of *Blue Octavo* was his sexual life in Siřem. In other times and other places, Kafka casually followed in words and deeds his heterosexual urges, showing no regret bedding numerous *femmes* (at least six of them since the start of the Great War), cavorting with prostitutes, mixing "a little bit of sulfur, a little bit of hell," or eventually dating the wife of his Prague compatriot Ernst Polak. In his novels, he also depicted women's loose ways but attached no emotional weight to it. In contrast, although his Siřem liaison was physical, "apprehensible to the senses,"[45] it was as much sinful and evil as delightful. In his new perspective, a struggle with a woman that "ends in bed" carried a stigma that he had never experienced before.

A student of the Old Testament well into his adulthood, Kafka had the Jewish image of God as the Lord of Revenge entrenched in his mind. In the fall of 1917, then, he began seeking a biblical dispensation for his conduct in Siřem. Thus, considering himself a target of seduction, he found particularly resonant the analogy in the original sin. "Sometimes I feel I understand the Fall of Man better than anyone," he quipped. He also reminded himself, and on occasion Max Brod, that the expulsion from the Garden of Eden was Eve's doing "with the mediation by the serpent." More than simply a payback for seduction, he also became inclined to accept that sinning is the universal condition regardless whether one is sinful, guilty, or not guilty.[46]

While his main psychological burden used to be drug addiction and stories such as "The Judgment," *The Metamorphosis*, *The Trial*, and "In the Penal Colony" ended with retribution, Kafka now disassociated guilt and punishment—and started reconciling with sin and evil. Here are his maxims in the Siřem period: "Once we have taken Evil into ourselves, it no longer insists that we believe in it"; "Evil is an emanation of human consciousness"; "The Diabolical sometimes assumes the aspect of the Good"; "The clear conscience is Evil"; and "No one can crave what truly harms him."[47]

This process of self-exoneration primarily concerned sexual matters. "Sexual love deceives us to heavenly love"; in fact, it contains within itself, "unknowingly, a germ of heavenly love." While the expulsion from paradise was eternal and irreversible, the ultimate outcome is that "not only we could remain forever in Paradise, but that we are currently there, whether we know it or not." Similar to Dante's treatment of hell, purgatory, and the earthly paradise, the writer of *The Blue Octavo* felt chained to both the earth and heaven and thus was prevented from leaving either one. As he would put it in retrospect, "Through a heaven of vice, a hell of virtue is reached. So easily? So dirtily? So unbelievably." Thanks to one seductress Kafka, this foresworn pessimist was now living both in sin and in paradise.[48]

Absorbed as he was in his private affairs, Kafka struggled to regain interest in reading let alone writing. His nirvana in Siřem was devoid of books. Not that he had been deprived of rich, opium-sponsored dreams. In a page-long fragment, for example, he wonderfully recreated the atmosphere during the battle of the Tagliamento that pitted the Austrians against Italians. But as on other leaves of absence, he was much too distracted to summon discipline for work.

Pestered with Brod's letters that apparently were far from calm, Kafka eventually consented to another meeting with Felice Bauer in Prague. The notice of her impending arrival came by telegram on December 18 and caused a storm in Siřem. Next day, Kafka reported having the worst day so far in the village. There was this "great tide of unrest" reminiscent of Genesis and involving another person who, he hoped, "will gradually cease to feel."[49] Almost certainly, he referred to a quarrel with the explosive Ottla over Felice Bauer.

He met Felice in a last attempt at reconciliation in Prague over the Christmas 1917. As on other occasions, they kept postponing serious talk. Despite his friends' intercession, however, a definite breakup was inevitable. On the morning of her departure, December 27, Kafka laid out the case. As he presented it both to Felice and his family, the formal reason for canceling the engagement was solely his disease. In a perceptive observation of a conventional biographer, this explanation 'clearly masked some more awkward and undeclared issues.'[50]

The very same morning of December 27, however, Kafka also wept more than any time since childhood. He would explain it by the calmness and kindness with which Felice received the ultimate breakup, but there clearly was more to his crying. Along with Max Brod, Felice pressed him into a healthier, more disciplined lifestyle. It was the path he knew he should but would not take alone. The breakup with her threatened to leave him exposed to the vagaries of drug addiction. Thus, he felt both depressed and yet with nothing to regret when, on December 27, in the final farewell, he took Felice to the main train station in Prague. In retrospect, he would call her an "unbreakable, Prussian-Jewish mixture, a strong, triumphant mixture."[51]

Max Brod was anything but pleased with the outcome: the follow-up evening he and Kafka spent together was not good.

Felice hardly left Prague when Kafka received a "love letter" that, he replied to Ottla, he could not answer with love, though feeling lonesome in the city.[52]

Major hurdles, however, still lay ahead. His return to Siřem was disapproved by his family and friends alike, and his "mental tuberculosis" had given him only a tenuous justification for leave extension on medical grounds. Back in September, Professor Pick recommended him for a furlough subject to an arsenic cure and voluntary reduction of drugs (outwardly manifested in weight gain). However, Kafka ignored the conditions, and another exam on October 19 confirmed his health had worsened rather than improved while living in the countryside. Rightfully, he feared Dr. Pick was ready to cut his leave short: "When I next see Dr. Pick, he will want to send me back to the Institute for the winter."[53] After spending almost four months in the fresh air of Siřem, Kafka coughed heavily on a date with Brod in Prague by the yearend.

On December 27, the very same day as Felice departed, then, Kafka willy-nilly went unannounced to see Pick again. However, the professor was unavailable until the following week, and Kafka presented himself instead to Dr. Mühlstein, the family doctor who denied him time off back in September. This time, Mühlstein could hear nothing at all, Kafka reported, even though he tried to cough and sniff more than usual. According to his not necessarily accurate claim, Mühlstein merely conceded him a moral right to request a pension. There was little chance Kafka's leave would be extended on bona fide medical grounds. But far more was at stake than a termination of his leave in December 1917. Since Kafka had after all been found fit for the home guard, he also needed to have his war-exempt status renewed to avoid the draft—and retain job.

Surprisingly, Kafka scaled these formidable barriers and more in short time. As, once again, no paper trail of this feat has been left in his employment file, an informed hypothesis must fill the gap. After the institute's head Oswald Přibram died in September 1917, the management split along the ethnic lines between Germans and Czechs, seriously weakening the central authority. The waning war prospect of Germany and Austria-Hungary added to the overall apathy and malaise. This gave more weight to particular interests and assertive individuals like Eugen Pfohl.

As we know, Kafka had a symbiotic relationship with his immediate boss, exploiting his health liabilities and possibly bisexual inclinations. Just as the imaginary head porter in *Amerika* vowed to never let Karl Rossman leave the "Hotel Occidental" he worked in, the real-life Pfohl also felt confident in November 1917 that he would prevent Franz from giving notice and let him stay in the country until something was decided.[54]

There may have been more to it, however: Pfohl also was on the hunt for material gains. Already prior to the Great War, he formally complained about inadequate pay and lack of respect. Struggling with war deprivations, during Kafka's days in Siřem, he invited himself to the village, asked for favors in the form of food articles, and solicited illicit trade of rabbits and partridges for money and tobacco goods. In addition, Pfohl had a son, Hans, who, like Kafka, was exempt from the draft, and his case was likewise due for review by early 1918. Bribery could keep both young men away from military service.

Pfohl's visit in Siřem in the critical December days, then, apparently led to a quid pro quo understanding that involved money. It prompted Kafka to gush about a "very friendly relationship" with the *Oberinspektor*.[55] Almost certainly, also, the prospective money-bag holder was Kafka's father, Hermann. Seriously in the money, in January 1918, he would buy an apartment building at 4 Bílkova Street for five hundred thousand crowns cash, the equivalent of several million U.S. dollars today. The junior Kafka had the habit of portraying him as an insensitive bully, but his disdain was opportunistic. Aware that his first book, *Meditations*, sold between one hundred and two hundred copies annually, he could hardly expect to earn decent living as a freelance. His father's support would have been expedient.

There is no doubt Herr Kafka was eager to keep his son out of harm's way. Along with his wife, however, he begrudged their children's Siřem adventure. In Prague for Christmas, the junior Kafka found the atmosphere at home very tense. It helped little that the father was so insensitive as to "tell . . . <u>everything</u>" to mother Julie, he reported to Ottla, stressing "everything." Frau Kafka, a caring and concerned mother, started eating very lightly and wondered aloud why Ottla needed to stay in Siřem any longer employing two maidservants. With the harvest completed, there indeed was no need for it. And now, her son proved keen on returning to the village as well.

There was again a "great fuss" at 6 Oldtown Square in the evening of Saturday, December 29, when it became obvious the two siblings intended to renew their relationship in Siřem. Kafka deflected the objections, arguing that their "abnormal behavior" was not so bad, compared to "normality" of the Great War.[56] In Kafka's microcosm, making love, any love, was more ethical than making war.

Next day, taking the blame on himself, the junior Kafka advised Ottla to push aside qualms and self-censures regarding their supposed craziness and desertion of their parents. What they had done to relieve themselves from the "burden" was proper. It was the urge of nature that had brought them into a conflict with social norm and kindled family revulsion.[57] His argument proved effective: on December 29, Herr and Frau Kafka apparently dropped resistance to their son's rejoining Ottla in Siřem, and Herr Kafka opened his valet.

There is a distinct tendency among biographers to accept uncritically Kafka's grumbling about the lack of support and mean-spiritedness of his father. In truth, Herr Kafka had rough edges but, in testimony of his granddaughter Věra, overall was a benevolent and loving family person. One cannot but concur with Frau Kafka's observation that anyone else in her son's place would be the "happiest of mortals, for his parents have never denied him any wish."[58]

On December 30, then, Franz advised Ottla important developments had taken place in prior days and expressed—for him a highly unusual—deference for their father's harping. As long as the siblings needed his help, they had to yield in some way. Saving appearances was important for this well-regarded family, and this now entailed allowing friends' visits in

Siřem. "Under the menace of Father," they needed to invite at least their blind friend Oskar Baum, Ottla learned. No matter how inconvenient, Kafka added, Baum's presence would be "trivial compared with the good that those last days have brought me."[59]

A major hurdle was overcome. However, as the war-exempt clerk, Kafka was ineligible for and unlikely to extract another leave from his doctors or his boss Marschner. Still in Prague, on January 2 (1918), he informed Ottla in Siřem that the director was raising objections. Perhaps he was too healthy and only giving notice would set him free, he wrote to Ottla cockily. Yet within a few days, Kafka was both exempted from the draft and had his vacation extended by a mind-boggling four months. Once again, he apparently accomplished this feat without any paper trail, supportive medical opinion, or petition to the director.

Deftness complemented with subornation would explain why Kafka achieved such a fabulous break and so fast. In a letter to Brod, he commented cryptically on favors he expected to receive from his superiors: "Certain things cannot be explained to certain people, especially by a certain person."[60]

Pfohl's son also avoided the draft—an occasion that, in turn, prompted Pfohl to thank Kafka for his assistance. The gambit worked for both sides well, and, to Kafka's relief, "no one seems to have noticed anything unusual."[61]

Kafka's days in Siřem followed the established routine in 1918. For his friends, he presented himself as entirely healthy except for a sore thumb. As expected from an addict, however, he felt hazy, weak, impatient, and stripped of desire to do anything. On occasion, he also recorded in *Blue Octavo* opiatic dreams straddling reality such as that of a horse that broke the roof of "our room."[62] Obviously, he still shared Ottla's quarters, but his *Blue Octavo* notes offer fewer steamy bedroom tidbits. Missing was the passion of the first months in Siřem.

In truth, remorse for engaging in uncouth sex asserted itself. In February 1918, Kafka observed that the "woman's glance into her bed leads to seduction—and this is "the worst thing" for it means that "Good has lured us into Evil."[63] His moralizing about "the great primal deception" was still anchored on the Bible and the fear of retribution but was giving way to musing about the tree of knowledge and tree of life. After another trip to Prague in mid-February 1918, he stopped using dates in *Blue Octavo* and confined his entries to philosophizing and short stories. In a parallel effort, he once again resorted to his favorite existentialist: "Kierkegaard is always in my mind."[64]

As his romance with Ottla was losing intensity in 1918, a sense of isolation started troubling him. How much he now missed Oskar Baum, and Brod needed to be told how lovely and serene it was in Siřem.

Judged by Ottla's casual remark, there also were more disputes between the siblings in the spring of 1918. Overall, however, Kafka complimented Ottla when on another visit to Prague in early March, "We do live or I live with you better than with anybody else."[65] He also came to appreciate both the simplicity of existence in Siřem, reporting with undisguised pride Ottla's carting goat manure, and his washing naked in freezing temperatures. "There is no more comfortable and above all freer life than that in a village," he claimed, repeating his wish to live there always.[66]

His appreciation was also growing for the villagers eking out living in modest circumstances. At one point and rather uncharacteristically for him, he even displayed his anarchistic bent: his page-long draft "The Brotherhood of Poor Workers" outlined a social order that, based on mutual trust, would do without money, property, and wages but would provisionally exclude independent persons, the married and women.[67]

His return to Prague promised to be hard, Kafka feared. But when the day arrived, he did not fight it. He departed from Siřem by the end of April (1918), leaving Ottla behind. From Prague, he assured her playfully that he would like to "bend your ear; I've tried it with Elli [his other sister] but it's not the right thing."[68] It did not portend well for his establishing a healthy relationship with another woman. When he came across a worthy prospect, Milena Jesenská, he still reminisced about his eight months in Siřem, the best time of his life, when he was "protected by . . . illness." And all his living in this paradise required was "very little change . . . merely to redraw the old narrow outlines of . . . [his] character a little more firmly."[69]

1918: MAYHEM IN PRAGUE

On May 2, 1918, Kafka at last resumed work at the Institute of Workers' Accident Insurance, richer in pleasant memories and poorer in social interaction. His lengthy seclusion in Siřem damaged his friendships; the contacts with Prague friends became less frequent. No longer in need of appeasing his father, Kafka also resumed treating him with truculence. The roots of antagonism were deep. As before, he also declined cooperation with a literary magazine. Unable to produce any serious bloc of writing in Siřem, he angered the publisher Wolff. "He does not answer, sends me nothing," Kafka lamented.[1]

Max Brod, who had so valiantly tried to rescue Kafka's body and soul, also became apathetic. In 1918, he published another novel, *Das grosse Wagnis* (*Great Risk*). Literary historians associate the novel's protagonist, the half-mad Dr. Askonas who leads a crowd of refugees from ordinary life, with the real-life psychologist Otto Gross. As we know, this heavy addict in 1917 contemplated a journal devoted to defying the will to power and discussed the project with the fellow traveler Kafka at Brod's. While Kafka showed keen interest, Brod was dismayed. The novel then meshed a spoof on Gross with a commentary on war, faddish contemporaries, Judaism, as well as dependence on dreams in writing, the "darkness of opium," and need for true love. "The real love is completely remote and totally independent of sensuous fire."[2]

Similar as Kafka in *The Trial*, Brod, so he claimed, portrayed himself in *Das grosse Wagnis* in three persons. Kafka likewise seems to be profiled here as a friend of Askonas, a poet, and the salient points of this book can be interpreted as a metaphor of Brod's objections to his friend's lifestyle.

No wonder Kafka responded with irony to three parts of the manuscript that Brod read him in late 1917.

Despite his literary silence, Kafka also returned from Siřem with his health at least as compromised as before. His insomnia was bad, and his breathing, about which he had already been complaining intermittently, turned worse. But tuberculosis was not the culprit. A new checkup by Dr. Pick confirmed his lungs were very good. Since he could ill-afford opium smoking in the family apartment, he apparently went back to opiates. As he confessed to Brod, "I consist only from needles that stab me and if I want to defend myself . . . I can only arrange the needles to stab me better."[3]

Within weeks of returning from Siřem, Kafka sought relief in manual labor once again. In the summer of 1918, he obtained yet another break, this time for gardening in Prague's northern suburb of Troja. Subsequently, in September 1918, he took three additional weeks off to work for a gardener in Turnov (Turnau), a town in Northeastern Bohemia.

Meanwhile, as if the war massacres were not devastating enough, a virulent pandemic engulfed the world. Known in history as the Spanish flu, it eventually killed twenty-one million, more than all war operations combined. In mid-October 1918, Kafka too fell ill with a high fever. In the three weeks he spent sick in bed, a momentous chain of events started taking place—the military collapse of Germany and Austria-Hungary ending the Great War, the redrawing of the political map of Europe, and the declaration of independence by nations hitherto under the umbrella of the Austro-Hungarian Empire.

On October 28, Czechoslovakia came into existence, a republic with the moralist professor T. G. Masaryk as its president, comprising Bohemia, Moravia, and Slovakia. Inhabited predominantly by the closely related Czechs and Slovaks, it was also a home to sizable minorities including Germans and Jews. The Jewish population, which during the war on the whole took the Habsburg side, faced a still more uncertain future.

There were also troubles in the Kafka family and not of the material kind. After buying the apartment building for cash in January 1918, Herr Kafka sold his wholesale business to a relative, Bedřich Löwy, intent on enjoying a worry-free retirement. There was no need for Ottla to tend the store again. Yet her brother-in-law Karl Hermann asked her to leave Siřem in the summer of 1918, and she complied in October of that year. It was supposed to be the moment of a joyous homecoming, but the family was far from thrilled with her in the fold. In fact, both parents showed displeasure if not anger. After a brief stay at home, Ottla left Prague again for the North Bohemian town of Frýdlant (Friedland), ostensibly to enroll in the local agricultural school. She contemplated a similar action in the past, but was it needed after her seventeen months of hands-on experience in Siřem and in such haste?

It appears that Ottla had enraged her parents by offensive behavior. As Frau Kafka would castigate her in retrospect, "You have done serious things that we did not think right."[4] Her moving out of sight was in compliance with her parents, but not her brother. Ten days after her departure and still fighting the flu, Kafka junior sent her warm words of encouragement, promising food parcels to keep her healthy. It would be admirable if she stayed in Frýdlant, but he would support her return home as well. With Siřem memories still fresh, he added a blunt warning against leaving half-written letters in her textbooks for fear they may fall out and be passed around the class. They could embarrass or discredit her.

The Kafkas were no doubt distressed by their children's cohabitation in Siřem and the aftermath. A month after Ottla left for Frýdlant and still troubled, Frau Kafka invited her innocently back home on November 14. But there was a catch: Ottla would have to accept changes in the apartment setup. While she would have her little room back, Franz had been moved into the parents' room for the sake of his comfort and peace. Comfort and peace? Franz's new chamber was accessible only through a connecting room now controlled by his parents. The rearrangement made it much harder for the siblings to catch unguarded moments. Ottla exploded in fury on getting this news, prompting her mother to pen a defensive response on November 20.

In search of defusing the crisis, the Kafkas stumbled on Josef David. One year Ottla's senior, he was one of three children of a modest Czech family and a Catholic. An ambitious hard worker who studied on the Kaiser's stipend and considered B mark a failure, he left for London in 1913 to earn money as a waiter and piano player in silent movies. Back in Prague just before the outbreak of the Great War, he worked as administrative clerk intent on becoming a lawyer. Ottla introduced him to Franz in the downtown park in March 1915, but David was soon drafted into the Austrian army to serve in a logistic depository on the Italian front. She had probably known him since prewar days and treated him merely as a friend.

Formally discharged from the military service on December 6, 1918, David was in Prague already in late November. On learning about his existence at last, the Kafkas invited him for a talk on short notice. They also contemplated bringing in Ottla from Frýdlant, but she rejected the invite angrily. She was neither informed about David's demobilization nor interested in meeting him now.

Franz Kafka was not a party to this. Trying to keep up with so many challenges, he suffered a mental collapse surpassing his suicidal mood in the fall of 1914 (which was brought about by Grete Bloch's pregnancy). On November 19, one day after his return to work from flu, his doctor Král issued a certificate suggesting a new lung inflammation had aggravated his lung catarrh and recommended at least a four to five weeks' rest in the country. In a cover letter to the head inspector, Kafka claimed that until the outbreak of the flu a month earlier, he had nothing to complain about his lungs. Ever since the flu gripped him, however, the inflammation and mild fever reappeared.

Thus, even though he had already spent five months on a paid leave in 1918, Kafka extricated himself once again from work and, on November 30, lodged at Pension Stüdl in Želízy (Schelesen), some fifty kilometers north of Prague. He was the only boarder there for a time.

With Ottla in Frýdlant and Franz in or about to be deposited in Želízy, the anxious parents met David without delay. Though this potential suitor spoke German in addition to French and English, he communicated with the Kafkas only in Czech. Frau Kafka subsequently reported that he came across as a goodhearted and intelligent person but struck the family as very alien. His small salary and religion, in particular, concerned her husband.

Far from being happy, however, Ottla was still in no hurry to meet David. Instead, she mailed him a letter from Frýdlant asking for forgiveness for her lack of interest. Since he had so far been unknown to her parents, which suited her fine, she did not expect them to issue an invite for serious talk and certainly not that fast. Ottla's heart was elsewhere. She reserved more resolute words of rejection for her parents. The mail exchange apparently angered but not deterred Frau Kafka and her husband. As Franz reported from Želízy on December 11, referring to her mother, there were follow-up meetings with David in Prague that went fine.

The family castaways now, the two siblings fell back on their Siřem memories. Christmas was approaching, for many Prague Jews a period of festivities. Should Franz travel all the way to Frýdlant to spend the holidays with Ottla there? On second thought, he suggested joint Christmas at Želízy or, alternatively, back home in Prague.

Kafka eventually returned for holidays to Prague, but Ottla did not. In late December, Frau Kafka conveyed her a generous offer: the family would buy her and David a farm in Šumava, the mountain range straddling Bohemia and Bavaria and one of the family's favorite vacation regions. That would have sealed the marriage of convenience, but Ottla was in no mood to accept. While quarreling with her parents, she wrote to David in early January 1919 that they were separated for an indefinite time. A week later, she confirmed her lack of interest: David needed to know she felt at ease only when alone or in the company of her cousin Irma and her brother Franz.

David also had reservations, fearing the Jewish community would shun him (to which Ottla answered that not all Jews view Gentiles negatively). But his social status was rising as the war veteran and member of the now dominant ethnic group in the country. He remained loosely associated with the Kafkas.

After about ten weeks of turmoil, emotions in the Kafka family showed an ebbing at last. Still in Frýdlant, Ottla relented somewhat, prompting Frau Kafka to express relief on January 10 (1919). She accepted gladly her daughter's admission that she had done a wrong thing. As the rumor of Ottla's possible marriage to David spread, the danger also receded of a possible embarrassment over her personal failings. That notwithstanding, while Frau Kafka took a conciliatory stand, the same could not be said about her husband, still resentful of Ottla and reserved about David. Thus, on January 24, when Ottla asked for permission to come home for a short while, the response obviously was not encouraging. She stayed put in Frýdlant.

In mid-February, Ottla, at last, met Josef David in a nearby town, but the outcome was inconclusive. In a follow-up letter to him, she regretted resisting her parents' prodding for nuptials but stood firm. She could not accept marriage and certainly not that quickly; therefore, she needed to find a job.

Thus, when she eventually paid a short visit to Prague in late February, her presence still strained her parents. Franz Kafka would report back to her, "Mother writes about her own distress and even greater distress on Father's part as if there still was much more to pass over in silence."[5] As far as the Kafkas were concerned, the crisis was contained but not resolved; Ottla remained the black sheep of the family.

Meanwhile, Franz returned to work on January 4 (1919). After the proclamation of Czechoslovakia several weeks earlier, the Institute of Workers' Accident Insurance underwent mainly cosmetic changes. His superiors, director Marschner and inspector Pfohl, were replaced by a Czech board of directors, and all written communication was in Czech. The German-speaking employees were reappointed provided they met the new requirements. The emphasis was on continuity. Since Kafka had been brought up by Czech nannies and took Czech lessons privately, he qualified, now going as František Kafka.

In addition, although more than a dozen exams between 1917 and his retirement in 1922 alone would confirm his nontubercular status, he was spared of the need to insinuate tuberculosis. The new director of the institute, Dr. Bedřich Odstrčil, a university professor and acquaintance of President Masaryk—in Kafka's view "an incredibly decent man"[6]—was himself unsound healthwise and died one year after Kafka at the age of forty-eight. With his superiors dedicated to sickness prevention and living in a society accustomed to Kafkaesque associations, Kafka was able to extract long absences from work on account of his "lung disease" and progressive health degradation.

Thus, shortly after resuming work in the reconstituted institute in January 1919, Kafka petitioned the management for three more months off for a stay in countryside. In his justification, supported by the institute's doctor Josef Popper, he stated, "I have been suffering from the inflammation of lung tips since 1917."[7] He was granted a three-week leave on the understanding he would resume work immediately if needed. The leave started on January 22—and less than two weeks later, Kafka requested another two-month extension, supported by another opinion of Dr. Popper. This time, though, the physician stipulated Kafka should place himself under medical supervision, preferably, if his financial means permitted, at an institute specializing in lung diseases.

Kafka was not tubercular: if he were, he would have been assigned to a specialized sanatorium—there were newly built ones around Prague and in the mountains—and his expenses could have been covered by the state. Still, the institute gave him four more weeks off to March 11.

Settled in Želízy again, Kafka resumed tender correspondence with Ottla still farther north in Frýdlant. Certainly, she was pleased reading his brief note suggestive of intimacy: in a dream, he heard her whispering "Franz" at the door of his room; he answered at once but nothing more happened. "What did you want?" he asked now. Ottla responded with another "very private letter," which prompted him to divert attention to her school assignment.[8] In another suggestive dream, he associated her with a small child he pushed around in a baby carriage. At the same time, he turned attention to her status and conceded that losing identity by marriage to a Gentile was such a difficult issue. Still, he was mildly supportive of her marrying David even though she would be stepping out of line.

Meanwhile, Frau Kafka reported on an evening attended by David and her nephew Robert Kafka. To her and Herr Kafka's satisfaction, both the nephew and his wife, Else, found David to be a talented and trustworthy man and surely an achiever. But Ottla remained unmoved. She dropped fast her vague interest in agriculture and announced nonchalantly she would join Franz in Želízy and look for a job there. Life is too short, she claimed. Caught in a precarious dilemma (more on this below), her brother, at first, showed reservation but eventually relented. He had nothing against her trip, "especially if you can guarantee me the anticipatory pleasure."[9] The siblings were still emotionally so close. But then, rather than inviting her to Želízy, he arranged a job interview for her in Prague.

He had a reason to be less than keen on welcoming Ottla in Želízy. On his latest stay there in Pension Stüdl, another guest caught his interest, Julie Wohryzek, age twenty-eight. A daughter of a shames in a Prague synagogue and a mild Zionist, she was livelier than Felice Bauer but also less sophisticated as a graduate of a junior commerce college. Kafka assessed her as a cheerful butterfly, hooked on the movies, operettas, and comedies: "If one wanted to classify her racially, one would have to say that she belongs to the race of shop girls."[10] Having lost her boyfriend in the war, she was available.

According to Kafka's biographers, Julie Wohryzek, who was quite thin, also suffered from tuberculosis. Yet, as we know, Kafka was nauseated by tubercular people. There is little doubt that if she had the disease, he would have stayed clear. In his early assessment, she had only a minor health issue. Wohryzek indeed shared his condition, pulmonary catarrh, and probably his taste for drugs as well. He positively found her attractive for resembling his onetime lover Grete Bloch, who struggled with the same. Modern research confirms anecdotal evidence that people with restrictive habits or handicaps prefer partners with similar conditions or lifestyle by far.

Reluctant to spoil his budding romance in Želízy, Kafka approached the local physician Dr. Ernst Fröhlich with a request for another extension of his leave. The doctor too refrained from calling the patient tubercular but confirmed an extension was desirable until at least the end of March 1919. The request granted, Kafka at last returned to Prague and resumed work at the institute by the end of that month. He also started dating Wohryzek openly. As the bond was getting stronger, his attachment to Ottla weakened. In anticipation of a new chapter in his private life, he probably also cleansed his diaries of indiscreet segments related to Ottla before starting a new log on June 27 (1919).

Kafka's parents had every reason to consider the Wohryzeks below their status, but they were not bigoted. The husband of their daughter Valli was also of modest means, as was the prospective groom, Josef David. In view of Franz's addiction, however, Herr Kafka found it expedient to remind him again and again that a marriage without financial resources is a misfortune. That notwithstanding, Franz and Julie Wohryzek became engaged in September 1919, and by the end of the following month, the Prague magistrate received notice of their impending wedding. It was slated for the first week of November.

Just before the wedding day, however, Kafka backed out. Taking his vacation time or another undocumented leave, he went again to Želízy on Tuesday, November 4, accompanied for a few days by Brod. The latter's presence suggests he disapproved of Julie for some reason. In this, we may assume, he was seconded by Ottla. She had been fairly detached lately but, on Brod's return to Prague, asked Franz for permission to visit him along with Oskar Baum. Her brother, however, at first, extended a rather casual invitation only, "If the impulse strikes you."

His lukewarm attitude can be ascribed to his flirt with another guest at the pension, Minze Eisner. The attractive eighteen-year-old teenager from the North Bohemian town of Teplice, however, was much too young and unsophisticated to make a dent in his emotional armory. More a mentor than a suitor, he would eventually keep epistolary contact with her, dishing out advice on health and life choices. On second thought, then, he urged Ottla definitely to come to Želízy with or without Baum. He was aching, barely able to write about her.

The prospect of Ottla's visit also made him still more assertive. On Friday, November 14, without much ado, Kafka advised his new department head Jindřich Valenta, "I meant to return to work on Monday . . . But if the weather should remain as nice as today and yesterday, and if I am inclined to stay here another three days, then please, dear Mr. Valenta, be so kind and excuse my absence. I would then return on Thursday."[11] Never mind the weather: Ottla did arrive, and the two spent several discreet days together in Želízy once again. As a result, he indeed postponed returning to work until Thursday, November 20.

While in Želízy, sharing life solely with Ottla once more, Kafka addressed the issue that had burdened the whole family at least since their Siřem adventure. He did so in a lengthy *Letter to His Father*, ostensibly a cathartic account of a troubled father-son relationship but in reality much more than that. The *Letter* opens with a grudging recognition that, thanks to father, the author could live "high and handsome" without showing any gratitude. Then, however, follows a litany of complaints against the paternoster, his imperiousness and insensitivity to his children, his success in business, and his superior physical and mental assets. Living under "heavy pressure" of the father's personality had led the son to "defiance, dislike and even hate." Herr Kafka was ultimately at guilt for ever walking on this planet.

Franz Kafka himself later characterized his whining letter as lawyerly constructed and dismissed it as bad and needless. Apart from hurling accusations at his father, it indeed carried, in Brod's characterization, "a general load of fear, weakness, and self-contempt."[12] Clearly, the two failed engagements to Felice Bauer and Julie Wohryzek added to Kafka's anguish. Circling around the most burning family issue, however, he conceded to his father, "You really suffered a great deal because of your children." By this concession, Kafka primarily meant him and Ottla: there still was a "terrible trial . . . tending between us and you," and it was not of Herr Kafka's doing. The rift concerned "things hard to confess" and imparted the son with a "boundless sense of guilt and shame." In this context, he alluded to Siřem and "accompanying circumstances." Overall, his sense of guilt and the source of friction stemmed from his "superhuman effort of wanting to marry."

One can hardly dodge the verdict that Kafka's principle motivation behind *Letter to His Father* was to atone for his illicit relationship with Ottla. However, with Ottla on his side, ultimately, he again turned the arrow against his father, declaring his quest for a mate and marriage to be the "most grandiose . . . attempts at escape" from harassment at home.[13] If this were the root cause of his resentment, needless to say, the thirty-six-year-old civil servant with a comfortable salary could easily afford living in a place of his own.

Kafka read the *Letter* to Ottla in Želízy and eventually passed it to his mother. However, there was little in this self-serving text that needed dissemination, and Frau Kafka returned it, probably unread by her husband.

Back at work in November 1919, Kafka also felt it desirable to justify his latest flop regarding Julie Wohryzek. In a long letter penned on the twenty-fourth and addressed to her elder sister Käthe, he claimed their marriage, despite his father's short-lived opposition, would have been that of love. But he also realized nuptials were not for him, and after the couple failed to secure an apartment on Friday, he backed out on Sunday. It was a silly replay of his treatment of Felice Bauer. In Julie's case, he was at least willing to try cohabitation outside marriage, despite all his weakness. He also felt it desirable to assure Wohryzek that Ottla was aware of his suggestion.

As Kafka's romance with Wohryzek was cooling off, Ottla reeled back into his mind. Retained in his Želízy memory was the bath that so delighted her, he would remind her. Subsequently, he also recorded in his diary reaching a "heaven of vice" through a "hell of virtue."[14] This was the same biblical, exculpatory language that, we know, he cultivated during his "small marriage" with Ottla in Siřem. But his perception of Ottla was changing again in the front weeks of 1920.

Ottla's Marriage

With the formation of Czechoslovakia in the fall of 1918, the pecking order in society also underwent subtle but perceptible changes. Even though the new country was a multinational state with fairly extensive and actionable minority and religious rights, Czechs and Slovaks became the leading nationalities. By 1921, only 354,000 citizens of Czechoslovakia, or 2.6 percent of the total population, declared themselves Jewish by religion, of which some 31,000 lived in Prague, amounting to 4.7 percent of the city populace. Thus, from Kafka's perspective, the Jews—still primarily German speaking—had "much in common such as industriousness" with Germans but felt like outcasts in the new state.[1] As he put it to Brod in 1921, "Most young Jews who began to write German wanted to leave Jewishness behind them, and their fathers approved of this but vaguely . . . But with their posterior legs they were still tied to their fathers' Jewishness and with their waving anterior legs they found no new ground."[2]

In addition, the general discontent in the wake of the Great War disproportionally impacted the Jews of Central Europe, now blamed for the failed war expectations and the postwar malaise. Anti-Jewish pogroms reoccurred in numerous places, nurtured also by the political prejudice associating Jews with the bogey of Bolshevism and communism.

Kafka, however, encountered no problems at work on account of his Jewishness. In fact, he continued to be pampered as ever by the new Czech management. In another gesture of accommodation, in 1920, he became a secretary dealing with legal matters. The new position relieved him from trips to various enterprises throughout the country and from communicating with clients, the responsibility made increasingly difficult by his worsening cough and physical weakness. Despite his sporadic work record, he also received a generous pay raise to 6,500 crowns monthly, the equivalent of US$6,000 today, to become the highest-paid non-Czech employee of the institute.

At work, Kafka also connected with his first Czech admirer, Gustav Janouch. A teenage son of his colleague, Janouch met Kafka for the first time probably in the spring of 1920. Restless and inquisitive, he kept coming back during Kafka's workdays to exchange ideas and books. His recollections, almost certainly written much later, were eventually published as *Conversations with Kafka* to the harsh response of some Kafka aficionados. True, his narrative is too rich in detail and fairly self-indulgent to be accepted verbatim. But Kafka's two intimates, Max Brod and Dora Diamant, found Janouch's account credible, and Brod even helped edit it. It represents a flawed but liveliest recollection of the writer by far.

The Kafka whom Janouch encountered was built for a robust person like his father, with "large, strong hands, broad palms . . . and prominent bones and knuckles. Just the flesh was missing. He spoke in a muted, melodious baritone," but his German had a hard accent similar to the German spoken by Czechs. His voice, demeanor, and personality all "radiated the peace of understanding and goodness," we learn. He also was "obsessively clean, and in the office washed his hands every other minute." Still, a dry, convulsive cough intermittently inhibited his speech and left him embarrassed. Neither Janouch nor anyone else, however, observed him spitting mucus characteristic of tuberculosis.

On the other hand, Janouch noticed Kafka's brown face, the marker of opium addiction. As in the past several years, Kafka also showed other external signs of degradation, primarily weight loss and occasional periods of immobility that kept him absent from work. On one of those occasions, Janouch visited him at home, to find him struggling again with "a hollow, ugly cough" and flu-like symptoms. For good reason, Kafka denied it was a real flu: opium addicts repeatedly suffer from a virtual flu, runny nose, and watery eyes. Apart from that, Janouch would testify, Kafka could no longer engage in exercise and sport activities he had cherished in the past. In fact, still in his thirties, he could not handle the 150-meter incline of steps leading from Malá Strana to the Prague Castle.[3]

In Janouch's presence, Kafka also displayed a fear of modernity, of the coming age of "frictionless thinking madness," as well as the attitudes that go with addiction—pessimism about the course of society, the feeling of his own entrapment in a cage, in a hopeless prison, of carrying "the bars within . . . all the time." As on past occasions, he also barely concealed disgust with his lifestyle: "I am so corrupt and shameless . . . a piece of deceit. But after all, I am a lawyer . . . So I can never get away from the devil."[4] Other writers indulgent in opium were on his horizon as well—Edgar Allan Poe and Robert Louis Stevenson, whose *Treasure Island* he kept in the drawer.

Janouch appealed to him for a similar reason. As his young admirer admitted in a moment of candor, he was addicted to hashish. This made him Kafka's spiritual younger brother, emphatic to his musings about devils and demons. But Kafka would not divulge details of his own private life, limiting himself to glosses over his published works. In truth, unknown to Janouch, he was engrossed in his private affairs and produced no memorable texts in the first postwar years.

His comfortable life at Oldtown Square was once again interrupted by a crisis in the front weeks of 1920, possibly concerning his relationship with Ottla. One night in January 1920, his hopes in a marriage of convenience were dashed, and he suffered a breakdown.[5] His diary might reveal more, but Kafka subsequently tore off and destroyed all diary entries between February 1920 and October 1921. At the same time, his stress level and probably also drug intake were rising. By the end of February (1920), he was skipping work and lying sick in bed with mild fever, out of his "old habit that I can no longer shake off." His routine was "not a real sickness" and, therefore, left the doctors helpless in dealing with it. This is as far as Kafka went in admitting drugs, not tuberculosis, was his real health issue.[5]

Similar as Josef K. in *The Trial*, on occasion, he still liked or wished to find appealing the security of his narrowly circumscribed life: "My prison cell is also my fortress."[6]

Concurrent with his breakdown, Ottla gave up hopes of joining him in Želízy or elsewhere. In disregard as before of Josef David, she resumed daydreaming about becoming a farmer in Palestine. This in mind, she eyed another program for agriculturalists, this time in the distant Rhenish city Cologne-Opladen. She must have received the promise of financial support from her parents. The urgency that marked their insistence on her nuptial in late 1918 had obviously receded. Franz was also mildly supportive of her Cologne project, but Ottla eventually stayed put, possibly because the program was fully enrolled.

A major event changed the Kafkas' perspective in April 1920, though. Josef David, now a doctor of law, was appointed the secretary of the association of Czechoslovak insurance companies. It was a plum job with a comfortable salary that raised the thirty-year-old's prestige and social status. In this situation, Kafka appears to have resumed nudging Ottla to marrying David and probably was seconded by his parents.

Parallel with this effort, he became restless and contemplated getting away from Prague. A new checkup by Dr. Kodym, the public health officer working on behalf of the institute, reported "symptoms of significantly advanced infiltration of both lungs"—the condition present in but not equivalent of tuberculosis. In Kafka's case, it probably signaled a gradual accumulation of allergens and toxins from opium smoke. His occasional presence in the family asbestos business may have been a contributing factor. Thus, he was once again spared of the dreaded verdict of tuberculosis, and consequently, the doctor did not prescribe any drastic measures. Kafka was recommended for up to three months at a sanatorium for lung diseases. As always on earlier occasions, the choice was his.

In testimony of Jean Cocteau, sanatoria were not keen on accepting addicts who rarely recovered and damaged the institution's reputation. Bypassing again a sanatorium cure, Kafka took the new leave as another holiday. He first eyed going with Julie Wohryzek to Munich or the Bavarian Alps. With Ottla not yet fully agreeable to the marriage, in early April, he eventually left for Merano, a resort town nestled under the peaks of the Tyrolean Alps in the northernmost part of Italy. In anticipation of two months' stay, he settled not in a lung clinic but in the Ottoburg Inn, a small pension catering to affluent clientele.

If he had tuberculosis, he would have been barred from the premises. However, a checkup by the resident doctor Josef Kohn, who happened to hail from Prague, revealed nothing disturbing about his lungs; in fact, they were "excellent." The physician recommended merely valerian tea against insomnia and condoned Kafka's vegetarian diet—a nonstarter for a tubercular.

Merano belonged to the Habsburg Empire until the end of the Great War, and its inhabitants spoke German, giving Kafka some comfort. An elevated degree of privacy was his standard demand, and the pension complied with a room and balcony that allowed nudity—and use of an opium pipe. He also chose to take his meals at a separate table, an arrangement supportive of his habit of lengthy chewing of food. However, unable to eat and losing weight, he gave up the solitary seating soon. This meant joining the other guests, an odd mixture of Austrian bourgeoisie and officers.

There was a lot to muse about at the dinner table given the political turmoil in the postwar world. The Bolshevik revolution in Russia of 1917, which Kafka disapproved of, reverberated internationally and inspired copycat communist experiments in Hungary, Austria, and Germany. If only because of his anarchist leaning, Kafka followed with interest the Bavarian Soviet Republic, proclaimed by a group of literati and itinerant adventurers in Munich in March 1919. Like in other instances, this revolt was quashed by regular troops and its leader Eugen Leviné executed. These postwar anarcho-communist attempts to subvert the 'bourgeois' society were associated with the likes of Leon Trotsky, Rosa Luxemburg, Bela Kun, and Leviné, and fueled the fear of both communism and Jewish dominance. The postwar years had sown the ugly seeds of intolerance and fanaticism that Hitler would exploit so skillfully during his rise to power. In 1923, he too attempted a coup in Munich that, though a failure, solidified Nazism as a political force in Germany.

The characters that Kafka encountered in Merano were in general polite, but anti-Semitism troubled him even in a disguised form. In an exchange with Max Brod, he made spirited observations of the slights he was receiving as a Prague Jew from the other guests. Venturing still further from his shell, he also commented on the infamous *Protocols of the Elders of Zion*, calling them "at once stupid and frightening" and declared exasperatingly what a "terribly barren preoccupation anti-Semitism is and everything that goes with it."[7]

As on other occasions, existential nihilism also flared up in this sensitive, insecure writer. If Max Brod's life had a solid foundation, Kafka claimed, he had "nothing but a few beams" to prop up with his head, and his life hung unstably in the air. He was also troubled by the "usual devils of my days and nights"—an obvious allusion to drugs he could indulge in more freely in Merano than in Prague. Hence, he wrote to Brod that the specifics of his life in Merano could not be conveyed by writing.[8]

While in the resort, Kafka also resumed correspondence with Ottla, urging her to write about herself, her dreams and concerns. She unloaded on him, prompting a sheepish response: he did not expect her to write about troubles all that earnestly. Despite her laments about receiving a harsh treatment, he also kept prodding her to marry Josef David. Never mind that she felt unwanted and her prospective groom was aloof. Ottla needed to understand David took pleasure in his job and was cheerful, healthy, and socially acceptable. She was wrong believing he did not need her or was better without her. If they saw each other more often than on Friday and Saturday, she would have no reason to feel unwelcome.

Miserable and incommunicative, in mid-May, Ottla, at last, consented to marrying Josef David. The wedding was eventually set for July 15. Both she and Kafka reacted by expressing a sentiment improper for ordinary siblings. She blamed herself for doing him wrong by the marriage. In soothing response, Franz acknowledged, "We should not both marry, that would be horrible . . . since you certainly are more suitable for marriage, you will be doing it for us. This is quite simple and everybody is aware of it." Their relationship was apparently not secret anymore, and Kafka wished to preserve the bond by remaining "single for the two of us."[9]

In a biographer's view, Kafka considered Ottla's pending marriage a 'substitute act . . . of a symbolical incest.'[10]

At the same time, in anticipation of the loss of Ottla, Kafka began reviewing his past romances. He could no longer imagine tying the knot with Julie Wohryzek, but Felice Bauer still intrigued him, even though she was already married. Using Ottla as an intermediary, he hoped to coax her into a new letter exchange. She seemed so solid, so conscientious, and caring now. The failure to reengage her, or perhaps by extension Grete Bloch, made him remorseful. He wrote to Ottla on June 11, "I have harmed her in the worst possible way . . . This is how I am playing with a living human being."[11] It is unclear whether his regret concerned Felice Bauer, Grete Bloch, or Julie Wohryzek. All three deserved of it.

In May, Kafka also resolved on extending his stay in Merano, preferably by two months. That would keep him absent from Ottla's wedding. However, without a convincing diagnosis by Dr. Kohn, Kafka scaled down his expectations from two months of sick leave to five weeks of his normal vacations. Instructed accordingly, Ottla successfully pleaded his case with Director Odstrčil. Kafka was approved for five weeks until July 2. His benign lungs notwithstanding, he now assumed that the director was willing to retire him on pension: "It after all makes no sense to keep a civil servant . . . [who] has to be granted one leave after another."[12]

With Ottla grudgingly focused on her wedding, Kafka was free to put his mind and time into another courtship.

1920: MILENA JESENSKÁ

In his romantic adventures, Kafka opted almost exclusively for Jewish dates. Christian females seemed exotica to him. When, during his stay in Riva, he dated a Christian girl, he found her different and lived "almost entirely within the sphere of her influence."[1] His encounter with another Christian temptress in 1920 proved to be even more memorable.

Born in August 1896, Milena Jesenská was the only child of a prominent Prague dentist and university professor. Growing up in a world of privilege, she felt deprived of parental attention, in particular after her mother died in 1913. Even before she graduated from a private lyceum for girls, she was showing signs of alienation and rebelliousness. As a precocious teenager, she started frequenting Café Arco and other establishments in downtown Prague and developed craving for drugs. Doctors and pharmacists were at a higher risk of becoming addicts because of their access to narcotics, and Dr. Jesenský himself was dependent on morphine. Milena invaded his medicine supplies and also found narcotics so alluring. When this source dried out, to feed her thirst for the fix, she raided her father's bank account, stole his clothing, and piled up debt. In addition, she was also having love affairs with both sexes and managed to become pregnant. No wonder that, though she enrolled in medicine in 1915, she dropped out fast, and her attempt to study literature and journalism was equally short lived. In retrospect, she called it "a period of moral collapse."[2]

Not yet eighteen, then, Milena started dating another steady at the café scene, Ernst Polak. Ten years her senior, eloquent and charismatic, Polak was the son of an affluent Jewish family with the reputation of a womanizer and big spender. In truth, though earning a high income as a bank official, he was constantly in debt because of his cocaine addiction.

Both he and Milena suffered from the recurring "disease" while essentially healthy, the typical predicament of addicts.

Polak's background and persona did not sit well with Milena's father, Jan Jesenský, a moderate Czech nationalist whose namesake, a physician and rector of Charles University, was among twenty-seven Czech leaders executed in 1621 for adherence to Protestantism. Using his connections, in June 1917, Jesenský had his wild daughter committed to a psychiatric institution near Prague on the grounds of moral deficiencies. She spent there nine months until her legal maturity. On release, she promptly married Polak and followed him to Vienna, for several months still the capital of the Austro-Hungarian Empire.

The marriage and new milieu added to Milena's woes. Though her husband again earned a substantial salary as a currency manager in a bank, his income again failed to meet the couple's expenses. While in Vienna, they rubbed shoulders with some of the city's premier bohemians and drug addicts including Otto Gross. According to a contemporary report, Ernest Polak lived in a nice apartment, but his cocaine habit was the only art-related expertise one could learn from him.[3] Surrounded by freewheeling literati, Milena struggled to make the ends meet amid the postwar chaos. She spent time in jail for theft of money and was fired as a housemaid for theft of jewelry in August 1919. Reportedly, she even ventured into carrying luggage for hotel guests. Her attempt to teach Czech was apparently stillborn.

At the bottom of her fortunes, by the end of 1919, Milena started sending small articles to Prague newspapers, primarily the liberal Prague daily *Tribuna,* and gradually established herself as a fashion writer and commentator on Viennese society. During her visit to Prague, she also met Kafka and eventually asked for permission to translate into Czech *The Stoker,* one of his stories that had seen the print. The translation appeared under her maiden name as a separate attachment of twelve pages in the journal *Kmen* in April 1920. It was the first ever republishing of Kafka's work in a language other than German. This put Milena on the path as a translator; she would render into Czech his other stories such as "Report to an Academy" and "The Judgment," as well as works of other German-writing authors.

Kafka, who knew Czech well, was duly impressed with her translation of *The Stoker.* From Merano, he instantly asked Ottla in Prague to buy twenty copies of the journal. He also started a mail exchange with Milena that was personal from the onset. While Milena addressed him as Frank and sent her letters to his workplace rather than home, he sent his poste restante and signed as Kramer. While her letters have not been preserved—and his have been sanitized—he clearly found his new pen friendship thrilling. According to a contemporary witness, Kafka and his Jewish peers perceived a baptized person with "quiet respect." In the testimony of Urzidil, then, Kafka's classmates "all regarded her [Milena] as a miracle." Among Ernst Polak's friends, his snatching of this daughter of a university professor was considered a coup.[4]

Milena proved to be a lively pen mate, responding with intelligence and disarming honesty. In early May 1920, Kafka confided to Brod, "She is a living fire, of a kind I have never seen before . . . Yet at the same time she is extremely tender, courageous, bright." In the process of ingratiation (Milena took no German classes in her gymnasium years), he asked her to write letters in Czech, claiming that although German was his mother tongue, Czech felt to him more intimate.[5] He also professed love for Božena Němcová, the author of the nineteenth-century Czech classic novel *The Grandmother*.

Still in Merano, Kafka also started probing her life and, as in Felice Bauer's case, suitability for a relationship. Health issues and underlying addiction naturally ranked high on his horizon. A few weeks later, a friend would report that Milena had been ruined by cocaine, but that probably was old news to him. The addicts frame their confessions and responses in a way understandable to each other. Thus, when she offered spilling the beans on herself, he was not interested even if they included appalling things, he answered on June 12.

When Milena reported a bout of hemorrhaging, he also showed little concern, noting that bleeding can have numerous causes. He was confident that in her case, it was not a symptom of tuberculosis but merely a warning. This gave him a chance to broadly hint at his own addiction. Yes, he also noticed a discharge from his mouth while in a swimming pool in August 1917, but none since; his concern for his lungs was merely spiritual. The underlying disease he suffered from was troublesome but neither real nor always disagreeable. There was a lot of "pleasure" in it that he tried to extract. On the whole, it offered more gratification than strain. Laments conveyed by her letters were basically his own.[6] Implicitly, Kafka assured Milena that he too was an addict rather than a tubercular. It surely raised the comfort level of both knowing they were coping with the same vice.

Meanwhile, he also tested Milena with yet another of his perceived liabilities, his Jewishness. He initiated it with the self-deprecating remark, "You must also consider, Milena, the kind of person who approaches you . . . a Jew." Milena apparently answered with the tactless query, "Jste Žid?" (You are a Jew?) The word can conjure up a pejorative connotation in Czech, and it did to Kafka as well. He recoiled in anger, accusing her of an anti-Semitic blow. In afterthought, he indirectly compared Milena to the attractive but naïve shop girl Mathilde whom Heinrich Heine met in Paris exile and made his wife. She believed that her husband was a Lutheran, and there were no Jews among his friends.[7]

When Milena found his reaction hurtful, Kafka reversed himself. His experience with fellow guests in Merano undoubtedly both heightened his sensitivity to anti-Semitism and further deflated his self-esteem. On June 13, he confessed he would not dare to offer Milena his "dirty hand" and soon thereafter put to paper damning words of self-condemnation: at times, he would like to stuff Jews, himself included, into the drawer of a laundry trunk and keep them there until they suffocated. On second thought, however, Kafka began retracting: the insecure position of Jews makes it understandable that they consider themselves lucky to be alive. "They are all threatened by threats." Confronted with Milena's bewilderment, he eventually withdrew the diatribe: "The 'Jewish question' was after all only a dumb joke."[8] But then, the conflicted Kafka expressed the bizarre fear that the Jews are "necessarily bound to fall upon you Christians, just as predatory animals are bound to murder."[9]

Kafka's innermost worries, revealed to the daughter of a Catholic traditionalist, in effect verbalized the gloomy sentiment of the Central European Jewry in the decades preceding the Holocaust.

As his Jewishness was put aside, epistolary romance between Kafka and Milena resumed and expanded to existential doubts, feeling of uselessness, self-hatred, and Milena's lack of cash. He offered money and, despite his stinginess, eventually began sending her some. Soon, Milena also started relegating Ottla and Felice Bauer into background, leading him to observe, "My world is collapsing, my world is rebuilding itself." On receiving her letters, he confessed, "I literally start to shake . . . I am unable to read them . . . trembling, totally unaware of the world."[10]

Meanwhile, Kafka and Milena began pondering a get-together. It made most sense to stop in Vienna on his return to Prague from Merano. However, he flinched, citing multiple reasons. He feared that he would not be able to cope with stress; his "mental disease" was overflowing his lungs; his hands were shaking, and, further, he was so much older than her, this "lanky, emaciated man . . . almost white-haired from the past nights and headaches." Above all, he was a "man plagued by his own devils."[11] Just as in the case of Felice Bauer, in retrospect, he admitted trying to frighten Milena away from him.

Apart from his growing physical frailty, a major source of Kafka's unease was Milena's husband. Evidently, he met Ernst Polak as early as 1912 and confided to him they were "surrounded by devils."[12] But he had little to recall in 1920 about his potential rival and hence was influenced by Milena's complaints. She portrayed her husband as a serial womanizer and egotist who spent his not-insignificant income on himself, placing his young wife into a disreputable position. Milena's marriage was indeed on the rocks from early days in Vienna, and she even tried to live separately.

However, Kafka eventually found the reality far more complex on inquiring among his friends. It turned out that Polak, apart from commanding the respect of Max Brod, among others, was in steady contact even with Milena's estranged father, the supposed anti-Semite Jan Jesenský. An apparent skirt chaser perhaps, but Polak also spent a night in 1919 trying to talk Milena out of a relationship with another man. Kafka's perception of Milena's husband was changing accordingly, from implied disrespect to grudging recognition. He entertained the idea of approaching him with a letter.

As he mulled all this in his head, Kafka proposed to Milena what he briefly considered an ingenious solution: she would leave her husband in Vienna and return—not to Prague but to "some peaceful part of Bohemia." He would loan her money on the understanding it may not be enough in some months. In retrospect, he dismissed it as a silly idea. Milena declined the suggestion anyway, claiming her husband's illness prevented her from leaving him even temporarily, but, she added, it was not the kind of disease that would last forever.

Her reluctance to part with Polak was a bitter pill to swallow, but Kafka was not entirely free either. Back in Prague, two women hoped to claim him in one way or another. Julie Wohryzek, the spurned fiancée, was still in his orbit, by her own words for as long as he wanted her. In the background, but potentially far more important, was his sister Ottla. Despite her impending marriage, Kafka felt the urge to disclose their entanglement to Milena, and he resolved to do it in a Kafkaesque form.

On June 21, prefacing it as an attempt to illuminate his prior life, he volunteered to send her the "massive letter I wrote to my father about six months ago." In it, as we know, he addressed his father's distress over his "abnormal" relationship with Ottla. Determined now to dispatch it once back in Prague, he implored Milena to keep it confidential and try to understand "all the lawyer's tricks, it's a lawyerly letter." And if she managed to decode the letter's message, she should not forget "your great Never Mind," *Dein grosses Trotzdem*—apparently a reference to Milena's pledge to treasure him no matter what. He liked and would repeatedly refer to Milena's Never Mind as a "magic word."[13]

As he pondered his return to Prague from Merano, Kafka first resolved to take a direct train, thus avoiding Vienna. Then he let Milena know that his Prague "girl" wished to meet him in Karlsbad on his way home. He dutifully accepted the stopover as well as an ensuing visit of his parents in nearby Františkovy Lázně. Then he changed his mind again: he would return directly to Prague. A day or two later, however, he could not rule out a stopover in Vienna after all. Strain and indecision apparently stimulated more doping and less food intake. Down to fifty-five kilograms in the nude, he felt even more unqualified to show up in Vienna. The darkening of his skin, the process he had been observing for several years, added to his discomfort.

At last, Kafka announced he might come to Vienna, but then he would need a stretcher to rest on for a while. Daydreaming about Milena yet trembling in anxiety, he boarded an overnight train and arrived in Vienna on June 29, 1920. Lodged in the Hotel Riva (today Congress Hotel) near the Polaks' apartment on Lerchenfelder Strasse, he reserved the first day for recovery. That left him and Milena four days for themselves. What transpired? It appears Kafka visited Milena's place and spent an intimate time with her. He would recall his whispering into her ear while lying in bed, "in a deep sleep for a good reason," and her unconsciously seeking his mouth. Another moment that stuck in his mind was his face lying in her crotch.[14] More expressions of physical closeness were to follow.

Milena's reaction was more restrained. Herself in poor shape, she would recall dragging him over the hills behind Vienna: "I went ahead since he was walking slowly—was hurting," and then he slept "like a bagpipe." Subsequently, she regretted not having received enough love from him.[15] Apart from that, observing him with an expert eye, she found his drug degradation irreversible. No sanatorium would cure him, she confided to Brod.

Those few days with Milena, however, certainly boosted Kafka's self-esteem. While he arrived in Vienna full of angst, "In the four days Franz was near me, he lost it. We even laughed about it," she would recall.[16] Kafka left for Prague on July 3, his thirty-eighth birthday, with the memory of Milena as staggeringly beautiful. Impressed both by her intellect and, undoubtedly, a well-proportioned body, he was ready to devote all his time for her, think about her, and breathe with her.

Back in Prague, the family doctor, as Kafka feared, was far from impressed with his health status. The apex of his left lung was still unhealthy. The constricted throat impeded his food intake as before, and hands disobeyed him because of tremor. He also suffered from virtual flu, and his hearing was sabotaged by a "little bell right inside the ear," other typical side effects of opium indulgence.In retrospect, Kafka would refer to his "wild time in Merano," admitting the damage was self-inflicted. In Dr. Král's view, his Merano vacation was a fiasco. Considering how Milena also squandered her health, Kafka commented, they could placidly rest beside each another to die.[17]

Brod likewise found Kafka in poor shape on his return to Prague and, aware of Milena's addiction, at first, feared the romance would further drag him toward an abyss. Thus, he chastised her in writing for tempest and for having the wrong influence. Kafka, who learned about this, denied Brod's claim that he was sick and in need of money—and asked Milena to cease corresponding with his best friend.

Brod and Milena, nevertheless, kept trading letters; in fact, they became benign plotters set on straightening Kafka out. She eventually destroyed all Brod's missives and asked that hers be destroyed as well. Fortunately, Brod would not comply fully. Eight of her letters penned between 1920 and 1924, all dealing with Kafka the man, have been preserved, albeit in a sanitized form. There is little doubt that the deleted passages did not conform to Kafka's image as a tubercular. Overall, these earthy letters are still to-be-mined texts for understanding the Jesenská-Kafka relationship.

Of interest here, they exude Jesenská's affection, mixed with a surprisingly sober, revealing characterization of Kafka as someone completely out of touch with reality. When Brod obviously attempted to pass a similar rationale to Milena as he did to Felice Bauer, presenting Kafka's health problems as a heroic struggle of a genius with destiny, she differed respectfully: his "asceticism"—meaning, primarily abstention from food and drink—"is completely unheroic . . . All 'heroism' is lying and cowardice." True, Kafka paid with his health for excellence in writing, but otherwise, she saw his future bleak. "Frank is unable to live. Frank isn't capable of living. Frank will never recover. Frank will die soon," she wrote prophetically.[18]

Meanwhile, Kafka was relieved on return to the Institute of Workers' Accident Insurance that he had not been dismissed. The flow of work was simply bypassing him. The first three days he had not written a line, and overall, he found his job lamentably easy. This freed his mind and time for private affairs that had accumulated up in the past three months.

Milena Jesenská's shadow activated the "girl" in Prague, as he put it. This "girl" already sent him a telegram in June asking for a date on his return from Merano in Karlsbad (he called it an "order"). Kafka, as we know, eventually traveled to Vienna instead. Meeting her in Prague on July 5, he was detached, feeling "dissolved" inside Milena. Confronted with the "girl's" laments, he gave her Milena's address only to realize how imprudent this was. The "girl" promptly mailed Milena a severe letter but retrieved it on his reprimand from the post office.[19]

Biographers identify this "girl" as Julie Wohryzek, Kafka's onetime fiancée. But the "girl's" traits—self-confidence, assertiveness, and impudence—match Ottla's character. In addition, the "girl" behaved as if belonging to the family, and her harping ended after Ottla's wedding. It cannot be precluded that Kafka, following the habit he had developed in *The Trial*, in letters to Jesenská, merged two real persons into the "girl." The real Julie Wohryzek soon backed off, devoting her time to a fashion hat shop she had opened in Prague.

The second woman Kafka had to contain in Prague was, of course, his sister Ottla. Prodded in May 1920 to marriage, she stopped communicating with him. Still in Merano, he inquired with Max Brod why. To the biographers' chagrin, his letters to her for June 12 to June 24 are not available either. On the twenty-eighth, then, he let her know he would be returning to Prague soon and recalled the great time they had together in Želízy—and added, "You probably have much to do . . . and won't find time to pay attention to me, and no one else is at home."[20]

He knew well, of course, that Ottla would be elated being with him alone if given a chance. As their parents were vacationing at Františkovy Lázně, on his return to Prague on July 4, Kafka indeed shared the family quarters with her (and the maid) only. However, the memory of his face in Milena's bosom still fresh, he struggled with restarting another romance. The atmosphere at 6 Oldtown Square was tense, prompting him to confess to Milena on July 6: "My apartment is making me restless, the evenings are making me restless, I'd like to be someplace different."[21]

In the evening of July 7, then, the parents returned home, and concurrently, Uncle Alfred Löwy arrived from Paris, intent on attending Ottla's wedding. To make room for him, Kafka moved to an apartment at 45 Mánesova Street, rented by Karl and Elli Hermann. It was about twenty-five minutes' walk from the Oldtown Square. Since the Hermanns were vacationing in Marienbad, Kafka lived there alone in the week preceding Ottla's marriage.

Already the first morning at Mánesova, Kafka would report to Milena the same day that his sister Ottla came the whole long way from the family apartment with breakfast—something he found unnecessary, for he intended to walk home for it. Arriving very early and unannounced, she had to ring for several minutes before he finally woke up. Obviously, Ottla hoped to repeat the breakfast-in-bed routine from Siřem days. Engrossed with Milena, was Kafka interested in rekindling the old flame? In the very same letter, expressing an overall sense of happiness in the apartment despite the noise, Kafka suddenly became very specific: he associated the place with the "lechery, the incest of dissolute bodies, thoughts and desires long uncontrolled," the dwelling where "improper accidental things take place, where illicit affairs occur, where illegitimate children are conceived, in every corner, between all the pieces of furniture."[22]

The context that stretches beyond this chapter suggests this was a Freudian confession of his renewed intimacy with Ottla in the days immediately preceding her wedding.[23]

On July 15 (1920), Ottla and Josef David married in a civil ceremony and departed on their honeymoon in Šumava, the mountain range between Bohemia and Bavaria. Also around that time, Ottla conceived her first daughter, Věra, who was born on March 27, 1921.

Besieged by conflicting impulses, Kafka was heavily distressed in the days of Ottla's nuptial. He flirted with revisiting Milena in Vienna, the city he dismissed on prior occasion as a decaying mammoth, and then encouraged her to leave the Austrian capital. Almost certainly in consequence of more drugs, he was turning incoherent and struggled again to retain the command of his fingers. His pains were raising fear in Milena that he might do something silly. In anticipation of that, or perhaps to start emancipation from Polak, Milena disclosed the romance to her husband.

It turned out, however, that the wedding changed little in Ottla's affection for her brother. She expressed remorse for deserting him and tried to cut short her honeymoon trip. Kafka calmed her down hastily, signaling his hope of maintaining the status quo: "I know well that I have lost nothing; could you say you've lost your ears since the wedding? And since you still have them, may I no longer play with them? . . . I'm remaining single for the two of us." At the same time, he wished all the best to both newlyweds.[24] Kafka began flirting with the idea of a triangular relationship that eventually impacted his other texts.

His renewed bond with Ottla was accompanied by an ebbing of his feelings for Milena. In part, it was also brought about by his three and a half hours' night walk with Max Brod in the wake of Ottla's wedding, followed by another meeting with "L," probably Arne Laurin, the deputy editor at Milena's journal *Tribuna*. Uncharacteristically, he then dispatched another letter castigating her for addiction. Milena was anguished. In a long reply, no longer available, she conceded the crux of her problems was her "disease" that, though not endless, for the time being precluded leaving her husband even temporarily. Her dilemma of choosing between Kafka and Polak could be solved in a third way, she believed, which meant staying with neither suitor but somewhere in solitude. She also invited Kafka for another meeting, either in Prague or Vienna.

Kafka found her letter unreadable yet devoured it four times and still was not sure how to respond. Eventually, on July 26, just a day after reaffirming his bond with Ottla, he settled on a harsh tone. He ruled out both his visit to Vienna and Milena's to Prague and, in response to her claim of having nothing to eat, also nixed sending her more money: "At noon I am going home and stuff the useless money into the kitchen stove." Reluctant to confirm his love for her, he also let Milena know they had drifted apart completely. They still had in common a death wish, he claimed.[25]

On second thought, however, Kafka decided to give the romance another chance. An apology followed: "I regret several things that I have written recently." Within days, he seemed to be deeply in love again, feeling like a giant warding off Milena's suitors with stretched arms. He also accepted her idea of another date.[26] But his affection was tainted now: in his first dream after visiting Vienna that involved Milena, he committed murder for her sake.

When, at his suggestion, they settled on a meeting in Gmünd, a border town between Czechoslovakia and Austria, it was a déjà vu for Kafka. More than six years earlier, in March 1914, as we know, he spent there a weekend or two with Grete Bloch and impregnated her with a son. He still felt vibes from that encounter now. But he also intimated to Milena that their tête-à-tête should offset them: "I like holding your hand in my own, I like staring in your eyes. That's about it, exit Grete!"[27]

When they met in Gmünd for an overnight stay on Saturday, August 14, however, it was under the shadow of Ottla and Ernst Polak. This alone doomed their weekend. Ottla rightfully considered Milena Jesenská—just as Felice Bauer—a competitor for her brother's tenderness and love. Conversely, Kafka noted, Milena hated almost all Jewish women. Yet on arrival in Gmünd, he had nothing more important in mind than sending Ottla a postcard. Unable to write because of another spell of hand tremor, he engaged Milena to pen it: "Dear Ottla, I am feeling well here, not coughing at all, and am coming tomorrow morning and all this has been dictated. Franz." The postcard closed with Milena's postscript: "He was not able to finish."[28] There was not much that recommended him as Milena's date.

The cumulative effect of Kafka's standoffishness since August 8 impacted Milena. Sensing his detachment, she asked in Gmünd whether he had been unfaithful to her in Prague. He denied it but uncomfortably. A moralist who admittedly lied when forced by circumstances, he was troubled by this denial in the aftermath. Little wonder Milena accused him of insincerity. But then, Kafka was aware that Milena had already committed to vacations with her husband. On that day in Gmünd, he would recall, "We spoke and listened to each other often and for a long time, like strangers."[29] With his mind elsewhere, the tryst in Gmünd was a near disaster. Almost certainly, there was no physical intimacy. Bitter and hurtful, Milena left the town on Sunday, the fifteenth, while he, contrary to his intention, delayed his departure until Monday morning. She would shortly join her husband for three-week holidays in the Austrian Alps.

Kafka's post-Gmünd letters turned mournful. With the image still fresh of her lying in bed and in the meadow, he confessed to so much pride in associating with her. Regretful he would not get another chance, he resorted to—for him so uncharacteristically poetic—words of tenderness and affection. He wished to cling to any part of her he could get hold of, loving her as the sea loves a pebble in its depths. In another letter, struggling with his injured masculinity, he also recalled trysts with a girl two decades earlier.

Milena, her letters to Brod reveal, had reservations about Kafka the man. Among them were his bad health, his lack of levelheadedness, and her desire to become a mother. Still, she was still trying to save the romance. Fragile as ever and overdosing, she wrote Kafka distressed missives while coping with headaches and fainting spells. In the hope of recovering in a sanatorium, she also approached her father for money but was rebuffed. Kafka offered himself as an intervener, yet it quickly became obvious that Dr. Jesenský had already advanced her a princely sum of ten thousand crowns and paid her a monthly allowance. That, along with her husband's large salary, was not enough? At this point, Kafka concurred with Jesenský's secretary that sending more money made no sense.

His romantic dispositions again started fading away by late summer 1920. Characteristically, he responded again by self-degradation, blaming himself for dragging Milena down to his dirty self, and his letters became less frequent and short of intimate passages.

There was more than Milena's attachment to her husband that held him back after Gmünd. When reconsidering the letter exchange with her in late August, he felt uncomfortable hiding something. "To send you cards full of lies is too silly [...] I am dirty, Milena, infinitely dirty, this is why I scream so much about purity. No one sings as purely as those who inhabit the deepest hell," he unburdened his conscience.[30] And again, "I am living in my dirt, that's my business."[31] Seen in the context of his renewed musing about Eve's plucking the apple and original sin, this suggests Ottla's return from honeymoon brought about another phase of in-house temptation.

After a lull of more than three years, as if seeking compensation for his waning passion for Milena, Kafka also returned to writing by the end of August 1920. This meant the resumption of opium smoking, or as he called it "my military service." Thus, once again, he slept in the afternoon and worked into late nightly hours: "The real treasure lies hidden in the deep of the night."[32] Much too distracted by his personal dilemmas, however, he failed to be consistently creative, producing merely bits and pieces of prose before his motivation fizzled again in the autumn of 1920.

Inevitably, Kafka's health took a turn for the worse in the fall of that year. Apart from the persistent cough, more than ever he struggled with raised temperature, shortness of breath, and recurrent immobility. He could not get out of bed because, he quipped, "I was too 'heavy,' this word keeps recurring, it's the only one that fits me."[33] In the grip of drugs, he found torture really important to him both as the tortured and torturer.

Little wonder his mind darkened again. A streak of masochism began affecting the tendermost parts of his psyche: love seemed to be morphing into a knife that he turned within himself. If love had become a burden, so had Milena. In one of his dreams, she somehow caught fire. Traces of his drug-induced cruelty and sadism also reappeared. Out of the blue, in one of his missives to Milena of mid-October, he imagined the situation when two poles are driven into a man's crotch and spread his legs wide until the man is torn apart in the middle. To make sure his sweetheart grasped it, he demonstrated it with a doodle. When she wrote that one day they would live together, Kafka responded once again, "No Milena, we don't have the shared possibility we thought we had in Vienna."[34]

In November 1920, he found even the mail exchange too traumatic for both sides, claiming his letters conveyed his incurable torment and caused the same.

In a parallel lane, Milena also struggled with weight loss and drugged herself to immobility because of painful limbs and lungs. She recovered somewhat in sanatoria paid by her father, but her love for Kafka could not surmount the circumstances. Late in 1920, she overdosed attempting a suicide but survived. The romance, however, was over. She and Kafka parted, facing the future each on their own.

In Matliary, Seeking "a Postponement of Sentence"

A century before Kafka, the great Romantic poet Samuel Coleridge sought relief from addiction to laudanum by confining himself to house arrest. In Kafka's days, institutionalization was still considered the most effective method of detoxification. Kafka fiercely resisted this venue. Barely back and degraded from the self-indulging days in Merano, in August 1920, he rejected the family doctor's suggestion that would effectively subject him to institutional care. He neither wanted nor was obligated to seek help in a sanatorium for tubercular. There was some justification in it, considering his health woes resulted primarily from his "choking throat," the inability to swallow food and drink.[1] But this affliction could be just as lethal as tuberculosis. Among his Prague acquaintances, an aspiring poet under the pen name Karl Brand died emaciated in 1918, and his demise attained for Kafka "an ominous prescience."[2]

The painful parting with Milena Jesenská in the autumn of 1920 apparently pushed Kafka beyond concern for his health. Looking back at the year 1920 in foreboding, he identified Merano as his last chance for recovery. His growing indifference and resignation alarmed even Ottla, who obliged him to visit Dr. Kodym in mid-October 1920. The latter's medical statement was worded cautiously: Kafka had "a double-sided infiltration of the lung apices" and claimed that his body temperature had somewhat increased. "It would be in his interest to attempt to improve or even cure his illness through treatment in a sanatorium." Kodym made it obvious that Kafka's health was a private, not a societal problem and not necessarily curable any longer. He still suggested at least three months of leave.[3]

Kafka's colleagues at work had already been exposed to his dry but heavy bouts of coughing and physical decline, both of which generated more pity than fear. Thus, three and a half months after his return from Merano, Director Odstrčil and the administrative board conceded him yet another three months of a "recuperative holiday" on October 21.[4] In his absence, they would also promote him to the department head in charge of setting up insurance premiums.

Never mind that Kafka had been so well treated at work and sang praises of Prague in exchanges with Milena. Modern research confirms the anecdotal evidence that addicts display increased tolerance to drugs in their customary places. Changing environments, therefore, results in an enhanced drug effect. Thus, Kafka now viewed Prague as the place where one was hated by anti-Semites so much that he needed to relocate. He was on the lookout for another location to renew his wild Merano days. It surely raised eyebrows of his family and friends.

Concerned about his growing abandon in the fall of 1920, those who cared about him—notably Max Brod and Dr. Král—still hoped to steer him into a reputable bona fide sanatorium. This would subject him to a disciplined lifestyle, restrict his drug intake, and give him a chance to regain weight. In October 1920, Kafka indeed considered a sanatorium in Grimmenstein, Lower Austria, but eventually ruled it out as much too expensive, not even counting "injections." He also nixed Dr. Král's recommendation of another bona fide but cheaper sanatorium in Nový Smokovec in the Upper Tatras Mountains and then the eastern part of Czechoslovakia. He was not keen on living in the mountains or at seashore, he claimed.

That notwithstanding, Kafka eventually selected as his next destination another locale in Upper Tatras, Tatranské Matliary (today Matliare in Slovakia). The choice defied both his preferences and the criteria of a lung patient. He decided to spend a predictably harsh winter in a hard-to-reach place, elevation of nine hundred meters, and in an establishment that was primarily a lodge catering to skiers, hunters, and hikers. But then, a recovery was not the prime factor in his decision. When Gustav Janouch asked why he would go there if he did not believe in a cure, Kafka answered, "The accused always endeavors to secure a postponement of sentence."[5]

On December 18, 1920, then, Kafka lodged in Villa Tatra, today a no longer existing building in a complex of recreational facilities nestled under the majestic Lomnický Štít, one of the Upper Tatras's highest peaks. The premises were Spartan, far below the standard he had been used to. In addition, he was lodged in a side wing, more private but still more primitive. His sister Ottla, now five months pregnant, at first, insisted on coming to Matliary as well—an uncomfortable prospect for him—but eventually, she reconsidered. This allowed him to move in a somewhat better room reserved for her.

In the same corridor and in charge of almost thirty residents in this primitive sanatorium resided Dr. Leopold Strelinger, who passed himself off as a lung specialist. Kafka described him as a handsome, red-cheeked man with a young wife and an exceptionally bright son. On examining Kafka, Strelinger suggested, "of course," an arsenic cure, the traditional treatment for opium addicts. The patient demurred. It turned out, however, that Strelinger was also walking around with a hypodermic needle inside a small leather case—and he did not dispense the dreaded tuberculin. In his sachet, Kafka reported to Brod, Strelinger "keeps the salvation of the world; and if the world wishes, he will inject it into the world's blood for twelve crowns . . . He pays me a daily visit; it is useless but not unpleasant."[6]

Unscrambling these cryptic lines, from his first days in Matliary, Kafka was injected with a stimulant, most likely morphine or heroin or the injectable opioid of his last years, pantopon. Invented in 1909 and nearly as potent as morphine, pantopon was cleaner and less prone to provoke allergy. Kafka loved this regime at Villa Tatra so much that, eventually, he struck with Strelinger a "wholesale contract under which he visits me daily—it costs six crowns."[7]

Brod, the recipient of Kafka's reports, saw his worst fears confirmed. Instead of seeking a way to curtail his drug dependence, his friend again opted for the opposite. Not given a chance to intervene against Matliary, Brod showed his displeasure after the exchange of first letters, only to be rebuffed. Despite the primitive conditions and noise in the building, Kafka liked it there. Why should he leave the place where "everybody makes an honest effort to give me all that I need"?[8]

Outwardly, Kafka insinuated a slight improvement in his health. In a letter composed in Czech to Director Odstrčil of January 27, 1921, he claimed to be avoiding physical exertion and reported a weight gain of four kilograms. "On the whole I feel better here than in Merano and hope to return with better results."[9] In truth, his health problems were accumulating in Matliary. Thus, he apparently arrived with good intentions to gain weight, and that presupposed an increased consumption of protein. He forced himself to eating meat but gave up soon. "To be sure, the Enemy intervened," he alluded to the fact that opium addicts develop an aversion to meat.[10]

As for many years past, Kafka's esophagus, cramped by opium and opiates, in general, allowed the passage of food and drink only with agonizing pain. Fighting hunger, he literally sweated seeing the "horror" of a full plate in front of him.[11]

The cornucopia of other side effects of addiction also accompanied him to Matliary. In response to Brod's query, he admitted in early March 1921 that he spent hours lethargic in the reclining chair, not doing well, experiencing such coughing, shortness of breath, and overall weakness as never before. More often than before, he could not even raise his hand to write.

Boils, his painful companions since 1910, were also coming back. At one point, a brutal abscess on his back kept him from lying down by day and sleeping at night, Kafka reported. He was also visited by hemorrhoids—another often excruciatingly painful side effect of opium consumption that forced Karl Marx to write sections of his masterpiece *The Capital* while standing. As for Kafka, after several uninhibited weeks in Matliary, he believed his health had reached nadir but not so: by mid-April 1921, he felt much worse than after all previous 'cures.'

Compared with this and his other supposedly health vacations, he realized that "the office kept the illness in check." It restricted the chance for drug consumption. But Strelinger also warned him, apparently having a withdrawal agony on mind, that his return to Prague could mean a "total collapse."[12]

The available bits of information suggest some effort to contain the ravages of opiates while in Villa Tatra. Thus, Kafka underwent a cold water treatment, the traditional fast remedy to bring under control a body overcharged by opiates. It was a cold bath, for example, that saved the life of Marx's first daughter born to an addicted mother. Chancellor Bismarck, on his part, used to wrap himself in wet towels. Kafka probably also took iron, another traditional antidote to opium that can cause havoc with the heart. A strong cardiac pain he experienced in his room, he accepted, was associated with another "torturer" that was milder and came faster.[13]

There was at least one resident in Villa Tatra who caught Kafka's attention, his Czech classmate from the primary school who reportedly suffered from tuberculosis of the larynx. The fastidious Kafka, as we know, avoided tubercular people because of what he considered their filthiness and the constant danger of infection. He could only watch them in disgust spitting into a sputum jar (which he, as a nontubercular, did not have to carry). Tuberculosis of the larynx is far less upsetting, and Kafka accepted his copatient's invitation to observe his self-treatment. Introduced in the 1860s and still used worldwide in Kafka's days, it consisted of a little mirror that, inserted deep into one's throat, exposed the larynx to sunrays. Even this dry, bloodless procedure nauseated Kafka, who beat a retreat at the first opportunity. The Czech patient eventually jumped or was pushed from a local train and died.

Never mind that the winter was so severe in Matliary and Kafka felt worse than ever after three months there. The unobstructed inflow of drugs was overruling his will to live. Bent on self-destruction, he expressed a wish to stay longer when his leave was about to expire by the end of March. But would the institute grant him an extension? A medical report that Dr. Strelinger wrote on March 11 noted some irregularities of his lungs, breathing difficulty, and half-dry cough. However, he did not attach a sputum test (which would have confirmed Kafka's nontubercular status), and his report offered no specific recommendation. This was the best (or worst) that Kafka could wring out of the doctor. Lungs were not his main problem; "this [other] illness" was, he noted.[14]

Kafka mailed Strelinger's report to Brod, pleading with him to negotiate on his behalf a leave extension with Dr. Odstrčil. Justifiably concerned the report was not convincing enough, he also gave Brod the discretion to accept whatever he would be offered, including an extension at half salary or using up his vacation privileges and retirement benefits.

Brod was unhappy about the situation. But he could ill-afford a trip to Matliary when, realizing he could not make a living as a writer, he eyed a regular job with the government. Supported by Dr. Král's view, once again, he urged Kafka to relocate to one of the true lung sanatoriums in Bohemia, Austria, or Germany. The aim was again to subject the patient to an institutional discipline. Kafka objected, claiming disingenuously in Bavaria, they accepted Jewish patients only to kill them. In fear of Brod not trying his best, Kafka also entrusted Ottla to negotiate a new deal for him. She found Director Odstrčil unusually accommodative. Without even seeing Strelinger's report (which arrived later through Brod), he arranged for the extension of Kafka's "holiday" until May 20, with full pay. Informing his parents about this, Kafka added he could change the location if need be. He did not.

In the front weeks of 1921, he found another argument against parting with Matliary, Robert Klopstock. A native of Budapest, this young German-speaking Jew with aspirations of becoming a physician instantly fascinated our Prague writer, and it was not mainly because of the shared interest in literature. Kafka wrote in cryptic admiration, "I have not yet seen so diabolical a spectacle from close up . . . In the Middle Ages, he would have been regarded as possessed." More importantly, Kafka discovered this red-cheeked, resourceful individual "shared direction" of some sort with him.[15]

What was Kafka alluding to? The ambitious Klopstock eventually established himself as a respected lung specialist in New York. As his ruddy face, health and mental problems similar to Kafka's, and constant shortage of money suggest, the shared "direction" were stimulants. In his later years, Klopstock became the trusted provider of morphine and other illicit drugs to the German novelist Klaus Mann and perhaps to his illustrious father, Thomas Mann. (Ruined by drugs, Klaus Mann eventually died by overdosing.)[16] Almost certainly rehearsing this role, Klopstock frequented Matliary to earn money by selling drugs—with his pal from Eastern Slovakia—and recruited Kafka as his client. "Whatever I want, they fetch it for me," the latter remarked. And to keep their service, Kafka was giving them "a lot of tips."[17]

Klopstock was to continue supplying Kafka even after Matliary. Back in Prague and elsewhere, be it Berlin or the Baltic, Kafka would be receiving parcels from Klopstock and be mindful that money was remitted to the sender by Herr Schmolka, apparently his father's business associate. At the same time, while in Matliary at least, Klopstock also performed a countervailing duty, treating patients with menthol sprays that relaxed their spasmodic larynx on swallowing. This might have helped Kafka control better his weight there. But he was still victimized by other side effects of opium, the most vexing of which were boils. Each took more than a month before healing superficially. Dr. Strelinger again suggested arsenic injections, the customary remedy, but Kafka again declined. In these circumstances, Kafka found in Klopstock a dependable companion and contact with the outside world.

Milena Jesenská was no longer welcomed in his world. Consumptive and sick, in April 1921, she visited her father in Prague but failed to make contact with Kafka. Though knowing his letters would not be coming anymore, she was unable to break the habit and still visited the post office daily. Nor could Kafka forget. On learning she had reconciled with her father and might come to a nearby sanatorium in Upper Tatras, he still experienced a senseless agitation. But he also trembled, guessing that his smelly bandaged boils would wreck any romance, and advised her sternly to avoid meeting him or even writing. Milena was torn apart, feeling guilty but not knowing the cause of rejection. This was perhaps the most difficult hour of her life, she would recall.

Meanwhile, as his extended "holiday" was coming to end, Kafka procured another medical judgment by Strelinger. Dated May 5, 1921, it identified Kafka as the sufferer of "a double-sized lung disease," but a sputum test was again omitted. On these mushy grounds, the doctor recommended another five-month period of "recuperation in the Upper Tatras." In addendum, Strelinger went as far as to suggest an indefinite extension of the "treatment" would be advisable. It read like another ticket to retirement.

Dispatched to Ottla in Prague, Strelinger's report had the desired effect. Kafka's leave was extended once again, by three months, to August 20, and not at half but at full salary. Once again, Kafka was granted more than he had asked for. This gesture of goodwill pleased him, even though, he commented cheekily, it reflected the fact he was so expendable at work now. In a thank-you letter to Director Odstrčil, he falsely claimed his general conditions had improved, resulting in a weight gain of eight kilos.[18] He repeated the same rosy make-believe to Brod, giving his weight at more than sixty-five kilograms.

When the extension was nearing the end, however, on August 16, Kafka informed Odstrčil in Czech that even though his lungs were overall in good condition, he had suffered a "considerable loss of weight" and had been confined to bed. Since he once again also struggled with ignominy of the most ferocious abscess he had ever had, he resolved to overstay in Matliary by another week. He was dealing with the Institute "the way a child would not dare to deal with its parents," he commented with disarming honesty.[19] On August 29, 1921, after more than eight months of absence, Kafka reported to work in worse shape than ever.

THE RETIREMENT

Not even a week on his job and Kafka was eyeing another three months' leave. On September 13, the institute's doctor Kodym confirmed the familiar diagnosis, an infiltration of upper lobes in the lungs, and recommended cure in a sanatorium. The patient ruled out revisiting Matliary. To return there would mean reinfecting himself with his own illness, he felt. Did he really wish to bid farewell to drugs? Not so. "I want to take the disease somewhere else," he claimed.[1] But, as on other occasions, he again ruled out a real sanatorium. In search of an alternate solution, Kafka's parents arranged for his examination by the trusted family physician Dr. Hermann. His report of October 19 (1921) echoed the past diagnoses. An X-ray confirmed the patient had a lung catarrh ending on the left side and receding on the right. Still, the doctor recommended that the patient underwent a several months' treatment away from work, not necessarily a sanatorium.

A few days later, the company physician, Dr. Kodym, also gave Kafka an exam, the second in three months. Once again, the X-ray found no tuberculosis. Kodym likewise called for "several months of complete physical rest" but dismissed a final cure as improbable. The doctor also wondered whether retirement would not be better for both the patient and the institute. Based on these reports, Kafka applied for a "medical holiday" not specifying the length of "systematic treatment" he needed. In another grand gesture, the institute granted him a three months' leave until February 4, 1922.

But he was in no hurry to go anywhere. One of the reasons for his sudden reluctance to leave his hometown was Milena Jesenská. On completion of a detoxification treatment of sort, she once more came to Prague in early October 1921. Thus, after fourteen months, they met again, this time as trusted friends. Kafka demonstrated it by handing her his diaries as well as the long-promised *Letter to His Father*. They had several other meetings, some at the Kafkas' home, which failed to reignite the flame. When Milena left Prague by December 1, Kafka felt "no sorrow at her departure, no real sorrow." Yet he was hesitant to start another diary and record a dreary reality. Besides, he claimed, there were other issues than his lungs that preoccupied him, but he preferred to keep them private.[2]

The "other issues" referred primarily to Kafka's uncontrolled health degradation. In moments of candor after Matliary, he felt shamed not being able to show "the faintest firmness of resolve" in his life. He had nothing, no tuberculosis or another act of God to blame for his health woes but himself. "It is astounding how I have systematically destroyed myself in the course of the years; it was like slowly widening a breach in a dam, a purposeful action."[3] He also observed growing social isolation evidenced by a number of those who considered him a nuisance or treated him with indifference. It appears that in these circumstances, Kafka consented to his first notable detoxification regime in October 1921, under the watchful eye of his family and caring doctors. The results were inconclusive.

Thus, when Dr. Kodym visited Kafka's family doctor and the two compared the patient's X-rays in January 1922, they found his lungs substantially improved. This may have been a reward for Kafka reducing his drug intake, but it left him indifferent. He would have preferred a serious inflammation, he claimed, to justify more time off work—and more opportunities for doping. Yet his physical appearance and cough were still worrisome, and Dr. Hermann recommended again three to four months off. Kafka promptly requested an extension of his "holiday" and, without delay, was granted one until April 1922.

By the end of January 1922, then, he left for Špindlerův Mlýn (Spindlermühle), a top ski center in Northern Bohemia, easily accessible from Prague. Lodged in a mountain hotel rather than a sanatorium, he found the location more congenial than the remote Matliary. Having written little of importance in the past few years and nothing in Matliary, he felt reenergized, undoubtedly driven by the attention his work was catching in Germany. Apart from Max Brod, who promoted him tirelessly, it was the reciter Ludwig Hardt (1886–1947), in particular, who included Kafka's texts in his performances. Already known in Prague, having performed there in October 1921, Hardt was scheduled to return in March 1922. In October 1921, the publisher Wolff also solicited a new major work that Kafka could not deliver.

Motivated obviously also by his recent personal crisis that he characterized as a period of insanity (more on this later), Kafka sought panacea in writing on arrival in Špindlerův Mlýn. Writing offered him the "strange, mysterious, perhaps dangerous, perhaps saving comfort . . . a leap out of murderers' row." As before, this meant an increased nightly intake of opium, or, as he put it, writing became again a "reward for serving the devil." Kafka regretted this latest "descent to the dark powers . . . these dubious embraces" unknown to those writing their stories in sunlight. But, he confided to Brod, there was no alternative: "I know only this kind; at night . . . I know only this kind."[4]

Throughout 1922, Kafka penned a few notable pieces of prose. Apparently, as he struggled with hand tremor, his handwritten characters had become less legible and smaller in size—another trend attributable to drugs. Directly or by implication, he again belabored the topics reflective of his growing premonition of death.

Mirroring this frame of mind, "Investigations of a Dog" is Kafka's highly original contribution to the inventory of tales depicting subhumans as humans—often an expression of low self-esteem on the part of drug addicts. In this instance, the narrator is a dog that, from his hiding hole, investigates other dogs "walking on their hind legs"—in other words, "dogs like you and me." He is "a lean dog, badly fed and neglectful of . . . [his] needs." His main interest is how the canine race feeds itself, Kafka writes.

But the text veers toward depicting the narrator's own experience. In the past, he was both pampered and ridiculed and treated like a silly puppy. People around also hoped to divert him, "without violence, almost lovingly, from a false path." But these would-be saviors failed, not being entirely convinced that violence was permissible in a case like his. For the first but not last time, Kafka voiced here the view that only strong-arming would cure him of addiction. The failure to subject him to discipline burdened him with a weak appetite, hunger burning in entrails, and social isolation: "Nobody [is] troubled about me . . . I [am] dying of their indifference."[5] Another lament of an addict blaming others for his woes.

The subject of dying helplessly from hunger is also the focal point of "A Hunger Artist," the short story written in May 1922. Kafka fathoms here a "professional faster" who sits from morning till night in a small circus cage, exposed to visitors curious to see someone dying by refusal of food. We learn that the artist's act was much more popular in the past when children came to see him as a special treat and the adults were buying season tickets to catch his gradual degradation, marveling at "his ribs sticking out so prominently." Lately, however, despite extensive advertising, people started losing interest in his self-sacrifice, and the friendly-looking ladies tending to him have turned out so indifferent. The artist himself finds nothing admirable about his act. "Why should not we admire it?" asks the manager to receive this surprising answer, "Because I could not find the food I liked. If I had found it, believe me, I would . . . stuff myself like you or anyone else." With these words, the "hunger artist" exhales for the last time.[6]

"A Hunger Artist" ranks among Kafka's most accomplished short stories. A deeply personal parable on the loneliness of an addict succumbing to consumption, it also lampoons commercialism and voyeurism, as well as indifference to sufferings of the individual. No wonder this jewel was an instant success. The top German literary journal *Die neue Rundschau* published it in October 1922 along with Brod's essay on Kafka, and the story was reprinted by other German periodicals. "A Hunger Artist" conclusively put Kafka on the literary horizon.

Aside from giving him an impulse to write, Kafka's detoxification cure in the fall of 1921 also helped revive his libido. This may be related to the fact that opium and opiates can function as aphrodisiacs but rarely in high dosages. Thus, he showed little interest in romantic escapades during his wild days in Matliary and, in April 1921, excluded wife and children from his wish list. On returning to Prague later the same year, however, he expressed envy of "all married couples . . . the happiness of married life," adding this may in fact apply to one couple only.[7]

Which particular couple did Kafka have in mind? The edited text does not contain the answer. With Milena Jesenská and Ernst Polak out of the picture, we need to consider his sister Ottla and Josef David as the possible subject of his jealousy.

Kafka's aficionados, in general, present his sister's marriage in a highly romanticized light of two people deeply in love. Only a few acknowledge that Ottla and Josef David had a tense relationship from the onset but tend to blame the husband. The matrimony, as Ottla's daughter Věra confirmed in retrospect, was "dystopian."[8] If anything, it tied together two young people of contrasting backgrounds. Though not unduly religious, the Kafkas on the whole confined their social intercourse to the Jewish community. The David family, on the other hand, was religiously Catholic. Ottla's father-in-law Antonín David was an undercastellan in St. Vitus cathedral and an unapologetic Czech patriot. Just like his wife, Marie, he disliked Germans and Jews. Their son and Ottla's husband, Josef, was educated and ambitious but, true to his Czech roots, patronized the national fitness club Sokol and felt affinity with Britain and France rather than Germany.

Ever since they met for the first time, possibly in 1911 or even earlier, Ottla and Josef David obviously harbored no strong attraction to each other. This continued after his return from the war. Ottla was in no hurry to see him and defiantly preferred her brother's company. David kept socializing with Czech friends who, as suggested below, may have included a mistress.

This aloofness extended into their marriage. Ottla met her in-laws for the first time only three days before wedding. At the time she became Mrs. Davidová in mid-July 1920, her parents were apparently readying a "new home" for the newlyweds. In defiance of their wish, however, Ottla was itching to terminate her honeymoon (her mother called it a "trip") and, on return to Prague in late July, continued to share the family apartment at Oldtown Square with her parents and brother Franz.

The arrangement troubled Max Brod, as always concerned about propriety. At first blaming Jesenská for Kafka's woes on the latter's return from the date with her in Vienna, he quickly reversed himself, noting in his diary that a relationship with Milena could save Kafka from sex— seemingly a nonsensical point unless Ottla is drawn into the context. On July 25 (1920), he observed that his friend Franz must do two things for his own good: to move out of his parents' apartment and to go to a sanatorium, possibly in Davos. Apprised of his dual-purpose drive, Milena Jesenská wholeheartedly assured Brod she would do everything to send Kafka away. It would effectively mean detaching him from Ottla and allowing David to move in.[9]

Kafka was irritated by Brod's suggestion. "Both"—that is, vacating the family apartment and Davos—"are wrong . . . You do not know the Letter to Father," he redirected the focus to address Brod's underlying desire to break his bond with Ottla in favor of Milena Jesenská. With reference to the term "never mind" (*Trotzdem*) that Jesenská had assured him with, Kafka tried to convince Brod that Jesenská adored him in spite of everything.[10] Indirectly but firmly, Kafka also signaled that his stay in the family apartment along with Ottla was also a nonnegotiable personal issue. Settling this yet another abnormal situation halfway, Ottla's husband, Josef David, moved as a subtenant to an apartment one floor below the Kafkas in late summer 1920.

On her part, Ottla struggled to preserve her controlling perch. In the fall of 1920, when Kafka considered an Austrian sanatorium with a stopover in Vienna and a chance to meet Milena Jesenská again, the four-months-pregnant Ottla promptly announced she would join him and spend several days in the Austrian capital as well. Kafka stayed put.

His follow-up decision to spend a lengthy time in the inaccessible Matliary may have in part aimed at chilling the flame. Five months into a difficult pregnancy, Ottla still planned on joining him there but eventually relented, obliging him to keep clear of women instead. At this point, Kafka once again felt uncomfortable with her sway. He tried to be on good terms with Josef David on whose flawless Czech he also relied on in contact with the institute. Shortly before the birth of Ottla's first child in March 1921, he sent him a reassuring postcard from Matliary.

It was a balancing act because Ottla continued wooing her brother. Three weeks before giving birth, she suggested that he resign from the institute and both—actually all three of them, including the still unborn child—move to Palestine. Kafka dismissed it as the "stuff of dreams."[11] On giving birth to her daughter Věra in mid-March 1921, she and the baby were driven straight to her parents' apartment at 6 Oldtown Square, where they would live, apart from David. The childbirth apparently failed to bridge the gap between the spouses.

In addition to uncertainty about Věra's biological father, the infant's religious identity turned out to be a major source of friction. In Jewish tradition, the mother imparts Jewishness to her children. Ottla hoped to bring up her offspring either as Jews or at least without a religious denomination. David objected and eventually prevailed. Both Věra and her younger sister Helena were christened. This would save them from death in Nazi camps but short term, we can be sure, further damaged the rapport between the Kafkas and the David clan. The two families would never be close. Above all, it was a bitter defeat to Ottla who was known for her thorny character. Since she and David differed in many ways but shared short temper, they were a mismatch also in this respect. Almost certainly, Ottla Kafka and Josef David started their common life in a marriage of convenience.[12]

This may explain why, oblivious to her marital status, Ottla continued seeking out her brother's company even after giving birth to her first daughter. Thus, as her husband was preparing for a business trip to Paris, she once again asked Franz—still in Matliary—to be her companion. Kafka junior recused himself again in early April (1921). He admitted his presence would really not endanger little Věra but still found a joint outing improper. "For that reason, I think we cannot travel together." Somewhat irritated by the pushiness of his "poor little sister," he ended the letter wishing good luck to her husband.[13]

Clearly, Ottla was anxious to avoid sharing her life and child with Josef David. Another idea that she eagerly embraced in April 1921 would have seen her and her brother immigrating to South Africa. At this point, she apparently engaged even Frau Kafka, who did some investigation about the ships. Kafka deflected her South Africa daydream as April Fool's joke unless Josef David joined them—and he would then feel odd man out.

In the first half of June 1921, the undefeatable Ottla made another eyebrow-raising suggestion, proposing her brother a joint summer vacation in the West Bohemian town of Domažlice (Taus). This time, Kafka replied from Matliary with a letter addressed to both Ottla and her husband, ruling out the invite for fear of infecting the child. Brod, who must have read the missive, promptly commented he could not take seriously his argument against Domažlice. Brod knew well his best friend was not contagious, and so did Ottla. Kafka's slap on the wrist made her angry, prompting him to exculpate himself with virtual kisses.

While sticking to his standoffish posture, Kafka, at the same time, treated as a gem Ottla's first daughter "Věruška," the Czech diminutive for Věra. On receiving their photo, he framed his response awkwardly to suggest he might be more than just an uncle. Thus, he identified Věra right off but had a trouble recognizing Ottla, "though your pride was instantly recognizable." His own pride on seeing the photo would "hardly fit on this card." Somehow, he also managed to praise the infant for its honest face and associate it with "openness, honesty and reliability." How much he would love to rest in a chair, read newspapers, and play with her, he added.[14]

There is no evidence Kafka articulated any remotely intense yearning for his other nieces. But as will be seen, nagging doubts about little Věra's paternity persisted and fueled his desire for progeny indisputably of his own.

In September 1921, Kafka returned from Matliary to the family apartment at the top floor of 6 Oldtown Square. Reflective of anomalous reality, the supposedly tubercular writer shared the space with his parents, Ottla, and her infant daughter. It does not appear that Ottla and her eventually two daughters resided anywhere else than at her parents' quarters during his lifetime. They would move with her husband, Josef David, to the family-owned apartment building at 4 Bílkova Street only in 1925—that is, a year after Franz Kafka's death.

The setup reignited Kafka's sensuousness in the fall of 1921. Owing also to other intervening developments, he experienced a meltdown by the yearend that revolved around sex. "What have you done with your gift of sex?" Kafka asked himself in a long soliloquy on January 18, 1922. Sex tortured him day and night, but a visit of a prostitute—to which he confessed to Brod—was not satisfactory. His mind was fixated on easy and welcoming sex available at close quarters. He was, after all, a shy and modest man who offered "little resistance to other people's aggressive impulses." However, his opportunities for sex were "vile," he conceded. To accept them, he would have to overcome fear and shame and perhaps also regret. As before, love was coming "hand-in-hand with filth." Sex as an evil act again preoccupied his mind, but this time without biblical inhibitions. Should he grab the chance? "I should at once take advantage of opportunities as they come."

Still, he struggled again with his reawakened libido and the implications. "As far as the 'law' is concerned, there is hardly anything to be said against **this,**" reads a truncated entry in his diary. Seen in the context, Kafka alluded to the fact that sex between siblings was a gray area legally in Czechoslovakia. On second take, however, Kafka conceded that "despite the fact that it satisfies the 'letter' of the 'law,' there is something detestable in it which must be unconditionally shunned." Then he corrected himself: "To be sure, one would have to force oneself to shun it."[15] Kafka was in a similar frame of mind as during his conjugal life with Ottla in Siřem. This time more firmly as ever before, however, he identified marriage as "the only thing with which I have any inclination to appease my longing."[16]

Just as in Siřem, he also looked beyond marriage. His ruminations, he clarified it for himself on January 19 (1922), "have the same meaning as yesterday . . . the infinite, deep, warm, saving happiness of sitting beside the cradle of one's child opposite its mother." His ultimate goal was parenthood that imparts a purpose to life, he implied. The fact that it may involve incestuous sex no longer mattered in 1922. "Evil does not exist; once you have crossed the threshold, all is good," he wished to believe. If earlier he discarded a marriage of convenience as illusion, now he dismissed this illusion as imaginary.[17]

Before long, however, the reality check deflated Kafka's daydreaming. Reflecting in April 1922 on his, as he put it, "heavenly *fata Morgana* in hell," he again leaned to realism: though it was in his genes to possess every girl, he admonished himself, "This girl you are not permitted to possess and for this very reason cannot." No matter how fierce was his longing for marriage and children, he could expect merely an "artificial, miserable substitute."[18]

Apart from Ottla's marital status, Kafka faced another major obstacle to his pipedream, his embedment at work. He could start a new life only if he were able to set himself free from the Institute of Workers' Accident Insurance. It was not a far-fetched prospect anymore. Both Director Odstrčil and the physician Dr. Kodym proved to be exceptionally accommodating. In anticipation of his retirement, Kafka received an unscheduled salary raise, and although Kodym found his "lung disease" at a relative standstill, he attested once again on April 26 that the patient could not resume his employment.

As he struggled with severe attacks of indisposition, occasional confusion, helplessness, and hopelessness, Kafka relied on health leaves and regular holidays to keep off work until June 1922. On his return at the end of the month, he sought again the assistance of Dr. Kodym. The diagnosis confirmed a progressing degradation of the lungs with a twist. The condition itself was not lethal, but, Kodym reported, a stay in an institution would not lead to a substantial improvement either. The patient may have needed "several years of appropriate therapy" to recover.[19]

Kafka could not ask for more. Based on Kodym's report, on June 30 (1922), the institute approved him for provisional retirement with a pro-rated pension, about a third of his salary. He was not yet thirty-nine years old. Impatient in the extreme, he did not wait for the decision. In haste and secrecy, he left Prague already a week earlier. "Appropriate therapy" was not on his mind. His destination was Planá nad Lužnicí, a small town of one thousand amid rolling hills some ninety kilometers south of Prague. The region served as a vacation spot for better-off Czechs and Prague Jewry including the Kafkas who had been coming for at least two decades. This time, Kafka's destination was the attic of a non-descript house at Příčná Street, a nondescript lane close to the town center. The flat consisting of two modest rooms of unequal size and a small loft was supposed to be occupied by Ottla, her fifteen-month-old daughter, and a maid. The shared kitchen was on the main floor facing the courtyard. The husband, Josef David, was expected to come for weekends.

Alas, this digression is due now: it is unthinkable that obsessed with hygiene as he was, Kafka would have risked sharing the confined space in Planá with a toddler if his cough were tubercular. It's equally unconceivable that Ottla and the family would have for a moment tolerated such a situation. All were unconcerned because the battery of tests Kafka had undergone on numerous occasions assured them as recently as the summer of 1922 that his "disease" was not communicable.

Ottla in her prime

Ottla's husband Josef David

The Strkov Castle in Planá nad Lužnicí –
Kafka's inspiration for *The Castle*

The house in Příčná Street in Planá – morphed into Bridge Inn
in *The Castle* (there were no backside additions in Kafka's days)

The walled (St. Wenceslaus) Church in Planá – a
fit with the walled church in *The Castle*

Ottla and her pre-teen daughters

THE CASTLE IN PLANÁ

A day after Kafka reached Příčná Street, Josef David apparently returned to Prague, and Ottla with her daughter moved to the smaller room, relinquishing to her brother the larger one with the table and spousal bed. Overall, the accommodation was poor and far below his standard. Even the renovated house as it stands today pales compared with the establishments Kafka frequented in the past (except Golden Lane that he also shared with Ottla). To make the matters still worse, the noise that bothered him everywhere was even more pronounced here, with Ottla's daughter next to him, children playing on the street, a large family collecting hay and a woodcutter splitting logs right under his windows, a sawmill across the street, and a railway station some one hundred meters away, the place where timber seemed to be constantly loaded on railway cars. It surely exasperated someone who professed not long ago, "The amount of quiet I need does not exist in the world."[1]

But Kafka had a table with chair and two windows that brightened up the space, and the Spartan noisy flat became both his writing preserve and playground in Planá. It was there and burning the midnight oil that he worked on his last and most intricate novel, *The Castle*.

The story line of the novel is so deceptively straightforward. A man identified only as "K." makes appearance in a village, claiming the aristocratic owner of a nearby castle had already engaged him as a land surveyor. Supposedly he seeks access to the castle and confirmation of his appointment. In the process, he encounters various village characters, the central of which is Frieda, the reputed mistress of the manager at the castle, Klamm. A hot romance quickly develops between Frieda and K., who just as fast redefines his focus from the surveyor job to wresting Frieda from Klamm's grip. He and Frieda briefly try living together but find the liaison unworkable. As Frieda resolves to return to the castle fold, K. is left pondering his future life alone. Just as other major works of his, the novel is unfinished.

Rudimentary elements of *The Castle* appeared in Kafka's writings as early as 1914. They were undoubtedly reinforced by his futile attempt to wrest Milena Jesenská from her husband, Ernst Polak, in 1920. Brod used the name Klumm in one of his works and published a book with a similar plot in 1920. In general, Kafka followed here his habitual pattern of mixing realism with reveries, this time drawing into the picture events or figures from the past. In addition, the manuscript underwent no corrections by the author and has been tendentiously edited and interpreted by Max Brod (to his credit, however, Brod preserved the logical flow of the novel). Still, this richly textured narrative is, on occasion, inconsistent and obscure even in the German original. In the best Kafka tradition, it leaves a lot to the imagination. Though Kafka never acknowledged James Joyce or Marcel Proust—or D. H. Lawrence whose *Lady Chatterley's Lover* was widely read in his circles—*The Castle*'s staging comes close to their style of storytelling. Overall, Kafka's last novel is an enormously complex work steadily inviting the search for intelligent meaning.

That said, the autobiographical allusions in this novel, opines a respected biographer, 'are clearer than in any other.'[2] There is little doubt that Kafka stands behind K. and *The Castle* reflects his personal experiences. However, unlike in *The Trial*, where the writer was able to work concurrently on the first and final chapter, this time, he penned much of the text on the go, on occasion apparently unsure what the next chapters would be.

Kafka started the novel in Špindlerův Mlýn in the front weeks of 1922 and read his creation to Max Brod on return to Prague in mid-March. However, the latter's response was less than enthusiastic, and the author obviously abandoned the manuscript to pen at least two shorter stories. He gave Brod a new batch of *The Castle* in mid-July, claiming it was much better. Brod's teasing response suggests that most if not all the text was new to him.[3] There are references in the novel to snow and sleigh, but this is another case of Kafka's playful camouflage of the location and time. Already in chapter 5, the weather is hot, and in chapter 8, it is so "extraordinarily warm" in the sleigh that it does not cool off even with the door wide open. Chapter 12 again mentions intense heat.

Further, *The Castle* renders an emotionally laden interaction among the main characters who go back and forth between two places. There is no grounding for it in Kafkas' life in the front months of 1922, when nothing extraordinary occurred either in Špindlerův Mlýn or in Prague. In contrast, overlooked by the biographers, the Kafkas went through a stressful summer in 1922 while commuting between Prague and Planá nad Lužnicí. Both, the text below shows, found echo in the novel.[4]

There are numerous markers supporting the claim that the bulk of *The Castle* was written in the summery Planá. Thus, the "village" in the novel can be matched with the "village," the term Kafka used to describe Planá, and similarly it stretches along the flat main street. Just as the house at Příčná Street, the dwelling K. seeks accommodation in is accessible by a flight of steps and has no indoor bathroom, forcing K. to use a portable basin (the bathroom was added to the Příčná house in 1941). K.'s living quarters too consist of two untidy rooms of unequal size in the attic.[5]

Other objects mentioned in *The Castle* still exist in the walking distance of Příčná Street today—the sawmill, the bridge (over the Lužnice River), the (elementary) school in a low-rise building, and the (St. Wenceslaus) church with a tapering tower. Just like in the novel, the church is actually a chapel without lodes, still covered by a reddish tile roof, still surrounded by a wall, and there still are "barn-like additions" nearby. In Kafka's description, also, there was an "old graveyard" between the wall and the church. Nearly a century later, the wall is still there—and outlines of the graves are still noticeable in the grass.

The dominant topographic feature of the novel is, of course, the mysterious, inaccessible "Castle," owned by an equally mysterious count Westwest. Biographers scour the countryside of Bohemia in attempts to identify the primary object of Kafka's inspiration and location of the novel. This "Castle" likewise exists in Planá. Built in 1903 on elevated grounds of the southeastern precinct Strkov, it connects with the town by a 1.5-kilometer-long side road (in the novel too, the castle is "within easy reach" by a road splitting from the main one). Erected as a summer retreat of the Harrachs, one of Bohemia's preeminent aristocratic families, it was owned in Kafka's days by Count Otto Harrach. The structure had a tower but lacked the character of a real castle—the fact described in the novel as a seemingly deserted "so-called castle," neither an old fortress nor a shiny new edifice. In addition, already in 1922, this Strkov castle was obscured by the surrounding buildup, leaving only the tower visible from the town.

Precisely this situation is described in the novel (the castle lacks a tower and hence is completely obscured today).

The reader of the novel may note that Kafka let the protagonist K. express little appreciation for this castle. Its tower paled in comparison with the church tower that dominated the town silhouette. Besides, Kafka also registered another castle-like structure in town, probably Villa Portika, located on elevated grounds above the River Lužnice and in a clear sight from town. It also was and still is topped by a tower. For Kafka's imaginative mind, all this was enough to start the novel with so masterly evocative castle motif.

Placing *The Castle* to Planá is a step that Kafka's interpreters persistently avoid. Max Brod himself, for example, willfully deleted a segment, intended by Kafka for introduction, that tethered K. to Kafka's accommodation in the town.[6] Why so? The cornerstone of the novel is a love triangle between K.—meaning, Kafka, the Castle manager Klamm, and Frieda, the reputed mistress of both. Mindful as ever of Kafka's standing, Brod also suggested this is an allegory on Kafka's relationship with Milena Jesenská and her husband, Ernst Polak. There is, however, precious little in the novel to support Brod's intervention.

For a start, Frieda has little in common with Milena Jesenská, the health-challenged intellectual with interests in literature, politics, and fashion rather than sex. Kafka's romance with Milena Jesenská was history anyway in 1922. That year, he ostentatiously reverted to addressing her "Dear Frau Milena." In addition, Frieda, Klamm, K., and the villagers interact far more intimately than Kafka ever did with the Jesenská-Polak couple. Neither Milena Jesenská nor Polak even remotely resembles Frieda and Klamm; in fact, they are not recognizable in any of the characters of *The Castle*. The mismatch constrains the biographers: out of all his important texts, this Kafka's masterpiece, in general, receives the weakest, the least insightful interpretation.

There is a much sounder attribution on hand that, however, requires perhaps more guts than knowledge to reckon with. Kafka started the novel in January 1922 when toying with the idea of a shared life with his married sister Ottla and wrote the critical parts of it living with her in Planá. Accordingly, the metaphor of the so-called land surveyor seeking acceptance in a territory dominated by someone else is deeply personal. As K. himself tells it, becoming a land surveyor is only a pretext; he has come to the village to claim the "promised wife," marry her, and integrate in the community.

Kafka adjusts the meaning of the "Castle" accordingly. It starts as an object gleaming in the air and then becomes the so-called Castle or simply a little town consisting of a huddle of wretched village houses and then morphs into an inscrutable authority, or in the words of a biographer, 'the grounding for the ethical and legal structure of the village.' Primarily symbolizing the institution of marriage, it is presented in the novel as women's holy grail, with men not missing this significance either. Even more specifically, another analyst has detected 'the chain of associations' in the novel linking the Castle to a womb.[7]

No wonder the narrative exudes eroticism. K. prefers to penetrate into the Castle undetected in the night, and when he accidentally meets a group of schoolchildren, their teacher switches to French once the talk turns to the Castle. Children should not be exposed to lecherous talk! In the biographer Marthe Robert's quip, the villagers have 'a jealously guarded secret: everybody talks about the Castle and thinks about sex.'[8]

While K. stands for Kafka, his counterpart Frieda bears the characteristics of Ottla, a street-smart female both submissive and aggressive, flirtatious and domineering. In one of the defining moments of the novel, Frieda pulls her lover K. through a barely noticeable side door into the recess open on two sides—apparently the feature of the house at Příčná Street in Kafka's day.

Similarities between Frieda and Ottla abound. Just as Ottla tended for her health-challenged brother (and Lena did for Dr. Huld), Frieda does the same for K. and performs some office work for him. While Ottla dreamed of living with her brother in Palestine, Frieda thinks of moving with K. undisturbed to Southern France or Spain. Just as Ottla and, for that matter, Leni in *The Trial* were rightfully uncertain of the reciprocal feelings of the man they coveted, Frieda doubts K. is genuinely in love with her. He is indeed both mesmerized and disgusted by her advances and views sex with her as unclean—ambivalence not dissimilar to Kafka's feelings toward Ottla. At the same time, however, K. also feels responsible for Frieda's predicament and makes no bones that every attack on her is an attack on himself.

Frieda also exhibits Ottla's character trait of a calculating risk-taker. In the famous passage that reads like a composite of truth and slapstick fantasy, she clears the bar with a whip—in other words, orders the maid to leave—in anticipation of intimacy with K. When the landlord walks in concerned about the possible violation of the house rules and K. hides under the counter, she keeps him down with foot and denies his presence. Far from being a stranger to K., she knows "all" about him, expects him to take her away from Klamm, and makes love to him passionately once the landlord leaves. Not accidentally, some authors speculate incest was on Kafka's mind when working on *The Castle* and find the traces of it in the novel itself.[9]

Symptomatic of this, Kafka started *The Castle* in the "I" form but switched to the third person, "K.," in the middle of a sentence in chapter 3, just as the main protagonist and Frieda become intimate. Clearly, he felt uncomfortable depicting what could be interpreted as sex with his sister. This obliged him to make retroactive corrections from the "I" form to the impersonal "K." in the preceding text. The original version of the lovemaking scene with Frieda was also stronger than the published one. Having the oversensitive Ottla in mind, Kafka also deleted a lengthy "report" mentioning K.'s disrespect for and abuse of Frieda. Further, Kafka's presentation of Frieda undergoes changes throughout the novel, corresponding to his changing relations with Ottla in the summer of 1922.

Ottla's husband, Josef David, is featured in *The Castle* under two names, Schwarzer and Klamm. Schwarzer is a guest in the Bridge Inn who confronts K. on his arrival there. Identified as the son of a castellan or undercastellan, he is unmistakably Kafka's brother-in-law. As we already know, Josef David's father held the position of undercastellan in the Prague cathedral. In one of his comic side swoops, Kafka describes Schwarzer's Catholic father as having a "strong hooked nose [and] . . . full beard." Similar to David, who was a squad leader in the gymnastic club Sokol, Schwarzer is a "moron" who does not like children and rarely speaks to them except when he takes over the gymnastic lessons from his girlfriend Gisa.

Klamm too is anything but Jesenská's husband, Ernst Polak, that sophisticated urbanite moving effortlessly in the literate circles of Prague and Vienna. *Klam* means "delusion" in Czech; *klamm* denotes "clammy" in German. In Kafka's unflattering portrayal, he is a middle-size man, at times a lowly and other times a distinguished bureaucrat who relishes smoking, beer drinking, and gymnastics. He too bears resemblance to Josef David, who, apart from being an office worker, also practiced gymnastics and smoked (as did Ottla and her eldest daughter, Věra, from age nine).

If David was a penny-pincher, so does Klamm have the reputation of a scrooge. Just like David, he is also a domestic despot making capricious decisions (remember the strife in the David family over children's baptism). His authority stems from his position in the Castle rather than his skills and extends to bedding Frieda.

Conversely, Frieda has a "title" that enables her to speak to Klamm whenever she likes. She enjoys the prerogatives of a wife. In a fragment of the text, the landlady mentions Klamm's signature on a marriage certificate, signed also by others, which was deposited with magistrate.

Far from living up to the status of an aristocratic bureaucrat, Klamm shares the lowly attic accommodation with Frieda. But it is not his permanent domicile. He resides in an "unacceptable dwelling"—probably an allusion to David's living in subtenancy—and is familiar with the narrow circle around K., including the freshly arrived K. himself.

K.'s obsession to be confirmed as a land surveyor to the Castle, the position he feels entitled to despite his lack of qualification, primarily reflects Kafka's bid to be accepted as a mate of his sister Ottla, the status he covertly held since the Siřem days in 1917. A testimonial to his living on the edge through that effort, Kafka suffered four emotional breakdowns between July and September 1922.

Among the supporting characters, the Barnabas family is featured most prominently in *The Castle*. It consists of the young man Barnabas and two young females, supposedly sisters, each pulling in a different direction but intent on helping K. This leads some authors to suggest the Barnabases are actually K.'s own family. True, Barnabas, whose appearance also changes as the story evolves, is a humble, submissive bachelor who always runs a fever, courts muses, and is afraid of life—the traits that Kafka might assign to himself. He also bears resemblance to K.'s "assistants," placing him effectively in K.'s family. Though mediating between K. and the Castle, he is not allowed to sleep there. On the whole, Barnabas is a fictional character, a composite Kafka that helps the author navigate the story in the desired direction.

Barnabas's sister Olga, Kafka tells us, was somehow crossed in the past. She approximates his ex-fiancée Felice Bauer. As we know, Felice was victimized by his affairs with Grete Bloch and Ottla before they definitely split in 1917. In the spring of 1922, then, Kafka learned from Brod that Felice, already married and expecting her second child, still harbored a tender spot for him. Accordingly, we learn that Olga preceded Frieda as

K.'s romantic interest but never met Klamm and has little to do with the Castle. She was disappointed by K. in the past but, despite her current relationship with Beutner, still dreams of him. Conversely, her touching eyes bring K. the feeling of happiness.

By the same token, just as Ottla had no affection for Felice Bauer, Olga also knows that Frieda does not like her. Frieda indeed considers Barnabas a hateful name and claims it was her love for K. that rescued him from Olga in the past. In the landlady's view, Frieda acted out of jealousy. These tidbits fit the situation around Kafka's definite breakup with Felice Bauer in 1917.

In the same time warp is Amalia, supposedly Olga's younger sister. She is not. As Kafka describes it in the text, they have different parents. While Olga's father is a relatively young man esteemed by others, Amalia's parents, three years later, are both senile and dependent solely on her care. Olga shows no interest in their well-being. Amalia stands for Grete Bloch, Felice Bauer's younger friend and mother of Kafka's child. In a touching reprisal of her story and personally pained, Kafka depicts Amalia in two chapters as still having a lock on K. but resisting his new advances.

Early in the novel, two "helpers" or "assistants" are introduced into the narrative as Arthur and Jeremiah. They come from the Castle supposedly to support K. in the land-surveying job for which they are not qualified either. At first, they are young adults but eventually start fooling around like kids, playful and undisciplined. They follow Frieda wherever she goes—even witnessing all night her copulation with K. When expelled from the room, they come back through the window, yet Frieda does not mind. They are "our friends . . . we don't need to have any mysteries before them," she assures K. while enjoying their company, laughing and joking with them from time to time. She has everlasting feeling for them. Klamm likes them too. Walking awkwardly, they travel in a "carriage" and do not even think of putting on their clothes. At night, K. almost rolls over one of them, who begins crying and awakens Frieda. Later in the text, we learn that despite their age, they are "mere children . . . only children." On parting with K., Frieda is left caring for them.

One would assume the "assistants" are indeed children, but then, did not Ottla, alias Frieda, have just one child in 1922? It is noteworthy that Kafka does not portray them as separate individuals and for good reason. Giving the reader just one clue, he writes that K. cannot tell them apart visually and, therefore, resolves to treat them as a single person and call them both "Arthur"; all their assignments have to be executed singly as well. It is a single child that stands behind "Arthur" or "assistants" in *The Castle*, Ottla's infant daughter Věra.

An identification of other characters and places in *The Castle* must likewise be attempted. Thus, so thoroughly dull accommodation at Příčná Street in Kafka's fertile imagination morphs into the Bridge Inn (*Wirtshaus zur Brücke*), the focal point of much action in the novel. Both the real and imaginary places are in the attic, both rated subpar by Kafka. It is the Bridge Inn that Frieda and K. cohabit in day and night, cook, make love . . . all the while she takes steps to make the Spartan place more pleasant for him—just as Ottla perked up the cubicle at Golden Lane.

The bar or taproom (*Auschank*) that Frieda works in as a barmaid—in the presence of assistants—refers to the kitchen, primarily in the rental unit where, just like the kitchen at Příčná, it is located one floor below the attic.

The other facility, *Herrenhof* or the Gentlemen's House, is more respectable. It is not an inn where strangers are welcome—and does not approximate any structure in Planá or the same-name café in Vienna frequented by Milena Jesenská's circle as some biographers speculate. It is the residence where both K. and Frieda first met and feel truly at home, having their rooms there. Herrenhof stands for Kafkas' apartment at Oldtown Square in Prague. This explains why K. dreads of being driven off; it would be a biggest misfortune that could happen to him.

K.'s residency at Herrenhof is dependent on the goodwill of the "landlady" (*Wirtin*) and her husband, "landlord" or "superintendent" (*Wirt*) or "chairman" (*Vorsteher*). Similarly, as the head cook in *Amerika* or Frau Grubach in *The Trial*—or for that matter Frau Kafka in real life—the landlady plays the lead violin. (In contrast, Milena Jesenská's mother deceased nine years earlier.) Both the landlady and her husband in *The Castle* are familiar with K., his past and present problems; they counsel him, chastise him, and seek out his advice. In a deleted passage of the novel, the landlady and K. address each other in the familiar German version of Thou (*Du*), and the landlady cuts him off with "Shut up."

Frieda too has a close relationship with the landlady, calling her "mother" and treating her with reverence; in turn, she is the subject of her "motherly care." Their meetings are affectionate, with kisses and long embraces. The family also knows well the elusive Klamm; in fact, apart from living in subpar conditions, he also frequents Herrenhof. In another passage eventually deleted by Kafka, the landlady exclaims she and Frieda love him, albeit more for his social position than persona. K. is also personally acquainted with Klamm and hopes to eventually meet him in Herrenhof regarding the release of Frieda.

Restating the attempt to identify the topography and major characters in *The Castle*,

- the village = Planá nad Sázavou, also the extended family of the Kafkas;
- the Castle = Strkov Castle in Planá;
- Count Westwest = Count Otto Harrach;
- K. or Sortini = Franz Kafka;
- Frieda = his sister Ottla;
- Klamm/Schwarzer = Ottla's husband Josef David;
- Arthur/assistants = Ottla's daughter Věra;
- Bridge Inn = the rental accommodation at Příčná Street in Planá;
- Herrenhof or Gentlemen's House = Kafkas apartment at 6 Oldtown Square in Prague;
- bar or taproom = the kitchen;
- the landlady in Herrenhof = Julie Kafka, mother of Ottla and Franz;
- the landlord/superintendent (in Herrenhof) = Hermann Kafka, their father;
- Olga = Felice Bauer;
- Amalia = Grete Bloch

With these associations in mind, let us attempt correlating *The Castle* story with a major crisis that befell Kafka and his family in the summer of 1922. The reader should bear in mind that the novel is not linear; it warps chronology and telescopes real events stretching over several weeks or years into a continuous narrative; numerous passages show the impact of his vivid drug-sponsored imagination that might have a tenuous link to reality. Similar to prior years, Kafka conceded in July 1922 that writing was his sweet and wonderful reward for serving the devil. What follows here is an interpretation of *The Castle*'s major blocks retaining most names of the text.

We can assume Kafka curbed his thirst for Ottla while living with the family in Prague. Impatient to renew intimacy, he hurriedly left for Planá one week before his retirement was approved and reached the house at Příčná on Friday evening, June 23. Probably unannounced, he was confronted by the landlord living on the main floor.

K. too arrives late and unexpected in the Bridge Inn and accepts the confused landlord's offer of a makeshift bed in the bar. But his is not an ordinary presence. His coming upsets another guest who identifies himself as the castellan's son Schwarzer (Kafka lets the landlord correct that to "undercastellan"). He confronts K., asserting the village is owned by the Castle and permit is needed to stay overnight. Schwarzer also blames the landlord for not enforcing this rule. When K. deflects the prompt to leave by suggesting he has already been engaged as the land surveyor, Schwarzer gets agitated. The ensuing "sharp encounter" sets in motion events (narrated in chapter 3) that, K. would concede in retrospect, vindicated his hostile reception.

Thus, Schwarzer makes a phone call—to his father, the undercastellan—and learns that K. indeed has the position of a land surveyor. Decoded, it means Kafka's intimate relationship with Ottla is no secret. The suddenly deflated Schwarzer pleads with K. to at least move into the landlord's own room, but the suddenly emboldened guest bounces him off. He settles in the bar presumably to sleep there the whole night.

At this point, Kafka diverts the reader to describing the features of the town and introducing other people. Among them is a young woman in a dimly lit kitchen, nursing an infant. She declares herself a "girl from the Castle," but she also knows K. and accepts in silence his claim of being the land surveyor.

Kafka then retells K.'s arrival in the Bridge Inn in chapter 2 with Olga as his escort. This time, he hints at his own unease when knocking on the door at Příčná. After all, he was an interloper with guileful intent.

Accordingly, the landlord is again hesitant to admit K. in view of the "disconcerting" fact—the presence of another gentleman. This time, he is identified not as Schwarzer but as Klamm, the Castle manager. The late arrival of K. assures the landlord he too has some influence in the Castle and will have still more; he also promises a full compensation for cooperation. But K. himself is ambivalent about Klamm.

As already mentioned, K. is not a stranger to the Castle manager. In fact, he feels gratitude to him, fears hurting his feelings, and hence gets a twinge of unease imagining a confrontation with him. These lines correlate neatly with real Kafka's mixed feelings he harbored toward Josef David and eventually relayed to Max Brod.

In chapter 3, K. is (again) assigned the bar as his sleeping quarters, but this time, Frieda is present. Clearly, they are not strangers to each other either, and she attaches to him instantly in expectation of being snatched away from Klamm. There follows the famous passage when Frieda shows K. the dozing Klamm through a peeping hole—and subsequently engages him in a steamy lovemaking in the adjacent room. As the lovers roll in disregard of circumstances, they eventually land with a thud on Klamm's door. Awoken in the breaking dawn, the latter calls for her in a deep, authoritative voice. It mortifies K., who, continuously worried by the presence of the rival next door, nudges Frieda to leave. Instead, she cries boldly, "I am with the land surveyor."

That makes K. both apprehensive and guilt conscious: "We are both ruined." Frieda, however, sees the silver lining: "No, it's only me that's ruined but I have won you." This ultimately pleases K. for he fears he would lose everything by letting her go.

The morning after is told in chapter 14, this time with Schwarzer substituted for Klamm. Remember, Schwarzer initially objected to giving shelter to K., the unapproved guest, but it was the confirmation of K. as land surveyor that truly upset him, and the follow-up nocturnal experience—unspecified in this chapter—added to his distress. Yet despite the sleepless night, Schwarzer still behaves with outward decorum of the aggrieved party and demands an immediate resolution. Getting none, he leaves for the arms of his beautiful girlfriend, the teacher Gisa.

The fracas K. has triggered makes even the landlord in Herrenhof fearful of consequences. He too is somehow involved. On consultation with him, K. eventually approaches Klamm with a personal communication. It is not about the land surveyor anymore—in fact, Kafka now drops the land surveyor symbolism from the novel. K. conveys to Klamm a proposal that is extraordinary and "somewhat crazy." He wants to talk to him as a private person and find out where he stands concerning his, K.'s, marriage to Frieda. Just as Schwarzer, however, Klamm is cross, in no mood to communicate after the humiliating night. In chapter 20, we learn that he does not come anymore to Herrenhof either. His silence frustrates K. and makes Frieda suspicious that he has given up on her.

This means the romance in the Bridge Inn can blossom. Chapter 4 narrates the idyll in the house, with Frieda fixing food on a stove and the "assistants" fooling on the stairs "like children." And when K. feels well enough to leave his bed, they are eager to serve him.

In the real world, Ottla's husband, Josef David, visited Příčná for the weekend of July 2, and the atmosphere there was tense. He meant to leave the next day, but the unresolved issues, we may assume, prompted him to return from the railway station and stay for at least one day longer. There is no evidence he reappeared at the rented flat until mid-August. Alone with Ottla, Kafka spared no praise of her, calling her "wonderfully solicitous" and commending her for treating him as tenderly as her daughter Věra. Life with her in Planá gave him the same pleasure as their cohabitation in Siřem. Indeed, thanks to Ottla, his life in this lazy locale, spent mostly in the skimpy flat, had become "dizzyingly turbulent . . . for someone like me."[10]

Thus, Kafka panicked when his old friend Oskar Baum announced that their planned trip to the Thuringian Forest could take place around July 20. He had given Baum his word he would surely come.

Sharing life with Ottla again, however, Kafka found the prospect of leaving Planá unappealing. Torn by conflicting impulses now, he suffered the first of four breakdowns. Eventually, with Josef David absent, he resolved to stay put in the town. Announcing his decision to Baum on July 5, Kafka justified it by the terrible fear of every change. It was a trifle excuse: after all, not long ago, he spent nearly one year combined in Merano and Matliary and would expend most of his remaining days away from his Prague. He passed the same argument against the trip to Brod, adding a "fear of attracting the attention of the gods." On second thought, he conceded his reasoning was odd; he simply could not accept the "horrible" notion of terminating "this happy situation" in Planá.[11] Never mind that the town now hosted for summer holidays some two hundred Prague schoolchildren, condemned by him as a scourge of humanity for generating "hellish" noise.

It was a déjà vu for Kafka's friends, a repeat of his Siřem effort to let no person or external circumstances interfere with his romance with Ottla. No wonder it provoked similar ironic responses. Baum attributed Kafka's cancellation to an "attack of exaggerated solitude," and the sarcastic Brod—reprising his Siřem stricture—suggested to Kafka a relocation to Western Europe so that he would not remain erotically unfulfilled. In response, Kafka claimed on July 12 that his relationship with Ottla was aboveboard: supposedly, she looked after everything with the result that "though we live wall to wall, I am not in the least disturbed by her, the child or the maid, either by day or by night."[12] More than a month later, August 16, Kafka, in turn, teased Brod—who, married, had a mistress in Berlin—to cut his Gordian knot by setting up a ménage à trois.

Meanwhile, Herr Kafka underwent navel hernia surgery on July 15, and his wife issued a call to children for visitation. Back in Prague, Franz Kafka was soon able to report (to Klopstock) that his father was recovering remarkably well. But his presence triggered ill-feelings in his parents. Another round of their children's cohabitation had driven them to despair. The father, already in the grip of terrible memories (probably an allusion to Siřem), now faced a torment that "exceeds all that has gone before." His respect for the freshly pensioned-off son had diminished day by day, Kafka reported, until he "could not get me out of the room quickly enough, while he forced my mother to stay." On his son's leaving, Herr Kafka somehow gestured the word "bitch." For Frau Kafka too, the visit started a "special, new, wearing period of suffering, even if everything [the surgery] goes on progressing as well as it has done so far."[13] Wow!

Treated by his parents with disdain, Kafka junior neglected trading views with Max Brod on their new texts and returned to Planá on July 19. His hasty departure, he would apologize, was motivated by a burning desire to get away from the bachelor's life. The time with Ottla in Planá was so rewarding.

The Castle offers more insights into the new crisis unraveling in the family. Thus, in chapter 3, K. placates the "assistants"—or Frieda's child—by promising to take them to the superintendent. In chapter 4, then, the location of the narrative changes accordingly. K., along with Frieda and the child, is at the landlady's place in Herrenhof. As expected, the latter displays motherly instincts for Frieda: she loves her and cares for her. This, however, is of little consolation to K., who wants to meet the superintendent. As the latter is absent, the trio eventually concurs they are all friends after all, and K. presents his case to the landlady. He wants to marry Frieda and make up for all she had lost for his sake and by her liaison with Klamm. Frieda hugs him in tears, clings to him, and kisses him wildly as if nobody else were in the room. Embarrassingly, she even falls on her knees to embrace his.

The landlady, also in tears, squarely blames Klamm for Frieda's straying. It is only his neglect of Frieda that K. can thank for this turn of events. Besides, she believes the rumor that Frieda is Klamm's lover is quite an exaggeration. She has no objections to K.'s plot but asks for guarantees. K. ought to realize how much Frieda would lose by associating with him.

K. agrees to guarantees, noting, however, that his intent to marry Frieda may trigger an intervention by the authorities (marriage between siblings was impermissible in Czechoslovakia). He envisages an informal relationship but must talk with Klamm first. The landlady counters it is next to impossible to convince Klamm into giving up Frieda, considering his "very high rank." Frieda has a privileged position with him, and the landlady is proud of it because he does not communicate even with people from the village. Asked for her opinion, Frieda claims it was entirely Klamm's fault that she and K. found each other under the bar counter but expects Klamm to have nothing to do with her anymore.

At this point, the landlady gets upset and turns against K. She does not understand how Frieda could allow this lowly stranger to lay hand on her and thus ruin her future with Klamm. She and her husband have so far kept a distance, but the latest affair may have consequences. They may ask K. to find lodging somewhere else. Frieda, however, belongs to her house.

In retort, K. claims he can get accommodation elsewhere but also warns the landlady that the "assistants" she finds so charming belong to him and he may bar them from talking to her. The threat drives the landlady to another outburst. Hurling accusations at him, she claims that Frieda, in her childish susceptibility, could not bear to see him with Olga, and, in consequence, she "deserted the eagle for the snake in the grass." K. concedes his intent to partner with Frieda indeed has "sinful consequences" but is prepared to put up with them. Besides, the landlady would always be able to take care of Frieda if need be.

In chapter 5, K. seeks out the superintendent, the self-styled "peasant"— probably a hint at Hermann Kafka's rural origin. Similar as Herr Kafka rested in postsurgery in the hospital, the superintendent is in bed, suffering from a severe attack of gout, and K. is surprised at how easy it was to access him. They chat amicably, as befits next of kin and muse about K's intent to extricate Frieda from Klamm. While K. tells the superintendent that Frieda's child—present at the meeting—has his smile, the latter shows awareness of K.'s affair with Frieda and concedes his paternity. When, however, K. produces a message from Klamm, the superintendent is unimpressed. It does not have the significance K. attributes to it. The superintendent has a connection with the Castle, but what he has heard so far is only humming, and that can be deceptive. He cannot agree to K.'s design anyway. The disappointed K. is at least assured he does not face expulsion from Herrenhof for now. He leaves this friendly encounter, pushing the child in front of him—that is, in a carriage.

The next meeting, narrated in chapter 6, is less congenial. This time, K.'s conversant is introduced as the landlord, but on close reading, he is identical with the superintendent in chapter 5. Apprised in the meantime of K.'s conflict with the landlady (who is not present), he reproaches him, noting his wife is unhappy on his account, "can't work, lies in bed and sighs." Since he does not want to act unilaterally, he directs K. to confer with her again.

On his revisit of the landlady, K. strikes a conciliatory tone, suggesting Frieda resembles her in stability of emotions. He also expresses hope that, considering how acrimonious their last talk was, this time he hopes to part in peace. The landlady is more composed but as adamant as before. She calls K.'s intent to marry Frieda both daring and shameful. If he insists on marrying her, he must find an accommodation on his own; he would no longer be welcomed in Herrenhof. As for Frieda, she can remain; the landlady would be very sorry if she followed him. That frightens K., who so far has no sound idea of the arrangement he seeks. But the landlady undertakes to contact Klamm and find out his response within a week. Frieda and the child do not seem to be present at this meeting.

The next chapter, the seventh, renders the events after Kafka's return from Prague to Planá on July 19. We learn that on arrival, K. hurries to Frieda to find that in his absence, she has greatly improved the space in the Bridge Inn. Also present is the "teacher," the superintendent's messenger who starts castigating K. for discourteous conduct. The superintendent is an old and experienced man, K. is told, and should be treated with respect. The more so since, by asking for something that has never happened before, K. is "damaging the reputation of the house" and his own honor as well. The superintendent and landlady think they would do the best to let K. do as he pleases. Showing instead compassion and kindness, the superintendent now offers K. a generous temporary settlement, the post of a school janitor with accommodation. K. should be able to handle it with the help of his wife.*

---

* *What did Kafka mean? Unless his following passage in the novel is just a figment of imagination, it would appear that Herr Kafka, conceding his wife's veto against lodging Franz and Ottla as a couple, found an alternative the outlines of which may be gathered from the superintendent's offer. Thus, children of Frieda and K. must*

The offer comes from the superintendent's exceptionally kind heart, the teacher points out in *The Castle*, for there really is no need for a caretaker, and K. is ignorant of that kind of work. Still, K. rejects the proposal. Frieda responds by dragging him through a barely noticeable side door on the adjacent loft open on two sides and implores him to accept, even if they start without salary. Otherwise, K. needs to know, the landlady would not tolerate him in her quarters for a day longer. It is a matter of honor. After a lengthy debate, K. accepts the offer. This defuses the situation somewhat. Would the landlady's mediation nudge Klamm into surrendering Frieda?

The narrative in chapters 8 to 11 veers into dreamland. Drugs continued to exact their toll on Kafka while he worked on *The Castle*; he was consumptive because of his "own fault" and, as his father quite properly saw it, had shown a "total incapacity for independence."[14] In consideration of Ottla's daughter, he probably curtailed opium smoking in favor of intravenous opiates in Planá. Thus, the novel still mentions "pipes" on a few occasions but no "smoke." On the other hand, Kafka inserted in this story about ordinary folks some fifteen references to needles and injections, in one instance as a happy moment.[15] The half-sleepy main character registers the words of a villager only in the state of semiconsciousness. A bottle of a sweet "perfume" or "sweet wine" has a magical effect stimulating reveries. The novel betrays the hallucinatory influence of opiates, but their impact is more diffused than in his past texts.

A mirror of the author's drug-induced fretfulness, K. anxiously envisions a meeting with Klamm, the purpose of which is solely Frieda. As his rival is absent and unresponsive, K. eventually sees his secretary

---

never be allowed to witness any "unedifying matrimonial scenes"—a stipulation reflecting the tacky relationship of their parents. Further, K. and Frieda would not cook—probably a response to vegetarianism of Franz and Ottla (Franz himself cautioned Ottla to feed her child properly). Along with their dependents, Frieda and K. would be getting free meals at the landlady's (that is what Franz Kafka was already getting at the family's apartment). Finally, Frieda would have to legitimize her status as soon as possible—in other words, shed Klamm. Suppose this reading is correct, Franz and Ottla were offered accommodation within walking distance of the Oldtown Square, probably a flat in the family-owned apartment block at 4 Bílkova Street, coupled with some paid management duties. Owing to his drug habit, Franz himself could not make ends meet with his pension—the fact alluded to in the novel by the landlady's mentioning K.'s dependence on gifts and donations. Similar as Ottla, Frieda is completely without means now.

Momus with the landlady present. However, K. senses his effort is hopeless and refuses to submit to Momus's interrogation (Momus is the Greek god of laughter). Instead, he issues a sort of an ultimatum to Klamm and retires with Frieda to the "school," which, similarly as the rental at Příčná Street, has only two rooms. Another letter eventually arrives from Klamm, merely congratulating K. for his work as land surveyor. It is a sarcastic response considering the above context that frustrates the recipient.

At the same time, problems start accumulating for K. and Frieda. Caught undressed by the teacher, they are summarily dismissed on account of their "dirty household affairs . . . scandalous things." Frieda suggests moving to France or Spain to avoid the stigma, but K. rules that out resolutely: "I cannot go abroad . . . but you too want to stay here, it is your country." A major obstruction to their cohabitation, however, proves to be the "assistants."

Kafka dreamed of his own children, but the duty of care served as a deterrent. He would be remembered as someone who scared his sisters' daughters by aloofness and eccentricity. Bothered so much by noise, he wished his home to be child-free. Noise and lack of privacy thus became a troubling issue in Planá. No matter how cute Ottla's infant Věra was, sharing the crammed space with her challenged Kafka's privacy, comfort, writing regime, and ultimately, his drug intake. The freedom to benefit from "on High" was embedded in his body and mind. Just like elsewhere in the past, his room needed to be aired regularly. To placate him, Kafka reported, Ottla dispersed children playing outside by carrot and stick; she also tried to discipline her daughter. It may have not been enough though.

We learn in the novel that K. fails to connect emotionally with Frieda's child. It watches him closely, demands attention in the least opportune moments, and takes his place in the bed when possible, raising concerns about being smothered; it can never stay quiet and behaves more and more impudently every day, encouraged by Frieda's attention. K. can only wonder why Frieda, so cutting with others, tolerates so much. During a night, he strikes it hard with his fist. The child becomes such a burden in chapter 13 that he tries to "dismiss" it, hoping that would draw Frieda closer to him. Frieda resists—as expected from a mother—at times with amazing patience but eventually capitulates. The novel suggests repeatedly that Frieda has deposited the child with her old friends, putting the blame on K. She conceals this from Klamm, who, of course, is absent anyway.

Thus, for a few chapters, K. and Frieda coexist without the child. She still shows much love and devotion to him, but it also is the time for recrimination and fits of jealousy. At one point, the frustrated Frieda suggests the child is a "messenger" of Klamm—meaning, his daughter. K. is astounded at this claim even though "it seems quite natural at the same time." Frieda retorts hastily that her invocation of Klamm is a mental exercise only not to be taken seriously—but then she adds coyly the child may be Klamm's after all; their eyes are similar. She would not be ashamed of that, and nor should K.

In real life, as Kafka's heavily censored banter on child education to his sister Elli also suggests in close reading, he was inclined to consider himself the biological father of Ottla's first daughter Věra.[16] Max Brod likewise interpreted Kafka's lavish praise of the infant as indicative of his paternity: "Reading your tender words about your sister's child, I am encouraged about your future. I can express it only so nebulously."[17] Somewhere in a fragment of the novel, Kafka assigns K. a wife and child.

Accordingly, K. now hotly contests Frieda's insinuation. It "proves nothing" that she sees the child's resemblance to Klamm; the little one has no real connection with him. Besides, Klamm's letter shows he is quite falsely informed about the child and apparently indifferent to it. In a change of heart, Frieda effectively denies being Klamm's mistress at all. It is a major confession, but K. pretends disbelief now—after all, she can see Klamm whenever she likes. "If you don't believe it, you can go . . . to Klamm and ask him," she retorts. "How cunning, how cunning," he replies.

More important, although Frieda indirectly also disclaims Klamm's paternity, K. still resists her wish to reclaim the child. It will never come back with his consent; he wants to get rid of it indefinitely. As both fight anger, K. becomes aggressive and accuses Frieda, who has done so much to please him, of being still Klamm's sweetheart rather than his wife.

The dispute mirrored the real Kafka's waning interest in women he had conquered. "I can love only what I can place high above me that I cannot reach," he wrote to Brod in the spring of 1921.[18] K. confesses exactly the same. In his mind, Frieda has lost sex appeal living with him; her "insignificant physique" has become obvious because of no fault of her own. It was her association with Klamm that had made her so foolishly seductive to him. It did not bode well for the couple.

As clouds gather in *The Castle*, Kafka takes a nostalgic detour to introduce Grete Bloch, his alluring lover and mother of his son Hans.

As we already know, the boy was born in December 1914 and given up for adoption to a Munich family, leaving Kafka off the hook. In October 1917, Grete apparently issued him a vague threat, but he rejected any blackmail on a prior occasion. The boy died just before his seventh birthday in December 1921. The sad news, we may assume, was responsible for or at least contributed to Kafka's puzzling personal crisis by the yearend of 1921 that sent him to Špindlerův Mlýn, rekindled his drive to write, and triggered his equally inexplicable yearning for a child and family in the front weeks of 1922.

In fact, just before leaving for Špindlerův Mlýn, Kafka registered in his diary what can be considered a nostalgic obituary of his son: it donned on him that a little boy B, in all his innocence stamped with his [Kafka's] traits, uncertain and aimless, would have wanted to go home with him in the evening. But this realization was too forced now, Kafka also noted, possibly alluding to the boy's death. A few weeks later, then, Kafka recorded "arresting and for unknown reasons liberating hysteria," indeed reveries concerning Bloch. We may assume he wished to communicate with her in the wake of their son's passing. She was back in his purview in 1922 and possibly even met him in Prague again.[19]

Grete Bloch and her son then get fair attention in *The Castle*. She is represented in two separate segments as the mother of a boy named Hans and as Amalia (the sister of Hans in Kafka's text of 1916). However, the first to make an appearance in the novel is Hans. A dead soul by the summer of 1922, Kafka hints having in truth no desire to remember him. Yielding to wistfulness, he nevertheless introduces him after the row in chapter 13 between K. and Frieda over the paternity of her child. In his imagination, a knock on their door opens it for Hans, the son of a mother known to K. He is a small, quiet boy with great brown eyes and overtly appealing character, "lively . . . confident . . . inquisitive," a delight to be with. He is also talkative until asked about his family; he divulges little on that score.

Kafka then sketches details that seem to throw additional light on his deceased son's short life. We learn that the boy lived with Lesemanns, friends of the Barnabases. The adoptive family had children of their own. His mother and K. visited the boy when he was still a toddler playing with the mother's foot. This claim in *The Castle* again complements both Grete Bloch's recollections and Kafka's above-mentioned fragments on Hans, Amalia, and the "stranger."

Back in the time zone of the novel, the out-of-worldly Hans offers K. help, yet he also seeks protection against his own father. In another of Kafka's patentable oxymora, Hans's father is identified as the owner of a big shoemaker business who frequents Herrenhof—very much a Kafka. Receptive to the boy's charm, K. is equally eager to establish affinity with him. Prodded gently, Hans professes the desire to become a man like K., despite the latter's current wretchedness. Based on what his mother and others have told him, Hans believes that K., in a distant future, in the "absurdly distant future," would outshine everybody. Deeply touched, K. starts caressing the boy. The two end up in a close relationship befitting father and son.

In this segment of chapter 13, K. also shows familiarity with Hans's mother. They were entangled in the past, and that has left him both remorseful and desirous of her. We learn that she is indefinitely sick with a trifling disorder that gives her a striking look and weakness; if untreated, it could lead to serious consequences. This characterization suggests again that Grete Bloch shared Kafka's taste for drugs, a powerful bond for addicts. Later, Bloch would indeed detail her affliction as lung inflammation or bronchitis "not dissimilar" to Kafka's illness.[20]

Thus, finding Hans's mother still irresistible, K. wants to see her again and help. He has some medical know-how and experience in handling sick people whom the conventional medicine fails. It turns out, however, that she likes hearing about him but does not want to meet. It prompts K. at least to express regret over the course of events since their last encounter and proffer apologies. Kafka apparently meant it as a closure of the Grete Bloch file, but it was not.

We may assume that, just as Ottla's daughter, Kafka's out-of-the wedlock son became an issue in Planá. As Frieda is reminded of Hans's existence, jealousy starts consuming her. She now understands the landlady's warning she has so far refused to believe. Then just as the real Frau Kafka visited Planá, the landlady too arrives at the Bridge Inn to talk with K. again and report to her husband back in the Herrenhof. She issues more caveats to Frieda, warning her among other points that K. views her as a pawn and contemplates a settlement with Klamm as a business deal, a "matter of hard cash." Giving credence to the landlady at last, Frieda accepts that K. betrayed Hans's mother and in his egotism does not care for her either. He may even ask Klamm to take her back. That may be the reason why he is not trying to reach Klamm anymore.

Upset by the growing discord with Ottla, Kafka returns to Grete Bloch in the chapters "Amalia's Secret" and "Amalia's Punishment." This time, he assumes yet another identity, that of Sortini, a clerk associated with the Castle but living in retirement. In a nostalgic disposition, Kafka lets Olga tell the story of Amalia, supposedly her sister, who is a healthy sick just like the mother of Hans, dazed at nights by the "sweet Castle wine." It was in a fairly distant past that Amalia received a summons from Sortini, to whom she was attracted and he still more to her, to come to Herrenhof.

On reading this, both the biographers and readers may conjure up an attempt at sexploitation.

As we know, however, Herrenhof was Kafka's synonym for the family home at Oldtown Square. Sortini's letter in truth refers to his invitation of the pregnant Grete Bloch to relocate to Prague—the step he took beyond any doubt. Making "Amalia's secret" still harder to fathom, Kafka presents the Sortini tale in a playful frame. His was not a love letter that Amalia received; on the contrary, Sortini wrote it while disturbed by Amalia's sight and distracted in his work—an allusion to Grete's pregnant profile. No wonder Sortini's letter had a threatening tone—"See that you come at once or else!"—and the recipient was dishonored.

In Kafka's self-mockery, Sortini is the typical official, abusive of his power, who made the offer cynically believing it would have succeeded completely on a "thousands of other occasions." Yet Amalia rejected Sortini's invite, feeling both anger and distress.

At this point, Kafka also effectively comments on Grete Bloch's visit in November 1914: "That was the morning which decided our fate . . . the decisive thing was Amalia's not going to Herrenhof." The author thereby acknowledges that had the pregnant Grete Bloch relocated to Prague, his life could have been vastly different. Just as the failure of her Prague mission brought Kafka to the edge of suicide, Sortini was shattered by Amalia's fate and became seriously sick out of desperation.

Amalia, we also learn, could still have pursued her case vigorously in the proper quarter—in other words, petitioned for support—or there was "a shorter and quicker way of doing it at Herrenhof"—that is, striking a private deal with the Kafka family. But neither of these has been attempted, and the opportunity has passed, Kafka writes. As brave as Amalia was by not seeking support from Herrenhof, we learn, she became a pariah, a social outcast. Worse still, even though people merely guessed at the nature of the transgression, it ostracized the whole family. They all were shunned because of the taboo that the "letter affair" had violated. The novel then depicts Amalia feeding her half-senile father in words conjuring up a mother nursing an unruly, uncoordinated child.

Despite Amalia's courage and honesty, however, asking himself if he would want her, K. concludes that if Frieda were not around, he would prefer Olga. By 1922, Ottla topped Kafka's pecking order followed by Felice Bauer, with Grete Bloch far behind.

It, therefore, suited Kafka fine that Ottla's husband stayed clear of Příčná Street for much of the summer. With Ottla's rearrangement of sleeping quarters that reserved him the larger room, there was no place for Josef David anyway. His absence allowed Kafka to pursue, as he put it in early August, an "unnatural life" in the nondescript flat in Planá.[21] In a sign of changing fortunes, however, a "thunderstorm" hit in mid-August. As Kafka reported to Brod, his brother-in-law, "someone at loose ends," reappeared on the stage, walked in his room, and took over his table. "My table? It is his table and it is incomprehensible magnanimity on his part that I am given the use of the fine room," Kafka conceded.[22] Behind this shift to normalcy in Planá was Ottla, of course. Kafka was losing her limitless goodwill. She even announced the intent to return to Prague by the month end. In a harsh blow to him, she indeed departed along with small Věra in early September.

Kafka followed her to Prague, pleading for reconsideration, and succeeded for a while. Ottla returned to Příčná Street for another month, "almost entirely for my sake," he reported. But it would not be the same in Planá. As the horizon clouded, he turned introspective again. In a long letter to Brod, the deflated Kafka claimed that, apart from his father's health problems and mother's concerns, he was "sad about several other, far less important but almost more oppressive things." As he feared, the road seemed to be breaking off at his feet with no prospect of his reintegrating in society. As on prior occasions, he still strained to assure Brod he was interested in other women than Ottla.[23]

The "thunderstorm" at Příčná Street also found its way into *The Castle*. In chapter 14, Schwarzer resurfaces, this time described by Kafka plainly as a rival. Though Schwarzer still commands a certain degree of respect, we learn, his actions have been "ridiculous rather than praiseworthy." It would be wrong to attribute him superiority over K. Schwarzer arrives in

Bridge Inn and, more assertive, greets K. with a mixture of embarrassment arising from their first evening and sheer contempt reserved for debtors.

Schwarzer's reappearance prompts K. to reflect on his own presence in Bridge Inn. He realizes the initial conflict with Schwarzer and night call confirming his position as land surveyor spared him of necessity of "lying and contriving." But this is a dubious consolation now. His coming here was highly improper, and the follow-up events have justified Schwarzer's objections to him, K. regrets. The head-on collision should and could have been avoided. Even arriving just one night later—after Schwarzer's departure—"might have made all the difference." He could have started living with Frieda "without making any shady moves" or could have backed out and left the village altogether.[24] Even though the authorities would have eventually figured him out, his chances of integrating in the village would have been much better.

However, K. still considers Schwarzer responsible for his wild romance and is not ready to give up on Frieda. Similar as Kafka in real life, he engages the landlord to give her a few hours to reconsider her departure. She cries, aware she would never become his wife, and her child, now back with her, begins to fear him. Tracing Ottla's steps, Frieda eventually returns to the Bridge Inn to serve in the bar but no longer as his mistress. She proclaims loyalty to Klamm. K. still cannot concede but eventually accepts the reality, "which he had been able to foresee but not to prevent."

It was in this situation that Kafka, in a fit of nostalgia, returned in chapters 15 and 16 to Grete Bloch to feature her as Amalia.

Chapter 18, both sad and increasingly hallucinatory, portrays Frieda again living with K. in Bridge Inn, but she is also seen with Jeremiah—the name of one of the "assistants," effectively Ottla's daughter Věra. In a flash of recrimination, Frieda finds K. responsible for the breakup. If he had not driven her child away, they might be sitting comfortably in the school now. He alone has destroyed their happiness. K. disagrees; in spite of everything, he does not regret pushing the child out. In truth, he feels even thankful to the family for playing some part in the split. It was particularly the landlady who kept inventing tales about his unfaithfulness, he claims. On hearing this, Frieda withdraws her hand from his, vowing, "Never, never will I go back to you. Go back to your girls!"

It would not be Kafka without taking a hard look at himself. The summer months in Planá had brought him closer to Ottla than ever before. In K.'s words, it was essentially all about Frieda. Anything else mattered to him only with regard to her, making the breakup so much more painful. He concedes he has brought it on himself with carelessness but would behave with the same abandon if Frieda changed her mind. Similar as Kafka, K. is almost unemployed and tired, and yearns for a complete unemployment. As consolation for losing Frieda, he finds a reciprocal interest in Pepi, a healthy girl and Frieda's would-be successor in the bar. Possibly another composite drawn on Kafkas' maid Marie Werner, Pepi treats him with compassion and understanding.

The closing chapters of *The Castle* are quite unique in Kafka's texts, amounting to the mean, visceral reaction of a jilted lover. Dropping his usual restraint, he unloads on Frieda. Just as Ottla was an indifferent dresser, Frieda is "not well dressed . . . not very beautiful . . . devoid of all taste." She is also domineering, mean to servants, cunning, and manipulative. "Nobody missed Frieda at the job . . . nobody could stand living with her." Her child may even not belong to Klamm but to his henchman Galater. And when she sent the child away to her friends, she begged them to say nothing to Klamm. She also abruptly bolted away from K., the man who still loves her, and thus endeared herself to the landlord. Nobody doubts any longer she is Klamm's mistress; "even those who obviously knew better" have become "too tired to doubt it." And the child who robbed him of Frieda sometimes gives the impression of not being properly alive.

Barely able to suppress *schadenfreude*, K. also notes that there is no more room for Frieda in Herrenhof and she has to move out—the remark suggesting Ottla was now expected to share accommodation with her husband, Josef David.

The real Kafka, back from a visit to Prague in early September, found the last weeks with Ottla in Planá bittersweet. He felt more serene than happy but still was "especially serene when . . . alone here with Ottla, without my brother-in-law and guests." That sentiment was challenged by reality. Sensing the change, his local landlady, so far cold and hostile to him, suddenly became cordial and friendly. "It's a complicated business," Kafka conceded.[25] She offered him to stay alone as a boarder over the winter, but Kafka realized he would feel completely isolated without Ottla.

Forfeiting the chance to stay until the end of September, he returned to Prague on the eighteenth. No matter how much he enjoyed the summer in Planá, at the end, he was almost glad to leave. He was still working on *The Castle* but not for long; his motivation fizzled again.

Just as Kafka rejoined the family, K. returns to Herrenhof and finds that his room has not changed. But the landlord and landlady inundate him with reproaches. They cannot understand what he has done. The landlord speaks privately with him in the kitchen, trembling with indignation. K. knows he was asking for something that has "never happened before" and that would damage the "reputation of the house." His failure, therefore, has averted a scandal—and has helped pave his way back.

On the last pages of *The Castle*, K. meets the landlady at her quarters accommodating several closets filled with dresses. Her wardrobe is of excellent quality—as one would expect from a lady in Herrenhof—but pretty dark and old-fashioned. When he dares to point this out, she reacts with dismay. But on leaving, he learns he may be invited to help her select a new dress next day. Kafka, alias K., is in the family fold again.

So is Ottla. She returns from Planá pregnant with her second daughter, who, probably conceived between late July and early August 1922, would be delivered on May 10, 1923.

Surrender to "Dark Forces"

The summer of 1922 was exceptionally vexing for the Kafkas and as such remained entrenched in the family's collective memory. As late as 2014, Ottla's ninety-three-year-old daughter Věra would know (obviously secondhand) and feel meaningful to relay that Josef David was not present in Planá and that Ottla's sisters and brothers-in-law teased her for "unconventional behavior" there.[1] But Franz Kafka, the real source of the family angst that summer, failed in his daring drive to secure a wife and place in society. As before, on return to Prague, he shared a life with Ottla and her infant daughter in their parents' apartment at 6 Oldtown Square. She also remained married to Josef David, who, living as a subtenant a floor below, continued to obstruct the siblings' intimacy. This was not the type of cohabitation Kafka had hoped for.

As reality donned on him, he suffered another emotional breakdown within a week of homecoming from Planá. Short of money, increasingly marginalized, fighting despair and depression, he became beset by "fear of the fear . . . fear of complete loneliness."[2] In a letter to Brod, he compared himself to Robinson Crusoe waving a white flag from the highest point of the island. Apparently no longer under a doctor-supervised regime, he also grappled with the same health problems as in Matliary—insomnia, frightening cough, fever, and immobility. With his temperature running at 37.5 Celsius in the evening, he sat at the desk but managed to get nothing done and hardly ever ventured into the street. More often than in the past, bed was his preserve.

Family correspondence for the period prior to September 1923 has not survived, and even Brod apparently liquidated numerous Kafka-related letters and notes in his possession. Kafka severely curtailed communication with friends and acquaintances anyway. Scanty evidence reduces a conscientious author to a tea-leaf reader. In that capacity, one could assume that, with another child of Ottla's on the way, a strange symbiosis developed in the Kafka household. According to the recollections of her younger daughter Helena, the one probably conceived in Planá, it was known in the family that Franz frequented Ottla's bed.[3] The bond between the siblings was weakened but not dissolved. It is hard to imagine Ottla's husband, Josef David, was pleased, but as before, he had a life apart. As before, also, Kafka sought to cultivate a relationship with him, addressing him affectionately as Pepa.

In the fall of 1922, Kafka rendered this anomalous situation in a parabolic tale, "The Married Couple." A sort of epilog to *The Castle* with a twist, it again features "K.," this time with a wife and a son, all living in a further unspecified "small company." He goes to his workplace on rare occasions only and is surprisingly thin, rundown, and unsure of himself; "Frau K." is lively but also vulnerable and in poor shape because of some condition (Ottla was pregnant again). The narrator is another Kafka alter ego, a visitor who is addicted to "cigarettes"—"a bad habit"—and strains to negotiate the staircase. He compliments Frau K. on resembling his own mother, who can do wonders fixing broken things. This is how Kafka insinuates the visitor and Frau K. are siblings with a mother who may still facilitate their cohabitation.

The visitor comes with a business proposal that totally absorbs him but has to square with a competitor, an agent already known to him. This "rival" has been crossed somehow in the past but still intends to plant himself in the family forever and—in the act of "unsurpassable insolence"—behaves as if he already belongs. He is a stand-in for Josef David. The proposal is intended in part for this agent—nay, it constitutes "a severe blow" to his designs. It is evening, however—the doping time—and K. experiences great strain as his body trembles and his face gets distorted. While his wife puts him in the bed next to his son with a mixture of tenderness and irony, the insouciant agent sits in a chair nearby "cold as a frog," confining himself to a few improper remarks.

K. eventually recovers enough to return to the proposal that is at once generous, shrewd, and distasteful. This is how Kafka codes his desire to replace David in Ottla's life. As we remember, K. was already suspected in *The Castle* of contemplating a removal of Klamm from Frieda's life "as a business deal, a matter of hard cash." This time, the agent himself responds bluntly that some compensation is due to him after what has happened. Circumstances, however, work in his favor. As the visitor notices on leaving, Frau K. has mixed him up with the agent. (About the same time, Ottla applied for a passport to accompany her husband on a business trip to France.) The visitor responds with lamentation over Frau K.'s unreliability: "Ah, how futile business affairs can be and yet one must carry the load farther."[4]

"The Married Couple" captured the essence of Kafka's life in the closing months of 1922. Uncomfortable with the image of Kafka living in a triangle, his literary executor Max Brod arbitrarily changed the designation of the protagonist from K. to N.

In bad shape both mentally and physically, Kafka also drafted another 'last will' in late 1922. His first, in the fall of 1914, as we know, was triggered by Grete Bloch's pregnancy that also led him to contemplate suicide. He had modest success as a writer since, and his renewed wish to burn his printed works was bizarre. The list of oeuvres he excluded from burning was longer now—*The Judgment, The Stoker, The Metamorphosis, The Penal Colony, The Country Doctor,* and *The Hunger Artist.* Spectacular omissions were the two unpublished manuscripts that would eventually elevate his reputation, *The Trial* and the recently abandoned *The Castle.*

This "last will" of November 1922 seems to have been motivated by the premonition of dying consumptive. As we already know, Kafka had struggled with this prospect since 1912, and his hunch was reinforced by real-life cases of that nature. In 1920, another addict with whom Kafka himself had developed an uneasy rapport succumbed to food deprivation, Otto Gross. This tarnished psychologist had been congregating in Vienna with Franz Werfel, Ernst Polak, and Milena Jesenská (who also wrote his obituary).

In 1922, Franz Werfel dealt with Gross critically in a play, *Schweiger,* featuring him as *Privatdozent* Dr. Otokar Grund, an eccentric who contemplates a revolution of the hungry. The main protagonist, however, is Franz Schweiger, a clockmaker and a Jew, who also copes with hunger and assorted afflictions but does not evoke empathy: his health issues are somehow un-German. "It's a miracle you have not died in fire," comments an accomplice contemptuously. Schweiger eventually dies believing there is no help for him, "but he is wrong." Werfel seems to suggest that addiction, the underlying cause, can be cured.[5]

Kafka felt offended in more than one way. Apart from his affinity with Gross, he obviously minded resemblance with Franz Schweiger and the implied linkage of drugs with death. Werfel touched his nerve so profoundly. The play, Kafka wrote in late 1922, "means a great deal to me; it hits me hard, affects me horribly on the most horrible level . . . these three acts of mud." He was agitated throughout the evening and all night, imagining the implication for himself.[6]

As was the case with other addicts, the prolonged indulgence in opiates also started sabotaging Kafka's writing aspirations. Thinking and writing had become quite difficult, he observed in the front weeks of 1923, and even when spared of sluggishness, his hand trembled, running blank over the page. Later in the spring of 1923, he observed that while his lungs had improved, his general condition had become much worse and excruciating headaches along with insomnia made him incapable of anything.

An escape from this cage crossed Kafka's mind when, in mid-April, his gymnasium classmate Hugo Bergman arrived in Prague for a visit. A librarian in Jerusalem now, Bergman spurred him to try "something radical," an immigration to Palestine. Motivated also by the Bergman's offer of accommodation in Jerusalem, Kafka restarted Hebrew lessons. His tutor, a young Palestine expatriate Puah Ben-Tovim, found him in very poor shape, distracted by coughing even during the instruction. He would have been barred from entering Palestine if tubercular, but that clearly was a moot point. His hope of starting a new life there was not even remotely realistic in view of his debilitating health condition. In fact, he was already voicing openly a presentiment of death. No wonder his Palestinian dream faded after Bergman's departure, and so did his interest in Hebrew classes.

As Ottla was due to give birth to her second child in May 1923, Kafka avoided possibly awkward moments and left the city temporarily. He settled on Prague's satellite Dobřichovice, but the seclusion failed to give him peace of mind. In a foul mood, he found the accommodation too expensive for the occasion. As drugs continued taking their toll, in June 1923, he recorded nasty spells of incapacity. Even when he managed to ply his pen, every word seemed to have become a spear turned against him. His encounter with Milena Jesenská in June 1923, which turned out to be the last, failed to get a single line in his diary.

The following month, Kafka traveled with his elder sister Elli and her three children to Müritz, a resort at the Baltic Sea. The family doctor expressed reservation on account of the northern climate but not tuberculosis. Considering his noninfectious status, Kafka was safe to mix with children.

On July 12, he met at Müritz Dwoyre Dymant, going as Dora Diamant (1898–1952), the daughter of a Hassidic factory owner in Breslau (today Wrocław in Poland). Twenty-five years old but claiming to be younger, she worked as a cook and Hebrew instructor in the nearby camp of Jewish children from the east. Though uneducated and uninterested in Kafka's literary work, she was a warm and caring creature who found him attractive as man and human being. She would remember him as tall and slim and so dark-skinned that she at first believed he was not a European but a half-breed American Indian—so much had opium darkened his exterior. She would also recall him as humorous but careful with his words, with eyes always cheerful, always ready for some mischief. In addition, she discovered him to be "sensuous like an animal—or like a child." Conversely, Dora, in Kafka's early assessment, was a "wonderful person."[7]

Still, no matter how appealing she seemed, Kafka left Müritz along with the family in mid-August and, after a brief stopover in Berlin, returned to Prague. Prior to departure and expecting to reunite with Dora shortly, he reserved a flat in Berlin and gave Dora money to cover the August rent. Once in Prague, however, his perspective changed fast. His sister Ottla just marked the end of postpartum after a difficult birth of her younger daughter and readied for another summer vacation. Within a few days in Prague, he accompanied her to Želízy, the place they shared as twosome in 1919. This time, Ottla took along her children, the twenty-six-month-old Věra and the two-month-old Helena.

Again, the mother, the family, their doctor . . . nobody objected to Kafka's sharing his heavy cough with two infants. Ottla's husband, Josef David, was supposed to come for weekends, but at least on one occasion, he excused himself on account of his "usual consideration for Franz."[8] Obviously, Kafka's preference for being with Ottla alone was at last respected by the family.

The Želízy setup was similar as that in Planá one year earlier, but this time, Kafka penned no chronicle thereof and no family correspondence is available. Circumstances suggest that, while Dora was paying rent for the reserved flat in Berlin, he tried to restore the romance with Ottla. Afterward, he would remind her of "Želízy bath which so delighted you" and caution against writing intimate letters. The siblings also broached again the subject of a common future, still tilting to "something radical." At the same time, Kafka sent regards to Ottla's husband.[9]

More than in the years past, however, Kafka struggled in Želízy with "too many counterforces" that "fight like the devil, or are it." In consequence of the obstructed food and drink intake, he recorded his lowest weight as an adult at 54.5 kilograms. "I shall never be able to understand . . . that an otherwise cheerful and essentially untroubled person can be destroyed by consumption alone," he observed.[10] As in the past, his head was muddled, a condition that also prevented him from writing. When a letter reached him from the Swiss editor Carl Seelig with a generous advance of one thousand Swiss francs for a new story, he kept the money but would not submit anything. Unlike the year earlier in Planá, however, it was he who eventually terminated the vacations in Želízy. He left after five weeks, while Ottla and her younger daughter stayed put until mid-October.

Herr Kafka spoke with great pride about his son to others but was enervated by his conduct in private. Thus, he was not enthused about this new Želízy escapade and gave Franz an earful on his return to Prague. Kafka junior at first considered canceling the trip to Berlin in consideration of Ottla, but this latest scolding obviously changed his mind. After less than two days in Prague, he boarded a train to Berlin on September 24. Those few notified in a hurry learned he was leaving for several days only. In truth, with Dora Diamant in tow, he settled down in Miquelstrasse in Steglitz, then a southwest suburb of the German capital.

If his sudden decision to live apart from the family caused consternation, it was understandable. So judicial a plodder in the past, Kafka was acting with abandon now. In prewar years, he was appreciative of the German capital as a center point of dynamism and creativity. In 1923, however, there was little that recommended Berlin over Prague. For one, the vexing issue of anti-Semitism had been much defused in his hometown. When German professors of Charles University protested the election of the Jewish historian Samuel Steinherz as university president, the Czechoslovak government in late 1922 quelled the protest with threats of restricting the university autonomy. The situation was far more explosive in Berlin. In June 1922, the German finance minister Walther Rathenau, a Jew, was assassinated there, and the city, just as much of the country, saw mushrooming right-wing groupings and paramilitary units that eventually became Hitler's backbone.

Even more burdensome, however, were living conditions. The Treaty of Versailles (May 1919) imposed onerous peace terms on Germany, the principal country of the defeated war alliance, including hefty war reparations. In response to German tardiness in payments, French troops occupied the industrial Ruhr region in January 1923, and the German central bank, out of desperation and spite, resorted to printing more and more paper money. The consequence was a hyperinflation of mind-boggling proportions. As the German mark depreciated by 20 percent in a day, the room Kafka initially rented for four million marks commanded approximately half a billion three months later. Bank savings had been wiped out, businesses closed, climbing unemployment gave rise to more social unrest, and the basic necessities were becoming prohibitively expensive, if available at all. In consequence, the Germans living on fixed incomes found it next to impossible to make ends meet.

In "The Departure," Kafka's short prose available as a fragment, the servant asks, "Where is the master going?" and receives this answer, "I don't know, just out of here, just out of here." In truth, Kafka's move to Berlin was foolhardy but not without motivation. Apart from reuniting with Dora, his dream was to break the fatuous dependence on drugs. As he put early into his Berlin days, he hoped to slip away from his demons so that they would not find him.[11]

Escape from addiction, so difficult under any circumstances, was not assisted by his new companion. Dora Diamant, apart from not sharing his living quarters, possessed neither the foresight nor the character of Felice Bauer to nudge him into changing the lifestyle. A resourceful scrapper, she was stricken by deep-seated unhappiness and pessimism that reinforced Kafka's apathy and resignation, exactly the opposite of what the situation asked for. Similar as Ottla, she was also willing to tolerate the drug regime of the man she did not quite understand but whom she worshipped. Precisely this made her desirable to Kafka—and placed him at increased risk.

Kafka sensed the young girl's devotion was also his major liability. He barely mentioned Dora's existence in letters to his family and friends. Under her passive care, his war against drugs also proved short-lived. The old sufferings found and attacked him again in Berlin. "The phantoms of the night have tracked me down," he confirmed a relapse into drug dependency to Brod. The grip was merciless, as his nights "destroy themselves on their own—more than ever."[12]

Like on other occasions, Kafka rendered this failure in prose, specifically in the short story "A Little Woman." The title refers to his landlady at Miquelstrasse, the place he liked, who terminated him after a few weeks. Why? Kafka here admitted that, though in no way intrusive, he engaged in nightly antics that left her "unslept, oppressed by headache, and almost unable to work." Without doubt, just as his parents since 1912, the landlady minded his lifestyle, the stench of opium smoke and his prolonged night coughing. His suggestion of how to defuse her sullenness wrought her up to such a rage that he would never repeat it. To avoid becoming the subject of public acrimony, he resolved to "change myself in time, before the world could intervene." The solution undoubtedly consisted of reducing opium intake, a major aim of his relocation to Berlin anyway. So he "honestly tried, taking some trouble and care," but even though the effort did him some good, ultimately, he failed. The landlady, being so sharp thinking, now understood how helpless he was, even with best intentions, in trying to placate her.[13] This marked the last time Kafka attempted to beat addiction; the failure left him reconciled with fate.

In addition to the constant need of fix, battling for food provisions, and the pain of prices had made his living a real challenge. Kafka experienced "the sadness of Berlin." He confided to Josef David in Czech, "Je to tu skutecně hrozné" [It really is terrible here]. After two weeks in the city, in a letter nostalgic about "Prague that I not only love but also fear," Kafka asked Ottla to come for a visit—or should he visit Prague first?[14] At the same time, he signaled it was no longer about intimacy. He also sent regards to her husband and the children. In a separate letter to Josef David, he bantered about soccer, his in-law's favorite topic, and directed regards to his [David's] parents and sisters. Fighting homesickness, he imagined a cozy atmosphere in the family and pleaded with Ottla for stories about Věra and Helena. He showed a particular concern that Věra would not forget him. "Who can provide me with a guarantee of that?"[15]

Kafka was smoothing a path for his return to Prague, but it remained a mere wish. After the less-than-joyful parting, his parents, in particular, were in no mood to accommodate him. In response to his pleas, he was warned not to expect cash advances. The purpose of this, he suspected, was to teach him about saving money. For the time being, he was dependent on his pension only—and also that meant fewer drugs. In addition, the family felt uncomfortable with Dora, whose capacity to care for Franz adequately was doubtful. Thus, Ottla herself, the ever-loyal Ottla, was not keen on traveling to Berlin, sensing the family would object to the trip. In truth, she even counseled him against homecoming. She gauged correctly the irreconcilable vibes on both sides. Almost certainly, the Kafkas expected him to return without Dora—the condition he found hard to swallow. When he nevertheless decided to take the trip to Prague by the yearend, even Frau Kafka ruled that out. With a stiffened upper lip, Kafka commented in a letter to Brod, "It's really better that way." He hoped to stay away long enough to be regarded as a family guest on return to Prague.[16]

In truth, Kafka, unwelcomed home, lost the last vestiges of self-confidence and started feeling, more strongly than ever, not in full possession of his mental powers. He joined other cultural icons that saw their mental capacity degraded by drug dependence. This enhanced the standing of his companion. Dora Diamant was becoming more assertive in everyday affairs. Under her influence, he also started paying more attention to religious issues, renewing some effort to attend Hebrew and Talmud classes. Characteristic of his split allegiances, Kafka learned Hebrew from a Czech textbook but wrote comments in German.

Meanwhile, Kafka left the place of his defeat at Miquelstrasse in mid-November and settled in a flat nearby, at Grünewaldstrasse 13. In a report to Ottla, he stressed the green character of the location and suggested that her visit—so far delayed—would be very welcome. This time, however, he made the trip conditional on her husband's consent. A challenge to his brother-in-law's spousal authority was no longer on his mind. Eventually, Ottla arrived in Berlin on November 25, "approving of everything she sees, I think," Kafka reported, not sure about her perception of Dora. As the prospect of living with Ottla fizzled, the photos of her daughters now caught his attention. Though having five nieces and a nephew, he found affinity with her elder daughter. He bought her a doll, and for the next several weeks his mind was focused on Věra, Věra, and again Věra. In response to Ottla's (apparently suggestive) letter, Kafka concurred, "You are right. I felt instantly recognized by her look."

The closing weeks of 1923 brought some financial relief to Kafka. For one, in a bid for survival, German society adopted an unofficial new currency, the so-called rentner mark. Pegged to the dollar, it stopped the madness of galloping inflation and made prices more predictable. Still better for him, after Ottla's visit in November, the family somewhat relented. Ottla and her sisters sent some money, while the parents now provided support in kind. This should have stabilized his situation just before winter, but it did not. In a letter to the institute's director, Kafka reported extreme insomnia not alleviated by sleeping drugs—that is, opiates—as well as an incapacity to take action of any kind. His hope that a "complete change of environment" would be beneficial proved futile.[17]

By the end of 1923, Kafka's health had taken a disturbing turn for the worse. In addition to an accelerating weight loss, he was incapacitated by fever, chills, insomnia, and cramps. A rigorous penny-pincher and no friend of doctors, Dora summoned one in early January 1924. He found little could be done and advised the patient to stay in bed. Since settling in Berlin, Kafka had been visited by several friends and acquaintances but rarely ventured outside. Nearly a total recluse now, he was also getting accustomed to living in an unheated room and cooking with Dora on a candle. The appeal of "warm, well-fed Bohemia" was undeniable, but he would not return to Prague without her.[18]

Meanwhile, his second landlady also minded his presence and asked him to leave after two months. Kafka found new lodging on Heidestrasse 25-26 in Zehlendorf, a more upscale suburb but less accessible by public transportation. His third landlady, Frau Busse, was the ex-wife of a deceased writer. This time, Kafka hid his identity, presenting himself under an assumed name and as a chemist. Chemists can be expected to experiment with odorous gases, cannot they? Coughing intensely as before and coping with obstructed swallowing and speaking, Kafka again tried to ply his night trade, writing. True, Kurt Wolff resigned as his publisher on account of slow sales, but Kafka followed Brod's advice and negotiated a new contract with another German company *Die Schmiede*.

In this stage of his life, Kafka was much too degraded to benefit consistently from his drug inspiration. "There are abysses into which I sink without even noticing . . . Such are not proper occasions for writing," he confided to Klopstock.[19] Still, despite his handicaps, he penned a number of stories, most of which, unfortunately, did not survive. Two extant texts show his ripened mastery in transforming his personal woes into sophisticated fiction. "The Burrow" is yet another allegory of his predicaments, this time revolving around a mole-like creature. Living underground as addicts often imagine themselves, the creature is supposedly free but struggles with Kafka's afflictions. "I have eaten nothing for a long time . . . And I spit out my food and would like to trample it underfoot," the narrator tells. Even worse, there is an intolerable noise everywhere in his labyrinth, day and night. An enemy "is boring his way slowly towards me." It is only a matter of time before this mysterious beast will have tortured him to death. That will be an act of liberation, Kafka intoned, for it is better to surrender to an unseen force than to endure a fearful existence.[20]

His last short fiction of note is "Josephine, the Singer, or the Mouse Folk." Completed in the spring of 1924, it amounts to a poignant, metaphoric epitaph of the writer bracing for grave. Ostensibly, it is a story of a fading mouse that squeaks, hoping to get a permanent recognition of her art, "going far beyond any precedent." Her supporters are still begging her to squeak, but her sad appearance—she "breaks down before our eyes"—makes her effort pathetic: "The sight of Josephine is enough to make one stop laughing." Existential loneliness permeates the story: "Josephine's squeaking . . . is almost like our people's precarious existence amidst the tumult of a hostile world . . . People are capable of presenting a stony, impenetrable front to one of their own."

No doubt, "Josephine" is a play on Kafka's growing inability to speak and the underlying cause. However, the critical verb the writer used, *pfeiffen*, has a multiple meaning in German, to whistle, to squeak, to sing, and to smoke a pipe (*Pfeiffe*). Confusing the reader with relish, Kafka himself noted that *pfeiffen* is not necessarily *pfeiffen*. This ambiguity allows him to mull mischievously on his favorite drug habit and its creative effect. Thus, he declares "piping" one of the pleasures that relieves people "from fetters of daily life and sets . . . [them] free too for a little while. We certainly should not want to do without these performances." Naturally, this piping is illicit. Josephine has always resorted to it "in the safest place and was always the first to whisk away quietly and speedily." It can be said that Josephine "stands almost beyond the law" in this respect. It also is in "direct contravention of laws" that she takes advantage of the "extraordinary gift" the piping grants her and applies it to another endeavor than singing.

Kafka does not elaborate, merely repeating that in her "artistic career," Josephine resorts to the "most unworthy methods." These are justified since, as she sees it, "honest methods are bound to fail" in this world. Equally exculpatory is her effort to avoid "general struggle for existence" and live at society's expense. The need of earning daily bread would siphon off her strength as an artist, Kafka effectively justifies his work truancy.

So far, we learn, Josephine's art is beyond the comprehension of the people even though they "marvel helplessly" about it. She should, therefore, wage the "last battle for recognition" before it is too late. Her ambition is already sabotaged by her frail body, and she has no one to blame but herself: singlehandedly, she "destroys the power she has gained over people's hearts." The story ends when Josephine has vanished, and the narrator opines her piping will also fade from memory. In *Josephine,* Kafka wrote a harsh, apocryphal account of himself and his drug-enhanced labors to score as a major writer.[21]

Meanwhile, Kafka's health continued to deteriorate. Tipped off by Max Brod, his uncle Siegfried Löwy arrived in Berlin by the end of February 1924 and urged a sanatorium treatment without delay. As before, Kafka resisted, fearing a loss of "freedom," seemingly an insanity grounded in his reluctance to submit to a detoxification regime. Dora supported him, knowing she could end up alone. For the same reason, she also claimed that Franz would be doomed if he stayed in his parents' care in Prague.

Eventually, Klopstock also arrived in Berlin, hauled Kafka up from the flat, and handed him at the railway station to Brod for the trip back to Prague. Dora was left behind out of fear his parents, in particular the father, would raise objections to her presence. She hoped to reunite with him at a yet-to-be determined place.

On March 14, Kafka saw his parents after six months' absence. In another comment on his real-life experience masked as prose, "Home-Coming," he registered the growing alienation: "Do you feel you belong, do you feel at home? I don't know, I feel most uncertain. My father's house it is, but each object stands cold beside the next . . . And I don't dare knock at the kitchen door."[22]

He was also drastically degraded and lost his voice the third day in Prague. An institutional care was called for, and Kafka at last consented to it. A sanatorium in Davos was selected as the place where, under the watchful eye of Uncle Löwy, his advancing morbidity could be reversed. His employer was advised accordingly. However, that meant a drastic reduction of drug intake and the absence of Dora. In a last-minute change of mind, after three weeks in Prague, Kafka settled on a sanatorium near Vienna. Ottla, now the mother of two young girls, promptly extended her passport to accompany him. However, he departed alone on April 5.

Alas, the biographers who blame Kafka's parents for this—what quickly turned out to be a disastrous—decision conveniently overlook the fact that Kafka was forty years old and acted against their wishes.

Austria was a rather unusual choice considering his lack of affection for that part of the globe. But then, Kafka never, not even among goats and pigs in Siřem, shed his lawyerly bearing, symbolized by a dark suit and tie, white shirt, and black hat. This public servant was also keenly aware and alluded to in his last story, "Josephine, the Singer," that his "piping" needed to be discreet. A disclosure of his root medical problem, drug dependency, could derail his early retirement on health grounds. In this respect, then, Austria was a safe heaven, the only civilized country not criminalizing narcotics yet (not until 1928). Only in this land on the Danube would Kafka be able to buy his contraband worry-free or have morphine injected by a nonqualified medical student. Little wonder that with Dora at his side, his Austrian adventure eventually also delivered his coup de grace.

The "Hunger Artist" Dies

Located in the rolling hills in Pernitz, seventy-five kilometers south of Vienna, Sanatorium Wienerwald was a well-regarded establishment for patrons recuperating from eating and breathing disorders. It was first suggested to Kafka by his doctor in 1920 and had Siegfried Löwy's colleague on board. On arrival, Kafka underwent admission exams, the record of which is no longer available. Their thrust can be established from his comments. Outwardly, in six months of Dora's easygoing care in Berlin, he lost an astonishing six to eight kilograms, and his weight dropped to a mere forty-five to forty-seven kilos, or less than one hundred pounds. He had become a walking skeleton. But there was no tuberculosis to account for it. In his last years, he had been repeatedly examined, had X-rays taken—yet there is no bona fide evidence he ever tested positive. In Wienerwald, he was once again diagnosed with infiltration of lungs rather than with their collapse. Overall, the grounds for his alarming weight loss were serious but not irreversible.[1]

Kafka's condition contrasted sharply with those suffering from cachexia, a metabolic disorder that blocks food digestion. A tubercular suffering from cachexia loses weight even if he eats abundantly. Kafka, on the other hand, was wilting because of the withdrawal of food and drink. He had been paying the price for drug abuse and its consequences, in particular spasmodic muscles, the affliction that prevented him from using his limbs and from swallowing. Specifically, the cramping of the feeding tube (esophagus) turns eating and drinking into an excruciating task. Only 1.5 centimeters wide, the esophagus on further constriction can push food and liquids back through the nose or into the adjacent breathing tube.

Unlike those suffering from another related affliction, anorexia nervosa, those dependent on opium have an appetite that cannot be satisfied. Never free of hunger and thirst, the addict becomes a "hunger artist." Preventing starvation thus may become his lifelong challenge. This explains why opium has often been taken with wine or other alcohol that, acting as a muscle relaxant, unlocks the esophagus. Countless Romantics of the previous generation had been taking laudanum, opium mixed with alcohol, and yet many were unable to consume even a simple meal or drink without experiencing intense agony.

Staying clear of alcohol, Kafka first expressed the premonition of death by starvation in *The Metamorphosis* (1912)—that is, long before the supposed breakout of tuberculosis—and during the next twelve years did little to reverse his drift downward. If pulmonary tuberculosis was not responsible for his morbidity, the real cause could be more easily uncovered and with it his source of writerly inspiration.

More was at stake than Kafka's conditional pension and his standing as a writer. The postwar society was regressing to an infantile stage, and that included creepy forms of anti-Semitism. To Max Brod's dismay, even his Berlin lover, Emmy Salveter, told him as the greatest praise, "But you are not a Jew."[2] The likes of the hypocritical Hans Blüher, the notorious German preacher of masculine homosexuality if not pederasty, was thundering against the supposed Jewish decadence and immorality (Kafka was both attracted and repelled by this character). Revelation of an aspiring Jewish author's drug dependence would serve Blüher and other anti-Semites well. After the Nazi takeover of Germany, a decade later, narcotics were formally denounced as Jewish depravity (that did not prevent Hitler from indulging in them privately).

As pulmonary tuberculosis had become a poor cover-up for his rapidly advancing health woes, Kafka revised his script on return to Prague in April 1924. He did so almost certainly in consultation with Brod, who had never reconciled with his friend's plunge into drugs. Thus, Kafka stopped insinuating lung tuberculosis and tried to present his inability to swallow as a result of tuberculosis of the larynx, the neck cavity channeling air to the lungs and food to the stomach.

This tuberculosis, manifesting itself in tubercles and polyps, was easy to detect already in Kafka's days. Almost always a migrant from the lungs, it also was uncommon and afflicted primarily females. Even if Kafka were to suffer from pulmonary tuberculosis, he would have stood no more than

1 percent chance of contracting it. A scholarly study published in 1924 reviewed the current understanding and cure of the disease. It acknowledged the laryngeal tuberculosis was very rare, easily detectable, and effectively treatable even in advanced stages by cauterization or excision of ulcers. The procedure merely left the patient's respiratory system with scars. Even before the age of antibiotics, those infected with laryngeal tuberculosis rarely died from it. Left untreated, the ulcerated tissue could produce similar discomfort as consumption of opium and opiates—difficulty in swallowing, chronic cough, and even loss of voice.[3]

Kafka, based on his noninfectious status alone, probably did not suffer from laryngeal tuberculosis either. But keeping himself abreast of health issues, he found in association with this disease a plausible explanation of his advancing morbidity. This was in line with other opium addicts who, rarely willing to confess to addiction, employed the tactics of diversion.

On arrival to Wienerwald, then, Kafka tried his new cover but was met with polite caginess. "I don't learn anything definite since in discussing the tuberculosis of the larynx everybody drops into a shy, evasive, glassy-eyed manner of speech," he described the doctors' reaction.[4] In truth, the Wienerwald doctors determined fast the root cause of his withering and advised him to seek the proper treatment in hospital. He did not like the message but complied. After five days in Wienerwald, he transferred to the Laryngological Clinic of the Vienna University on April 10.

Headed by Prof. Markus Hajek, the clinic was highly regarded, the place where Sigmund Freud was operated on a year earlier. Kafka was assigned to a room with two other patients and found the hospital atmosphere depressing. But the clinic had a roof garden overlooking the city, and the quality of care was impressive. As he reported to his parents on April 11, he was "under the best medical supervision available in Vienna" and needed not summon specialists at extra cost. "As long as I cannot eat any more, I must naturally stay here."[5] Eating disorder was his critical concern now.

However, the admission interview and physical checkup shows Kafka—probably with Dora Diamant's help for he could only whisper—was framing his medical past to support the claim of laryngeal tuberculosis. Thus, the patient conceded there was no tubercular in his family but asserted having been diagnosed with pulmonary tuberculosis six years earlier. Yet again, explaining his drastic weight loss of six kilograms in so few months, he admitted the inability to eat was the culprit. Naturally,

Kafka also felt very weak and suffered from constipation. Judging by two unannotated words in his health sheet, "nicotine" and "alcohol," he also confessed to some form of intoxicant intake.

The examination of Kafka's larynx revealed that his vocal cords were indurated, impeding his speech, but no malign growth obstructing the air passages was recorded, no sign of tuberculosis. The second test, conducted by an internist from the General Hospital in Vienna on April 11, noted that the patient was drastically emaciated, and his bronchial breathing pointed to a densification of the lungs. However, no follow-up exam—such as X-ray and sputum test—was recorded to clear up any suspicion of tuberculosis. Respiratory system was not the main culprit of Kafka's ill health.[6]

The Laryngological Clinic routinely treated similar cases of weight loss. Just as the Wienerwald sanatorium, Professor Hajek's staff needed little time to identify the root cause, the swollen, spasmodic muscles in his larynx and esophagus. Thus, Kafka was spared of cauterization to remove obstructions from his breathing tract that sufferers from laryngeal tuberculosis undergo. He was in little danger of choking. His pain on swallowing could be relieved by injections of alcohol or aromatic oils into the upper laryngeal nerve. Precisely, this expected him. On April 12, he received the first treatment of menthol oil, followed by two more on the fourteenth and fifteenth. The procedure required a skillful professional to locate the nerve and was far from pleasant for the patient, but the results came instantly (that would not be the case with tuberculosis). To Kafka's great relief, his pain subsided; he started eating again. The food in the clinic was to his taste and varied, and Dora even received permission to cook for him.

That concession probably reflected his rising status in the clinic. He had been admitted on the intervention of his relative, a Viennese architect, and in the following days, the clinic was approached on his behalf by others, including Franz Werfel, his Prague friend now residing in Vienna. Though already an established author, Werfel's inquiry reportedly prompted Professor Hajek to quip sarcastically, "I know who Kafka is, he is the patient on Number 12. But who is Franz Werfel?"[7]

Active in his way was also Max Brod. When Kafka wrote from Wienerwald, "As for me, it's evidently the larynx," Brod, as if waiting for the clue, eagerly stretched this in his diary into the melodramatic, "Tuberculosis of larynx confirmed. Terrible, unlucky day."[8] It was a contrite response penned in view of posterity. In truth, tuberculosis of the larynx would have been far more preferable to lung tuberculosis, which still killed 50 percent of the diseased. There is little doubt that Brod, just as he had tirelessly promoted Kafka's work, now operated behind the scene to save his life and pristine reputation. The immediate benefit to Kafka was the clinic's promise to move him into a private room.

Not everything was to Kafka's liking at the Laryngological Clinic. He would feel better, he reported on April 12, if he could be spared of a "few petty issues." Thus, he was asked to undergo treatment with an arsenic compound—the substance used to counteract opium deprivation. As on other occasions, he declined. Almost certainly, Kafka was also expected to reduce or stop intake of opium. That resulted in excruciating withdrawal pain. In a letter from Vienna, Dora Diamant indeed mentioned harsh restrictions on Kafka in the clinic. But quite uncharacteristically, Kafka was in a positive mood, willing to trade temporary adversities for a new lease on life. He certainly expected to endure the injections for several weeks until he regained weight. Preparing for the long haul, Dora asked his parents for a feather quilt and pillow to replace those in the clinic.

On the sunny day of April 16, Kafka had the large window in his room open the whole day and drank a lot of water, he reported. As even better weather was forecast, he was looking forward to spending time on the roof enclosure with panoramic views of Vienna. "I like the life here . . . very much," he wrote, comparing the regime in the clinic to a softer version of "military life that I have hitherto missed."[9] Did he mean it?

Much depended on Dora Diamant. She was impressively resilient but in the wrong way as Kafka's companion. Infatuated with him but unable or unwilling to rein in his taste for drugs, already in Berlin, she displayed a sense of resignation to forces that could not be challenged easily. The consequence, Kafka's debilitating weight loss, did not recommend her to his family. In the first letter to his parents from Wienerwald of April 7, Kafka complained that nobody communicated with her, but "it is no misfortune."[10]

For her part, Dora also had a rebellious streak that eventually turned her into a communist active both in Soviet Russia and Britain. In the spring of 1924, her resentment of authority and conventions made her distrustful of the medical establishment and eager to subject Kafka to homeopathic treatment. In her messianic belief, Kafka would be doomed if taken away from her care. Money woes reinforced her conviction. In Wienerwald, she lodged separately in a farmer's house, fearing she would have to return to Berlin soon because of a shortage of cash. Under her spell, Kafka quickly reversed his initial appreciation of the sanatorium and started echoing her words: "That awful, depressing sanatorium in Wienerwald . . . excessively expensive . . . disgustingly expensive"; of two doctors there, one was tyrannical and the other weak-minded, and both, believers in medicine, were unhelpful.[11]

Dora eventually followed Kafka to Vienna but lodged alone outside the Laryngological Clinic, restricted to two hours of visitation daily. "Completely dependent on myself," as she put it, she was running out of money. Living in tandem with Kafka would be to her advantage, even more so that his resources were also limited. After he left Prague for Austria, his parents once again showed displeasure with his life choices by withholding financial support. Kafka, so uncharacteristically of him, pleaded with Max Brod to find a publisher for his short story "Josephine, the Singer." A few days later, he also asked for a visit by someone from the family, probably in an effort to regain goodwill. His brother-in-law Karl Hermann arrived on April 12, but if he advanced any cash, it did not cover Kafka's and Dora's expenses.

Concerned about her dwindling resources and blinded by self-interest, Dora also put down the Laryngological Clinic on the very first day in Vienna: "The clinic that Franz comes in is revolting. It will speed up his end . . . The doctors have become powerless. An absolute surrender. The despair has led me to the idea of homeopathy or similar healing methods. There is nothing to be lost," she wrote to Klopstock. Driven by the desire to reclaim Kafka, she dismissed Hajek's conduct as inacceptable and vowed to do everything in her power to find a better solution. She also asked the letter recipient for advice in finding an alternate place.[12]

After five days in Vienna, Dora indeed discovered a much cheaper accommodation for both. But Kafka was far from ready to move again. Next day, April 16, as we know, in a letter to his parents, he expressed satisfaction with the military discipline imposed on him at the clinic and was looking forward to staying. Dora, however, boldly overruled him, informing his parents in the postscript, "A great undertaking has meanwhile ripened. On Saturday Franz goes into a sanatorium, 25 minutes from Vienna. The doctor will be visiting him there. I was there today and reserved a beautiful room with balcony facing south."[13] In her selfish love and ignorance, Dora Diamant was perfectly willing to nurture Franz Kafka to his grave.

Professor Hajek put up a stiff resistance, arguing that a sanatorium could in no way match the resources and treatment available to Kafka in the hospital. Staying put was the only possibility open to the patient. Klopstock, who held Hajek in high esteem, was also alarmed. In a long letter to Ottla, he implored her to dissuade Dora from taking Kafka away from the clinic or, at least, move him to a sanatorium nearby that Hajek could visit.

Kafka himself was torn apart by conflicting impulses. Apparently, he either summoned Brod by telegram or asked him for advice, but before Brod could act, a patient with whom Kafka shared the hospital room died overnight on April 17–18. In itself a traumatic event for Kafka, Dora exploited it to buttress her argument: "I do not believe doctors a single word any more." Guessing Klopstock would not condone her next step, she advised him not to come to Vienna for the time being. She worked first on getting Kafka to accept her decision to leave the clinic. In an emotional backlash to his copatient's death, the latter indeed agreed to it despite the offer of a private room. He advised the family of the transfer to the sanatorium in Kierling on Saturday, April 18, pointedly omitting criticism of Hajek's center. In a letter to his family, Dora claimed brazenly the move was "with the agreement of the doctors and friends."[14]

On Kafka's hospital sheet, someone else than the examining doctor wrote down "Released into home care" (which was untrue) and scribbled "Tuberculosis of larynx" into the window Diagnosis. It was another dubious statement supported neither by the admission exam nor by his cure in the clinic. The association with tuberculosis, however, came to Kafka as a relief: "Once the fact of tuberculosis of the larynx is accepted, my condition is bearable."[15] This diagnosis was made to order, as the Laryngological Clinic's last service to the writer on the path of self-destruction but mindful of his legacy.

Brod's intervention was called off by a telegram; Kafka apologized for "the epistolary and telegraphic noise . . . It was largely needless, prompted by weak nerves."[16] Another friend Franz Werfel, whose drama *Schweiger* had earned Kafka's wrath for depicting the addict's slide to death because of hunger, was outright an unwelcomed guest. He made three attempts to visit Kafka and talk him out of leaving the clinic, and three times he was turned back at the gate. Dora or Kafka himself denied him visitation rights. Werfel asked Hajek's colleague to investigate and learned it was doubtful that Kafka had contracted a laryngeal tuberculosis. It made sense, considering malnutrition that was sapping his life had been his nemesis for many years past. Kafka's impairment, Werfel realized, could still be reversed in the controlled environment of a hospital, just like Professor Hajek claimed. Leaving the Laryngological Clinic for a sanatorium in Werfel's view, therefore, was a "sickening disaster."[17]

It needed not come that far. Felix Weltsch, a close friend and mentor, in Kafka's words, also struggled with "hypochondria lodged in his lungs and larynx,"[18] and his finer forms of smoking earned him opiatic boils and rocky marriage. Like countless others, however, he learned to live with addiction to become a respected university librarian and editor from 1919 to 1938 of *Selbstwehr* (*Self-Defense*), the weekly of Central European Judaism.

Another contemporary, Jean Cocteau (1889–1963), relapsed into opium smoking in 1923 after the death of his young lover. Experiencing a cornucopia of problems, he sought institutional care and managed to beat the dependence—the feat he recounted in *Opium: Journal of Drug Rehabilitation* (1930). Referring to other luminaries such as Moliere and Picasso, Cocteau also correlated firsthand the opium intake and creativity—and confessed to feeling empty and suicidal once cured. Apart from being no longer able to fly on the "magic carpet" creatively, he also missed the drug's uplifting effect. "Opium leads the organism towards death in euphoric mood. The tortures arise from the process of returning to life against one's wishes." In his quip that also applies to Kafka seamlessly, opium induces euphoria that is "superior to that of death."[19]

Cocteau, of course, was a Renaissance man who would imprint himself on French culture in more than one way without opium. In contrast, Kafka was a Gothic figure, much more focused, unique, yet also irresolute. He repeatedly wished for the strict military discipline that could cure him of addiction, but his sense of self-preservation was sabotaged by excruciating withdrawal pains as well as by the belief he needed assistance of "foreign hands" or "weeds" as a writer. Ultimately, caught in a "grey, hopeless prison cell," he reconciled with the warped view he expressed a few years earlier, "Man is condemned to life, not to death."[20]

Other stars followed the path of self-destruction, perhaps most closely related of whom was Robert Louis Stevenson (1850–1894). Addicted to opium and morphine, Stevenson produced such signature works as *Treasure Island*, an imaginative fantasy that Kafka kept in his drawer, as well as *The Strange Case of Dr. Jekyll and Mr. Hyde*, the tale that can be plausibly interpreted as belaboring the addicts' two parallel minds, the realistic (good) and the drug-induced (evil). Always concerned about his creative vein, Stevenson also struggled with poor health that his contemporaries attributed to tuberculosis. In all likelihood, he suffered from bronchitis or degradation of the upper respiratory system just like Kafka. Similarly, like Kafka, he died consumptive at the age of forty-four.

In more recent times and in another field of creative endeavor, Janice Joplin could not image sustaining her awesome talent as a singer and songwriter without heroin—and succumbed to overdose in 1970, age twenty-seven.

Still in the Laryngological Clinic, Kafka himself plunged into depression realizing the implication of leaving it. "I have been feeling better; the procedures in the hospital (except for details) have done me good . . . I can swallow again," he reckoned now. His stay in the hospital was in many respects a gift, he conceded ruefully. Clearly, Kafka felt the clinic was his last genuine hope but no longer possessed the fortitude to overrule Dora. He cried the whole day uncontrollably—the situation that would prompt a less single-minded companion to a change of heart. On departing for Kierling, he also penned what amounted a farewell letter to Max Brod: "Many thanks for all the laborious literary affairs you've so splendidly taken care of for me. All the best for you and for everything relating to your life."[21]

On Saturday April 19, Kafka and Dora transferred to Dr. Hoffmann's sanatorium in Kierling, today a section of Klosterneuburg, just north of Vienna. The two-story building on the main street was anything but luxurious inside, but Kafka's room on the second floor had a balcony overlooking the garden and forest in the distance. The sanatorium of twelve units was a family business run by an ailing doctor, a nurse, and a cook. In addition, a freshly graduated doctor who worked in Vienna but lived nearby moonlighted there. Considering the rudimentary care that Dr. Hoffman offered, his facility was more a retirement home and turned into one on his death three years later. What appealed to Dora was that she could stay in another room on the premises, and the total cost, between eleven and sixteen kronen a day, should have been affordable to Kafka, whose monthly pension was 1,450 kronen.

By happenstance, this son of a multimillionaire still eligible for salvation spent the last weeks of his life in one of the cheapest, least appropriate establishments money could buy.

Problems started piling up right on arrival. Thus, Dora learned fast that homeopathic healers she hoped to engage were not allowed on premises, and services such as night care and drugs were an extra expense. The doctors considered alcohol or menthol-oil injections just as desirable as their Viennese colleagues, but there was no one qualified to administer them. Similar to Kafka's past health providers, Dr. Hoffmann also proposed a treatment with arsenic only to run into the patient's resistance. That confined Kafka to a palliative medicine for treating fever and inflammation, principally in the form of pantopon. This toxic substance further attacked his mental faculty already eroded by other narcotics.

As on previous occasions, Kafka ultimately opted for what he called "freedom" over discipline by his transfer to Kierling, and this meant a chance to engage in his favorite trade, opium smoking. As we know, he addressed this issue in his customary cheekiness in his last prose, "Josephine, the Singer," penned when he could no longer talk. Playing on the ambiguous noun *Pfeiffen* that can mean squealing, whistling, or smoking a pipe, he noted, "We have resumed piping, a little bit of piping here and there, that is the right thing for us."[22]

Apart from the comfort of narcotics' legality that Austria offered, Kafka could expect support and understanding of his "piping" by his companion Dora Diamant. We can assume that in her railing against the medical establishment, she was ready to accept opium as a form of natural remedy (in a quip of Jean Cocteau, opium is an expression of the "anti-medical elegance").[23] Little wonder she dared to convey the allure of opium smoking even to Kafka's family in Prague. When the sun sets over his balcony, she wrote from Kierling, "There slowly rises from the depth a wonderful intoxicating vapor which works like balsam. Towards evening it gains an unbelievable almost unbearable strength . . . All senses become organs of breathing and all together spell healing and grace."[24]

A few hours of fix could not compensate for Kafka's advancing degradation. Without the counterbalancing treatment to relieve the larynx and esophagus, cough and pain on swallowing returned, depriving him fast of the freedom to eat and drink he had enjoyed at Hajek's clinic. The attendant weight loss also meant long hours of fever. After a mere six days in Kierling, Dora herself conceded the patient was doing poorly. A few days later, she confessed to failing in her ardent wish to see Kafka getting better and please his family: "I do not think much. My capacity to feel and think is terribly limited."[25]

Kafka tried to stage a revolt. The owner of the sanatorium is a sick old man, he complained, who could not be expected to render much help, and the other doctor is a highly disagreeable character of a questionable interest in patients. A transfer to another sanatorium was considered, but Dora, now unabashedly making decisions on Kafka's behalf, would not go along. Succumbing to fatalism, she claimed Kafka's recovery was a matter of will: "He carries salvation in himself."[26] Alternatively, she held on a faint belief that her Franz could replicate the experience of another patient of Dr. Hoffmann, a young baroness who had her appetite restored there and was gaining weight rapidly.

Kafka was also open to believing in recovery against all odds. In the not too distant past, he quipped, "There is no hope, apart from miracles."[27] No longer able to speak, he was still scanning history on this issue. Otto von Bismarck, the towering German politician of the nineteenth century, provided inspiration. Dubbed an "Iron Chancellor" for his bold gun diplomacy, Bismarck was an undisciplined epicure in private life, consuming inordinate amounts of wine and cigars. He was also beholden to opium smoking and morphine—the secret craving that inflicted him with cough and insomnia and kept him out of public life for extended periods. Like other addicts, he had no problem with swallowing or weight loss, possibly because of his countervailing indulgence in alcohol and the antiopiatic treatment by arsenic that he, unlike Kafka, accepted. However, as his intake of narcotics reached a dangerous level at five teaspoons of morphine nightly, his days seemed counted in 1882. In dire straits, Bismarck summoned a young doctor from Munich, Ernst Schwenninger, who was also treating his son Wilhelm. Schwenninger ordered a strict detoxification regime that reversed the customary but fatuous routine of fighting the penalties inflicted by opium with more opium. Almost miraculously—it seemed at that time—Bismarck recovered to live sixteen more years.[28]

Kafka used a cryptic language typical for addicts to pay tribute to Schwenninger, presenting him as a discoverer of "natural therapy . . . a great man who had a hard time treating Bismarck, . . . a magnificent glutton and a heavy drinker." Kafka uttered no word about Bismarck's addiction or the sense of Schwenninger's mission, just repeating the accolade of "a great man."[29] Longing for his Schwenninger but a narcissist to the bone, Kafka lacked the will and discipline to reform himself.

Meanwhile, the family and friends had become alarmed about the inadequate care he was receiving in Kierling. Dora started dispatching postcards with his postscripts, but they failed to dispel fears. Since he objected to a return for proper treatment in Prague, the family wanted him to visit another specialist in Vienna, Professor Tandler. Resigned to his fate, Kafka declined the suggestion, claiming he was too weak to travel.

After he declared himself unfit to visit Vienna, Felix Weltsch arranged for the Viennese specialist Dr. Oskar Best to examine him in Kierling. Kafka was upset, knowing another patient in Kierling had paid a substantial sum for the exam (he would have been spared of these worries at Hajek's clinic). Unknown to him, Dora sent a postcard—not to his parents but to his sister Elli—telling her without much ado she needed money for the doctor and other expenses. In contrast, she told Kafka they had enough to carry on for five more months.

The exam, conducted by Dr. Beck and his colleague Dr. Wilhelm Neumann, took place on Friday, May 2. The doctors were treated in an indifferent if not hostile manner. In her obscurantism, Dora wished to believe that "medicine has no more to offer" to Kafka.[30] Both she and Kafka were more concerned about the bill than the outcome, but Beck provided a friendly service rather than a thorough exam and asked for a modest charge. In his follow-up letter to Weltsch that we know only from Brod's rendering of it, Beck acknowledged Kafka's main problem was impossibility to swallow because of a sharp pain in the larynx. Allegedly, he attributed it to a disintegrating tubercular tissue in Kafka's larynx cavity and claimed the condition was inoperable. He gave Kafka an alcohol injection into the laryngeal nerve, but Dora reported next day that the pains had returned.

The two prior exams in Wienerwald and in Hajek's clinic, as we know, found no tuberculosis in Kafka's larynx. An exam subsequent to Beck's by another expert, Professor Tschiassny, showed a "substantial improvement" of this cavity. Almost certainly then, Beck's claim in a private letter of Kafka's untreatable tuberculosis—if made at all—was, like the parting "diagnosis" in Hajek's clinic, a gesture made at Kafka's behest. Whether the patient developed laryngeal tuberculosis in 1924 is a moot point anyway, of course. He had been struggling with weight loss at least since 1912, tuberculosis or not, and all agreed that he could still be saved under institutional care. Beck probably hoped that the ring of tuberculosis would make Dora agreeable to Kafka's transfer to a hospital in Prague, which he recommended, giving Kafka about three months to live without proper treatment. The case was not lost if handled expeditiously.

Dora, however, ruled out the relocation instantly, knowing she would be sidetracked again. If Kafka were to stay in Kierling, Beck insisted, the family should be informed how serious the situation was. The palliative treatment in the sanatorium with ice patches, pantopon, and—increasingly—morphine offered no realistic chance of recovery. Kafka faced a certain death. Instead of taking any action, however, Dora advised Elli Hermann on May 5 that her only wish now was keeping Kafka pain-free. In another letter, this time to Ottla, she renewed a cash call, claiming she had prepaid a week in the sanatorium and had little else to spare. Masking her fatalism, she still kept reporting how much Franz enjoyed the sunny weather and the moments of contentment.

Her tranquilizing reports nevertheless troubled the Kafkas. If their son was not to return to Prague, perhaps the family could visit him? Frau Kafka expressed a desire to come, fearing this could be her last chance. Dora resolutely nixed the idea. "Nobody should come," she advised Elli bluntly.[31] Yielding to her tenacious defense of the turf, the Kafkas agreed on someone more acceptable to her, Robert Klopstock. This handler of Kafka in Matliary had been driven by anti-Semitism from his native Hungary and, in 1922, matriculated in medicine in Prague. However, Kafka shunned him while vacationing in Planá that year, and the relationship cooled off.

After Dora removed Kafka from Hajek's clinic in April 1924, she saw in Klopstock a potential ally against the medical establishment and consented to his presence. Summoned from Matliary again, he arrived in Kierling on May 6. Sincere but undereducated—he would graduate from medicine four years later—he joined the stubborn Dora in tending for Kafka in the last month of his life. Aware of the Hippocratic duty of care, Klopstock found the do-nothing palliative approach depressing. He begged Dora to transfer the patient to a sanatorium in Vienna where Professor Hajek could supervise him or, at worst, subject Kafka to substitute—or force-feeding. Hitting the wall, he summoned the professor to Kierling. But a single alcohol injection Hajek administered no longer helped: Kafka's larynx had swollen too much since leaving the clinic to locate the proper nerve. Hajek recommended daily injections to stabilize the patient's conditions and avert the worse.

Rather than taking Kafka back to Vienna, Klopstock searched for a visiting doctor but, probably deterred by the cost, eventually took it upon himself to care for Kafka. That meant a continuation of palliative treatment. As the patient continued to wilt, Klopstock adjusted fast to Dora's fatalism and perception of Kafka as a prized trophy. In the future, they would both use him to pad their egos, Klopstock boasting of the writer having died in his arms, Dora signing herself as Dora Kafka.

She indeed may have intended to become Mrs. Kafka while in Kierling. According to her recollections, the inspiration came from the sanatorium's owner, Dr. Hoffmann, who—himself motivated by the young baroness's betrothal—even summoned a rabbi from Vienna to perform the ceremony. But Kafka, mindful of etiquette, asked Dora's father for his blessing, who in turn deferred to his trusted rabbi. The request was denied—obviously a major blow to Kafka's psyche.

Meanwhile, the correspondence between Kierling and Kafka's parents almost dried out or was of such a nature that it has been destroyed. No letters seem to have been preserved for the period May 6 to 19. It was Klopstock who started sending to Prague long, rambling reports on Kafka's conditions, in general evasive or supportive of Dora's failing efforts.

Around mid-May, Franz's relatives arrived in Kierling, Uncle Dr. Löwy and probably also Ottla. Brother-in-law Karl Hermann may have paid a return visit as well. We know that the uncle found the sanatorium inadequate to provide effective care. Kafka faced a concerted effort to return him to Prague or move to a proper establishment. Subsequent to Professor Tschiassny's visit, Dora would recall, Kafka himself wished for life and health more than ever before, but ultimately, he deferred to her. His relatives returned to Prague without him.

Max Brod also arrived, probably around May 11, pretending—similarly as in Siřem seven years earlier—he had business dealings in the area. It was his second visit to Kafka in several weeks and quite depressing. During this last meet, Kafka communicated merely by gestures, pantomime, and written notes; he also joked with Dora, but the "angel of death" (Kafka's term) was lurking behind. Besides, he was not entirely lucid because of the cocktail of drugs he was taking. Subsequently, he would apologize to Brod for his behavior: the visit that he had been looking forward to so much turned out so dismal.[32] Behind his back, Brod may have accepted that the patient should stay in Kierling and be allowed to die with dignity. He must also have opened his valet for Dora, who was suddenly in the money. As Brod bade farewell, Kafka's hope to have him at his deathbed seemed questionable at best.

In the aftermath of Brod's call, an express letter from Frau Kafka reached Kierling on May 19. She and her husband also wished to come for a visit. Herr Kafka, mixing affection with nostalgia, added a desire to drink beer with his son. In a postscript to Dora's lengthy reply, Franz mused nostalgically about sipping wine and beer with his father but extended no invitation. Nor did Dora, who instead pretended there was no need for worries: "There is not much to report." In another letter a week later, she flattered Herr Kafka but ignored the request to visit again. Instead, she claimed, "Franz has become a passionate drinker. Hardly a meal without beer or wine." It was a sheer fabrication. In Kafka's version, "The trouble is that I cannot drink a single glass of water, though the craving itself is some satisfaction."[33] When the confused Frau Kafka requested information from Klopstock, he did not answer.

Finally, probably on June 2, Franz once again penned the main letter to his parents, full of nostalgia and musing about the pros and contras of their visit. He admitted further deterioration of health, made worse by a new problem, painful liver (another curse of addicts). But he claimed that, apart from Klopstock, he was in good care of more than one doctor and regretfully asked his parents to delay the trip. Dora rudely interrupted his letter-writing with a brief postscript: "I took the letter from his hand. It was already an achievement. Only a few lines, but what he is asking seems very important."[34] It was "very important" that Kafka's parents would not get the chance to see their son alive.

On June 2, Kafka also worked on proofs of "Hunger Artist," a metaphoric self-portrait of the man who never finds a food of his liking. In Klopstock's testimony, at this time, Kafka was "literally starving to death," and his physical condition was truly ghastly. When he finished the proofs, "tears rolled down for a long time." Never before did Klopstock see such an overt display of emotions in his idol.[35]

Next morning, June 3, Dora woke up Klopstock to report Kafka in poor shape. He, in turn, alerted the resident doctor, who administered two camphor injections in succession. They proved ineffective. The organs of Kafka's emaciated body were shutting down. Based on the recollections of his nurse and reported by his friend Willy Haas, Kafka had contemplated ending his life unnaturally and even gave Dora permission to depart with him.

When the moment arrived in late morning on June 3, however, she was sent to the post office to spare her the agony of seeing him dying, and

Klopstock faced the thankless task of administering the coup de grace. Just like his inspiration, Sigmund Freund, would, Kafka opted for assisted suicide by morphine. As two doses of the opiate failed to knock him out, he pleaded with Klopstock for more: "You are torturing me . . . kill me or otherwise you are a murderer."[36] The third injection left Kafka half-conscious for long enough to notice the return of Dora. He mistook her for his sister Elli. As she held up flowers to his face, he sniffed the bouquet and stopped breathing.

**Kafka's compassionate bosses, Robert Marschner
(up to 1918) and Bedřich Odstrčil (1919-1924)**

Dora Diamant

Last photo of Ottla, 1941

Ottla's adult daughter Helena

Robotic Kafka in Prague

EPILOGUE

In the golden century of narcotics, 1820–1920, when their circulation was unregulated or restricted sluggishly, millions died of their side effects—consumption, degradation of the respiratory system, or failure of internal organs such as lungs and liver. Very few if any of these deaths were registered listing narcotics as the cause. Unlike today, society lived in denial when it came to addiction. It was a different story with infectious diseases such as tuberculosis. A strict reporting protocol was in place in those cases, to be followed by an autopsy. The Kierling sanatorium, however, needed not to be concerned about that. Since the formal cause of Kafka's death was given as cardiac arrest, no autopsy was done, and his uncle Siegfried Löwy returned with the body to Prague on June 5.

The funeral was held at the Jewish section of the cemetery in Strašnice, attended by one hundred mourners. Dora Diamant was present, although she had already received curt treatment by Dr. Löwy at Kierling. Hermann Kafka refused to shake hand with her and frowned on her theatrical display of grief. For a few years thereafter, Dora struggled to establish contacts with the Kafka family, primarily with Elli Herman and Ottla David. However, her belated mea culpa failed to impress. In vain did she foreswear, "Ottla! Damn me not!"[1] Klopstock likewise started shunning her. Restlessly seeking her place in society, she subsequently qualified as an actress but, disenchanted with Germany, immigrated to the Soviet Union. She was allowed to exit the Stalinist totality under suspicious circumstance in 1938 to spend the rest of her life in London.

Robert Klopstock fared somewhat better in the judgment of the family before he too eventually faded away to further his medical career in the United States. Kafka's parents, Hermann and Julie, died in the

1930s, as did their granddaughter Lotte and son-in-law Karl Hermann. Most of Franz Kafka's schoolmates and casual friends dispersed, finding greener pastures away from their hometown. Perhaps most adventurous was Franz Werfel, who narrowly escaped the Nazis in 1940 and settled in Los Angeles to confirm his reputation as a poet, novelist, and playwright. Another Kafka's peer, Johannes Urzidil, commented in retrospect and not without justification, "The intellectual Prague of the Czech-German-Austrian-Jewish synthesis which had sustained . . . the city and inspired it throughout centuries, came to an end with Kafka."[2]

Kafka's closest friends, Brod, Weltsch, Oskar Baum, and Jesenská, stayed put, however. The humanist Max Brod, who had been on a tear prior to the Great War, was out of sync with the postwar world. He earned a living first as a communication officer in the Czechoslovak government and then as a journalist for German-language newspapers in Prague. Weltsch, as the editor of *Die Selbstwehr*, wrote numerous perceptive articles on politics and culture, just as Brod was increasingly concerned about Hitler's advances and fate of European Jewry. Milena Jesenská divorced Ernst Polak after all and returned to Prague to work for progressive Czech periodicals. She remarried, gave birth to a daughter (who too was an addict), split with her second husband, and under the influence of her lover joined the Communist Party for a few years, as ever struggling with addiction and always broke. It was her first husband, Ernst Polak, who reportedly supported her with money.

When the Munich Agreement of September 1938 exposed Czechoslovakia to Nazi encroachment, immigration to Palestine became a timely but pricey consideration. The cost of the British certificate for travel to Palestine was prohibitive, one thousand British pounds. Brod could afford the fee for himself and his wife, but his brother Otto, Oskar Baum, and Weltsch could not. The Weltsch's in-laws eventually sold their business to cover the road to safety for their daughter's family, while they resigned to facing the uncertain future in Czechoslovakia. So did Oskar Baum, who would die in Prague in 1941.

Just as Hitler's armies were about to occupy Czech lands on March 15, 1939, Weltsch and Brod, the latter carrying a luggage with Kafka's manuscripts, boarded a train that eventually took them through Poland and Rumania to the Black Sea. On board of *Bessarabia*, they passed through the straits and, after a stopover in Athens, landed in Tel Aviv. Both Weltsch and Brod spent the rest of their lives in Israel, both dying in the 1960s.

Felice Bauer also escaped the looming disaster. After she married a prosperous German businessman in 1918 and gave birth to two children, the family moved to Switzerland in 1931 and immigrated to the USA in 1936. She passed away there by a natural death in 1960.

Two nieces of Franz Kafka also avoided the Holocaust. Elli's daughter Gerti Kaufmann and her husband were fortunate enough to reside in India in the critical time, while Valli's daughter Marianne Steiner, a woman of exceptional beauty, managed to escape to London along with her husband and son. Elli's son Felix was last reported in the internment camp in French Pyrenees in July 1940 and subsequently died either from typhus or while fleeing the German-occupied France into Spain.

The rest of the family stayed put in what had become the German "Protectorate" of Bohemia and Moravia, and was caught in the Holocaust. Elli Hermann, along with her daughter and her son-in-law, was deported to the ghetto in Lodz already in October 1941. The family of Valli Pollak followed ten days later. None of them ever returned. The younger brother of Max Brod, Otto, a reserve officer of the Czechoslovak army, likewise perished along with his family in a Nazi concentration camp. The actor Isaak Löwy died in the death camp of Treblinka in 1942. Kafka's onetime fiancée Julie Wohryzek, who had moved with her lawyerly husband to Rumania, perished in Auschwitz in 1944.

From other persons profiled here, the retired "country doctor" and Kafka's uncle Siegfried Löwy committed suicide rather than submit to the Nazis. The writer and physician Ernst Weiss, considered by Kafka as the model of an emancipated Jew, also took his life, in Paris, after the city fell to the Germans in 1940.

Grete Bloch started a new job in December 1915 with Adrema, a company producing label printers. She disclosed the existence of her out-of-wedlock son to the manager/owner, Julius Goldschmidt, and fared well under his aegis. Reportedly, she became the highest-paid female executive in Germany in the 1920s but never married (eventually, she declared Goldschmidt her husband). Deteriorating health, in particular inflammation of lungs, Kafka's affliction, sapped her energy and optimism. The Nazi takeover of Germany in 1933 and the passing of Goldschmidt three years later left her bewildered and without means. After a brief stay with Felice Bauer/Marasse in Geneva, she traveled to join her brother in Palestine but returned to Europe to settle in a colony of German expats in Florence. As the Nazi dragnet reached the German-occupied Northern

Italy, she sought refuge in the countryside but not for long. In May 1944, she was arrested and transported to her death in Auschwitz.

Milena Jesenská matured in the 1930s into a respected journalist, editor, and translator known as much for her association with progressive causes as for drugs and affairs. In reaction to the rising threat of Hitler, she behaved with exemplary fortitude. In the critical times of 1938–1939, she helped Jewish and political refugees including her past husband Ernst Polak. In November 1939, however, she too was arrested by the gestapo and eventually deported to the concentration camp Ravensbrück. In one of her last preserved letters, she expressed respect to her father, the "fabulous" Jan Jesenský. She died in the camp of kidney failure in May 1944. Her two cousins were executed along with their wives, the victims of the brutal Nazi drive to eliminate potential opponents with spine.

Meanwhile, as the infamous Nuremberg Laws had been extended to the Protectorate Bohemia and Moravia and Jews were being increasingly excluded from public life, Ottla and her husband, Josef David, legally separated in February 1940. It was her decision, according to her daughter Věra, and an act of potential self-sacrifice. It gave her daughters a much better chance of survival and lessened the risk Aryanization of the family property, but separation from her Christian husband entailed a high risk. While she, along with Věra, stayed at Bílkova Street, caring for her several dogs and hiding whenever the bell rang, David and the underage daughter Helena registered on a street nearby, but apparently, all strained to live as a family. The arrangement was risky both to both sides, but the ordeal obviously bonded them at last. In early August 1942, as roundups and deportations of Jews were at a high point, Ottla was summoned to and interned in the concentration camp Theresienstadt (Terezín), some fifty kilometers north of Prague.

The following year, in July 1943, she reportedly still managed to organize there a commemoration of Franz Kafka's sixtieth birthday. A few months later, a call was issued in Terezín for volunteers to accompany 1,200 Jewish orphans, supposedly for a trip to Palestine or to neutral Sweden, in exchange for cash. Ottla registered if only because of her instinctive need of caring for someone. Possibly a ruse from the onset, the transport with the orphans and fifty-three volunteers ended in Auschwitz, where all were gassed on arrival on October 5, 1943.

With Ottla's departure, the David's family ran into turbulences. As we know, the paternity of both Ottla's daughters was spurious. In particular, the elder one, Věra, felt estranged from her formal father, Josef David. Early on, her mother, Ottla, impressed on her how wonderful Franz Kafka was, and her aunt Elli repeatedly stressed how much she resembled him: "Just like Franz, completely Franz." The eight-year-old was "so proud" hearing it.[3] She grew up more a Kafka than a David and asserted her independence by a court decision just one day after turning eighteen. She also stopped communicating with David's parents, annoyed by their anti-Semitism.

Disapproving also by what seemed Josef David's opportunism, Věra did not return home on Ottla's departure to Theresienstadt in August 1942. With Helena in tow, she considered following her but failed being formally only half-Jewish. Though Ottla included surreptitious greetings to her ex-husband in letters from Theresienstadt, she dodged the David household by marrying an elderly suitor of her mother.

After the war, Věra remarried a respected translator of Shakespeare, Erich Saudek, who died prematurely. She earned a living as an editor and translator from German, taking care of their four children. A perennial resident of Prague, she lived at the Bílkova Street building that her grandfather Hermann bought in 1918 until her death at age ninety-four in August 2015. Her children and grandchildren have been residing primarily in Prague.

Věra's younger sister, Helena, followed a different path. She studied medicine and, another family version of the "country doctor," ended up practicing in Kašperské Hory, a small town in the Šumava Mountains, one of the family's favorite vacation regions. While one of her sons immigrated overseas, the other set up medical practice in the same district. A kind, cultured, and unassuming individual, Helena died in 2009. Throughout the years, her family maintained a warm relationship with Josef David, whose visits to Kašperské Hory are remembered to this day.

Kafka was German-writing but not the German man of letters. Despite similarities with German confreres, he had much more in common with his Bohemian—mainly Jewish—contemporaries and even in this context was unique in the selection and presentation of his topics. In the words of Urzidil, "Kafka was Prague and Prague was Kafka."[4] Considered an idiosyncratic wordsmith, his appeal was rather limited prior to the Second World War. Understandably, there was a tinge of strangeness attached to his name. In an obituary published in Czech shortly after Kafka's death, Milena Jesenská noted deprivations leading to his demise had been self-inflicted—she called them "asceticism"—and "totally unheroic." Kafka not only failed to treat his lung disease medically but also even "consciously encouraged it" being "too weak to fight." His world was "full of invisible demons that tear apart and destroy defenseless people." Jesenská effectively conceded that drug addiction was a major factor in Kafka's life and work.[5]

Max Brod, however, struck a different tone with his biography first published in 1937: Kafka was not a perfect saint but "was on the road to becoming one . . . absolute truthfulness was one of the most important and distinctive features of his character." Apart from his conscientiousness and thoroughness, he also showed interest "in every kind of reform . . . in the methods of natural healing, in modern methods of education, such as the Montessori system."[6] Kafka, needless to say, may have been all this but was also much more. In a striking contrast to his sober understanding of Kafka's health problems in the past, Brod also became instrumental in assigning them to tuberculosis.

Much too eccentric a writer at the time of his death, Kafka was slowly gaining recognition in afterlife. It was the major catastrophes of the twentieth century, the two world wars, the Great Depression of the 1930s, and the rise of murderous totalitarianism in Germany and Soviet Russia that cumulatively imparted a much deeper symbolism to his work—or made it more obvious. In this brave new world, nothing seems to make sense or has a clear-cut ending anymore; life has become an endless string of disappointments and defeats. The individual striving for self-realization can expect no mercy in a world stacked against him.

Once Kafka entered the banquet room of eternity, his work attracted a plethora of biographers linking him to other authors from Kleist to Sartre and to the trendy tenets of Marxism, totalitarian ideologies, existentialism, psychoanalysis, expressionism, and Dadaism, to name a few. As is the case with other celebrities, his interpreters often display a casual relationship with reality and romanticize or gloss over his flaws. What an irony considering Kafka himself observed there are ridiculous features even in great men. He would surely be dismayed by being treated with veneration bordering on hagiography.

In truth, Kafka neither expected nor was in need of favors. Speaking through his deceased son in *The Castle*, as we know, he expressed conviction that his sorry state notwithstanding, he would become famous in the distant, very distant future. Has that future arrived? The answer is as transparent as Kafka himself, but does it matter? As he also remarked midway through his short life in 1917, "A man cannot live without a steady faith in something indestructible within himself, though both . . . may remain permanently concealed from him."[7]

ENDNOTES

Preface

1   Ernst Pawel, *The Nightmare of Reason: A Life of Franz Kafka*. New York: Farrar, Straus, Giroux, 1984, 449.

2   Gustav Janouch, *Conversations with Kafka*. London: Deutsch, 1985, 25.

3   Louis Begley, *Franz Kafka: The Tremendous World I Have Inside My Head*. New York: Atlas & Co., 2008, 280; also Walter H. Sokel, *The Myth of Power and the Self Essays on Franz Kafka*. Detroit: Wayne State UP, 2002.

4   Roberto Calasso in *The Zürau Aphorisms of Franz Kafka*. New York: Schocken, 2005, 123.

5   Reiner Stach, *Kafka: The Decisive Years*. New York: Harcourt, 2005, 3, 13f; also Reiner Stach, *Kafka: The Years of Insight*. Princeton, NJ: Princeton UP, 2013, 429.

6   James Hawes, *Why You Should Read Kafka Before You Waste Your Life*. New York: St. Martin's, 2008, 57. Hawes's book, one of a few that dared to challenge Kafka's sparkling image, has met with indignation of Kafka biographers.

7   Franz Kafka, *Letters to Ottla and the Family*, ed. by N. N. Glaser. New York: Schocken, 1982 (hereafter *LOF*), 8.

8   Franz Kafka, *Letters to Felice*, ed. by Erich Heller and Jürgen Born. New York: Schocken, 1973 (hereafter *LF*), 321. Subsequently, Kafka again conceded, "I also falsify and withhold"—ibid., 379.

9   Franz Kafka, *Letters to Friends, Family, and Editors*, transl. by Clara and Richard Winston. New York: Schocken, 1977 (hereafter *LFF*), 387.

10 Begley, 187; also Peter-André Alt, *Franz Kafka der ewige Sohn*. Munich: C. H. Beck, 2005, 510; and Stach, *The Decisive Years*, 466.

11 George Fabian, "Was Franz Kafka Tubercular?" in *Oxford German Studies*, vol.45 (2016), issue 4, 434.

12 Johannes Urzidil, *There Goes Kafka*. Detroit: Wayne State UP, 1968, 127, 135.

13 Jean Cocteau, *Opium: The Diary of a Cure*. London: Peter Owen, 1968, 48.

14 Klaus Mann, preface to Franz Kafka, *Amerika*, translated by Edwin Muir. NY: Schocken, 1946, x-xi. Preempting his conventional interpreters, Kafka himself noted, "The written and handed-down history of the world frequently utterly fails"—Franz Kafka, *Abandoned Fragments*. London: Sun Vision Press, 2012, 200.

Kafka's 'Tuberculosis'

1 Bohumil Vacek, *Zákony a nařízení jakož in důležitá rozhodnutí o organisaci zdravotní a epidemické služby v Čechách a na Moravě*. Prague: 1916, 525-50.

2 Ibid., 576-583.

3 An equally strict regime existed in Germany—see Sylvelyn Hähner-Rombach, *Sozialgeschichte der Tuberkulose: vom Kaiserreich bis zum Ende des zweiten Weltkrieges unter besonderer Berücksichtigung Württembergs*. Stuttgart: Franz Stener, 2000.

4 *LOF*, 18f.

5 Stach, *The Decisive Years*, 346. For this misconception, see also the editorial comment in Franz Kafka, *Briefe 1918–1920*, ed. by Hans-Gerd Koch. Frankfurt: S. Fischer, 2013, 411, 417.

6 Josef Thomayer, *Pathologie a terapie nemocí vnitřních*. Prague: Bursik & Kohout, 1923, 560ff and 613ff.

7 Stach, *The Years of Insight*, 187-92; also Rotraut Hackermüller, *Kafkas letzte Jahre, 1917-1924*. Munich: P. Kirchheim, 1990, 108.

8 The issue is further addressed in chapters "1917: Mental Tuberculosis" and "The Hunger Artist Dies."

9 *LFF*, 286f.

10 In communication with this author, the foremost Kafka biographer R. S. has claimed the existence of Kafka's positive sputum test, but his assertion cannot be corroborated by Kafka's employment file.

11 This issue was first raised by Fabian, "Was Franz Kafka Tubercular?" in *Oxford German Studies*, vol. 45 (2016), issue 4, 434–443.

12 *LF*, 544f.

Background

1 Max Brod, *Franz Kafka a Biography*. New York: Schocken, 1973, 48.

2 Franz Kafka, *Diaries 1910–1923*, ed. by Max Brod. New York: Schocken, 1976 (hereafter *Diaries*), 397.

3   *LF*, 271; also Franz Kafka, *Letters to Milena*, transl. by Philip Boehm. New York: Schocken, 1990 (hereafter *LM*), 136.

4   *Briefe 1918–1920*, 325.

5   Brod, *Kafka*, 19, 51, 75, 86f, 122.

6   Ibid., 229.

7   Urzidil, 102.

8   Brod, *Kafka*, 40; also *LF*, 271.

9   *LFF*, 17.

1902: Resorting to "Saw Dust"

1   Sabine Fellner and Katrin Unterreiner, *Morphium, Cannabis und Cocaine: Medizin und Rezepte der Kaiserhauses*. Vienna: Amathea, 2008.

2   Martin Green, *Otto Gross, Freudian Psychoanalyst, 1877–1920*. Lewiston, NY: Ed Mellen, 1999, 42.

3   *LFF*, 167.

4   Alt, 209.

5   *Diaries*, 397.

6   *LFF*, 1, 4.

7   *LM*, 163.

8   Franz Kafka, *Letter to His Father*. New York: Schocken, 1974, 95.

9   *LFF*, 4.

10 Ibid., 6f. Cocteau, among others, also expressed the peculiar symbiosis of good and evil in the addict's mind: "Without the devil God would be inhuman"—Cocteau, 65.

11 *LFF*, 15, 12.

1907: The Faustian Compact

1   For pioneering studies in English on opium and its impact on the nineteenth-century Romantic men of letters, see J. Emanuel and J. Mickel, *The Artificial Paradise in French Literature. The Influence of Opium and Hashish on the Literature of French Romanticism and Les fleurs du mal*. Chapel Hill, NC, 1969; Althea Hayter, *Opium and the Romantic Imagination*. London, 1971; and Molly Lefebure, *Coleridge, a Bondage of Opium*. London, 1974.

2   See George Fabian, *Karl Marx Prince of Darkness*. Indiana: Xlibris, 2011, 453.

3   *Diaries*, 38.

4   Brod in epilogue to Franz Kafka's *The Trial*, translation by Willa and Edwin Muir, in *The Complete Novels of Franz Kafka*. Harmondsworth: Penguin, 1983, 173. Kafka also apocryphally conceded that he had started using

drugs for creative purposes to Felice Bauer (*LF, 413*) and in his last prose, "Josephine the Singer or the Mouse Folk."

5   *LF*, 414.

6   *Diaries*, 10.

7   Ibid., 34.

8   Ibid., 27.

9   Cocteau, 35. "You misunderstand me nicely if you think that striving for the ideal usefulness is consonant with my nature," Kafka claimed in self-defense—*LFF*, 31.

10 Ibid., 26.

11 *Letter to His Father*, 103.

12 *Diaries*, 199.

13 Brod, *Kafka*, 86; also Hans-Gerd Koch, ed., *"Als Kafka mir entgegenkam . . ."* *Erinnerungen an Franz Kafka*. Frankfurt: S. Fischer, 1995, 203.

14 *LFF*, 24.

15 Judging by their realistic narrative, several of Kafka's undated short stories may have originated prior to 1907: "Children on a Country Road," "Clothes," "Rejection," "Absent-minded Window-gazing," "The Way Home," "Reflections for Gentlemen-Jockeys," as well as fragments of "Wedding Preparations in the Country"—see Franz Kafka, *The Complete Stories*. New York: Schocken, 1971, (hereafter *CS*), 52ff and 379–390.

16 These include "Excursion into the Mountain" expressing contempt for others ("these nobodies") and food deprivation common to addicts ("our throats swell"); "The Street Window" and "On the Tram" conveying the sense of alienation in a city; "The Tradesman" describing a flight in the staircase; "Passers-by" mentioning murder of an innocent man (as in *The Trial*); "Unhappiness" imagining that "the cart horses down below on the paving stones were rising in the air"; "Bachelor's Ill Luck" proposing "to lie ill gazing for weeks into an empty room from the corner where one's bed is" (as in *The Metamorphosis*). *CS*, 379–395.

17 All quotations from *CS*, 9–51.

18 Ibid., 49.

19 Sokel, 254.

20 *CS*, 442f.

21 Ibid., 52–76.

22 Brod, *Kafka*, 58, 60. Brod claimed to have written *The Kingdom of Love* with Richard Farda representing Kafka.

23 *LFF*, 27f.

24 Ibid., 41f.

25 Ibid., 45.

26 Ibid., 47.

27 Brod's respect for Kafka increased on reading "Description of a Struggle," but "it was not the first of his works that K showed me"—Brod, *Kafka*, 61.

28 *Diaries*, 13f.

1910: "The General Uproar within Me"

1 *Diaries*, 21.

2 *LFF*, 65.

3 *Diaries*, 12; Brod, *Kafka*, 89.

4 *Diaries*, 15f.

5 *LFF*, 70.

6 *Diaries*, 14, 16.

7 Ibid., 12.

8 Ibid., 19f.

9 Ibid., 15.

10 *LFF*, 66.

11 Ibid., 65.

12 See Fabian, *Karl Marx*, 419, and passim; also Charles E. Terry and M. Pellens, *The Opium Problem*. New York, 1928, 456.

13 *LFF*, 67.

14 *Diaries*, 29.

15 Ibid., 37f.

16 Franz Kafka, *Briefe April 1914-1917*, ed. by Hans-Gerd Koch. Frankfurt: S. Fischer, 2005, 656.

17 *Diaries*, 37f.

18 *LFF*, 277.

19 *Diaries*, 55.

20 Ibid., 62.

21 Ibid., 61.

22 Ibid., 101.

23 Ibid., 118.

24 *LFF*, 129.

25 *Diaries*, 124f.

26 Ibid., 122.

27 Ibid., 134.

28 Ibid., 141.

1912: 'Civilizing the Ape'

1 *LFF*, 423.

2 Nicholas Murray, *Kafka*. New Haven: Yale UP, 2004, 97, 263.

3   *LM*, 276.

4   Pharmacists, along with doctors and career soldiers, were, because of their easy access to drugs, at a higher risk of developing addiction. This may have been the case with Frau Fanta. When she died relatively young at fifty-five, Brod remarked in January 1918 that she had "waged a passionate war against her minor flaws." Malcolm Pasley, ed., *Max Brod, Franz Kafka, eine Freundschaft*, vol. 2, Frankfurt: S. Fischer, 1987, 254.

5   *Diaries.*, 162; *LF*, 185.

6   *Diaries*, 176.

7   Ibid., 198.

8   Ibid., 200.

9   "A Report to an Academy," *CS*, 250-59.

10 Ibid., 261.

11 *Diaries*, 200.

12 *CS*, 397f.

13 *LF*, 237.

14 *LFF*, 81.

15 Ibid., 52.

16 *LF*, 185.

17 Sander L. Gilman, *Franz Kafka: The Jewish Patient*. New York: Routledge, 1995, 247.

18 Stach, *The Decisive Years*, 97.

19 *Diaries*, 206.

20 Franz Kafka, *Tagebücher*, ed. by Hans-Gerd Koch, Michael Müller and Malcolm Pasley. Frankfurt: S. Fischer, 1990, 431f.

21 *LF*, 13.

22 Cocteau, 54. In an attendant reprieve from needles, Kafka also stopped being ashamed of his body in swimming pools.

23 *LF*, 5.

"The Judgment"; *The Metamorphosis; Amerika*

1   Terry, 55.

2   For a more detailed overview of the issue, see Fabian, *Karl Marx*, 26ff, 119ff, 269ff, 452f.

3   Terry, 487.

4   Among the bearers of these characteristics were the medical doctor and writer Ernst Weiss (1882–1940), the modernist writer and editor Robert Musil (1880–1942), the poet and novelist Rainer Maria Rilke (1875–1926), and the illustrator and writer Alfred Kubin (1877–1959). Perhaps most distinguished in this group was Karl Kraus (1874–1936), a son of a well-to-do Jewish

manufacturer in Czech town of Jičín who suffered from spinal deformity like Brod. Transposed to Vienna, he became a writer and essayist of surprising originality and foresight, the qualities that earned him Nobel Prize for literature. Known as a satirist, he also expounded suicidal and apocalyptic notions—as befitted a night owl inspired by his nightmares. In 1919, he confirmed his reputation as Central Europe's foremost nihilist with *The Last Days of Mankind*, foreseeing society destroyed by a push of a button.

5   Franz Kafka, *The Metamorphosis and other stories,* transl. by Joachim Neugroschel. Toronto: Maxwell, 1993, 59ff.

6   *LF*, 297; Brod, *Kafka, 114.*

7   Hartmut Binder, ed., *Kafka-Handbuch,* vol. 1. Stuttgart: Kröner, 1979, 429.

8   Stach, *The Decisive Years,* 114.

9   *LF*, 107; Brod, *Kafka,* 128f.

10 Stach, *The Decisive Years,* 114 and 529n; Murray, 101.

11 *Diaries*, 213. Kafka's involvement with opium helps explain why Felice Bauer never got the chance of watching him write, and when his last amour, Dora Diamant, caught him plying pen in the middle of the night, he was someone else, a possessed man with a contorted face. Kafka himself observed similar profound changes in the face of his smoking mentor Felix Weltsch.

12 Peter Selg, *Rainer Maria Rilke und Franz Kafka.* Dornach: Pforte, 2007, 117; also Janouch, 31.

13 Stach, *The Decisive Years,* 117, 148; also Murray, 127.

14 Cocteau, 66.

15 *LF*, 107.

16 Ibid., 21f.

17 Franz Kafka, *The Metamorphosis and other stories,* transl. by Christopher Moncrieff. Richmond, Surrey: Alma Classics, 2014, 49–112.

18 Hartmut Binder, *Kafkas "Verwandlung."* Frankfurt: Stroemfeld, 2004, 118.

19 Janouch, 35. Stach surmises Kafka committed indiscretion by disclosing the existence of bugs in the family—*The Decisive Years,* 201.

20 *LF*, 156; also 271. The entrapment in an underground cavity seems to have been the opium addicts' nightmare rendered first in Plato's famous simile and most notably in De Quincey.

21 *LF*, 136.

22 *LM*, 204.

23 *LF*, 31.

24 Urzidil, 18.

25 *The Metamorphosis* (2014), 105.

26 Ibid., 108.

27 Elias Canetti, *Kafka's Other Trial.* New York: Schocken, 1974, 20.

28 *Diaries*, 253.

29   *Amerika*, translated by Willa and Edwin Muir, in *The Complete Novels of Franz Kafka*. Harmondsworth: Penguin, 1967, 441–638. Kafka referred to this novel by its first chapter, "The Stoker."

30   Cocteau, 44.

31   *Diaries*, 209f; also *LF*, 239; Janouch, 30.

32   *Synoptische Konkordanz zu Franz Kafkas Nachgelassenen Schriften und Fragmenten*, vol. 3, ed. by Ralf Becker et al. Tübingen: M. Niemeyer, 2003, 980-82, 1381, 1416f.

33   *Amerika*, 480, 537.

34   *Letter to His Father*, 109. Years later, Kafka recorded the aging Bailly's visit of Kafkas in Prague.

Felice Bauer

1   *LF*, 21. On another occasion, Kafka confessed, "I am dragging myself out of bed when I am tired almost to death"—*LFF*, 91.

2   *LF*, 31.

3   Stach, *The Decisive Years*, 131; *LF*, 43.

4   *LF*, 58.

5   Ibid., 145.

6   *LFF*, 77.

7   Ibid., 263.

8   *Amerika*, 480.

9   *LF*, 112.

10   *Synoptische Konkordanz*, vol. 2, 1004f.

11   *LF*, 185; Canetti, 30.

12   *LF*, 212, 217.

13   Ibid., 222.

14   Ibid., 226.

15   Ibid., 95.

16   Ibid., 256.

17   Ibid., 238.

18   Ibid., 251f.

19   *Diaries*, 221.

20   *LF*, 257f.

21   Ibid., 255.

22   Ibid., 260f.

23   *Diaries*, 222.

24   Canetti, 46.

25   *LF*, 292f.

26   *Diaries*, 225.

27 *LF*, 304.

28 *Diaries*, 228.

29 *LF*, 308.

30 Ibid., 314.

31 Ibid., 298.

32 Ibid., 311.

33 *LFF*, 100.

Grete Bloch

1 *LF*, 35.

2 Max Brod, *Der Prager Kreis*. Frankfurt: Suhrkamp, 1977, 115f.

3 Wolfgang A. Schocken, "Wer war Grete Bloch?" in *Exilforschung: Ein internationales Jahrbuch*, vol. 4, *Das jüdische Exil und andere Themen*. Munich, 1986, 83–97.

4 Stach, *The Decisive Years*, 435; Saul Friedländer, *Franz Kafka the Poet of Shame and Guilt*. New Haven: Yale UP, 2013, 68.

5 *LF*, 325.

6 *Diaries*, 237f.

7 Ibid., 248. Weltsch married in 1914, and Kafka's visits—meaning, unbearable stink and smoke—were cordially detested by his wife.

8 Ibid., 244.

9 *LF*, 345f.

10 *Diaries*, 259.

11 *LF*, 352f.

12 Ibid., 354.

13 Ibid., 356.

14 Ibid., 360. This undated fragment is tentatively attached by the editors of *Letters to Felice* to his letter of March 11 or 12.

15 *LM*, 154.

16 *Diaries*, 265f. Emphasis added.

17 *LF*, 358f.

18 Ibid., 362.

19 Ibid., 341, 411. The word "furs" implies two previous meetings, dated here November 1913 and March 7–8, 1914. Later, Kafka mentioned "three different phases," apparently meaning three stages in their relationship, the friendship, the courtship, and parenthood—ibid., 431.

20 Ibid., 365f, 371. Emphasis added.

21 Ibid., 378f.

22 Ibid., 388.

The "Tribunal" in Berlin

1   *LF*, 384f.
2   Ibid., 388.
3   Ibid., 391.
4   Ibid., 386.
5   Ibid., 397.
6   Ibid., 414.
7   *Diaries*, 275.
8   *LF*, 418.
9   Ibid., 422.
10 Ibid., 425f.
11 Ibid., 426f.
12 Ibid., 428.
13 Ibid., 429.
14 Ibid., 430.
15 Ibid., 431.
16 Ibid., 109.
17 Reconstructed from *Diaries*, 293f.
18 Ibid., 301f.

Ottla Kafka

1   Stach, *The Decisive Years*, 423. For an opposing—and much maligned—view, see Hawes, 185f.
2   *Diaries*, 192f. About three years later, Kafka returned to the subject of rape in "The Country Doctor," a dreamy fantasy. This time, it was presented as a violent act against a servant girl Rose by a brute who emerged from the pigsty "on all fours." On close reading, the rapist represents the story's protagonist.
3   *LOF*, 31.
4   Pasley, *Brod-Kafka*, vol. 2, 176, 200. For Kafka and sex, see also Hawes, 185f; Murray, 187f; and Reiner Stach, *Kafkas erotischer Mythos*. Frankfurt: S. Fischer, 1987.
5   *The Trial* (1998), 249.
6   Brod, *Der Prager Kreis*, 116f.
7   The nudity aspect is ignored by biographers—see, for example, Binder, *Kafka-Handbuch*, vol. 1, 326.
8   *Letter to His Father*, 63.
9   This embarrassing entry, for long excluded from publication, is now available in Franz Kafka, *Tagebücher*. Frankfurt: S. Fischer, 1990, 538. Symptomatic

of scholarly self-deception, Elli is deemed to have directed this intimacy at her husband, Karl Hermann, serving on the front at World War I—see Bettina von Jagow und Oliver Jahraus, eds., *Kafka-Handbuch: Leben, Werk, Wirkung.* Göttingen: Vandenhoeck & Ruprecht, 2008, 413. In truth, Kafka registered his sister's yearning for his "elastic body" in June 1914, about one month before World War I started.

10 *Diaries,* 210.
11 *LF,* 164.
12 *LF,* 166.
13 Stach, *The Decisive Years,* 32f.
14 *Diaries,* 164.
15 *LF,* 153, also 184.
16 *The Metamorphosis* (2014), 112.
17 *LF,* 186, 269.
18 *Diaries,* 223.
19 Ibid., 225f, 231.
20 Ibid., 254f.
21 *LF,* 416.
22 *Diaries,* 276.

1914: The Second Burst of Creativity

1   *Diaries,* 222.
2   *LF,* 390.
3   *Diaries,* 302.
4   Ibid., 313.
5   Janouch, 32.
6   *LFF,* 95.
7   *LF,* 235.
8   *LFF,* 124.
9   *The Metamorphosis* (2014), 113-48.
10 Ibid., 146.
11 *Diaries,* 303-13.
12 Ibid., 321.
13 Ibid., 322f.
14 *CS,* 183–205.

1   Sokel, 251.
2   All references are to the classic translation of *The Trial* by Willa and Edwin Muir in the *Complete Novels of Franz Kafka*. Harmondsworth: Penguin, 1983.
3   *Synoptische Konkordanz*, vol. 3, 1381, 1417.
4   Stach, *The Years of Decision*, 478: 'Since we have had access to Kafka's diaries, we know that the "tribunal" in the Hotel Askanischer Hof spawned the key images and scenes.' See also Begley, 178; and Binder, *Kafka-Handbuch*, vol. 1, 292. In truth, there is nothing in Kafka's diaries to substantiate this claim.
5   The Šviha affair was covered in the book form in *Zrádce dr. Karel Šviha před porotou: stenografický protocol*. Prague, 1914; and *Dr. Karel Šviha, národněsociální zrádce národa*. Prague, 1914; also Bohumil Nuska and Jiří Pernes, *Kafkův Proces a Švihova aféra*. Brno: Barrister & Principal, 2000.
6   *LF*, 436.
7   *The Trial*, 74-82; also Franz Kafka, *Der Process*, ed. by Malcolm Pasley. Frankfurt: S. Fischer, 1990, 315–326.
8   The latest volume of Kafka's letters erroneously dates Bloch's childbirth to the late summer of 1914—*Briefe 1918–1920*, 799.
9   *Diaries*, 318f; *LF*, 441.
10 Ibid., 318.
11 *Trial*, 265f; also *Diaries*, 314f.
12 Resorting to the same ploy, Max Brod—so he would claim—presented himself in three personae in his novel *Das grosse Wagnis*. Leipzig: Kurt Wolff, 1918.
13 An "ostensible acquittal . . . artificially restricts" the "charge" (drug use) and its knowledge by the outside world but the "accused" (addict) is never free. It also involves great "strain and agitation" and may lead to new "arrests" (relapses") and court appearances. Surmising this option would not appeal to K., Titorelli then outlines another one, "postponement" of the "case." It "taxes your strength less but means a steady strain," K. is told. Decoded, it probably means the addict does not reduce drug consumption and hence suffers no excruciating withdrawal pain provided the drug consumption does not spiral.

Wartime: "What a Muddle ... with Girls"

1   *Diaries*, 331f.
2   Ibid., 325.
3   *CS*, 419.
4   *LF*, 499.

5 Franz Kafka, *The Blue Octavo Notebooks*, ed. by Max Brod. Cambridge, MA: Exact Change, 1991, 8. See also *Synoptische Konkordanz*, vol. 2, 1004f, and "Josephine the Singer, or the Mouse Folk," *CS*, 360-78.

6 *Diaries*, 327. Kafka eventually commented with disrespect on morphine habits of Otto Gross and Milena Jesenská's close friend Jarmila Reinerová.

7 *LM*, 156.

8 "Fratricide," *CS*, 402f; "The Bridge," *CS*, 411; The New Advocate, *CS*, 414f; An Old Manuscript, *CS*, 415-17; also "A Country Doctor," *CS*, 220-25.

9 *Diaries*, 331.

10 Ibid., 230.

10 Pasley, *Brod–Kafka*, 238; *Diaries,* 230; *LF*, 502.

11 The birth of Hans Werner Bloch was registered in Berlin-Mitte under No. 2323/1914/Berlin 12b.

12 *Briefe April 1914–1917,* 510.

13 *Diaries*, 318, 325f.

14 Ibid., 329.

15 *LF*, 457; Stach, *The Decisive Years,* 502.

16 *Diaries*, 362.

17 Franz Kafka, *Amtliche Schriften*, ed. by Klaus Hermsdorf and Benno Wagner. Frankfurt: S. Fischer, 2004, 625.

18 *Amerika*, 568-70, 573.

19 *LF*, 319.

20 *Diaries*, 245.

21 "Public Prosecutor" in Franz Kafka, *The Trial*, transl. by Breon Mitchell. New York: Schocken, 1998, 244-50.

22 *The Trial* (1998), 254-58.

23 *Diaries*, 253.

24 *LF*, 449; also Koch, *Als ich*, 114; *Zürau Aphorisms*, 10; Murray, 237.

25 *LF*, 470.

26 *Diaries*, 361f.

27 Ibid., 363.

28 *LF*, 117.

29 *Diaries*, 364.

30 *LF*, 437.

31 *LFF*, 117.

32 *LF*, 473.

33 *Diaries*, 357-60.

34 *LF*, 485.

35 Ibid., 494f.

36 *Abandoned Fragments*, 145f.

37 *Diaries*, 368f.

The Golden Lane

1 *Diaries*, 325.
2 *LOF*, 11.
3 Ibid., 13; also *LF*, 464.
4 *LF*, 495.
5 Ibid., 497.
6 *Diaries*, 362f.
7 *LF*, 527.
8 Ibid., 527.
9 Ibid., 536.
10 Ibid., 533f.
11 Ibid., 541f.
12 *Abandoned Fragments*, 170-73.
13 *CS*, 432. Kafka's another variation on this legend is "Vulture" in which the storyteller is attacked by the bird and drowns in blood—ibid., 442f. This issue is reviewed in Fabian, *Karl Marx*, esp. 39f.
14 *CS*, 230. Karl Kraus published a book of the same title, *Die chinesische Mauer*, in 1910.
15 *CS*, 223.
16 *Abandoned Fragments*, 181-91.
17 Brod, *Kafka*, 164.

1917: A "Mental Tuberculosis"

1 *Diaries*, 192.
2 *LM*, 115.
3 *LFF*, 137.
4 Ibid., 138.
5 Murray, 256.
6 *LOF*, 21f.
7 *LFF*, 137.
8 Terry, 215.
9 *LOF*, 23.
10 *LFF*, 142.
11 *LOF*, 23; *Briefe April 1914–1917*, 318.

The Paradise in Siřem

1 Hartmut Binder, "Kafkas Briefscherze. Sein Verhältnis zu Josef David," *Jahrbuch der Deutsche Schillergesselschaft*, vol. 13 (1969), 542n.

2   *Briefe April 1914–1917*, 660.

3   *LFF*, 138.

4   Ibid., 154; Hartmut Binder, "Kafka und seine Schwester Ottla," *Jahrbuch der Deutsche Schillergesselschaft*, vol. 12 (1968), 445.

5   Ibid.

6   *LF*, 543.

7   *Diaries*, 385.

8   *LF*, 546.

9   *LFF*, 153.

10 *Briefe April 1914–1920*, 319f.

11 *LFF*, 149.

12 *LF*, 545f.

13 *LFF*, 137, 143f; *LF*, 543.

14 *Briefe April 1914–1917*, 755.

15 *Diaries*, 383.

16 Sokel, 123.

17 *Zürau Aphorisms*, 10.

18 *Abandoned Fragments*, 222.

19 *Blue Octavo*, 16, 18, 31.

20 *LFF*, 154.

21 Ibid., 159.

22 Wagenbach, 119.

23 *LFF*, 141; *Briefe April 1914–1917*, 323.

24 *Diaries*, 386.

25 Pasley, *Brod-Kafka*, vol. 2, 165f, 179. Also *Briefe April 1914–1917*, 750f. Kafka readily admitted Ottla had "limitless willingness to grant me a vacation on the slightest pretext"—*LFF*, 194.

26 *LFF*, 156.

27 Ibid., 155.

28 *Blue Octavo*, 19f.

29 Ibid., 21f.

30 *Diaries*, 389, and *Blue Octavo*, 22.

31 *LFF*, 163.

32 *Blue Octavo*, 91.

33 *LFF*, 178.

34 *Briefe April 1914–1917*, 771, 775, 778.

35 *LFF*, 170.

36 *Briefe April 1914–1917*, 775, 778.

37 *LFF*, 176, 178.

38 Ibid., 183.

39 Ibid., 167.

40 *Diaries*, 387.

41 Terry, 459.

42 *LFF*, 166.

43 *Blue Octavo*, 23f; also 29f.

44 Ibid., 9, 17.

45 Ibid., 49.

46 Ibid., 9, 50.

47 Ibid., 18, 23, 33.

48 Ibid., 28, 65f, 78; *Diaries*, 391.

49 *LFF*, 180.

50 *LOF*, 24; Murray, 265.

51 *LM*, 23.

53 *LFF*, 177.

54 *LOF*, 102.

55 *LFF*, 180.

56 *LOF*, 25.

57 Ibid., 26.

58 *LF*, 46.

59 *LOF*, 26.

60 *LFF*, 177.

61 Ibid., 197f.

62 Památník národního písemnictví [Monument of National Literature], Prague, Franz Kafka Collection, item 381. Emphasis added.

63 *Blue Octavo*, 50.

64 Ibid., 53.

65 *LOF*, 29.

66 *LFF*, 193.

67 *Blue Octavo*, 56f.

68 *LOF*, 28.

69 *LM*, 27.

1918: Mayhem in Prague

1 *LFF*, 201.

2 Památník národního písemnictví, Franz Kafka Collection, items 107, 109, 110.

3 Brod, *Das grosse Wagnis*, 183.

4 *LOF*, 29; Selg, 138.

5 *LOF*, 39.

6 *Briefe 1818–1920*, 79.

7 *LOF*, 107.

8 Ibid., 33.

9   Ibid., 38.
10 *LFF*, 213.
11 Gilman, 256.
12 Brod, *Kafka*, 23.
13 *Letter to His Father*, 115.
14 *Diaries*, 391.

Ottla's Marriage

1   Janouch, 111. Max Brod accepted Janouch's *Conversations* as "the only detailed account" of Kafka by his contemporary next to his own Kafka-biography—*Der Prager Kreis*, 193.
2   *LFF*, 289.
3   Janouch, 176f, 14.
4   Ibid., 103, 25f.
5   *LFF*, 227.
6   *Tagebücher*, 859.
7   *LFF*, 236.
8   Ibid., 234.
9   *Briefe 1918–1920*, 138f.
10 Alt, 545.
11 *Briefe 1918–1920*, 175.
12 Ibid., 152f.

1920: Milena Jesenská

1   *Diaries*, 232.
2   Buber-Neumann, 25.
3   Urzidil, 161f.
4   Emil Utiz in Hugo Siebenschein et al., eds. *Franz Kafka a Praha: vzpomínky, úvahy, dokumenty*. Prague: 1947, 28.
5   *LFF*, 237.
6   *LM*, 22. This edition is not completely satisfactory in terms of translation and sequencing of the letters. It has been complemented here by the authoritative German edition of Kafka's letters, *Briefe 1918–1920*.
7   *Briefe 1918–1920*, 149f, 162.
8   *LM*, 44.
9   *LM*, 51.
10 Ibid., 43, 45.
11 Ibid., 48.

12 Hartmut Binder, "Ernest Polak—Literat ohne Werk: Zu den Kaffeehauszirkeln in Prag und Wien," *Jahrbuch der Deutsche Schillergesselschaft*, vol. 22 (1979), 393.

13 *Briefe 1918–1920*, 190-92, 202f, 585, 599f.

14 Ibid., 200f.

15 Ibid., 223.

16 Ibid., 585.

17 Ibid., 218.

18 Brod, *Kafka*, 229.

19 *LM*, 76f.

20 *Briefe 1918–1920*, 199.

21 *LM*, 70.

22 Ibid., 74.

23 On July 8, Kafka also called off seeing Julie Wohryzek, probably never to date her again.

24 *Briefe 1918–1920*, 249.

25 *LM*, 109.

26 *Briefe 1918–1920*, 262-64.

27 Ibid., 301. In the ongoing campaign to blot out Grete Bloch from Kafka's life, the editor of this authoritative collection of letters dismisses Kafka's association of Gmünd with Grete as a mere "play of words"—ibid., 622.

28 *LOF*, 53f.

29 *LM*, 166.

30 Ibid., 169.

31 Ibid., 214.

32 Ibid., 169.

33 Ibid., 199.

34 Ibid., 214.

In Matliary, Seeking "a Postponement of Sentence"

1   *LM*, 215.

2   Urzidil, 95.

3   Gilman, 259.

4   Ibid.

5   Janouch, 178.

6   *LFF*, 247, 263. Kafka resolutely rejected injections of the detested tuberculin.

7   *LOF*, 56.

8   *LFF*, 252; Stach, *The Years of Insight*, 388.

9   Gilman, 260.

10 *LFF*, 252.

11 Ibid., 263.

12 Ibid., 261f.

13 Ibid., 254f.

14 *LOF*, 69.

15 *LFF*, 259.

16 Hugo Wetcherek, ed., *Kafkas letzter Freund: der Nachlass Robert Klopstock (1899-1972)*. Vienna: Inlibris, 2003, 86f; *LFF*, 252f.

17 *LOF*, 67.

18 Gilman, 263f.

19 *LOF*, 76.

1922: The Retirement

1 *LFF*, 303.

2 *Diaries*, 397.

3 Ibid., 393.

4 *LFF*, 333f.

5 *CS*, 278–316.

6 Ibid., 268–277.

7 *Diaries*, 393.

8 Hana Benešová," Kafkova krev—Věra Saudková" ("Kafka's Blood—Věra Saudková"), in *Reflex* (Prague), August 22, 2011; also Alena Wágnerová, *Im Hauptquartier des Lärms: die Familie Kafka aus Prague*. Berlin: Bollmann, 1997.

9 Pasley, *Brod-Kafka*, vol. 2, 361; *Tagebücher*, 208.

10 Ibid., 363.

11 *LOF*, 63.

12 A partial account of the dysfunctional marriage can be found in Josef David's petition for divorce of February 1940, in Krajský soud civilní v Praze, CK VIIIa 95/40, National Archives, Prague.

13 *LOF*, 63.

14 *LOF*, 76.

15 *Diaries*, 399f.

16 In his early thirties, Kafka excerpted the Talmud stricture to the effect that a man without a woman is no person—*Diaries*, 126.

17 *Diaries*, 401.

18 Ibid., 418.

19 Gilman, 271.

1   *LOF*, 73. The layout and surrounding of the Příčná Street house have not changed much since Kafka's days almost a century ago.

2   Wagenbach, 140; also Stach, *The Years of Insight*, 428.

3   Pasley, *Brod-Kafka*, vol. 2, 390.

4   The authoritative German analysis of *The Castle*'s genesis, dating it primarily to the first half of 1922, is narrowly conceived and short of accuracy—*Das Schloss: Apparatband*, ed. by Malcolm Pasley. Frankfurt: S. Fischer, 1982, 61–72, esp. 68.

5   The references here are to the classical English translation of *The Castle* by Willa and Edwin Muir, in the *Complete Novels of Franz Kafka*. Harmondsworth: Penguin, 1983, 9-176.

6   See Matthias Schuster, *Franz Kafkas Handschrift zum Schloss*. Heidelberg: Universitätsverlag Winter, 2012, 124.

7   Karoline Krauss, *Kafka's K. versus the Castle: The Self and the Other*. New York: P. Lang 1996, 24.

8   Marthe Robert, *The Old and the New: From Don Quixote to Kafka*. Berkeley, CA: University of California Press, 1977, 290.

9   Stach, *Kafkas erotischer Mythos*, 99–124, esp. 117, assigns Kafka's incestual tendencies to his Oedipus complex—an attribution not born out of documentary evidence.

10 *LFF*, 341.

11 Ibid., 332f.

12 Ibid., 338.

13 Ibid., 343.

14 Ibid., 347.

15 *Synoptische Konkordanz*, vol. 3, 613, 642 and passim.

16 *LFF*, 290-97.

17 Pasley, *Brod-Kafka*, vol. 2, 400.

18 *LFF*, 273.

19 *Diaries*, 411, 417; Friedländer, *Franz Kafka*, 9.

20 Schocken, 96.

21 *LFF*, 352.

22 Ibid., 353.

23 Ibid., 357-60.

24 *The Castle*, 311.

25 *LFF*, 357.

The Surrender to "Dark Forces"

1 Hana Benešová, "Zemřela Věra Saudková," in *Reflex*, August 4, 2015; also Hana Benešová," Kafkova krev—Věra Saudková," *Reflex*, August 22, 2011.
2 *LFF*, 358f.
3 This author's interview with a close family friend M. P. on May 29, 2012.
4 *Nachgelassene Schriften und Fragmente*, vol. 2, 534–546; *CS*, 451-56.
5 Franz Werfel, *Schweiger*. Munich: Kurt Wolff, 1922, 111, 118f, 152.
6 *LFF*, 365, 481.
7 Ibid., 375.
8 Binder, "Kafkas Briefscherze," 557.
9 *LOF*, 71.
10 *LFF*, 377. In addition to Klopstock or instead of him, while in Berlin, Kafka was receiving further unidentified parcels from Weltsch and had his sister Ottla pay for them.
11 Ibid., 383.
12 Ibid., 386.
13 "A Little Woman," *CS*, 317-24.
14 Bodleian Library, Kafka Collection, file 50, folio 7r; also *LOF*, 79.
15 *LOF*, 85.
16 *LFF*, 401.
17 *LOF*, 89.
18 Ibid., 87f.
19 *LFF*, 404.
20 Ibid., 402.
21 *CS*, 360-78.
22 Ibid., 445.

The "Hunger Artist" Dies

1 *LFF*, 411.
2 Pasley, *Brod-Kafka*, vol. 2, 319.
3 R. S. Pentecost, "Symptoms of Upper Respiratory Tract Disease Simulating Tuberculosis," in *Canadian Medical Association Journal* (July 1924), 591f.
4 *LFF*, 411.
5 Franz Kafka, *Briefe an die Eltern aus dem Jahren 1922–1924*, ed. by Josef Čermák and Martin Svatoš. Frankfurt: S. Fischer, 1990, 66.
6 Hackermüller, 117f.
7 Max Brod, *Über Franz Kafka*. Frankfurt: S. Fischer, 1966, 178.
8 *LFF*, 412; Stach, *The Years of Insight*, 554.
9 *Briefe an die Eltern*, 73.

10 Kathi Diamant, *Kafka's Last Love: The Mystery of Dora Diamant*. New York: Basic Books, 2002, 98.

11 *LFF*, 413; *LM*, 205f.

12 Wetcherek, 254.

13 *Briefe an die Eltern*, 73f.

14 Wetscherek, 72, 74, 254; Diamant, 99.

15 Hackermüller, 108f; *LOF*, 120; LFF, 413.

16 *LFF*, 412.

17 Wetscherek, 38, 69, 74n.

18 *LF*, 184.

19 Cocteau, 22, 24.

20 Janouch, 98, 156.

21 *LFF*, 413. Presaging his own health problems, Kafka also observed Weltsch's "hypochondria lodges in his lungs and larynx"—*LF*, 185.

22 *CS*, 371.

23 Cocteau, 35.

24 *Briefe an die Eltern*, 77f.

25 Josef Čermák, *Franz Kafka: Život ve stínu smrti Dopisy Robertovi* [Franz Kafka: Life in the shadow of death Letters to Robert]. Prague: Mladá Fronta, 2012, 95.

26 Bodleian Collection, Kafka Collection, file 51, folio 51r; *Briefe an die Eltern*, 79.

27 *LFF*, 419.

28 For this secret aspect of Bismarck's life, see Fabian, *Karl Marx*, chapter "Bismarck Strikes," 569–580.

29 *LFF*, 418.

30 *Briefe an die Eltern*, 76.

31 Diamant, 108.

32 *LFF*, 415.

33 LOF, 91f.

34 Ibid., 93.

35 Brod, *Kafka*, 211f.

36 Ibid., *Kafka*, 76.

Epilogue

1   Bodleian Library, Kafka Collection, file 50, folio 52v.

2   Urzidil, 190.

3   Benešová in "Kafkova krev—Věra Saudková," *Reflex*, August 22, 2011.

4   Urzidil, 192.
5   Brod, *Kafka*, 47, 51.
6   Ibid., 51.
7   *Zürau Aphorisms*, 50; *Blue Octavo*, 91.

BIBLIOGRAPHY

Archival Sources

Bodleian Library, Oxford
  -Franz Kafka Collection
National Archives, Prague
    -Police Headquarters, files of Franz Kafka, Hermann Kafka, Ottilie
     Davidová-Kafková, Josef David, Max Brod, Felix Weltsch, Eduard
     Goldstücker
    -Files of the Institute of Workers' Accident Insurance, 1919–1925
     Památník národního písemnictví [Monument of National Literature],
     Prague
    -Franz Kafka Collection

Primary literature

BROD, Max,
Franz Kafka A Biography. New York: Schocken, 1973
Das grosse Wagnis. Leipzig: Kurt Wolff, 1918
Der Prager Kreis. Frankfurt: Suhrkamp, 1979
Über Franz Kafka. Frankfurt: S. Fischer, 1974
BUBER-NEUMANN, Margarete, *Milena: The Tragic Story of Kafka's
    Great Love.* New York: Seaver, 1988
ČERMÁK, Josef, *Franz Kafka: Život ve stínu smrti Dopisy Robertovi*
    [Franz Kafka: Life in the shadow of death Letters to Robert]. Prague:
    Mladá Fronta, 2012
COCTEAU, Jean, *Opium: The Diary of a Cure.* London: Peter Owen, 1968

Dr. Karel Šviha, národněsociální zrádce národa [Dr. Karel Šviha, a populist-socialist traitor of the nation]. Prague, 1914

JANOUCH, Gustav, *Conversations with Kafka.* London: Deutsch, 1985

KAFKA, Franz,

Abandoned Fragments: The Unedited Works of Franz Kafka 1897–1917. London: Sun Vision, 2012

Amerika (The Man Who Disappeared), transl. by Michael Hofmann. New York: New Directions Books, 2002

Amtliche Schriften, ed. by Klaus Hermsdorf and Benno Wagner. Frankfurt: S. Fischer, 2004

The Blue Octavo Notebooks, ed. by Max Brod. Cambridge, MA: Exact Change, 1991

Briefe an die Eltern aus den Jahren 1922-1924, ed. by Josef Čermák and Martin Svatoš. Frankfurt: S. Fischer, 1990

Briefe 1900–1912, ed. by Hans-Gerd Koch, Frankfurt: S. Fischer, 1999

Briefe 1913–1914, ed. by Hans-Gerd Koch, Frankfurt: S. Fischer, 2001

Briefe April 1914–1917, ed. by Hans-Gerd Koch, Frankfurt: S. Fischer. 2005

Briefe 1918–1920, ed. by Hans-Gerd Koch, Frankfurt: S. Fischer, 2013

The Castle, transl. by Wilma and Edwin Muir, in *The Complete Novels of Franz Kafka.* Harmondsworth: Penguin, 1983

The Complete Stories, ed. by Nabum M. Glatzer. New York: Schocken, 1971

The Diaries 1910-1923, ed. by Max Brod. New York, Schocken, 1976

Letters to Felice. New York: Schocken, 1973

Letters to Friends, Family, and Editors. New York: Schocken, 1977

Letter to His Father. New York: Schocken, 1974

Letters to Milena, ed. by Willy Haas. New York, Schocken, 1965

Letters to Milena. New York: Schocken, 1990

Letters to Ottla and Family, ed. by N. N. Glatzer. New York: Schocken, 1982

The Metamorphosis and other stories, transl. by Christopher Moncrieff. Richmond, Surrey: Alma Classics, 2014

The Metamorphosis and other stories, transl. by Joachim Neugroschel. Toronto: Maxwell, 1993

Nachgelassene Schriften und Fragmente I, ed. by Malcolm Pasley. Frankfurt: S. Fischer, 1993

Nachgelassene Schriften und Fragmente II, ed. by Jost Schillemeit. Frankfurt: S. Fischer, 1992

The Office Writings, ed. by Stanley Corngold et al. Princeton: Princeton UP, 2009

Der Process, ed. by Malcolm Pasley. Frankfurt: S. Fischer, 1990

Der Process: Apparatband, ed. by Malcolm Pasley. Frankfurt: S. Fischer, 1990

Das Schloss, ed. by Malcolm Pasley. Frankfurt: S. Fischer, 1982

Das Schloss: Apparatband, ed. by Malcolm Pasley. Frankfurt: S. Fischer, 1982

Das Schloss: Roman; in der Fassung der Handschrift. Frankfurt: Fischer Taschenbuch, 1994

Synoptische Konkordanz zu Franz Kafkas Nachgelassenen Schriften und Fragmenten, 3 vols., ed. by Ralf Becker et al. Tübingen: M. Niemeyer, 2003

Tagebücher, ed. by Hans-Gerd Koch, Michael Müller and Malcolm Pasley. Frankfurt: S. Fischer, 1990

Tagebücher: 1909–1923: Fassung der Handschrift. Frankfurt: S. Fischer, 1997

The Trial, transl. by Willa and Edwin Muir, in *The Complete Novels of Franz Kafka.* Harmondsworth: Penguin, 1983

The Trial, transl. by Breon Mitchell. New York: Schocken, 1998

Der Verschollene, ed. by Jost Schillemeit. Frankfurt: S. Fischer, 1983

The Zürau Aphorisms of Franz Kafka, ed. by Roberto Calasso. New York: Knopf, 2005

KOCH, Hans-Gerd, ed., "Als Kafka mir entgegenkam . . ." *Erinnerungen an Franz Kafka.* Frankfurt: S. Fischer, 1995

MAREŠ, Michal, *Vzpomínky na Kafku* [Recollections of Kafka]. Prague: 1946

PASLEY, Malcolm, ed., *Max Brod, Franz Kafka, eine Freundschaft*, 2 vols. Frankfurt: S. Fischer, 1987

SCHOCKEN, Wolfgang A., "Wer war Grete Bloch?" *Exilforschung: Ein internationales Jahrbuch*, vol. 4, *Das Jüddische Exil und andere Themen.* Munich, 1986, 83-97

SIEBENSCHEIN, Hugo and al, eds. *Franz Kafka a Praha: vzpomínky, úvahy, dokumenty* [Franz Kafka and Prague: recollections, thoughts, documents]. Prague: 1947

ŠVIHA, Karel, *Zrádce dr. Karel Šviha před porotou: stenografický záznam* [Traitor dr. Karel Šviha before jury]. Prague, 1914

TERRY, Charles E. and PELLENS, M., *The Opium Problem.* New York, 1928

THOMAYER, Josef, *Pathologie a terapie nemocí vnitřních* [Pathology and therapy of internal diseases]. Prague: Bursik & Kohout, 1923

URZIDIL, Johannes, *There Goes Kafka.* Detroit: Wayne State UP, 1968

VACEK, Bohumil, *Zákony a nařízení jakož i důležitá rozhodnutí o organisaci zdravotní a epidemické služby v Čechách a na Moravě* [Legislation and directives as well as important decisions concerning the organization of health and epidemiological services in Bohemia and Moravia]. Prague: 1916

WERFEL, Franz, *Schweiger.* Munich: Kurt Wolff, 1922

WETSCHEREK, Hugo, ed., *Kafkas letzter Freund: der Nachlass Robert Klopstock (1899-1972).* Vienna: Inlibris, 2003

WOLFF, Kurt, *Briefwechsel eines Verlegers, 1911–1963,* ed. by Bernhard Zeller and Ellen Orten. Frankfurt: Scheffer, 1966

Secondary literature

ALT, Peter-André, *Franz Kafka Der ewige Sohn.* Munich: C. H. Beck, 2005

BEGLEY, Louis, *Franz Kafka the Tremendous World I Have in My Mind.* New York: Atlas & Co, 2008

BENEŠOVÁ, Hana, "Kafkova krev—Věra Saudková" [Kafka's Blood—Věra Saudková], in *Reflex* (Prague), 22 August 2011

BENEŠOVÁ, Hana, "Zemřela Věra Saudková" [Věra Saudková Died], in *Reflex* (Prague), 4 August 2015

BINDER, Hartmut, "Ernest Polak—Literat ohne Werk: Zu den Kaffeehauszirkeln in Prag und Wien," *Jahrbuch der Deutsche Schillergesselschaft,* vol. 22 (1979), 366–415

BINDER, Hartmut, ed., *Kafka-Handbuch,* 2 vols, Stuttgart: Kröner, 1979

BINDER, Hartmut, "Kafka und seine Schwester Ottla," *Jahrbuch der Deutsche Schillergesselschaft,* vol. 12, 1968, 403–456

BINDER, Hartmut, "Kafkas Briefscherze. Sein Verhältniss zu Josef David," *Jahrbuch der Deutsche Schillergesselschaft,* vol. 13, 1969, 536–559

BINDER, Hartmut, *Kafkas "Verwandlung."* Frankfurt: Stroemfeld, 2004

BINDER, Hartmut, *Kafkas Wien Portrait einer schwierigen Beziehung.* Prague: Vitalis, 2013

CANETTI, Elias, *Kafka's Other Trial.* New York: Schocken, 1974

ČERMÁK, Josef, *Franz Kafka: výmysly a mystifikace.* Prague: Labyrint, 2005

ČERMÁK, Josef, "Pobyt Franze Kafky v Plané nad Lužnicí," *Světová literatura* (Prague), 1989, no. 1, 219–239

ČERNÁ, Jana, *Kafka's Milena.* Evanston, IL: Northwestern UP, 1993

DIAMANT, Kathi, *Kafka's Last Love: The Mystery of Dora Diamant.* New York: Basic Books, 2002

FABIAN, George, *Karl Marx Prince of Darkness*. Bloomington, IN: Xlibris, 2011.

FABIAN, George, "Was Franz Kafka Tubercular?" in *Oxford German Studies*, vol. 45 (2016), issue 4, 434–443.

FELLNER, Sabine and UNTERREINE, Katrin, *Morphium, Cannabis und Cocain: Medizin und Rezepte des Kaisershauses*. Vienna: Amalthea, 2008

FRIEDLÄNDER, Saul, *Franz Kafka the Poet of Shame and Guilt*. New Haven: Yale UP, 2013

GILMAN, Sander L., *Franz Kafka: The Jewish Patient*. New York: Routledge, 1995

GRANDIN, John M., *Kafka's Prussian Advocate: A Study of the Influence of Heinrich von Kleist on Franz Kafka*. Columbia, SC: Camden House, 1987

GREEN, Martin, *Mountain of Truth: The Counterculture Begins, Ascona 1900-1920*. Lewiston, NY: E. Mellen Press, 1999

HACKERMÜLLER, Rotraut, *Kafkas letzte Jahre, 1917–1924*. Munich: P. Kirchheim, 1990

HÄHNER-ROMBACH, Sylvelyn, *Sozialgeschichte der Tuberkulose: vom Kaiserreich zum Ende des zweiten Weltkriegs unter besonderer Berücksichtigung Württembergs*. Stuttgart: Franz Stener, 2000

HÁJKOVÁ, Anna, "Die Jahre der Verbitterung," in *Süddeutsche Zeitung*, 24 November 2015

HAWES, James, *Why You Should Read Kafka Before You Waste Your Life*. New York: St. Martin's, 2008

HOCKADAY, Mary, *Kafka, Love and Courage: The Life of Milena Jesenska*. London: Deutsch, 1995

Kafka-Handbuch Leben-Werk-Wirkung, ed. by Bettina von Jagow and Oliver Jahraus. Göttingen: Vandenhoeck & Ruprecht, 2008

KAUTMAN, František, *Franz Kafka*. Prague: Rozmluvy, 1996

KOCH, Hans-Gerd, *Kafka in Berlin*. Berlin: Wagenbach, 1995

KUNA, Franz, *Kafka Literature as Corrective Punishment*. London: Elek, 1979

KRAUSS, Karoline, *Kafka's K. Versus the Castle*. New York: P. Lang, 1996

KURZ, Gerhard, ed., *Der junge Kafka*. Frankfurt: Suhrkampf, 1984

MÜLLEROVÁ, Radana, "Franz Kafka a Siřem," in *Sborník Okresního archivu v Lounech*. Louny: 2001, 199–228

MURRAY, Nicholas, *Kafka*. New Haven: Yale UP, 2004

NORTHEY, Anthony, *Kafka's Relatives: Their Lives and His Writings*. New Haven: Yale UP, 1999

NORTHEY, Anthony, "Franz Kafkas Selbstmörder," *Sudetenland*, 2007, 267–294

NUSKA, Bohumil and PERNES, Jiří, *Kafkův Process a Švihova aféra* [Kafka's *The Trial* and Šviha's affair]. Brno: Barrister & Principal, 2000

PAWEL, Ernst, *The Nightmare of Reason; a Life of Franz Kafka*. New York: Farrar, Straus, Giroux, 1984

ROBERT, Marthe, *As Lonely as Franz Kafka: A Psychological Biography*. New York: Harcourt Brace Jovanovich, 1986

ROBERT, Marthe, *The Old and the New: From Don Quixote to Kafka*. Berkeley, CA: University of California Press, 1977

ROBERT, Marthe, *Seul, comme Franz Kafka*. Paris: Calman-Lévy, 1979

SAUR, Pamela S., *Ernst Weiss Life, Works and Legacy of a Czech Literary Master and Friend of Franz Kafka, 1882-1940*. Bethesda, MD: Academic Press, 2012

SCHMIDT, Carsten, *Kafkas fast unbekannte Freund: das Leben und Werk von Felix Weltsch (1884-1914)*. Würzburg: Konighausen & Neumann, 2010

SCHUSTER, Matthias, *Franz Kafkas Handschrift zum Schloss*. Heidelberg: Universitätsverlag Winter, 2012

SELG, Peter, *Rainer Maria Rilke und Franz Kafka: Lebensweg und Krankheitsschicksal im 20. Jahrhundert*. Dornach: Pforte, 2007

SOKEL, Walter, *The Myth of Power and the Self: Essays on Franz Kafka*. Detroit: Wayne State UP, 2002

STACH, Reiner, *Kafkas erotischer Mythos*. Frankfurt: S. Fischer, 1987

STACH, Reiner, *Kafka: The Decisive Years*. New York: Harcourt, 2005

STACH, Reiner, *Kafka: The Years of Insight*. Princeton, NJ: Princeton UP, 2013

STACH, Reiner, *Kafka Die Frühen Jahre*. Frankfurt: S. Fischer, 2014

TAUSSIG, Pavel, "Ottla Davidová," in *Xantypa* (Prague), 20 January, 2010

UNSELD, Joachim, *Franz Kafka a Writer's Life*. Riverside, CA: Ariadne Press, 1994

WAGENBACH, Klaus, *Kafka*. Cambridge, MA: Harvard UP, 2003

WÁGNEROVÁ, Alena, *"Im Hauptquartier des Lärme: die Familie Kafka aus Prag*. Berlin: Bollmann, 1997

WÁGNEROVÁ, Alena, ed., "Ich hätte zu antworten Tage –und nächtelang." *Die Briefe von Milena Jesenská*. Mannheim: Bollmann, 1996

WÁGNEROVÁ, Alena, *Milena Jesenská*. Mannheim: Bollmann, 1996

WÁGNEROVÁ, Alena, "Die Welt ist ja nicht zum Aushalten," in *Frankfurter Allgemeine Zeitung*, March 25, 2011

GERMAN-CZECH TOPOGRAPHY

-Alchimistengasse = Zlatá ulička (Golden Lane)
-Altstädterring = Staroměstské náměstí (Oldtown Square)
-Am Graben = Na Příkopě
-Belveder = Letná
-Ferdinandstrasse = Národní třída
-Heinrichgasse = Jindřišská ulice
-Josefsplatz = Náměstí republiky
-Laurenziberg = Petřín
-Langenstrasse = Dlouhá ulice
-Niklasstrasse = Pařížská ulice
-Spindlermühle = Špindlerův Mlýn
-Theresienstadt = Terezín
-Schelesen = Želízy
-Triesch = Třešť
-Wenzeslausplatz = Václavské náměstí
-Zeltnergasse = Celetná ulice
-Zürau = Siřem

INDEX

Printed in the USA
CPSIA information can be obtained
at www.ICGtesting.com
CBHW031232200524
8813CB00023B/407/J

9 781796 020564